The US Supreme Court and the Centralization of Federal Authority

SUNY series in American Constitutionalism

Robert J. Spitzer, editor

THE US SUPREME COURT AND THE CENTRALIZATION OF FEDERAL AUTHORITY

Michael A. Dichio

SUNY PRESS

Published by State University of New York Press, Albany

For information, contact State University of New York Press, Albany, NY
www.sunypress.edu

Library of Congress Cataloging-in-Publication Data

Names: Dichio, Michael A., 1986– author.
Title: The US Supreme Court and the centralization of federal authority /
    Michael A. Dichio.
Other titles: U.S. Supreme Court and the centralization of federal authority |
    United States Supreme Court and the centralization of federal authority
Description: Albany [New York] : State University of New York Press [2018] |
    Series: SUNY series in American constitutionalism | Includes bibliographical
    references and index.
Identifiers: LCCN 2018003724 | ISBN 9781438472539 (hardcover) |
    ISBN 9781438472522 (pbk.) | ISBN 9781438472546 (ebook) Subjects: LCSH:
United States. Supreme Court—History. | Federal government—
    United States—History. | Constitutional history—United States.
Classification: LCC KF8742 .D53 2018 | DDC 342.73/042—dc23
LC record available at https://lccn.loc.gov/2018003724

10 9 8 7 6 5 4 3 2 1

To my parents, Anna and Anthony, and
To my grandparents, Michelina and Antonio

Contents

List of Illustrations   ix

Acknowledgments   xiii

Introduction   xv

Chapter 1   Conceptualizing Supreme Court Power   1

Chapter 2   Discerning Incremental Changes in Constitutional
             Development   27

Chapter 3   Strengths of the Early American State, 1789–1864   67

Chapter 4   Building a Modern National Government, 1865–1932   93

Chapter 5   Legal Developments in the Modern American State,
             1933–1997   115

Chapter 6   Comprehending Supreme Court Influence   139

Appendix 1   Coding Decisions   153

Appendix 2   List of Cases in the Data   169

Appendix 3   List of Constitutional Casebooks Used for
             Data Collection   187

Appendix 4   Characteristics of Constitutional Expansion   193

Notes   199

References   239

Index   251

Illustrations

Tables

2.1	Bensel's Dimensions of Central State Authority	35
2.2	Constitutional Issue Areas	37
2.3	Central State Dimensions Frequency of Federal Expansion	44
3.1	Constitutional Issue by Effect on Federal Authority, 1792–1864	72
3.2	Frequency of Central State Dimensions, 1792–1864	74
4.1	Constitutional Issue by Effect on Federal Authority, 1865–1932	97
4.2	Frequency of the Dimensions of the Central State, 1865–1932	98
5.1	Constitutional Issue by Effect on Federal Authority, 1933–1997	119
5.2	Frequency of Dimensions of the Central State, 1933–1997	121
A.1	Cross-Tabulation of Level of Government Action under Review by Effect on Federal Authority	194
A.2	Cross-Tabulation of Ideology of Decision by Effect on Federal Authority	195

Figures

1.1	Typology of Judicial Decisions	15
2.1	Casebook Distribution	31
2.2	Distribution of Cases Affecting Federal State Authority, 1792–1997	39

2.3   Effect on Federal Authority by Year, 1792–1997   40

2.4   Cumulative Frequency of Constitutional Decisions' Effect on
      Federal State Authority, 1792–1997   41

2.5   Federal State Expansion across Historical Eras   42

2.6   Central State Dimensions and Effect on Federal Authority   43

2.7   Central State Dimensions and Effect on Federal Authority
      across Time   45

2.8   Cumulative Frequency of Citizenship Dimension, 1792–1997   46

2.9   Cumulative Frequency of Centralization Dimensions 1792–1997   47

2.10 Constitutional Issues, Early Republic Era, 1789–1828   48

2.11 Level of Government Action under Review, Early Republic Era   49

2.12 Constitutional Issues, Jacksonian Era, 1829–1860   51

2.13 Level of Government Action under Review, Jacksonian Era   53

2.14 Constitutional Issues, Civil War and Reconstruction Eras,
      1861–1876   54

2.15 Level of Government Action under Review, Civil War and
      Reconstruction Eras   56

2.16 Constitutional Issues, Republican Era, 1877–1932   57

2.17 Level of Government Action under Review, Republican Era   59

2.18 Constitutional Issues, New Deal and Great Society Eras,
      1933–1968   60

2.19 Level of Government Action under Review, New Deal and
      Great Society Eras   62

2.20 Constitutional Issues, Contemporary Era, 1969–1997   63

2.21 Level of Government Action under Review, Contemporary Era   64

3.1   Cumulative Frequency of the Effect of Federal Authority,
      1792–1864   71

3.2   The Effect on Federal Authority across Chief Justice Tenures,
      1792–1864   73

3.3   Constitutional Issue Areas and Effect on Federal Authority,
      1792–1864   74

3.4   Most Abundant Constitutional Issues, 1792–1864   75

4.1   Cumulative Frequency of the Effect of Federal Authority,
      1865–1932   96

4.2   Effect on Federal Authority across Historical Eras, 1865–1932   98

4.3   Constitutional Issue Areas and Effect on Federal Authority,
      1865–1932   99

4.4   Most Abundant Constitutional Issues, 1865–1932   100

5.1   Cumulative Frequency of Effect on Federal Authority,
      1933–1997   117

5.2   Effect on Federal Authority across Historical Eras, 1933–1997   118

5.3   Constitutional Issue Areas and Effect on Federal Authority,
      1933–1977   120

5.4   Most Abundant Constitutional Issues, 1933–1997   120

A.1   Coding Process Flow Chart   154

A.2   Distribution of Landmark Decisions across Years, 1792–1997   193

A.3   Effect on Federal Authority by Constitutional Issue, 1792–1997   196

A.4   Constitutional Issues as a Subset of Centralization   197

A.5   Constitutional Issues as a Subset of Citizenship   198

Acknowledgments

I've long loved reading acknowledgments because they are one of the few places in academic literature where we get to see the author as a person. To see the people and the values the author cherishes and to dedicate a space for humility allows us to recognize that virtually nothing in life—even things that seems like yours, such as a book—are not just your own creation.

This project first began in graduate school at Cornell University, where I was fortunate enough to assemble a committee who provided support, much-needed criticism, and perhaps most importantly, genuine curiosity about my project.

So let me begin by thanking those who contributed most directly to the intellectual development of this project in graduate school. Elizabeth Sanders offered invaluable historical references and incredible attention to the prose while treating me to long lunches and coffee. Her warm and generous guidance has made me a better adviser to my own students. Aziz Rana's persistent curiosity and excitement over my project renewed my intellectual energy when I struggled the most. Each time we met, I left feeling revived and eager to tackle additional questions—the sign of a gifted adviser. As one of my professors during my undergraduate years at Boston College, Ken Kersch generously agreed to sit on my dissertation committee. This gesture and enormous undertaking is something I don't think I can ever fully repay. From the beginning, Ken not only took great interest in my research ideas, but took interest in me as a person and as a professional.

Of all these wonderful advisers, however, none were more integral to my development as a scholar than my dissertation chair, Richard Bensel. Richard's attentiveness to his students is truly extraordinary. He read *every-thing*—down to the very last, tiny footnote in this project—and he did it with remarkable speed while still providing extensive commentary. By the end of my time at Cornell, I had only become more amazed at Richard as an adviser and as a scholar.

Richard and Ken, especially, have remained a font of support and an invaluable source of feedback as I developed this project into a book, and I'm so grateful to have them as advisers.

Beyond my dissertation committee, I have had the help of many others. The late Ted Lowi and his John L. Senior Chair of Institutions provided generous support so I could hire four excellent research assistants—Dan Marcus, Eric Silverberg, Malhar Naik, and Julius Kairey. Their help in data collection and coding made this project far more manageable than it would have been otherwise. Early on in graduate school, Ted Lowi and Isaac Kramnick fostered my love for public law and American political thought, and guided me through my public law course of study. Along with Ted and Isaac, Michael Jones-Correa provided invaluable feedback when I first created this project as a dissertation prospectus. While at Cornell, I was also lucky to meet a number of colleagues who offered support along the way—Nolan Bennett, Paul Herron, Desmond Jagmohan, Julianna Koch, Danielle Thomsen, Martha Wilfahrt, and Alexis Walker. Over countless late-night conversations, Jason Hecht and Igor Logvinenko, in particular, provided support and encouragement when I most needed it. I owe a special thanks to Phil Rocco, who read the entire revised manuscript.

While at Fort Lewis College, I have benefited immensely from the collegiality and from spirited discussion with my colleagues, especially Ruth Alminas, Brad Clark, Paul DeBell, Justin McBrayer, Dugald Owen, and Sarah Roberts-Cady. The college's Faculty Development, especially its chair, Ryan Smith, and the Fort Lewis College Foundation have generously supported my research endeavors. I owe a special thanks to Stacey Sotosky for providing never-ending encouragement and creative perspective, and for renewing my energy when I needed it the most. I also appreciated the thorough and thoughtful feedback from SUNY Press's anonymous reviewers, which have undoubtedly improved this book.

Finally, I would be nowhere without the ceaseless support and unbounded love from my family—especially my parents, Anna and Anthony, my siblings, Justin and Alexa, and my grandparents, Lina and Tony, and Uncle Michael. They help keep everything in perspective and remind me of life's most precious gifts.

Introduction

On June 26, 2015, Justice Anthony Kennedy wrote the majority opinion in a landmark gay-marriage case, *Obergefell v. Hodges*, for the US Supreme Court. "The fundamental liberties protected by [the Due Process] Clause include most of the rights enumerated in the Bill of Rights," he wrote. "In addition these liberties extend to certain personal choices central to individual dignity and autonomy, including intimate choices that define personal identity and beliefs." In ringing language, he concluded, "The Constitution, however, does not permit the State to bar same-sex couples from marriage on the same terms as accorded to couples of the opposite sex."[1]

The four dissenters made clear their vociferous opposition. Quoting in part from *Federalist* No. 78, Chief Justice Roberts said, "But this Court is not a legislature. Whether same-sex marriage is a good idea should be of no concern to us. Under the Constitution, judges have power to say what the law is, not what it should be. The people who ratified the Constitution authorized courts to exercise 'neither force nor will but merely judgment.'" According to Chief Justice Roberts, the majority's opinion was "an act of will," which would transform the marriage laws of "more than half the states" and alter "a social institution that has formed the basis of human society for millennia, for the Kalahari Bushmen and the Han Chinese, the Carthaginians and the Aztecs. Just who do we think we are?"[2]

Apparently, the members of the Supreme Court think they comprise an institution that has the ability to consolidate and centralize authority, shifting decision-making power from the states to the federal government. Yet it also maintains the right to contract central state authority by leaving power with the states or invalidating federal laws. In *Obergefell*, the Court extended the protections of the Fourteenth Amendment, requiring all fifty states to recognize a marriage between two people of the same sex that was legally licensed and performed in another state: "The Court, in this decision, holds same-sex couples may exercise the fundamental right to marry in all States.

It follows that the Court also must hold—and it now does hold—that there is no lawful basis for a State to refuse to recognize a lawful same-sex marriage performed in another State on the ground of its same-sex character."[3] This action is nothing new: requiring that states do something because the federal government mandates it typifies the expansion of central state authority. The Court has taken such actions persistently over time and across most, if not all, issue areas—in railroad regulation, taxation, abortion rights, and healthcare, to name a few.[4]

The language of federal authority is at the very root of American constitutional law, all of which addresses questions about the federal government's reach. The judiciary's central responsibility is to determine the boundaries of this authority. As it does so, it expands and contracts federal power. This is the basic pattern of constitutional development. Shaping the federal government in this way places the Court at the center of American state-building. In other words, the Supreme Court will always crucially influence American political development. The interesting question is when, where, and how the Court has influenced federal authority over time. Until now, we have not systematically studied this across constitutional issues and across American history. If we better understood these patterns of expansion and restriction, we could then better understand the constitutional underpinnings of changes in the American state.

Expansion of the reach of federal power often encounters resistance at the state level. After *Obergefell*, Rowan County Clerk Kim Davis refused to issue same-sex marriage licenses to eligible couples in Kentucky, citing her Christian beliefs. When a federal district judge ordered her to comply with the Supreme Court, she still refused and was then jailed for five days. Ultimately, her actions resulted in Kentucky having to pay $224,000 in legal fees and costs associated with Davis's refusal to comply with an order handed down by a federal judge.[5] Something similar happened to Alabama's former state Supreme Court chief justice and Republican senatorial candidate, Roy Moore. Moore ordered the state's probate judges to refuse applications for same-sex marriage licenses, which resulted in Alabama's Court of the Judiciary suspending him for the remainder of his term, finding him in violation of the canon of judicial ethics.[6] Whereas in Kentucky, a federal court ordered a state official to do something, in Alabama, the state itself enforced the federal ruling against its own chief judge who dissented. Such political controversy has often marked the boundary between federal and state authority.

This book charts and interprets the complicated relationship between American constitutional law and changes in federal governmental power from the 1790s to the 1990s. It demonstrates that the Court is an institution that continuously defines and redefines the boundaries of federal authority, not one that expands or contracts that authority during neat, specific eras. This book moves us away from interpreting constitutional outcomes with respect to "original intent" or "judicial activism," as liberal or conservative, or "right" or "wrong." Instead, this book tracks the political outcomes and effects of legal decisions. It looks beyond historical eras and the ideological motivations of individual justices to consider the Court's overall effect on federal authority.

Constitutional issues involving federalism provide the primary avenue through which the Court advances the federal government; the judiciary thus influences the public's understanding of the limits of constituent state power. In the less-common cases, when the Court overrules a congressional statute, it restricts federal authority because it has constricted the ability of the federal government to enforce its preferences through that statute.

As evaluated through judicial rulings, federal power has grown dramatically, and has done so across each historical era. Because the limits of federal authority constantly expand and contract, and because its overall strength has varied across time, it makes little sense to dub the federal government at any given point as either strong or weak or big or small (Novak 2015). This enduring pattern of constitutional change challenges an overarching assumption both liberals and conservatives share, which is that the federal government only began to exert significant influence over the lives of citizens in the early twentieth century. To hold this assumption belies the patterns of constitutional change—and their concomitant effect on the federal government.

The US Supreme Court and the Centralization of Federal Authority unearths when the authority of the federal government expands and contracts and what issues prompt these changes. It also contends that political characterizations of the national state miss the nuanced ways both the state and constitutional law have evolved over time. Uncovering when and how the federal state's authority grew in size and scope ultimately causes us to revise our understanding of American state-building.

As an institution not deeply connected to the democratic will or the power of the purse or sword, the Court has gradually enhanced its own authority and the authority of the coordinate government branches over time. This book argues that (1) there is persistent expansion of federal state authority, and defines such expansion of authority as any Court ruling that invalidates a state law or affirms a federal law; that (2) this expansion happens gradually and incrementally over time, often through invalidating lower-level state laws; and (3) expansion occurs through extending federal authority to make decisions concerning citizens and people.

When the federal judiciary upholds a *state* law, the Court has restricted central state authority. The Court, in effect, has said federal power (i.e., the

Constitution) does not apply to the state-level action before the Court. Likewise, when the federal judiciary strikes down a state law, then the Court has expanded central state authority: the Court, in effect, has said that federal power (i.e., the Constitution, or a superior federal statute) applies to the state-level action before the Court. When the federal judiciary affirms a federal law, then the Court has expanded central state authority, allowing a coordinate branch to extend its reach. And when the judiciary invalidates a federal law, it restricts central state authority because the Court has explicitly impeded a coordinate branch from continuing to exert authority.

Central State Authority Defined

In charting the growth and development of the American state, American Political Development (APD) scholars have often drawn comparisons to European state systems, leading "many scholars to focus on things that did not happen in the United States, such as the absence of strong social democratic movements in the late nineteenth and early twentieth centuries." With these comparisons, scholars have "reinforce[d] a continuing preoccupation with European experience" and thus overlooked facets of American state formation (Bensel 1990, ix). A burgeoning movement in APD argues that equating the absence of centralized bureaucratic Weberian structures with a weak or absent central state-building "is false and no longer tenable analytically" (King and Lieberman 2008, 371; Bensel 2000; Howard 2007; Brian Balogh 2009; Sparrow 2011; Murakawa 2014).

In this regard, many scholars have too-narrowly defined "central state authority" and "central state building," seeing it as only the creation of bureaucratic and administrative capacity and movement toward a European Weberian kind of central state, one with strong social welfare and administrative capacities.[7] Weberian understanding of state authority is simply one way to define the state and its development. While the growth of Weberian structures certainly counts as "central state expansion," this traditional approach juxtaposes judicial power against the national political branches. The interpretation of judicial decisions summarized above understands central state expansion as an assertion of jurisdiction over some area of government. In this way, jurisdiction and authority are synonymous. One of this book's chief assumptions is that state-building consists of centralizing, consolidating, expanding, and asserting federal authority, which builds off William Novak's (1996) understanding of nineteenth-century state development.[8] Therefore, when the federal judiciary invalidates state-level laws, it expands central state authority. Thus, the term "central state expansion" means the advancement, growth, and affirmation of federal state authority toward any end.

Note: this book uses "central state," "federal state," "American state," and "federal/national/central government," interchangeably. They all represent the actions of the highest level of government in the United States. This conception requires one to think about the supervisory role the Court plays as part of the central state in a federal system.

In most federations such as the United States, courts are crucial in that "they can affect centralization and decentralization directly by ruling on the constitutional distribution or powers and indirectly by ruling on social issues, individual rights, economic affairs, and other matters" (Aroney and Kincaid 2017, 3). Indeed these types of governments typically require written constitutions, which invites judicial interpretation, so this book is primarily interested in uncovering whether the Supreme Court, through its interpretation, centralizes federal authority (fostering a "unitary" state) or whether the Court tends toward supporting constituent states (contributing toward a "federalist" state).

The American Constitution marked the origin of modern federalism because it combined both a traditional "confederal" understanding and a national or unitary understanding, described by James Madison as a "compound republic" (Ball 2007, 253).[9] This national understanding, embodied in what the framers called the "general" government, gave significant authority to the general government: to raise an army, levy taxes, regulate trade and businesses, and prosecute citizens who violated federal law. These newfound powers required a federal court system with strong judicial review precisely because the framers lacked "the political ability to displace states' courts" and recognized "the liabilities of relying only on the states' courts to adjudicate federal matters" (Aroney and Kincaid 2017, 8). While the power of judicial review during the Early Republic era, as Alexis de Tocqueville remarked, was "the only power peculiar to an American judge," this power is found in nearly 83 percent of the world's constitutions (Aroney and Kincaid 2017, 8).

Therefore, a crucial part of state-building in federal systems is the development of constitutional judicial review. So part of American state-building rests on the Supreme Court's use of judicial review to centralize federal authority. However, the centralizing tendency of the Court's decisions does not always build the state in the European sense; nevertheless, the Court's centralization constitutes an accretion of federal power unique to federally designed countries. Centralization always means some sort of growth of federal authority, but it does not always translate into "state-building" in the European sense. Still, this book views centralization and state-building as synonymous because centralization contributes to a nation-state's capacity to govern.

Debating the Boundaries of Federal Authority

American political development has revealed the growing expansion of the federal government relative to states' autonomy. Congress has become more involved in virtually every policy area, from economics to social realms, while the Court has become central in policing and protecting individual rights. Nevertheless, today, as in periods before, the scope and boundaries of federal power remain a central political debate.

In the United States, political arguments rest on a discourse regarding constitutional rights. While a relatively recent phenomenon,[10] the dominance of rights argumentation necessitates that we understand the shape and trajectory of constitutional rights and authority over time. Conservative critics of the Affordable Care Act (ACA), for example, claimed it reached beyond the constitutional powers of the federal government. Indeed, Republicans calling for a repeal of the ACA were a dime a dozen in the 2014 midterm elections. Similarly, the Senate's nonrenewal of the federal assault weapons ban in 2013 revealed the power of constitutional rhetoric in determining policy. Sen. Charles E. Grassley (R-Iowa) attacked the measure as a "slippery slope of compromising the 2nd Amendment."[11] Progressive political thought often invokes the Constitution, too, but in a different way. Some, such as Georgetown law professor Louis Michael Siedeman, encourage constitutional disobedience as a way to remedy federal government dysfunction and congressional gridlock.[12] Both sides of the political aisle see engaging the Constitution (either maintaining or revising our understanding of it) as a panacea for the policy issues facing the United States, because there is no single understanding of what the Constitution means.

Moreover, because reliance on and reverence for the Constitution have defined US political debate, we need to better understand how the Court has shaped our understanding of the Constitution and the limits of federal power. America's reliance on constitutional rhetoric stands in contrast to other Western democratic states, whose constitutions are much younger and, in some cases, unwritten. Indeed, as French sociologist Alexis de Tocqueville opined back in the mid-nineteenth century, many political problems eventually become legal, though not always constitutional, questions in the United States.[13] The United States has a more extensive constitutional discourse on political power than Western European nation-states, a feature that requires a thorough exploration of constitutional development and its connection to political discourse.

The reason for this unique American discourse has much to do with a written constitution, but it also has to do with the institution of chattel slavery and the rights-claims it produced (Shklar 1998, 111). More specifically, these claims necessitate that the Supreme Court play a vital role in defining the relationship between the federal government and society. Since this written constitution inscribes all citizens' *federal* rights, each citizen can claim her rights before the judiciary. The Supreme Court, as an institution, has traditionally defined what it means to be a citizen and what counts as legitimate state authority. As such, the study of the Court and its pivotal cases sheds light on far more than jurisprudential changes, because the Court has shaped the rights of peoples and governmental authority more than any other institution. The United States's reliance on a written constitution has enabled the Court to serve this role.

In sum, US political rhetoric suffers from an incomplete understanding of the constitutional changes to the federal state. Contemporary conservative and libertarian political thought concerns itself with limiting federal power, thus creating a smaller federal government. Conservative public intellectuals and politicians bemoan "big government" for many reasons, but chief among them is that big government limits individual rights and freedoms.[14] By contrast, political liberals seek to expand the role of the federal government. Yet neither side of the political debate maintains consistency: conservatives might favor expanding federal power (e.g. for military and defense spending) while liberals sometime seek to maintain state-level autonomy, devolving power from the federal government. Clearly, neither side can agree on where the boundary between federal and state authority lies.

Therefore, I will examine whether, as the federal government has grown in strength and size, civil liberties and governmental protections of these liberties have kept pace. I will also examine how long "big government"— or a powerful, active federal government—has existed in this country. The public—not just conservatives—views big government as an artifact of the twentieth century because the public tends to assess federal power through the limited perspectives of the social-welfare and national-security states. By employing this myopic lens, however, we overlook the myriad aspects of federal government that the Supreme Court advanced and consolidated steadily throughout the years, rather than through momentary bursts of expansion, as punctuated equilibrium models posit. Preoccupied with the size of government, US political debate turns on questions about the constitutional boundaries of the federal government. The rhetoric of "big" versus "small" government, however, misses the nuanced ways in which the federal government has evolved through the Court's constitutional interpretation. That is why it is important to examine precisely where, when, and how the national government constitutionally expanded and narrowed. Understanding these changes will help produce more intelligent political discussion about the role of the federal government in American lives.

The Court's Role in State-Building

Like political parties, presidents, legislators, and bureaucrats, the Supreme Court plays a major role in expanding the American state.[15] To understand the Court's impact on and proclivity toward expanding central state authority, we need to broaden our notion of "development" beyond development toward a European-style welfare state.

A "developed" national state can do other, less egalitarian things. For example, it can protect national marketplaces (Bensel 2000), make war (Sparrow 2011), imprison minorities (Murakawa 2014), and act as a clearinghouse for rent seekers (Mettler 2011). The state can also move toward becoming a European-style welfare state in covert ways (Balogh 2009; Novak 1996; Howard 2007). It is critical to note that levels of government below the federal level can have important social-welfare state functions, such as that of protecting positive rights (Zackin 2013).

Recognizing the impact of the legal branch on the growth of the federal government adds to the literature on how the judiciary contributes to central state growth.[15] It also emphasizes the importance of judges to federal state formation. I make my case not by focusing on institutional changes within the Supreme Court, but by examining the impact of the Court's ideational and constitutional decisions on central-state development and authority over most of its history, from 1789 to 1997. The end date of this book is 1997 because of the inductive method of case selection, which I discuss in chapter 2. I am not alone in arguing that the law and courts have successfully enhanced, and not just constricted, national and state regulatory power (Frymer 2003; Farhang 2010; Novak 1996). I also have company in my view that the federal courts are part of broadening both the national regime and electoral politics through expanding the powers of national governing coalitions (Gillman 2002; Graber 1993; Whittington 2007). But I break new ground in looking at constitutional change over the long term rather than vis-à-vis specific critical junctures and moments such as the Founding, Reconstruction, and New Deal eras (Ackerman 1991, 1998). Moreover, I apply traditional understandings of state development—the Weberian definition of state power—to the Court's constitutional output, merging public law and new state research agendas. In this way, this book uses new state frameworks to understand constitutional development, a primarily ideational rather than institutional perspective on the judiciary. I use an agnostic or neutral definition of central state expansion, seeing it as the advancement of federal authority irrespective of ideological or normative aims. Thus, judicial decisions that invalidate state laws expand and centralize federal authority.

Taking an expansive look across American history and across constitutional issues adds important texture to our understanding of the Supreme

Court's role in developing central state authority. This book is the first attempt to illuminate that role by systemically collecting and cataloging the Court's influence on the American federal government across all of US history. In doing so, I return repeatedly to two questions: How has the Court affected central state authority? And when and in what areas of the central state has the Court facilitated state development? These questions are important because, as *Obergefell* demonstrates, the Court continually shapes government authority. Indeed, before *Obergefell*, the Court had first upheld state statutes restricting same-sex marriage and then, beginning with *Lawrence v. Texas* (2003), started to expand central state authority by invalidating laws regulating homosexual conduct. With a more rigorous and systematic examination of Supreme Court decisions, we can develop a stronger foundation on which to assess the Court's influence on American state development.

To uncover this influence, I compile an original database of landmark constitutional decisions spanning from the 1790s to 1990s, which I derived from constitutional law casebooks and treatises published between 1822 and 2010. With these data, I discern patterns of expansion and restriction in constitutional development that historical institutionalist approaches to the Supreme Court do not fully reveal. These patterns support arguments that judges are important state-builders (Forbath 2008), that regime politics have important influence on the Court (Whittington 2007), and that federal courts are significant forces that extend central state power to the periphery (Shapiro 1981; Gillman 2002).

Analyzing the Evolution of Constitutional Law

Constitutional change is the product of persistent contestation over the meaning of the values and institutional powers that the Constitution enshrines. This contestation produces a tension that any fallible institution, like the Court, would have difficulty resolving in an evolving society.

But what does constitutional development look like? That is, *how* has the Court shaped the federal government since 1789? If the Supreme Court turns out to have been an engine for (rather than a bulwark against) the expansion of federal authority, what uses of central state authority has the Court supported? If the Court varies over time in its impact on federal authority—that is, if it at different times restricts and expands that authority—we would expect to see variation in the kind of central state that the Court entrenches during any moment in political development. Rather than impose a teleological, progressive understanding of "the state" on constitutional authority, I recognize that the balance between expansion and restriction may change during different eras and in relation to different models of central state formation. I set aside consideration of the ideological and political makeup of the Court and simply track the Court's oscillation between restricting and expanding the federal government. In doing so, I explore three things: (1) whether the Court's impact on federal authority has been gradual and accretive or, conversely, has expanded at flashpoints; (2) whether the Court has affected federal power in consistent or inconsistent ways across all constitutional issues; and (3) whether in the aggregate the Court has expanded federal state power.

This systematic approach illuminates three theoretical concerns about constitutional and state development: how strong or weak the early American state was; how the Court affected the modern American state around the turn of the twentieth century; and why it is important to develop a narrative that examines the Court's constitutional development between the typically recognized watershed cases and moments.

These findings and the theoretical claims on which they rest give us a new understanding of the evolution of constitutional law and the American state. I discern patterns in the ways the judicial branch acts—how it expands federal authority when it does so, and how and when it allows states to control civil and political rights. The Court's interpretation of the federal government's authority forms the constitutional foundation for governance. The story of the American state is not necessarily about strong versus weak federal government, but rather about federal versus state power. The contestation over the meaning and authority of the Constitution, at bottom, concerns one question—does the federal government have the authority to regulate whatever issue is before the Court? Through uncovering the national state's constitutional patterns, the judiciary's precise role in building the American federal government can be more fully comprehended.

Methodology and Epistemic Foundations

While I detail the research design in chapter 2 and in the appendices, a brief word on the epistemic foundations of this book's approach remains necessary. This book employs a trans-historical notion of state authority because of the book's chief purpose: an examination of the Supreme Court's role in national state expansion since the founding. As this chapter's opening anecdote about implementing the same-sex marriage ruling suggests, Americans continue to debate the scope of federal authority. Because of this basic fact, the broad developmental patterns surrounding the Court's position on the boundaries of central state authority need to be revealed and examined. The macro perspective of this book has merit because the scope of federal and state-level authority under the Constitution has pervaded political debates since the country's founding.

This macro perspective, in some ways, differs from the more fine-grained, historical approaches of the studies to which this book speaks—historical institutionalist literature on law and courts, and studies concerning the development of American state. In contrast to judicial behavioralist and rational-choice scholars,[17] historical institutionalists are less concerned with the behavior of actors with fixed preferences, and are concerned instead with the behavior of actors who also have historically constituted beliefs involving the norms of their institution.[18] Thus, historical institutionalist studies attempt to illuminate the long-term processes that lead to the construction of both judicial preferences and of the institutions that constrain a judge's preferences.[19] Yet, while this book contributes to these literatures, it does not examine, in the same historical detail as they would, all the explanations and reasons for why the Court behaves as it does. Instead, this book seeks to empirically catalog and systematically describe the Court's broad attitude toward the central state across time, which resembles the work done by judicial behavioralists. Such a goal warrants closer investigation given the centrality of these debates about political boundaries. Through this book, I incorporate APD's concern with how the construction of authority is formed, shaped, and changed over time, but I examine this through the systematic and empirical approach followed by behavioral studies.

Looking Ahead

The primary focus of chapter 1 is to provide the reasoning behind my interpretation of constitutional decisions and their effect on central state authority. Chapter 1 also explains why I believe decisions that overturn state laws concerning liberty rights do in fact expand central state authority.

Chapter 2 provides an overview of the research design and original, historical database compiled for this book, defining key variables used throughout the book. It presents the overall findings and explores the effect of the Supreme Court's constitutional interpretation on central state authority across time and across constitutional issue areas. In this chapter, I offer a detailed overview of the outcomes of the Court's rulings, and I identify which constitutional issues expanded and which restricted federal power.

Chapters 3 to 5 situate these findings to revise conventional understandings of the historical development of the federal state, the varying interpretations of central state strength and weakness by period, and the nature of the major challenges facing the American federal state (as evidenced by the focus and orientation of the Supreme Court during each period). Here, with newly gathered evidence, I add to the literature that sees the Court as more supportive of state-building than is commonly portrayed, and that sees the federal state as building authority across a longer period than is generally thought.

Chapter 3 analyzes constitutional development up to 1864, paying close attention to the framers' constitutional design, which facilitated a judiciary that would largely support federal supremacy and thus tend toward national government expansion. The Constitution's design created inherent tensions that the Supreme Court would have to navigate. Focusing largely on Chief Justice Marshall's and Taney's Courts (1801–1864), this chapter evaluates the judiciary's role in advancing the authority of the early American state and examines the effect of the constitutionally ambiguous design of federalism.

Chapter 4 centers on building a modern national government from 1865 to 1932. This chapter considers the Court's role in the rise of this state and the reduction of state-level sovereignty in the individual rights realm and in commerce and economic decisions. The recurring issue the central state faced during this period was the reduction of state autonomy, and thus, conflicts over competing models of federalism were paramount during this time.

Chapter 5 takes the reader up to the twenty-first century. It explores how the Court's doctrine outlined in chapter 4 helped establish the distinctive administrative and welfare-state apparatuses advanced throughout the twentieth century. This chapter emphasizes development beyond watershed landmark cases and moments[20] and demonstrates a shift in the purpose of the central state within and across various periods of development.

Chapter 6 concludes with a discussion of how this book adds to the APD literature, looking beyond the constitutional moments approach and showing the Court to be collaborator in national state expansion. Chapter 6 also reemphasizes my broader definition of state-building and the judiciary's supervisory role over constituent states.

Overall, this book adds to the literature concerning the Court's influence on state growth, looking beyond New Deal efforts to expand federal government powers. My interpretation considers the many ways the justices have acted as state builders and shows how the Court's constitutional interpretation helped construct a powerful national government that has grown steadily over time through constitutional doctrine.

Chapter 1

Conceptualizing Supreme Court Power

Introduction

The chief argument and finding of this book—that the Supreme Court has persistently expanded federal authority—depends on a particular conception of both the Court and the American state. Traditionally, the American state is defined by the existence of centralized, growing, and insulated bureaucracies, as measured against the European Weberian model. As a result, scholars have typically viewed the American federal state as fragmented, decentralized, "weak," and "stateless" (Nettl 1968, 561, 564).[1] In some ways, the federal judiciary presents an exception to this view; the Supreme Court performs judicial review of both federal and state laws, creating a shared consistent legal context for the entire nation—in other words, the Supreme Court persistently promotes unitarism, not federalism and state autonomy.[2] Recognizing this fact, this chapter offers an explanation of the judicial behaviors that count as expanding the authority of the federal state.

Briefly, I advocate for a more expansive understanding of the judiciary's integral role in shifting governing authority away from subnational units (i.e., constituent states) upward into the federal or central state. This redefinition of the judiciary's role in consolidating federal power takes heed of recent scholarship that expands understandings of "the state" and its evolution, growth, and strength. These revisionist scholars argue that a lack of centralized bureaucratic Weberian structures does not mean a weak or absent central state, and that the equation of the two "is false and no longer tenable analytically" (King and Lieberman 2008, 371). This book thus contributes to the body of literature seeking to broaden our understanding of what counts as "central state development" and as "state-building" (Baldwin 2005; Mettler 2011; King and Stears 2011; King and Lieberman 2008, 2009, 2016).

1

My interpretation rests not on a Weberian conception of the state but on what Desmond King and Robert Lieberman call "a Dahlian procedural conception of democracy"; in this model, "the state acts as a guarantor of democratic rights alongside its role as a maintainer of internal order and external integrity" (King and Lieberman 2008, 371). Let me be clear: this book defines state-building neither as the growth of individual rights protection (a model in which change entails a telos toward progressivism) nor as the expansion of a European-style welfare state (the Weberian model), but simply as the expansion of federal power over constituent state power and citizens.[3] If we think about state-building primarily in Weberian terms, we are prevented from seeing how the Court extends the power of the federal state in other ways. Instead, I consider how a powerful judiciary advances federal power for any purpose whatsoever.[4] Constitutional decisions that advance welfare-state powers are not the only way to understand central state development and expansion. In what follows, I take a broad view of how the Court expands the Dahlian procedural state.

The history of the role played by the Supreme Court, from the founding until the turn of the twenty-first century, in constitutional development (or state-building) has not yet been systematically analyzed.[5] Perhaps more importantly, citizens and politicians alike have never agreed on precisely where the boundaries between federal and state authority lie (Somin 2017, 442). This book deliberately takes a broad, macro-level approach to understanding the Court's role in state-building and the development of central state authority by coding the Court's leading constitutional decisions across issue areas and across American history. Constitutional development is the ebb and flow of *all* forms of central state authority, not simply the advancement of welfare-state powers, and we need a theoretical framework that allows us to interpret judicial decisions in terms of their effect on advancing the myriad kinds of central state power across time. This broad definition of the "state" (and the state powers the Court could advance) allows us to see how the Court has decided constitutional cases in ways that advanced or impeded the development of the American state across history.

Understanding State Expansion, Capacity, and Development

This book rests, in part, on recognizing the Court's role as a key centralizer of federal authority throughout American political development and understanding expansive judicial authority as an important facet of state building. The federal judiciary expands the federal state when it invalidates a state/local action *or* when it affirms a federal action. Judicial invalidation of a state action expands federal authority through the assertion of federal judicial power; judicial affirmation of a federal action affirms the authority of the coordinate branches. Every time the Court expands federal authority through one of these actions, it engages in state-building, as it is delineated in Richard Bensel's (1990, 107) taxonomy of central state authority. Bensel's taxonomy—which is discussed further in chapter 2—recognizes that one major component in state development is the centralization of authority, which he defines as "all measures that concentrate decision-making authority within one of the institutions of the central state" (Bensel 1990, 107). When the Court's decisions extend congressional or executive power, or when the Court extends federal judicial power by limiting the legal authority of individual states and the rights of people, it engages in a crucial component of state development: centralization of authority.[6]

This book's major contentions are connected to recent scholarly under-standings of state development and state capacity. These new, non-Weberian definitions lean on the importance of the centralization of federal authority. For example, Karen Orren and Stephen Skowronek define "political development" as "a durable shift in governing authority," or "the exercise of control over persons or things that is designated and enforceable by the state" (Orren and Skowronek 2004, 123). I argue that this governing authority is shifted, in part, through the Court's decisions; even decisions that do not concretely alter federal authority in the typical way, such as by establishing bureaucratic control over a policy area, still shape the boundaries of accepted federal authority. Similarly, Suzanne Mettler and Richard Valelly have recently defined "state capacity" in terms of centralized state authority: state capacity means, "Government being able to do what its various legitimate principals want it to do when they want it to" (Mettler and Valelly 2016, 9). Of course, this definition of capacity also entails the enforcement power of the state, something the Court has little to do with (the Court does not even have power to enforce its own decisions). However, the importance of central state authority to Mettler and Valelly's definition is what I am interested in, for it is precisely the business of the Court to specify the authority of the central state—to expand or limit it through its published opinions.[7] The Court does not implement its own decisions, it only expands (or diminishes) state authority, as opposed to capacity, through a text. Whenever the Court expands or restricts the authority of the central state, it engages in central state development, or constitutional development, which means simply the accretion or diminishment of central state authority over time. The term "development" does not imply an increasingly progressive central state;[8] it only suggests that authority has shifted.

A relatively passive political institution, the Court gradually builds the federal state as it rules on cases that come before it. The Court can construct federal power either actively, by invalidating a state law, or passively, by let-ting a federal law stand—in other words, by deferring to another political authority.[9] When the Court invalidates state-level laws, this increases the reach and scope of the federal state. Striking down a state-level law thus tends to increase the power of the central state and thus represents a type of state-building. Therefore, we must consider both validation of federal law and invalidation of constituent-state law to have equal importance in building the central state.

Why the Supreme Court's Decisions Centralize Federal Power

The Supreme Court builds the American federal state across non-Weberian understandings of state capacity; in its rulings, the Supreme Court declares itself or other parts of the central state to be the supervisor over particular policies and issues. Because the US Supreme Court is America's highest judicial tribunal, the Court's actions are actions of the central state and tend to increase its power. The Fourteenth Amendment—the mechanism through which the Court has invalidated the lion's share of state-level laws—has produced significant central state expansion; judicial invalidation of state laws grants additional authority to the central state by enabling the Court to supervise myriad state actions.

The Court as a Central State Actor

Constitutional rights cases often involve two stages, jurisdictional and sub-stantive. The first stage is jurisdictional: this stage decides whether a federal court will hear a particular claim. The second stage is substantive: this stage decides whether the federal judge will recognize the litigants' rights claim in this particular case. One might wonder, then: does every Supreme Court case granted certiorari—the mere judicial assertion of jurisdiction—expand federal authority, regardless of the case outcome? No. To interpret the act of jurisdictional assertion itself as expanding the central state would disregard the substantive ruling of the case at hand. The substantive matter of a ruling is concerned with what the Court allows a government to do (or not do) to its citizens; a ruling expands the power of the central state when it affirms a coordinate branch of government or invalidates a state-level law. The *only* time that the Court's simple assertion of jurisdiction expands central state authority is when the actual *substantive* question before the Supreme Court is a jurisdictional one: does the Court have the right to hear this type of case?[10] In the federal system, constitutional courts' decisions are a zero-sum game: what increases federal power reduces constituent state power, and vice versa. The Supreme Court's authority is thus often in tension with the governing authority of constituent states, and the Court's rulings on Fourteenth Amendment rights cases emanating from constituent states must be interpreted substantively. Only substantive interpretation can reveal whether the Court has restricted federal authority (by holding that the plaintiff's rights claim is beyond the scope of the Constitution) or expanded federal authority—in other words, expanded the Constitution's reach—by recognizing a rights claim in the particular case before the Court. To put it another way, virtually all cases ask the Court to define the extent of central state authority.

Despite the Supreme Court's clear role in defining central state authority, the construction of American state authority has often been understood only in terms of the growth of administrative authority.[11] Few studies of the American state consider the Court's centralizing tendency to be a form of state-building; studies of American state-building typically focus on the advancement of administrative capacity and on America's differences from the European, Weberian ideal–type state (Skowronek 1982; Carpenter 2001; Novak 2008; Balogh 2009). But, as Kimberly Morgan argues, "There is no reason why the European ideal–type should be the dominant starting point" for examining state-building and authority (Morgan 2016, 175). This narrow definition of state building has led some scholars to view judicial invalidation of Progressive-era laws as anti-statist: when Orren (1991) analyzes judicial restrictions on legislative sovereignty as feudal holdovers, she argues that judicial authority opposes "state" or "national" governing authority. Similarly, when Skowronek (1982) characterizes the late nineteenth century as an era of "courts and parties," he implicitly argues that strong judicial authority acted as a substitute for state-building in the European, Weberian sense. In other words, the American federal state is understood by some scholars as only "the administrative structures created in the federal bureaucracy and executive branch" (King and Lieberman 2016, 239).

But why should the American state and state-building be defined so narrowly? The particularities of the US Constitution—its federal system and independent judiciary—require that, at least where the Court is concerned, we should broaden our definition of state-building to include the centralization of authority along various dimensions of the American state. When the Court issues a ruling that reduces state-level autonomy, the judiciary centralizes federal power and creates uniformity, *even when* the ruling inhibits the building of the Weberian ideal–type state. Perhaps, then, what is most distinctive about the American state-building story is not its unusually fragmented, decentralized bureaucratic capacity, but rather its powerful and independent federal judiciary. The judiciary's tendency to centralize federal authority over time represents a crucial dimension in the construction of political authority.

This judicial tendency to centralize is not entirely unique to the United States; it is described in comparative analyses of constitutional courts in many Western democracies, especially federal states. Legal scholars have previously noted the tendency toward centralization of authority in federal states such as Australia, Austria, post-1949 Canada, Germany, and India.[12] In a study of forty-two countries, including the United States, Roland Vaubel finds that the judiciary reinforces this centralizing tendency: he argues that "constitutional judges have a vested interested in centralization," especially if the judges of the court are "independent" and if there are high barriers to constitutional amendments—both conditions that exist in the United States (Vaubel 2009, 203).[13] Other studies of Western democracies conclude, "constitutional courts predominantly tend to expand the power of central institutions in the economic sector," another example of the tendency of judicial branches to centralize (Von Brunneck, quoted in Vaubel 2009, 205).

Viewing the Court's invalidation of state laws as expanding federal authority dovetails with a burgeoning movement in American political development that argues equating a lack of centralized bureaucratic Weberian structures with a weak central state "omits the state's complexities" (King and Lieberman 2008, 371). This recent scholarly movement finds that American state capacity reveals itself in a multitude of ways, ranging from the traditional administrative bureaucracy (Skowronek 1982) to the "submerged" aspects of the federal tax code (Mettler 2011) to assertions of federal judicial jurisdiction over various issues and policies.[14] The Supreme Court's constitutional decisions fall into this last category, tending toward centralizing federal authority and limiting constituent state autonomy. Yet some scholars still argue that the judiciary, and its practice of judicial review, *constrains* American state development—a conclusion based on the narrow Weberian definition of the state (King and Lieberman 2016, 239–40).[15] However, the vast majority of the Court's decisions review state and local laws, and the Court strikes these laws down far more frequently than it does federal laws; the judiciary thus engages in two of Skowronek's four "organizational qualities" that define a state actor: concentrating authority at the national center of government, and centralizing authority within the national government (Skowronek 1982, 19–20). To conclude that the judiciary engages in state-building, we must recognize that state-building consists not only of constructing administrative capacity but also of taking authority from subnational units and lodging it upward in the federal government.

The US Supreme Court Rests at the Top

The Court's tendency to centralize federal authority grows out of a particular institutional feature of the Supreme Court, judicial finality, and on the Court's hierarchical place in American politics. During constitutional ratification debates, anti-Federalists recognized that judicial finality—meaning that the Court is the final interpreter of the Constitution; after judicial review, there is no further recourse or appeal—posed a threat to state rights. The anti-Federalists saw that the Court's decisions could expand central state authority by invalidating state laws. These anti-Federalist fears suggest that they saw judicial invalidation as constituting an expansion of central state authority.[16] For example, the anti-Federalist Brutus worried that when the Court extended its jurisdiction—its authority to decide particular questions and issues—state-level autonomy and authority would be more likely to be diminished. Brutus feared that the Court's power would lead to the "entire subversion of the legislative, executive, and judicial powers of the individual states. Every adjudication of the supreme court . . . will affect the limits of the state jurisdiction."[17] Anti-Federalists' fear of judicial review of state laws suggests that they recognized judicial invalidation as an expansion of central state authority, creating what Storing has called "a consolidating aristocracy" (Storing 1981, 50).

But for the most part, the framers thought that judges should have the power of judicial review to void at least state laws should they violate the US Constitution (Gillman, Graber, and Whittington 2017a, 56).[18] Indeed, James Madison went so far as to propose a federal veto of state legislation, which would allow federal courts to directly invalidate state laws without need for a lawsuit to establish jurisdiction. The other delegates rejected his proposal; instead, on the next day, the delegates adopted the Supremacy Clause language, which asserted that the Constitution would be "the supreme Law of the Land." According to Woody Holton, the Supremacy Clause "was obviously intended as a more palatable substitute" for Madison's direct invalidation proposal (Holton 2007, 186). This decision indicates that the delegates understood that the Court was likely to engage in judicial review of state laws, and that they foresaw its ability to extend the sphere of central state authority and thereby reduce constituent-state authority.[19] Just a couple of decades later, the Marshall Court (1801–1835) established the judiciary's position as "the final arbiter and interpreter of the Constitution"[20] (Balogh 2009, 250–51). In so doing, it "spearheaded the movement toward nationalism" (Ellis 2007, 15). President Thomas Jefferson even bemoaned "the Judiciary," which he saw as "on every occasion still driving us into consolidation."[21]

Because the Court rests at the top of the judicial branch in the hierarchical structure of a federal system, judicial finality allows the Court to expand national governing authority by invalidating state laws; in other words, the Court drives "us into consolidation" by reducing state-level autonomy through judicial review. Whenever the Court, from its institutional position as the final interpreter of the Constitution, blocks a state-level action or turns back a state or individual challenge to a federal law, it incrementally expands the accepted boundary of central state authority. As chapter 2 will show, Brutus was largely right: the Supreme Court would, over time, "lean strongly in favour of the general government," and it would indeed interpret the Constitution to "favour an extension of its jurisdiction."[22] And the passage of the Fourteenth Amendment in 1868 would enable the Court to further expand central state authority.

The Fourteenth Amendment Expanded Federal Authority

Passed in 1868, the Fourteenth Amendment provides one of the primary ways the Court has centralized federal state authority. Its interpretations of the Fourteenth Amendment have, over time, incorporated or nationalized the Bill of Rights under the Fourteenth Amendment. Whether those Reconstruction Republicans who formulated the Fourteenth Amendment intended to nationalize the Bill of Rights remains unclear.[23] Nevertheless, the empirical reality is that the Fourteenth Amendment "transformed the structure of constitutional protection for political and civil liberties in the United States and . . . profoundly altered the nature of the federal system," enabling the federal judiciary to supervise states' policies in expanding ways (Cortner 1981, 279).[24]

The Fourteenth Amendment established a structure of active federal supervision, through the Supreme Court, over a growing number of legal issues and policy areas, including economic policy and the creation of a national marketplace (Bensel 2000, 289–355).[25] The Fourteenth Amendment gave the Court the power to supervise states to ensure that no laws deprived "any person of life, liberty, or property without due process of law." But in 1886, the Court declared that, for purposes of Fourteenth Amendment consideration, a corporation was a "person"; this expansive interpretation of the Fourteenth Amendment enabled the Court to protect corporate and property interests in addition to the interests of individual citizens.[26] In arrogating to itself the power to determine economic and regulatory questions, the Court levied a major "blow to state regulatory power" and took on the task of "supervising legislators' policy judgments" (Wiecek 1998, 154).[27] Under the Fourteenth Amendment, the Supreme Court now had the discretionary prerogative to decide how (and how much) central state expansion would happen through its interpretive decisions, which reduced states' regulatory power and bolstered the regulatory authority of the central state. Although the central state actually imposed fewer regulations than some constituent states preferred, this was still an expansion of central state power.

The Court's interpretations of the Fourteenth Amendment through the end of the nineteenth century transformed the judiciary into a supervisor of nation-building. The Court's decisions imbued the Due Process Clause with substantive meaning; this clause, broadly speaking, offered the basis for the Court's striking down of regulatory laws that prevented people *and* corporations from receiving a "reasonable return" on their invested capital (Bensel 2000, 334).[28] Before the passage of the Fourteenth Amendment, state and local governments had overseen and regulated economic and infrastructural development (McCurdy 1978, 634; Balogh 2009, 339), and Congress's parochial interests had "forestalled vigorous" federal action over national marketplace regulation (McCurdy 1978, 634). After the passage of the Fourteenth Amendment, the Supreme Court stepped in to act as the primary state-builder of the national market economy, imposing meaningful restrictions on state-level economic regulations.[29] For example, in 1890, the Court handed down two decisions that invalidated two local railroad regulations imposed by the Railroad and Warehouse Commission of Minnesota. The Commission had attempted to levy charges and rates for switching cars in a Minneapolis railroad yard and transporting goods from Minneapolis to smaller cities within Minnesota. The Court's majority opinion held that "If the [railway] company is deprived of the power of charging reasonable rates for the use of its property, and such deprivation takes place in the absence of an investigation by judicial machinery, it is deprived of the lawful use of its property, and thus, in substance and effect, of the property itself without due process of law in violation of the Constitution of the United States."[30] During this period, many state-level regulations collided with the "liberty of contract" doctrine that the Court read into the Fourteenth Amendment.[31]

Each Supreme Court decision on the meaning of the Fourteenth Amendment decided how and in what ways central state authority would be exercised. Because political actors (Congress and the president, primarily) have historically sought to make the federal judiciary the ultimate arbiter of the Constitution (Whittington 2007), the nature of American federal courts makes them desirable places for outside groups to advance their political agenda. In appealing to the Court's interpretation of the Fourteenth Amendment, in particular, these groups, like railroad companies and the NAACP Legal Defense Fund, have helped extend central state authority.[32] When the Court stated that the Fourteenth did not apply to the state action in question, the

Court refrained from applying the US Constitution to the state law—a decision that restricted central state authority. When the Court ruled the other way, stating that the Fourteenth did apply to the state action in question, it expanded both central state authority and the reach of the Constitution. The key element in these Fourteenth Amendment cases is that there were no previous interpretive positions on these issues; the Court's rulings could therefore only either expand or restrict federal authority. The Court's initial rulings on Fourteenth Amendment cases did not advance the Weberian ideal–type state; the Court itself, rather than a centralized bureaucracy, effectively became the primary supervisor. Yet the Court's decisions during the late nineteenth century assuredly expanded federal power: the Court "facilitated a concentration of governing authority," and with its liberty of contract decisions, the Court "sought to sharpen the boundaries between the public and private spheres [and] to provide clear and predictable standards for gauging the scope of acceptable state action" (Skowronek 1982, 41).

Judicial Review's Influence over States

Although the American national government is seen as being decentralized and localized, the federal judiciary, and its power of judicial review, is not; in the US federal system, judicial review generally promotes unitarism, not federalism.[33] As it is practiced (often through the Fourteenth Amendment and other liberty cases), judicial review expands central state authority without constructing centralized bureaucracy or building administrative capacity. Judicial invalidation of state laws expanded central state authority by substantively limiting the freedom and authority of state-level governments. Even when judicial enforcements of limits on state-level power do not advance the traditional Weberian state, they do advance another of Bensel's seven dimensions of central state[34] authority: jurisdiction over a policy issue in government.[35] So how do these judicial invalidations contribute to central state development? The answer is that the Court's use of judicial invalidation, especially since the passage of the Fourteenth Amendment, usually establishes the federal government as the supervisor over particular legal and policy issue areas, even if national regulatory efforts to guarantee rights and liberties do not soon follow.

The Commerce Clause and liberty cases of the *Lochner* era laid the groundwork for the centralized and powerful Weberian-style federal government that would emerge decades later, in the postwar era. The initial assertion of these federal powers, however, was antiprogressive and anti-Weberian.[36] In the late nineteenth century, manufacturing giants such as I. M. Singer & Company used their "legal defense war chests" to spearhead a "doctrinal revolution" that made the Supreme Court the "umpire of the nation's free trade network" (McCurdy 1978, 642, 649).[37] These manufacturing corporations' legal cases had implications for the development of civil rights and the Court's supervisory role over these rights in the mid-twentieth century: "What the NAACP Legal Defense Fund accomplished for black Americans under the Fourteenth Amendment in the twentieth century, the legal-defense war chests of I. M. Singer & Company and the 'Big Four' meatpackers accomplished for vertically integrated corporations under the commerce clause between 1875 and 1890" (McCurdy 1978, 649). In other words, the Court's development and expansion of central state authority were used to protect both corporations and individual civil rights; state development is the advancement of federal authority irrespective of its ideological or normative aims.

During the Early Republic era, before the passage of the Fourteenth Amendment, the Court restricted state governments and advanced central state authority. In *Fletcher v. Peck* (1810),[38] for example—the first case in which the Supreme Court invalidated a state law on constitutional grounds—the Marshall Court's Contracts Clause cases prevented states from impairing obligations of contracts to spur land and economic development. At issue in *Fletcher* was the Georgia legislature's 1794 sale of 35 million acres of state land to four private companies. In 1796, the legislature passed an act aimed at rescinding the previous sale. The Supreme Court interpreted the original grant to private land companies as a contract within the meaning of the Contracts Clause of the Constitution and ruled that, once made, such a grant could not be repealed—an example of "judicial nationalization" and an extension of central state authority (VanBurkleo 2005, 352). In a four-one decision, Marshall invalidated the Georgia law repealing the original land-grant sale. Marshall's decision produced a public outcry, especially from states' rights advocates, who claimed that the Court's decision pandered to land speculators and developers (VanBurkeleo 2005, 352). In fact, *Fletcher* and other Contracts Clause cases did exactly that: they facilitated land and economic development at the expense of state-level autonomy. More importantly, they expanded the accepted limits of national power by establishing that the Court, a branch of the central state, could supervise state laws.

Later in the nineteenth century, during the antebellum era, Supreme Court judicial invalidations also centralized federal authority. The Court invalidated some northern states' attempts to protect escaped slaves from the far-reaching federal Fugitive Slave Acts; in *Prigg v. Pennsylvania* (1842),[39] the Court struck down a Pennsylvania law that prohibited the removal of African-Americans from the state for purposes of enslaving them. Similarly, in *Ableman v. Booth* (1859),[40] Chief Justice Roger Taney's Court unanimously blocked the Wisconsin State Supreme Court from issuing a writ of habeas corpus for an escaped slave held in federal custody in Milwaukee.

The Court also expanded central state authority through a variety of rulings on the dormant Commerce Clause. Between 1872 and 1932, the Supreme Court invalidated 180 state laws via the dormant Commerce Clause, and the judicial interpretation of this clause prevented states from enacting legislation that the Court ruled was prohibited by the Constitution (Greve 2012, 93, 111). These decisions interpreted the Commerce Clause—which granted Congress the authority to regulate interstate commerce—as an implicit restriction on states' abilities to regulate interstate commerce, even if Congress had not chosen to regulate the activity in question. These rulings invalidated state regulatory laws, thus advancing central state authority.[41] Michael Greve argues that these dormant Commerce Clause case decisions instituted "judicial dominance" over interstate commerce and facilitated the "rise of a competitive federal Constitution"—a constitution that constructed a national market (Greve 2012, 92). Throughout the nineteenth century, the national market comprised a "rivalistic state mercantilism"; no federal branch but the Supreme Court acted as a "meaningful political check" on these behaviors (Greve 2012, 94).

The best-known of the Court's judicial invalidations of state laws during the late nineteenth and early twentieth centuries are *Lochner* and its progeny. In 1905, the Court used the "liberty of contract" interpretation that it had read into the Fourteenth Amendment to declare unconstitutional a New York law mandating maximum working hours for bakers. The so-called *Lochner* era imposed significant restrictions on state economic and labor regulations, centralizing federal decision-making authority in the judiciary (Somin 2017, 468). While most see *Lochner* and similar cases as simply restricting central state authority (these judicial invalidations prevented state governments from intervening in the private sphere and altering societal arrangements), *Lochner* also expanded national state power: the Court's contraction of state-level legislative authority produced the expansion of the reach and scope of the Constitution; *Lochner* is two-sided in this way. The judiciary used central state power to even more explicitly control labor and economic policy; this period, according to William Forbath, marked the introduction of the labor injunction, an important state-building judicial initiative. Forbath argues, "The labor injunction marked a new era of rapidly expanding regulation—and suppression—of strikes and boycotts. . . . Surveying the injunction's varied uses, political scientists concluded it was the only effective means of executing 'the will of the state'" (Forbath 2008, 656).[42] Although *Lochner* prevented development of some aspects of the modern Weberian ideal–type state, which is responsive to workers' rights and labor welfare issues, it remained an act of state-building: it centralized federal authority, removing it from states and placing it in the hands of the federal government—in the hands of the judiciary itself.

The *Lochner* era review of state laws also helped to build the Progressive, Weberian modern American state; the "substantive" Due Process rights defended and extended during the *Lochner* era set the precedent for the advancement of other civil liberties later in the twentieth century. For example, this reasoning led the Court to invalidate a Nebraska law that prevented teaching German to grade school children[43] and a state law that mandated that children attend public schools instead of private religious ones.[44] Substantive due process also led to the Court's unanimous overturning of a Louisiana residential segregation law in *Buchanan v. Warley* (1917).[45] *Buchanan* certainly did not abolish residential segregation, but it allowed African Americans to move into neighborhoods previously barred to them (Somin 2017, 468–469). These examples provide a glimpse into how the Court used Due Process to expand central state authority over the individual rights issues that are presumed to be part of the Weberian ideal–type strong central state: civil liberties and civil rights protection. These Weberian advancements of central state authority relied upon the Fourteenth amendment Substantive Due Process mechanism used throughout the *Lochner* era. The *Lochner*-era decisions also built the central state by extending the Constitution's reach.

After the New Deal, the Court moved away from judicial review of economic regulations and instead centralized federal authority over the states in other realms, primarily in civil rights and liberties issues. For example, like *Lochner*, *Brown v. Board of Education* (1954) used the Fourteenth Amendment to strike down a state-level law; *Brown* invalidated the state's assertion that it could segregate its public schools.[46] Because after *Brown*, unlike *Lochner*, a national regulatory effort to guarantee rights and liberties soon followed, some consider *Brown* (but not *Lochner*) to be an example of national state expansion, although the two cases advanced their logic via similar constitutional interpretational moves.[47] Since the jurisprudential reasoning in cases like *Brown* resemble that in *Lochner*, it is difficult to maintain that the former expands the central state while the latter does not. Whether a national regulatory effort follows a ruling—as it did for *Brown* but not *Lochner*—is not the Court's doing, and it should not influence whether the *judicial decision itself* expanded or restricted federal authority.[48] Clearly, *Lochner* did centralize federal authority; other post–New Deal liberal jurisprudence followed *Lochner* by applying a variety of rights, enumerated and unenumerated, against the states via the Due Process Clause (Bernstein 2011, 124).

Yet another example of judicial review expanding central state authority can be seen in the Court's gradual incorporation of the US Bill of Rights against state governments. Only three amendments have not been incorporated: the Third Amendment, which prohibits quartering soldiers in private homes, the Fifth Amendment, which gives the right to a grand jury in criminal trials, and the Seventh Amendment, which guarantees a jury trial in civil cases. The various incorporation cases force "states to adhere to unitary national standards" in a variety of policy areas (Somin 2017, 473).

The Supreme Court's incorporation doctrine significantly centralized federal authority with respect to criminal procedure and rights. The Warren Court incorporated the Fourth,[49] Fifth,[50] and Sixth Amendments[51] precisely because it "recognized that the Bill of Rights offered national standards for criminal procedure regardless of how the states wished to conduct trials" (Powe 2000, 412).[52] As it had with *Brown*, the Court imposed national uniformity and standards on issues faced by the nation as a whole, centralizing federal authority (Powe 2000, 443). The Court's frequent uses of judicial review to examine state-level laws were not just the province of liberal judicial "activism" during the Warren Court; subsequent conservative courts, especially the Court led by Chief Justice Rehnquist, continued the use of judicial review to extend and entrench federal authority (Keck 2004, 2007).

The Court also extended incorporation to free speech. In *Brandenburg v. Ohio* (1969), for example, the Court established an interpretation of speech that makes it difficult for states to censor it.[53] Here the Court struck down the Ohio Criminal Syndicalism statute used to convict a Ku Klux Klan leader for "advocat[ing] . . . the duty, necessity, or propriety of crime, sabotage, violence, or unlawful methods of terrorism as a means of accomplishing industrial or political reform."[54] Without evidence that speech "is likely to incite or produce" "imminent lawless action," states cannot silence the people.

Similarly, the Court has extended incorporation to the Establishment Clause; the Court has, for example, outlined strict limits on the display of religious symbols on state public property. In *Allegheny County v. ACLU* (1989),[55] the Court held that the crèche inside the courthouse "unmistakably" endorsed "a patently Christian message: Glory to God for the birth of Jesus Christ" and thus violated the Establishment Clause (*Allegheny*, 598, 601).[56] The Court has also used the Establishment and Free Exercise Clauses to invalidate Bible reading in Pennsylvania public schools and recitations of the Lord' Prayer.[57] These types of Establishment Clause decisions have remained controversial among people in more socially conservative states where residents prefer religion to be integrated with public life. As legal historian Ilya Somin notes, "Since education policy in the United States has historically been controlled largely by local governments, there is sometimes considerable resentment over federal court intervention in this field" (Somin 2017, 474).[58] The state residents resent these Court invalidations of state or local laws because they reduce state and local authority and expand federal authority. When the people on the ground view a federal action as intrusive, that indicates that central state authority has expanded beyond its previously accepted boundaries: the federal government—as represented by the Court—has prevented a state, and its people, from doing something that at least part of its community wants to do.

A Typology of Decisions and Their Effect on Federal Authority

Having provided a broad overview of how the Court's decisions centralize and expand federal state authority, I now offer some more tangible case interpretations of the Court's expansion and restriction of the federal state in the following typology (see Figure 1.1). The Court cases examined in this section illustrate how this book interprets constitutional decisions with respect to federal authority. These decisions represent all possible outcomes on central state authority: restrict, neutral, and expand. The decisions represent different moments in American constitutional history and typify the effect on federal authority, illuminating the typology I propose in this section and the interpretation of a constitutional decision's effect on federal authority.

Two types of decisions—found in the top-left box of Figure 1.1—raise complicated questions about how to interpret the effect of judicial decisions on central state authority: decisions involving individual rights (economic or civil rights and liberties) and decisions involving individual state governments (federalism). Cases about individual rights are centrally about the expansion

	Invalidate	Affirm
State/local	**Expand** Examples: *Lochner v. New York* (economic rights) *Brown v. Board* (civil rights)	**Restrict** Examples: *Barron v. Baltimore*
Federal	**Restrict** Examples: *Coyle v. Smith*	**Expand** Examples: *Julliard v. Greenman*

Level of government under review

Figure 1.1. Typology of Judicial Decisions

or contraction of the Constitution's reach and scope. For example, when the Court strikes down a state law as a violation of a "right," this expands central state power (whether or not the same right prevented Congress from similarly acting) because the Court asserted both the primacy of the Constitution over the constituent state and its own ability, as part of the central state, to supervise that right. Alternatively, when the Court upholds a state law as not violating a "right," this limits federal power (whether or not the decision similarly empowered Congress) because the Court asserted that the central state cannot supervise this issue. Decisions that relate to federalism—to the competing jurisdictions of the federal and state governments—are relatively straightforward when they do not involve "rights"; in these cases, a finding for federal jurisdiction advances central state authority, and a finding for state jurisdiction contracts federal authority. But, as the next section about *Lochner* will show, many federalism decisions do in fact involve rights.

The rights cases are complex because, according to the interpretation set out below, expansion of federal authority can occur even when the judicial outcomes are normatively different. For example, if the Court sustained a federal law that silenced dissenting speech but in a different decision struck down a state law that discriminated against certain people from speaking, both of these decisions—even though one limits speech and one protects speech—count as an expansion of federal authority. This agnostic interpretation is simply a way to measure the degree to which the Court's decisions centralize federal power, regardless of the normative underpinning of the case outcome (whether to allow or disallow speech, for example).

The Controversial Case of *Lochner v. New York* (1905)

Applying my understanding of state development as the centralization of power in the federal state to *Lochner* and its progeny—the *Lochner* era—produces a different interpretation of the Court's role in national state expansion. Scholars often see the *Lochner* era as symbolizing the Court's embrace of a "laissez-faire" interpretation of Constitutional rights that prevented state governments from regulating the labor market.[59] However, *Lochner* represents an expansion, not a restriction, of central state authority understood agnostically—as simply the centralization of federal power; *Lochner* enhanced the primacy of the federal judiciary over state legislatures (Bensel's centralization dimension) and over substantive labor policy and contracts (Bensel's property dimension).[60] The Court's decision in *Lochner* reveals the need to understand judicial power as endogenous to the development of federal state authority.

In *Lochner*, the Supreme Court held that a New York law forbidding bakers to work more than sixty hours a week was unconstitutional. New York fined Joseph Lochner $50 for allowing an employee to work more than that at his bakery in Utica, New York. Lochner was sentenced to county jail for 50 days or until he paid the fine.[61] The New York Court of Appeals upheld the statute, but Lochner appealed to the Supreme Court, claiming that the New York labor law was unconstitutional.

In a five-four decision, the Court held that the law "interferes with the right of contract between the employer and employees" and declared that "the general right to make a contract in relation to his business is part of the liberty of the individual protected by the Fourteenth Amendment of the Federal Constitution."[62] Writing for the majority, Justice Peckham maintained that the Constitution prohibits the states from interfering with most employment contracts because these contracts represent the fundamental freedom to buy and sell labor, which the Fourteenth Amendment protected. The amendment's Due Process Clause prohibited states from depriving any person of life, liberty, or property without due process of law; to the Court, the right to buy and sell labor through contract was a "liberty of the individual" protected under the amendment.[63]

By invalidating the New York statute, the Court centralized decision-making authority over labor questions in the judiciary, which is part of the central state, advancing the central state's authority to determine the boundaries of state-level regulation. While this interpretation prevented the development of the *welfare* state at the state level, it nevertheless helped create a stronger central state, illustrating my contention that constitutional development is not necessarily the advancement of progressive welfare state ideals but the advancement of national governing authority over state governments and citizens. *Lochner* thus embodies an important feature of American state-building: judicial supervision over state-society relations. This case and its progeny also underline that judicial power is not separate from the federal government itself.[64] The effect of *Lochner* was to impede state autonomy; the ruling stymied New York's maximum-hour legislation and centralized supervisory authority in the federal judicial branch. If the Court had ruled in the opposite direction, it would have decentralized decision-making authority and substantively refused to wield supervisory and jurisdictional power over similar cases.

According to the standard historical narrative, early-twentieth-century Progressive jurists defended the powerless from ever-expanding corporations and their unjust practices against the "reactionary" judges of the Gilded Age, with their outmoded jurisprudential ideas; the heroic Progressive judges are seen as replacing the laissez-faire ideology that stymied the growth of the regulatory state with modern constitutional interpretations. *Lochner* revisionists do not claim that the case advanced the central state, instead situating it within the nineteenth-century tradition of "class legislation" (Gillman 1993).[65]

But the primary drive behind *Lochner* was the Court's duty to protect fundamental, enumerated constitutional rights (Bernstein 2003, 12). To defend and protect those fundamental rights, the Supreme Court established itself as the ultimate guardian and supervisor of state-level regulations—a clear expansion of federal authority.

Juilliard v. Greenman (1884)—Expansion by Validating Congressional Statute

In this case,[66] Mr. Juilliard made a contract with Mr. Greenman to sell 100 bales of cotton for $5,122.90, a price agreed to by both parties. Greenman, the defendant, agreed to pay that sum on delivery of the cotton, at which time Greenman paid Juilliard $22.90 in gold and silver coins and the remaining $5,100 in US currency, one note of $5,000 and one note of $100, but Juilliard demanded that the $5,100 be paid in coin. Greenman refused, claiming that the US paper currency provided was as good as coin and that the notes should be taken for their respective face value for all debts, public and private.

Upset by Greenman's refusal to pay in coin, Julliard appealed to the Supreme Court, contending that the Legal Tender Acts that created paper currency were an unconstitutional exercise of Congressional power. Juilliard claimed that Greenman's payment was a breach of their original contract because the US notes were not equivalent to gold and silver coin. The question before the Supreme Court was whether US treasury notes were a tender of lawful money in payment of Greenman's debt.

In an eight-one ruling, the Court held that, yes, US treasury notes were a tender of lawful money in payment of debt, because the Congressional Act of May 31, 1878, under which the treasury issued the notes, was constitutional. The majority opinion argued, "The constitutional authority of Congress to provide a currency for the whole country is now firmly established."[67] It went on to say, "The power of making the notes of the United States a legal tender in payment of private debts, being included in the power to borrow money and to provide a national currency, is not defeated or restricted by the fact that its exercise may affect the value of private contracts. If . . . a particular power or authority appears to be vested in Congress, it is no constitutional objection to its existence, or to its exercise, that the property or the contracts of individuals may be incidentally affected."[68] Finally, the Court concluded that the issuance of treasury notes for payment of private debts is "conducive and plainly adapted to the execution of the undoubted powers of Congress" and within the meaning of the Necessary and Proper Clause.[69]

Juilliard is a quintessential example of federal power being expanding by the Court's support of another coordinate branch of the national government; this case expanded federal power both jurisdictionally and substantively, first by deciding to hear the case, and then by affecting contracts all across the United States.[70] And by validating this Congressional act, the Court also extended federal authority over another policy dimension: "creation of client groups," which increases the dependence of citizens on the viability of the federal government; controlling currency increases citizens' dependence on the federal government (Bensel 1990, 161–62).

Brown v. Board of Education (1954)—Expansion by Invalidating State-Level Statute

Juilliard expanded federal power through Court validation of a Congressional act, an active use of judicial power; *Brown v. Board of Education* (1954) offers an example of the Court's expanding federal power by striking down state law.[71] In the 1950s, the Topeka, Kansas, school board denied black children admission to public schools attended by white children; local laws permitted racial segregation as long as the facilities provided were equal. White and black schools in Topeka were assessed for equality in terms of objective factors such as buildings, curricula, qualifications, and teacher salaries. The central question in Brown was whether racial segregation of children in public schools deprived minority children of the equal protection of the law guaranteed by the Fourteenth Amendment. Although the school claimed to be equal as measured by objective factors, the Court held that intangible psychological issues foster and maintain inequality. More specifically, it stated that racial segregation in public education has a detrimental effect on minority children because they interpret segregation as a sign they are inferior. Consequently, the Court rejected the long-held doctrine, first promulgated in *Plessy v. Ferguson* (1896),[72] that separate facilities were permissible provided they were equal. The unanimous decision invalidated all forms of state-maintained racial separation.

    Brown expanded central state authority. First, it conferred rights on blacks by expanding their national citizenship rights; in diminishing the authority of constituent states to pass and enforce segregationist laws, the Court engaged in what King and Lieberman call the "standardizing project in civil rights" (King and Lieberman 2016, 248). The Court rested its justification on the importance of public school education in shaping democratic citizens: "Today, education is perhaps the most important function of state and local governments. Compulsory school attendance laws and the great expenditures for education both demonstrate our recognition of the importance of education to our democratic society. It is required in the performance of our most basic public responsibilities, even service in the armed forces. It is the very foundation of good citizenship."[73]

Any state policy that obstructed the creation of "good citizenship," then, was unconstitutional. In *Brown*, the state-mandated segregation policy impeded the education of African Americans:

> To separate [African-Americans] from others of similar age and qualifications solely because of their race generates a feeling of inferiority as to their status in the community that may affect their hearts and minds in a way unlikely ever to be undone. . . . Segregation of white and colored children in public schools has a detrimental effect upon the colored children. The effect is greater when it has the sanction of the law, for the policy of separating the races is usually interpreted as denoting the inferiority of the negro group. A sense of inferiority affects the motivation of a child to learn.[74]

The *Brown* decision therefore affects citizenship, one of Bensel's seven dimensions of the federal government (discussed at length in chapter 2). Second, the *Brown* decision explicitly centralized authority, moving the authority to determine citizenship (education) rights away from state/local governments and consolidating this authority in the federal Supreme Court, putting a new policy area (education) under federal supervision. Thus, *Brown* both expanded the private rights of African Americans and consolidated authority over questions of education in the hands of the central government, removing it from local governmental authority. The Court's ruling substantively affected the lives not only of schoolchildren but of policymakers and administrators throughout the United States.[75]

Coyle v. Smith (1911)—Restriction by Invalidating Federal Statute

In 1907, Oklahoma was admitted to the Union as a state and chose Guthrie, Oklahoma, as its capital. Three years later, Oklahoma enacted the Oklahoma Act, a law that moved the state capital to Oklahoma City. The Congressional statute that had admitted Oklahoma to the Union had declared the temporary capital to be Guthrie and stated that the capital could not change until 1913. W. H. Coyle, who owned a large property interest in Guthrie, attempted to prevent the enforcement of the Oklahoma Act by suing Oklahoma. According to Coyle and other petitioner citizens, the state's Oklahoma Act violated the Congressional Act—the Enabling Act of Congress of June 16, 1906. Thus, the Court was required to decide whether Oklahoma had the authority to relocate its seat of government when Congress had imposed conditions limiting that location.

The Court upheld in the affirmative, arguing Congress had overstepped its power.[76] States, the Court held, are on an equal footing to determine their own location for the seat of government. The constitutional duty of Congress to guarantee a republican form of government does not give Congress the authority to impose on a new state, as a condition to its admission to the Union, restrictions that render that state unequal to the other states, such as limits on its power to locate or change its seat of government. When the Court restricts federal authority it does not just mean an existing authority—like guaranteeing a republican form of government—was cut back or clarified. Restricting federal authority could also mean that the Court prevented new exercises of federal power.

The Court determined that Congress did not have the authority to mandate the location of a state's capital, thus restricting federal authority along Bensel's "centralization" dimension; in other words, the Court left authority over this issue with Oklahoma. The Court's decision did not confront any other substantive policy issue, adjudicating only where decision-making authority for this issue lay. This case restricted central state authority because the Court invalidated a Congressional statute, holding that the Constitutional guaranty of a republican form of government does not necessitate that the central state determine lower states' capitals. This decision highlights the important distinction between a substantive and jurisdictional understanding of the Court's rulings. The Court's decision to hear this case (jurisdiction) does not make this an expansion of power, and to interpret it in this manner would ignore the effect (substantive) of the Court's decision—a clear limit on Congressional power over states.[77]

Barron v. Baltimore (1833)—Restriction by Allowing a State Law to Stand

Like Coyle, *Barron* also represents a restriction of federal power, but a passive one: in this case,[78] the Court refused to extend a constitutional Amendment to the states. The case, which was decided shortly before Chief Justice John Marshall's tenure ended in 1835, concerned John Barron, the co-owner of a successful wharf in Baltimore's harbor. As the city developed its infrastructure, it deposited sand and earth from a road construction project into the Baltimore harbor, making the water too shallow to dock most vessels and depriving Mr. Barron of the deep waters he needed to maintain his profitable business. Barron sued, claiming that the city ruined his business and violated his Fifth Amendment rights, which provide that the federal government may not take private property without just compensation. The Court was asked to adjudicate whether the Fifth Amendment also denies the states the right to take private property for public use without justly compensating the property's owner.

In a very brief, unanimous decision, Marshall held for the Court that the limitations on government articulated in the Fifth Amendment were intended to limit the powers of the national government, not state governments: "The constitution was ordained and established by the people of the United States for themselves, for their own government, and not for the government of the individual states."[79] Citing the framers' intent and the development of the Bill of Rights[80] as an exclusive check on the national government, Marshall argued that the Supreme Court had no jurisdiction in this case, since the Fifth Amendment did not apply to the states.

In declaring that the Court (part of the central state) had no jurisdiction to hear this case, the Court left power with the constituent states, limiting the reach of the Bill of Rights. *Barron* thus restricted federal authority along Bensel's "centralization" dimension. The Court also restricted the federal government's power along the "control of property" dimension; although the Court decided to hear the case, the substance of the decision left power in the hands of the Maryland state legislature to control property rights as it saw fit. In other words, the central state—in this case the Supreme Court—declared that it had no authority to remedy Barron's property claim. By confronting questions about both decision-making authority and property, *Barron* thus interacted with two of Bensel's seven policy dimensions, the centralization and property dimensions, restricting the central state authority in both realms.

Barron demonstrates why we must view both uses of judicial review—the affirmation of federal law and the invalidation of state law—as expanding federal power. Marshall plainly declared, "The fifth amendment must be understood as restraining the power of the General Government, not as applicable to the States."[81] (Substantively, then, the Court's refusal to act in this case restricted the application of federal protections through the Bill of Rights for thirty-five years, until the passage of the Fourteenth Amendment in 1868.) And since scholars have understood incorporation—the slow process of applying the Bill of Rights to the states through the Fourteenth Amendment[82]—as an extraordinary expansion of federal authority, then the reverse—the Court's refusal to apply the Constitution to state-level laws—necessarily restricts the federal government's authority. Similarly, because we have interpreted cases such as *Brown*, above, as expanding federal power by invalidating a state law, the opposite—letting a state law stand—must be interpreted as restricting the authority of the national government.

A Word on Neutral Cases

While neutral outcomes make up 3% of the data (21 of 624 decisions), they remain a necessary category because some cases simply have nothing to do with central state authority; other cases, like the example discussed below, simply shift central state authority among the federal branches, but have no net effect on central state authority. Thus, many interbranch conflicts between the Congress and president fall into the neutral category.

Humphrey's Executor v. United States (1935): Neutral

On December 10, 1931, President Herbert Hoover nominated William Humphrey as head of the Federal Trade Commission (FTC); the Senate eventually confirmed Humphrey. When Franklin Roosevelt assumed the presidency in 1933, he asked for Humphrey's resignation, believing that Humphrey, as a conservative, might be unsympathetic to Roosevelt's New Deal policies, over which Humphrey had jurisdiction. When Humphrey refused to resign, Roosevelt fired him. However, the FTC Act[83] allowed a president to remove a commissioner only in the case of "inefficiency, neglect of duty, or malfeasance in office" (623). Humphrey died shortly after being dismissed, and his executor sued to recover Humphrey's lost salary. The Court was asked to determine if section 1 of the Federal Trade Commission Act unconstitutionally interfered with the executive power of the president to remove appointees.

The Court unanimously said the FTC Act was constitutional and that President Roosevelt, given the circumstances, did not have the authority to dismiss Humphrey.[84] The Court reasoned that the Constitution had never given the president "illimitable power of removal"; instead, authority rested with Congress to create agencies of the central government that were independent of executive control: "We think it plain under the Constitution that illimitable power of removal is not possessed by the President in respect of officers of the character of those just named. The authority of Congress, in creating quasi-legislative or quasi-judicial agencies, to require them to act in discharge of their duties independently of executive control cannot well be doubted; and that authority includes, as an appropriate incident, power to fix the period during which they shall continue in office" (629).[85]

Humphrey thus limited the power of one branch of the central government, the executive, while expanding the power of another branch, the legislative. *Humphrey* thus typifies a net "neutral" effect on overall central state authority: the decision merely said that Congress, not the executive branch, has the authority to determine when an agency head may be discharged from her duties. The overall central state, as an entity, lost no authority.[86] Ultimately, *Humphrey* left the authority to control administrative agencies with the less statist branch of the national government—the Congress. *Humphrey* therefore restricted the administrative capacity of the state.

Potential Objections to My Interpretation

Two possible objections to my interpretation schema warrant examination. First, some might argue that when the Supreme Court invalidates a state-level law, it expands not "national governing authority" or "federal state authority," but federal judicial authority. These readers might argue that I should differentiate between the Court's expansion of its own authority and its expansion of national governing authority—expansion vis-à-vis the states and expansion involving co-equal branches of the national government. Second, some might believe that I should disentangle cases involving rights claims and/or federal judicial authority vis-à-vis the states from cases involving congressional or executive authority. These readers may believe that the Court's invalidation of rights claims brought by a person—the mere assertion that the federal Constitution protects the individual making the rights claim—is not the same type of central state expansion as when the Court affirms federal action or law. Others might make a more nuanced argument, contending that only some judicial invalidations of state laws count as central state expansion: only invalidations that assert the presence or need for national state-building and regulatory activities expand the central state, not judicial invalidations that are merely self-executing.

To the first objection, I am skeptical that disentangling "judicial" and "state" authority is feasible in any kind of rigorous, scientific way. In the cases that pit the *federal* judiciary against a *state*-level government, the trade-off is clear: the Court either sides with the federal level (the central government and Constitution) or it sides with the states. When interbranch conflicts arise, the coding schema in this book provides a solution: a neutral category. Even if I could make this distinction, nuancing my dependent variable to somehow disentangle "judicial" authority from "federal" authority, doing so would undercut the reality that the judiciary plays a crucial supervisory role over constituent states—an important fact when trying to understanding the growth and development of the American central state (the chief aim of this book).[87]

To the second objection, I do not believe that one could accurately distinguish between decisions that entail regulatory efforts and those that self-execute; judicial decisions rarely lay out the presence or need for national state regulatory activities in any specific manner. More often than not, enforcement activities only occur when a Supreme Court decision is seen to manifestly not self-execute. Even in the landmark desegregation case *Brown v. Board of Education* (which some might classify as an example of a case that calls for national state-building activities), the Court does not call for enforcement; it merely asserts that segregation violates the Fourteenth Amendment. Even in *Brown II*,[88] the follow-up case that details enforcement, there are only vague mentions that schools must desegregate with "all deliberate speed."

Desegregation occurred in earnest only after the executive and the Congressional branches got involved, years and decades later, but the Court's decision never specifically called for these enforcement interventions (Rosenberg 2008, 42–72). These interventions occurred only when it became evident that some Southern schools defied the Court's orders. Had those schools followed the Court order on their own, federal enforcement interventions would not have been needed, and Brown might now be seen as self-executing.

By recognizing that the judiciary's supervisory role, we can understand that when the Court exerts its power to uphold a federal statute or strike down a state law (i.e., interpreting the substance of a ruling), this expands and develops the reach of broad central state authority, not only the reach of federal judicial authority. Separating federal judicial authority from national governing authority leaves us with only the traditional definition of central state development—one that defines expansion only as the advancement of certain goals or capacities of the political branches, captured by the European Weberian administrative state. In opposing this traditional definition, I join many APD scholars who seek to broaden our understanding of what counts as "central state development" and "state-building" (Baldwin 2005; Mettler 2011; King and Stears 2011; King and Lieberman 2008, 2009, 2016).

I understand *Lochner v. New York* (1905) and other individual liberty cases as expanding central state power because the "state" cannot be reduced to a unidimensional model of strong to weak, a model based only on a Weberian conception of federal government rooted in centralized bureaucracy and administration. *Lochner* and the liberty cases, generally speaking, established the federal government as supervisors over particular legal and policy issue areas. *Lochner* laid the groundwork for the centralized and powerful federal government seen decades later in the postwar era, even though the initial assertion of these federal powers was antiprogressive and anti-Weberian. In other words, "state expansion" can be understood as the advancement of federal authority regardless of its ideological or normative aims. By reinterpreting *Lochner* and other liberty cases, I place APD scholars who are concerned with state development in conversation with those APD scholars who are concerned with legal development. With my broader definition of "state authority" and "state-building," we can better understand the ways in which the Court has advanced as well as obstructed federal authority.

Conclusion

This chapter has centered on justifying this book's interpretation of judicial decisions and their effect on central state authority. It has examined why rulings such as *Lochner*, which emphasize liberty rights and thwart regulation, serve to expand federal authority and build the central state. To recapitulate the argument of this chapter: in a federal system, the Court's rulings that invalidate state laws centralize power in the federal government. By striking a state law down, the Court asserts its primacy as supervisor over subnational units. Despite the lack of a centralized bureaucracy in the United States, the Court's decision helped expand federal state authority immensely across the nineteenth and twentieth centuries. This suggests that the "state's importance cannot be captured on a one-dimensional strong-weak continuum or through a model that builds central on a Weberian conception" (King and Lieberman 2008, 378). The Court has largely expanded federal power through means other than Weberian-style bureaucracy.

While the Supreme Court has embraced a largely negative reading of constitutional (individual) rights by invalidating state laws that infringe on those rights, the Court has still contributed a great deal to the positive expansion of the central government's right to coerce and its tendency to increase its own power. Therefore, the next chapter will empirically detail the Court's historical effect on federal authority.

Chapter 2

Discerning Incremental Changes in Constitutional Development

That the judicial power of the United States will lean strongly in favour
of the general government, and will give such an explanation to the
Constitution, as will favour an extension of its jurisdiction, is very evident
from a variety of considerations.

—Brutus, Letter XI, 31 January 1788

Introduction

On October 18, 1787, the *New York Journal* published the first of sixteen
letters by the New York anti-Federalist "Brutus" (a pen name inspired by
the Roman Marcus Junius Brutus, who assassinated Julius Caesar to try to
save the republic). Soon after, James Madison worried that this "new Com-
batant . . . with considerable address & plausibility, strikes at the foundation
[of the proposed constitution]."[1] Brutus did indeed become one of the Constitution's most vociferous critics, not least because of his opposition to the
"judicial power of the United States," the focus of four of his sixteen letters.
Historians' best guess is that Brutus was Robert Yates (1738–1801), a well-
regarded jurist from New York and one of three New York delegates attending
the Philadelphia Constitutional Convention in 1787. When it became clear the
Convention sought not to revise the Articles of Confederation but to write a
new constitution, Yates left in a "fury" (Ball 2007, 436).[2]

Regardless of Brutus's identity, he hinted at the trajectory of constitutional development given an institution that is "totally independent" and

"authorised to determine all questions that may arise upon the meaning of the constitution in law" (Ball 2007, 501, 503): constitutional development would shift gradually and incrementally in favor of the federal government. He argued, "The judicial power will operate to effect, in the most certain, but yet silent and imperceptible manner, what is evidently the tendency of the constitution: . . . . Every adjudication of the supreme court, on any question that may arise upon the nature and extent of the general government, will affect the limits of state jurisdiction" (Ball 2007, 504).

An institution not deeply connected to the democratic will, and lacking the power of the purse or sword, the Court has gradually enhanced its own authority and the authority of the coordinate branches over time. This chapter lays out the precise details of this book's primary argument: (1) there is persistent expansion of federal state authority, centralizing power upward; (2) it happens gradually and imperceptibly over time, often through the Court's use of its negative powers, invalidating lower-level state laws; and (3) it occurs through extending federal authority to make decisions concerning citizens and people. Before discussing these primary arguments, let's turn to the research design and methods through which I make these arguments.

Research Design

Case Selection Method

The US Supreme Court has handed down over 31,000 decisions since 1754.[3] My goal was to evaluate some of the Court's most salient constitutional cases, those that have affected state-society relations most visibly. Given the ever-changing nature of the canon, the first challenge was to identify cases worthy of study.[4] To create an unbiased list of landmark decisions and uncover their relationship to national state development, I began by selecting fifty-eight constitutional law casebooks and treatises published between 1822 and 2010.[5] Collectively, the casebooks described 12,192 cases, from which I extracted the 624 constitutional decisions that appeared most frequently.

By using the casebooks (textbooks used to teach constitutional law in law schools), I considered the canon as snapshots in time and avoided the hindsight bias that would occur if I chose cases according to modern scholars' opinions about their landmark status.[6] While this selection mechanism depends heavily on legal education (and its potential biases),[7] the cases included for analysis are both representative of the Court's landmark decisions and important in guiding lower courts across the country (see below in this section for a discussion of external validation). I thereby developed not only a stronger foundation from which to assess the Court's position toward the state but also uncovered constitutional law cases that legal scholars once considered salient but present-day scholars consider superseded or defunct. Even if these cases have been superseded, they still shaped constitutional development when they were decided.

I selected the fifty-eight constitutional law casebooks based on their influence on the instruction of law students. Appendix 3 lists, in chronological order, all the books I used to construct the data set; these are all the earliest editions of a casebook or treatise. To find these books, I used Cornell University's library catalog.[8] My initial search for titles with "constitutional law" in the title yielded 1,853 books. I then ran an advanced keyword search for "constitution* law" and specified desired publication dates. I included virtually every pre-1876 treatise or constitutional law book I could find as long as it had an index, which I needed to create the database, as did Mayhew's model (2000, 31). For pre-1825 casebooks not available on campus or via Interlibrary Loan, I employed the *Making of Modern Law*[9] database, which contains electronic copies of old treatises. I searched that database by specifying "constitutional law" in the "full text" section, "treatises on American law" in the "body of law" section, and my desired years in "years of publication" section. The legal community considers casebooks authoritative and representative of the important decisions spanning America's constitutional history. Indeed, many of the casebooks used in this study have appeared in many revised editions, thereby indicating the legal community's high regard for these sources.

There are roughly three periods of legal education in the United States, and my selection methodology changed accordingly with each period. In the first period, before 1876, legal training was built on an apprentice model. Casebooks began being published in 1876 as universities started to offer law degrees and modern legal training began to take root.[10] This second period lasted until about 1920 when the Association of American Law Schools and the American Bar Association "created the institutional mechanism for defining, if not fully implementing, national standards for legal education" (MacGill and Newmyer 2008, 36). The third period continues today.

To represent the first period before the rise of casebooks, I incorporated widely read legal treatises, such as James Kent's (1826) *Commentaries on American Law* and Joseph Story's (1833) *Commentaries on the Constitution of the United States*, in my casebook list. Legal treatises were the primary way individuals learned how to practice law before the advent of law schools.[11] For this period, I used books by constitutional scholars such as Kent and Story, who scholars consider important today.[12] From the casebooks published between the 1870s and 1920, I once again selected books that contemporary scholars believe made important lasting contributions to legal thought. Thomas

Cooley, James Bradley Thayer, and Westel Willoughby are among the twelve I selected from this period.[13]

For the final period, after 1920, I selected books that are often still in circulation, available today as much later editions and still central to teaching lawyers. For example, the eighteenth edition of Kathleen Sullivan and Noah Feldman's *Constitutional Law* follows from the original text by Noel Dowling in 1937.[14] For this more contemporary period, I accessed syllabi from leading law schools and I included all the casebooks recommended on a widely read legal academic blog, "Choosing a Constitutional Law Casebook."[15] In each instance, I consulted the first edition because many of the casebooks are still in print and used throughout the most prestigious law schools in the United States, and thus, if I used later editions I would not have a proper casebook distribution in the modern period. In addition to using first editions of each book, I distributed casebooks fairly evenly across American history (weighted toward the present day) and chose only casebooks used to train lawyers, the individuals who would most likely shape the development of American law. I weighted the casebooks I selected to the present day because there were many more books to choose from in the twentieth century, and I wanted up-to-date coverage. Most, if not all, the major casebooks law schools currently use are on my list (Sullivan and Gunther, Brest et al., Choper et al., Stone et al., and Varat et al.). The authors of these major casebooks have taught at some of the most well-regarded law schools around the country—Balkin (Yale), Brest and Sullivan (Stanford), Choper (Berkeley), and Varat (UCLA)—and they often use their books in their respective institutions. The casebook list thus includes the most authoritative and contemporary casebooks used to teach constitutional law. Ultimately, across all three periods, I selected books that contemporary scholars considered some of the most important treatises and casebooks of constitutional law.

Because I am unable to include *all* casebooks ever published, there might be a selection effect on the casebooks I included in the database. This concern pertains especially to the latter part of twentieth century, when casebook publication proliferated. Accordingly, I selected more casebooks from the twentieth century to mitigate this problem (see the distribution of casebooks in Figure 2.1). Still, many books have been omitted, which is less of a problem considering that scholars and practitioners of the law have externally validated my selections as important in terms of the citation counts of my selected cases. Moreover, from the link referenced above,[16] it appears that law schools in a given period use only a handful of casebooks to teach constitutional law, and I have included the ones most widely used today.

With the casebooks selected, the next step was to select the landmark judicial decisions I would study. First, I created a single spreadsheet, includ-

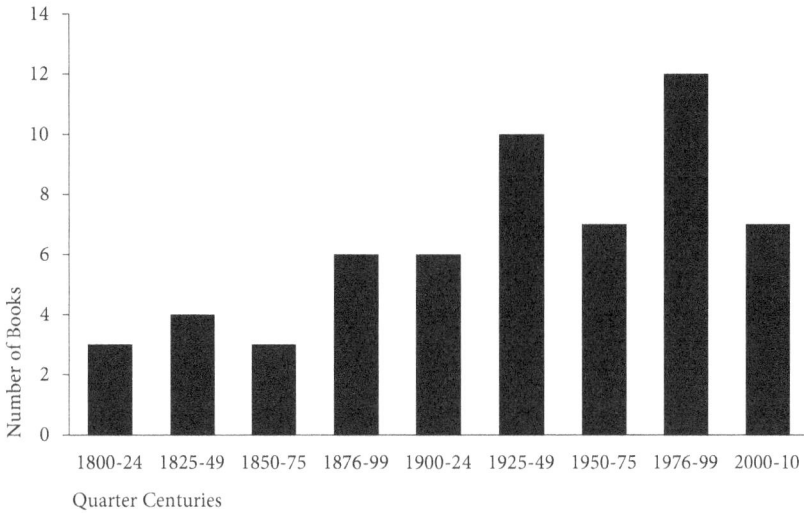

Figure 2.1. Casebook Distribution.

Note and Source: Compiled by author. This is the distribution of the fifty-eight casebooks and treatises used to derive the landmark decisions in my database. I outline the selection criteria for these books in the text.

ing all the cases found in each casebook's index.[17] I then noted the overlap of cases across the books and considered the cases cited most often across books to be leading decisions in constitutional law. Using this case listing method, I extracted 12,192 cases from the fifty-eight casebooks and treatises, of which the vast majority were not Supreme Court cases. Moreover, 8,391 of these 12,192 cases were cited in only one book.[18] From this collection, I selected the 624 decisions (of which all but 5 were Supreme Court cases) that overlapped across the books six times or more. With 624 decisions selected, each quarter-century period included at least 30 decisions, thus ensuring even distribution and capturing sufficient variation.

This six-book cutoff number produced a manageable data set and prevented bias against decisions handed down later in American constitutional history. (These decisions have had less opportunity to be published in casebooks.) The selection criteria intentionally ended the case sample date at 2000, but the casebook sample date ends in 2010. As eight casebooks that I used appeared after 2000, a 1999 decision, say, would have to appear in six of the eight twenty-first century casebooks to appear in the data set. Thus, 1997 ended up being the latest case in these data because of this inductive case selection method. Since over 8,000 of the cases appeared in only one casebook or treatise, for a case to be in six or more books proved to be a relatively high rate of appearance. I also analyzed the data with a cutoff point of seven and eight, and in all three cut points, the results of this study, in particular the ratio of expansion to restriction in constitutional decisions, remained stable. The robustness of this cutoff number demonstrates that the casebooks, too, can be considered reliable. That is, results do not change much, if at all, when I require a case to appear in seven or eight casebooks rather than six before including it in the database.

While the list is weighted toward contemporary casebooks, I drew from almost two centuries of casebooks, which allowed me to track changes in the constitutional law canon. I chose casebooks beginning with the earliest publication I could find (1822) and ending with the most recent (2010). Figure 2.1 on page 31 illustrates the distribution of casebooks used in the data set.

There might be a case selection bias with using casebooks: these books are edited by legal scholars to train budding lawyers, and thus they might oversample particular types of cases, such as those that are not particularly important to lower courts and to the broader American polity. In using a casebook selection method, I did not seek to select decisions that only lawyers thought were salient so I externally validated the case selection method. My goal was to collect a sample of important cases that avoided contemporary bias as to what counts as landmark. By "important," I mean not what law professors viewed as crucial. Instead, important cases are ones that guided lower federal and state courts and that the Court and other scholarly communities viewed as salient; my case selection, as detailed below, captured a sample of such decisions.

External validation puts these selection bias concerns to rest. While the casebook design I used does rely on what legal scholars view as important, my decisions also dovetail with non–legal scholars' opinions. In particular, Jerry Goldman conducted a study in 1992 of twelve leading constitutional law casebooks, some by legal scholars and some by political scientists, used in undergraduate classrooms. He attempted to identify a constitutional law canon—"a widely accepted body of rules, principles, and norms exemplified in a common set of Supreme Court opinions" (J. Goldman 1992, 134). As I did in my research, Goldman found very little overlap in the cases that comprise these casebooks (J. Goldman 1992, 137). In 2005, he conducted a similar study of thirteen casebooks by political scientists for undergraduate teaching. Using his loosest definition of "canonical," Goldman identified forty-nine constitutional law decisions. My database includes forty-six of his forty-nine decisions (J. Goldman 2005). This begins to show that lawyers' own educational experiences and their intellectual beliefs do not systematically bias the cases my method identifies. Using a more thorough external validation method also dispels any selection biases that might result from using lawyer-edited casebooks.

To validate my case selection and demonstrate that these cases guide lower courts, I used the "authority scores" generated by James Fowler and Sangick Jeon's (2008) study. In that article, Fowler and Jeon create an "authority" score for every single Supreme Court majority opinion from 1754 to 2002. According to them, "The authority score of a case depends on the number of times it is cited and the quality of the cases that cite it" (Fowler and Jeon 2008, 17). In other words, they gather citation counts for all decisions the Supreme Court handed down, which allows us to see if lower federal and state courts follow the Court's decisions. The mean authority score for the cases in my data is 0.01469, and the mean authority score for the universe of all Court cases is 0.00130. A one-sample t-test, with the population mean set at 0.00130, reveals my sample cases have a p-value $< .001$; thus they are significantly different from the population. In sum, the cases in my data can be considered as important and salient to both the Supreme Court and lower-level courts, not just to legal academics training budding lawyers.

By using casebooks that describe the canon at snapshots in time, I avoided the hindsight bias that would occur if the list of landmark decisions were grounded in the opinions of modern scholars. I thereby developed not only a stronger foundation on which to assess the Court's position toward the state but also uncovered constitutional law cases once considered salient by legal scholars that present-day scholars now consider superseded or defunct. Even if these cases have been superseded, they still shaped constitutional development when they were decided.

Key Variables Studied

After identifying the judicial decisions that constituted the data set, I coded for several variables, three of them crucial: "central state dimensions," "effect on federal authority," "constitutional issue areas," and one less crucial, "level of government action under review." To determine whether a judicial decision expanded or constrained central state authority, I followed Bensel's (1990) seven-point central state authority framework (see Table 2.1 detailed in the next section). I coded each decision for its overall effect on central state authority—expanding, restricting, or neutral—and I also coded which of the seven policy dimensions of the central state the Court expanded or restricted, the constitutional issue areas central in each decision, and which level of government action the Court reviewed.

Effect on Federal Authority

This categorical variable measured the overall effect a judicial decision had on federal authority, whether the decision expanded, restricted, or remained neutral toward central state authority. This measure consists of three points: "−1" represents a judicial decision that restricted the extent of central state authority; "0" represents a decision that was neutral toward and did not affect central state authority; "1" is a decision that expanded some aspect of central state authority. When the Court's decision invalidates a state/local action *or* upholds a federal action, the decision expands the boundary of federal power. Conversely, if a Supreme Court decision upholds a state/local action, *or* invalidates a federal action, then this decision restricts the extent of federal power.

Most importantly, I restricted coding to the text of the majority decision for three reasons. First, that is the position of the Court and thus the law of the land. Second, Court opinions are not simply public rationales for a ruling but also bureaucratic rulings that guide the decisions of the lower courts and, at some remove, litigants generally. Moreover, when political institutions and legal actors respond to the Court they are responding to the directives found within the Court's formal decision; that too necessitated restricting my coding to the text of majority opinions. And last, because this book uses Orren and Skowronek's definition of political development as a "durable shift in governing authority," the coding focuses on majority Court rulings, the only opinions that can specify and distribute authority "among persons or organizations within the polity at large or between them and their counterparts outside" (Orren and Skowronek 2004, 123). Since Court rulings embody formal statements of constitutional interpretation, they warrant close investigation for their effect on central state authority. Still, the subsequent effect of these rulings on the practice of government might sometimes differ from their formal statement. For example, *Brown v. Board of Education*[19] (1954) meant one thing as a formal interpretation of the Constitution (an expansion of central state authority), but to realize that interpretation took another decade or more, in terms of its effect on government practice.[20] In this book, I confine my coding to the majority opinions of the Supreme Court in the singular case before the tribunal.

Central State Dimensions

The central state authority framework that I applied includes seven dimensions of the federal government. Like the framework itself, I derived these areas of the central state—a term interchangeable with "federal" and "national" state—from Bensel's work.[21] This book uses these seven dimensions as the interpretative framework through which to assess a constitutional decision's effect on central state authority and to discuss the primary findings of these data. Table 2.1 enumerates Bensel's exhaustive framework.

The first two dimensions—centralization and administrative capacity—are structural, dealing with the design of the federal state and the location of decision-

Table 2.1. Bensel's Dimensions of Central State Authority[22]

1. **Centralization of Authority:** Measures involving the transfer of decision-making authority from subordinate governments and the citizenry to the central state. In the case of individual citizens, such measures do not involve a substantive expansion of central state activity, but only the allocation of influence and control over that activity. In the case of subordinate governments, such measures include the review of subordinate government decisions by central state institutions and the form of subordinate government participation in central state decision-making.

2. **Administrative Capacity:** Measures involving a broadening or narrowing of bureaucratic discretion and long-term planning capacity within the central state; these measures affect only institutions within the central state itself; in analyzing policy, reference is made to a hierarchy based on relative insulation from societal or outside political influence.

3. **Citizenship:** Measures involving the religious practices, political beliefs, ethnic identity, and rights and duties of citizens in their relations with the state; this category excludes measures affecting property but includes all measures concerning the physical movement and labor of citizens (such as conscription).

4. **Control of Property:** Measures involving the control or use of property by individuals or institutions other than the central state itself, including expropriation, regulation of the marketplace, and labor contracts between private parties.

5. **Creation of Client Groups:** Measures that increase the dependence of groups within society on the continued existence and viability of the central state; includes only measures that provide income or income substitutes to individuals (pensions, employment by central state institutions, welfare, and price-control programs for specific groups in society); that establish future-oriented obligations that depend on state viability (the issuance of long-term debt); and that control the value of the currency (the gold standard and redemption of paper money).

6. **Extraction:** The coercive dimensions of material resources from society into the central state apparatus; extraction measures skim wealth and resources from the flow of commerce and marketplace transaction without significantly redirecting or influencing the volume of these transactions (unlike otherwise similar measures falling under the property, client-group, or world system dimensions); primarily forms of light taxation or manipulations of the financial system such as gradual inflation of the currency.

continued on next page

Table 2.1. *Continued.*

---

7. **The Central State in the World System:** Measures concerning the relationship of the central state and nation with other states and the world economy; these include access to foreign markets (licensing, import quotas, export subsidies, and tariffs), diplomatic relations (membership in international organizations, treaties, and military conflict), immigration restrictions, and broadly conceived polices of internal development (the construction of a railroad to the Pacific Ocean, the Homestead Act, and administration of territorial possessions).

---

making within the state (Bensel 1990, 111). The remaining five dimensions concern the "substantive content of central state policy" (Bensel 1990, 109).

These seven dimensions of state authority identify the specific policy areas that the Court could expand or restrict in a particular decision. The central state authority variable is a categorical variable coding of these seven areas, any of which could be coded "not applicable" if the dimension was not relevant to the decision. The coding is not cumulative (e.g., expansion on two dimensions does not indicate greater effect on federal authority than a decision that only affected one dimension of central state authority). Very rarely does a decision expand along one dimension and constrict along another.[23] That is, "effect on federal authority" is not a scale variable. I aimed to capture variation in areas of the state that the Court expanded or restricted in particular eras of American history. This variable allows me to say, for example, what areas of the state the Court expanded or restricted in the Early Republic, in the New Deal Era, in the regulatory era, and so forth.

Level of Government Action under Review

Since the Court can expand federal authority through invalidating state action, as well as through sustaining federal action, this variable considers the level of government action in question before the Court. It falls into three categories: state/local action, federal action, and unspecifiable. This variable offers a way to understand how the Court centralizes federal authority: either through judicial monitoring of constituent states or through cases involving the national state.

The coding protocol for the variables above is both accurate and reliable. I provided and explained this coding protocol to three undergraduate research assistants, who remained anonymous to one another. After choosing these assistants and explaining the coding protocol, I randomly selected ten constitutional decisions from the data set, asking each assistant to code each decision along the nine variables—the effect on federal authority, the level of government action under review, and the seven dimensions of the central state, thus yielding a total of ninety outcomes. The research assistants matched my coding with 86% to 93% similarity. I also performed an interrater reliability analysis using the kappa statistic to determine consistency among the three raters. I found substantial agreement among the raters where kappa = 0.756 ($p < .000$), 95% CI [0.644, 0.868].[24]

Constitutional Issue Areas[25]

As Table 2.2 shows, the issue areas comprise fifteen legal issues from Harold Spaeth's widely used Supreme Court Database. The Database codes every Supreme Court decision from 1791 to 2015 across dozens of variables, including "constitutional issue areas." Since Spaeth's variables are presentist in defining and applying "issue areas," the Database coders have included several more common-law-related issues, which helps mitigate the presentist bias as the researchers backcoded these data.[26] Like the central state dimensions, the constitutional issues consist of an exhaustive list of issues that may arise under US constitutional law.

Table 2.2. Constitutional Issue Areas[27]

1. **Criminal procedure** encompasses the rights of persons accused of crimes, except for the due process rights of prisoners. These rights concern such matters as involuntary confession, habeas corpus, plea bargaining, search and seizure, self-incrimination, contempt of court, Miranda warnings, right to counsel, cruel and unusual punishment, double jeopardy, and retroactivity (of newly announced or newly enacted constitutional or statutory rights). Often includes Amendments 4, 5, 6, 8, and 14.

2. **Civil rights/liberties** includes cases that pertain to classifications based on race (including American Indians), age, indigency, voting, residency, military or handicapped status, gender, and alienage. Often includes Amendments 13, 14, 15, and 19. Civil Rights Acts of 1866, 1870, 1871, 1875, and 1964.

3. **First Amendment** includes both speech and religion clauses.

4. **Due process** is limited to civil guarantees (but does include criminal due process). Concerned with such issues as prisoners' rights and defendants' rights, government taking of property for public use (Takings Clause), having an impartial decision-maker at trial, and due-process rights as written in Amendments 5, 14, or both, encompassing procedural as well as substantive due process.

5. **Privacy** relates to noncriminal privacy, abortion, use of contraceptives/birth control, right to die, the Freedom of Information Act, and related federal or state statutes or regulations.

continued on next page

Table 2.2. *Continued.*

---

6. **Attorneys' or governmental officials' fees** covers compensation or licensees for attorneys and government officials.

7. **Unions** encompasses issues involving labor union activity.

8. **Economic activity** is largely related to commerce and business; it includes tort actions (suing business entities) and employee actions in relation to employers.

9. **Judicial power/jurisdiction** concerns the exercise of the judiciary's own power. To the extent that a number of these issues concern federal and state court relationships, they may be included in the federalism category.

10. **Federalism** pertains to conflicts and other relationships between the federal government and the states, except for those between the federal and state courts. It often includes the Interstate Commerce Clause, Amendments 10 and 11.

11. **Interstate relations** are not related to interstate commerce, but include boundary disputes between states, miscellaneous interstate conflicts, and non–real property disputes (anything that is non–real property is personal property, and personal property is anything that isn't nailed down, dug into, or built onto the land. A house is real property, but a dining room set is not).

12. **Federal taxation** concerns the Internal Revenue Code and related statutes and the general extraction of material resources from citizens. Often includes Amendment 16.

13. **Miscellaneous.**

14. **Private action** relates to disputes between private persons involving real and personal property, contracts, evidence, civil procedure, torts, wills and trusts, and commercial transactions. This category also pertains to slavery, land claims (mostly state and territorial), and incorporation of foreign territories. The passage of the Judges' Bill of 1925 gave the Court control of its docket, as a result of which such cases have disappeared from the Court's docket in preference to litigation of more general applicability.

15. **Executive power** pertains to the authority of the president to execute his/her office. Often includes Article II.

The Court's Effect on Federal Authority: Overall Findings

This section presents the macro findings from the book while the next section introduces some specific case examples across various periods of American political development. While punctuated equilibrium models contrast "normal" politics with moments of exogenous disruption, pinpointing continuity in constitutional development allows us to understand shared characteristics of politics and political change. The findings below reveal that the Court has consistently supported state-building largely through centralizing power in the national government.

This continuity has manifested in the Court's constitutional decisions; it has incrementally expanded federal authority, evidenced by the persistence of decisions that expand authority, but it has never drastically changed the rate of expansion across common historical eras. I make this statement based on a rich sampling of landmark decisions from 1792 to 1997. Each quarter-century contains at least sixty decisions.[28]

More importantly, a significant majority of these decisions expand federal state authority, revealing an important trend of American constitutional development: that it generally expanded the powers of the federal government. The trend in Figure 2.2 demonstrates that the Court did much to expand federal power through its constitutional interpretation. Of the 624 decisions, 231 (37%) restricted authority, 21 had a neutral effect (3%), and 372 (60%) expanded governing authority. It is important to note that the graphic displays only the *overall* effect on federal government power; I present the effect on each of the seven central state dimensions later.

Breaking down the Court's behavior across time provides a more detailed view of the Court's effect on national power. Constitutional decisions

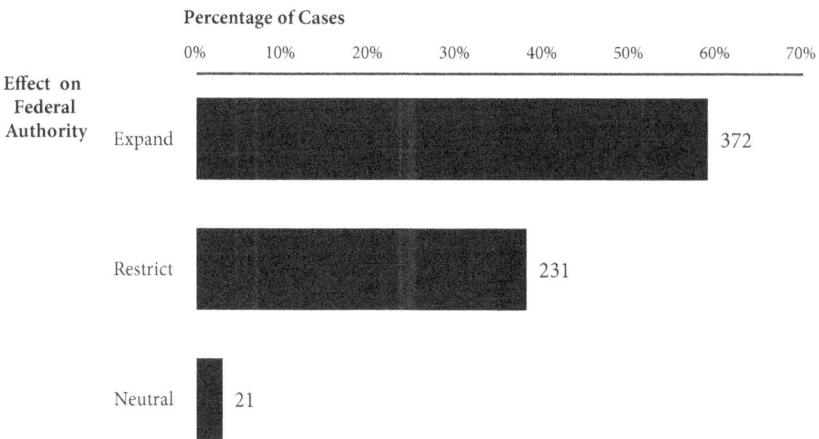

Figure 2.2. Distribution of Cases Affecting Federal State Authority, 1792–1997.
Source: Compiled by author. N=624.

persistently both expand and constrict federal power; never are restrictive cases absent, but rarely do restrictive decisions outweigh expansive ones. Only a few brief periods witness a majority of restrictive cases—around 1825, 1880, and 1895. After 1900, decisions that expand federal power almost always outweigh those that restrict it.

Nevertheless, the story of American constitutional development rests largely on the gradual, expansive changes in the power of the federal state. While restriction declined in the twentieth century, it has remained a prominent feature throughout constitutional development. Somewhat surprisingly, and contrary to well-known accounts, the Court handed down many decisions that expanded central state authority between 1875 and 1920. Often, the Court is depicted as inhibiting central state growth, but Figure 2.3 demonstrates the opposite: the Court was active in advancing important dimensions of central state authority.

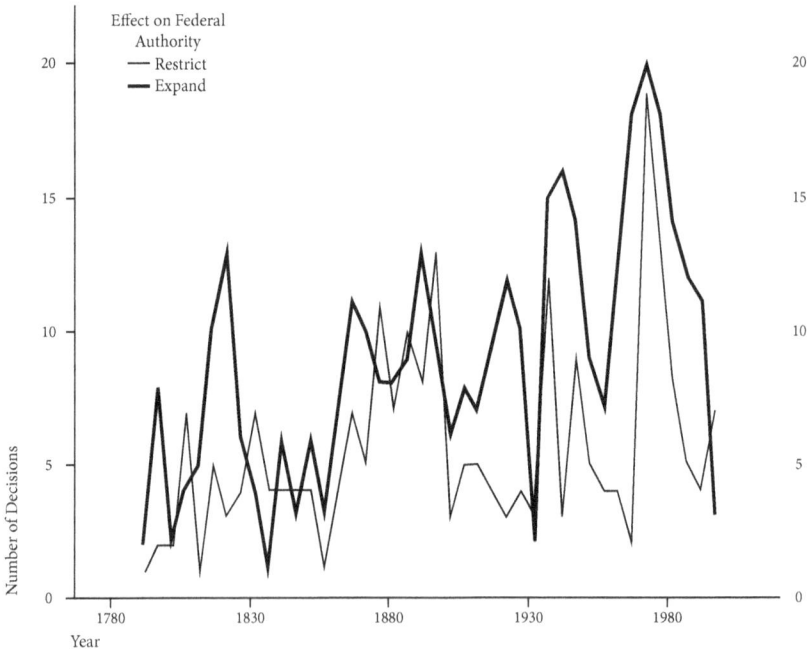

Figure 2.3. Effect on Federal Authority by Year, 1792–1997.

Notes and Source: Compiled by author. Expanding decisions persistently outweigh restricting ones, especially after 1900. Neutral decisions not included. N=603.

The numbers of expansive and restrictive decisions,[29] however, consistently grow farther apart over time. Below, Figure 2.4 maps constitutional decisions' influence on overall state authority over time. Around 1820, and 1870, and then consistently after 1900, the Court handed down more decisions that extended federal authority than restricted it. More than that, Figure 2.4 demonstrates that expansive decisions grow at a faster rate than restrictive decisions throughout all of American constitutional history. The line chart shows us that constitutional development persistently expands governing authority throughout history.

Constitutional changes in federal authority have remained relatively stable across time, in terms of the percentage of decisions that have expanded

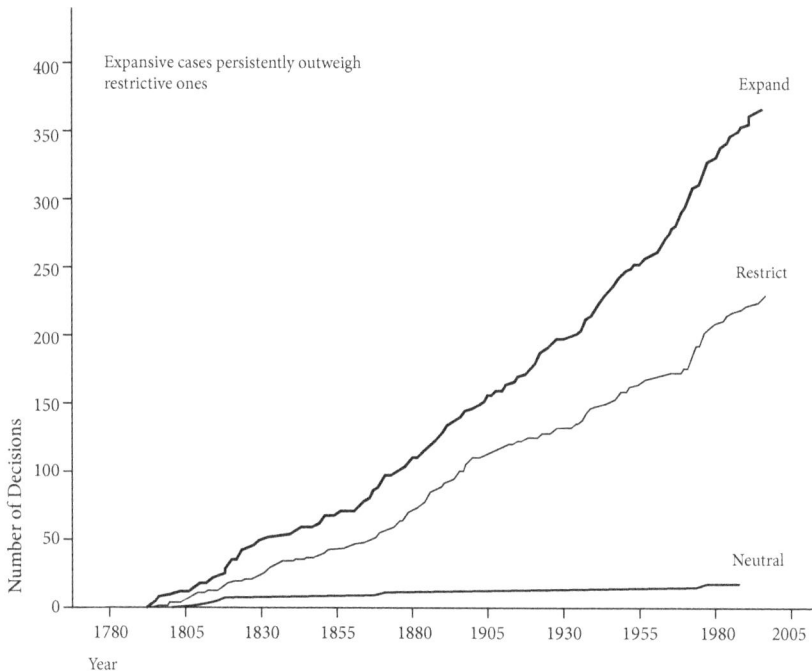

Figure 2.4. Cumulative Frequency of Constitutional Decisions' Effect on Federal State Authority, 1792–1997.

Notes and Source: Compiled by author. This cumulative frequency chart shows the relatively steady growth of decisions that both expand and restrict federal government power. Around 1900, decisions that restrict experienced a more gradual growth rate while expansion decisions experience a faster growth rate. N=624.

this authority. The Court advanced federal authority at an average rate of .61, and it never strayed far from this average. Even during the slowest periods of state-building, the Court's decisions expanded governmental power over half the time. Figure 2.5 shows that some supposed periods of restriction (e.g., the Republican Era, 1877–1932) show more expansion of power than scholars think, and other periods (such as the New Deal era, 1933–1968) do not stray far from the mean rate of central state expansion.

The proportion of state-expanding cases tells us a great deal about the evolution of constitutional interpretation pertaining to state authority: it has been steady over time. Certainly, the interpretation of the federal government's specific authority has changed immensely, but the overall effect on the growth of the state has not. Taking the long view, the Court has persistently expanded federal power, steadily advancing into new policy areas. The rate of central state expansion has implications for the standard interpretation of the New Deal as a critical juncture, which, it is held, witnessed an abrupt shift in federal government authority.[30] On the contrary, the process of change was far more gradual than typically posited.

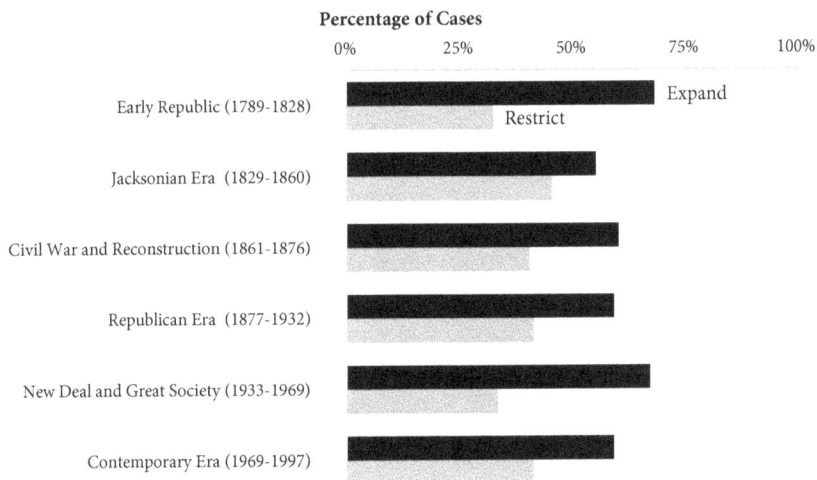

Figure 2.5. Federal State Expansion across Historical Eras.

Notes and Sources: Compiled by the author. The average rate is a function of the number of decisions that expanded authority over the total number of decisions in a given quarter-century era. Neutral decisions were not included in the proportion. The mean percentage of federal state expansion is 61%. N=603.

Central State Dimensions: Overall Findings

Because individual rights and economic activity comprise 72% of all the decisions, it is worth exploring the two central state dimensions that touch closely on these constitutional issues: the centralization and citizenship dimensions. Centralization involves the transfer of decision-making authority from the individual states or citizens to the national government. And citizenship pertains to issues concerning individual rights. Consequently, these two dimensions interact with civil rights and economic activity frequently.

The seven dimensions I drew from Bensel's (1990) work comprise an exhaustive list of both the structural design and substantive policy dimensions of the central state. 64% of all decisions interact with two of the seven dimensions (401 of 624), while 25% of decisions deal with three of the dimensions (158 of 624). Only four decisions deal with five dimensions, and eleven decisions deal with zero dimensions (i.e., are neutral). Of the seven dimensions, centralization and citizenship are the most frequent—nearly 50% of all decisions interact with citizenship while 91% of all decisions interact with centralization, as Figure 2.6 illustrates. Indeed, the development of the

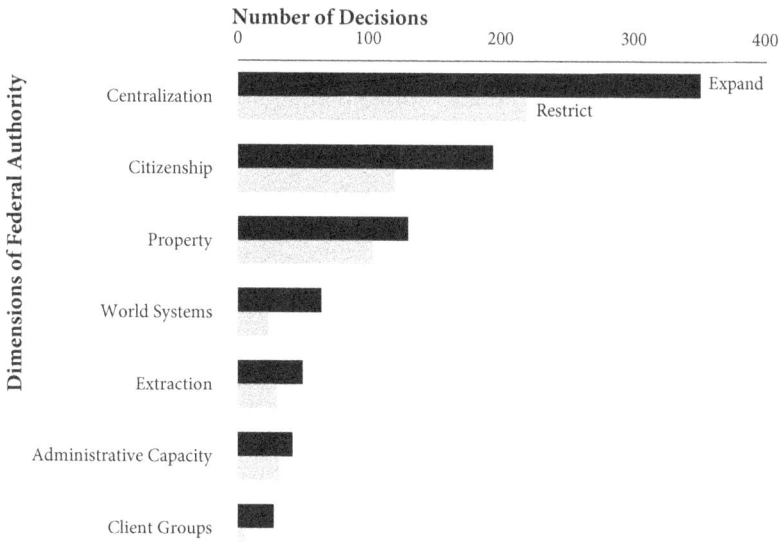

Figure 2.6. Central State Dimensions and Effect on Federal Authority.
Source: Compiled by author. N=603.

centralization dimension looks identical to the development of the overall effect on central state authority seen above in Figure 2.4.[31] The property dimension expands federal authority least frequently, proportionally, with 129 of 231 decisions, or 56%, expanding authority. The creation of client groups expands federal authority most frequently, 84% of the time, with 27 of 32 decisions tending this way (see Table 2.3 below).

Looking across time gives us a better understanding of the frequency of these dimensions. Figure 2.7 compares the number of decisions that expand versus the number that constrict federal authority for each of the seven dimensions. For the most part, constitutional development charts a gradual course, and only the citizenship dimension sees a sharp spike in federal expansion, in around 1950. The remaining six dimensions, by contrast, often outweigh restrictive cases, but not by drastic amounts on a year-to-year basis, lending credence to the "imperceptible" and incremental expansions of federal authority to which Brutus alluded.

Centralization and citizenship stand out in frequency and thus warrant closer investigation. The graphs in Figure 2.8 on page 46 and Figure 2.9 on page 47 juxtapose the development of these dimensions. Like many of the graphs above, Figures 2.8 and 2.9 indicate that both central state dimensions fluctuated between expansion and restriction. Nevertheless, expansion is the predominant outcome over time, especially within the centralization dimension. Indeed, virtually all Court decisions involve a transfer of power from lower to higher levels, or vice versa. Expansion is persistently the more frequent outcome for centralization, while expansion and restriction stay much closer together in the citizenship dimension until around 1920, when decisions that expand federal power rise dramatically.

From the foregoing discussion, we see that the Court's interpretation of constitutional law consistently advances the federal government's authority, and it does so primarily through the medium of individual rights and economic activity. That the central government's authority expands more frequently than

Table 2.3. Central State Dimensions and Frequency of Federal Expansion

Dimension	Percent Expanding Authority
Client groups	84.38%
World systems	73.26%
Extraction	62.82%
Citizenship	61.86%
Centralization	61.55%
Administrative capacity	56.94%
Property	55.84%

Source: Compiled by author.

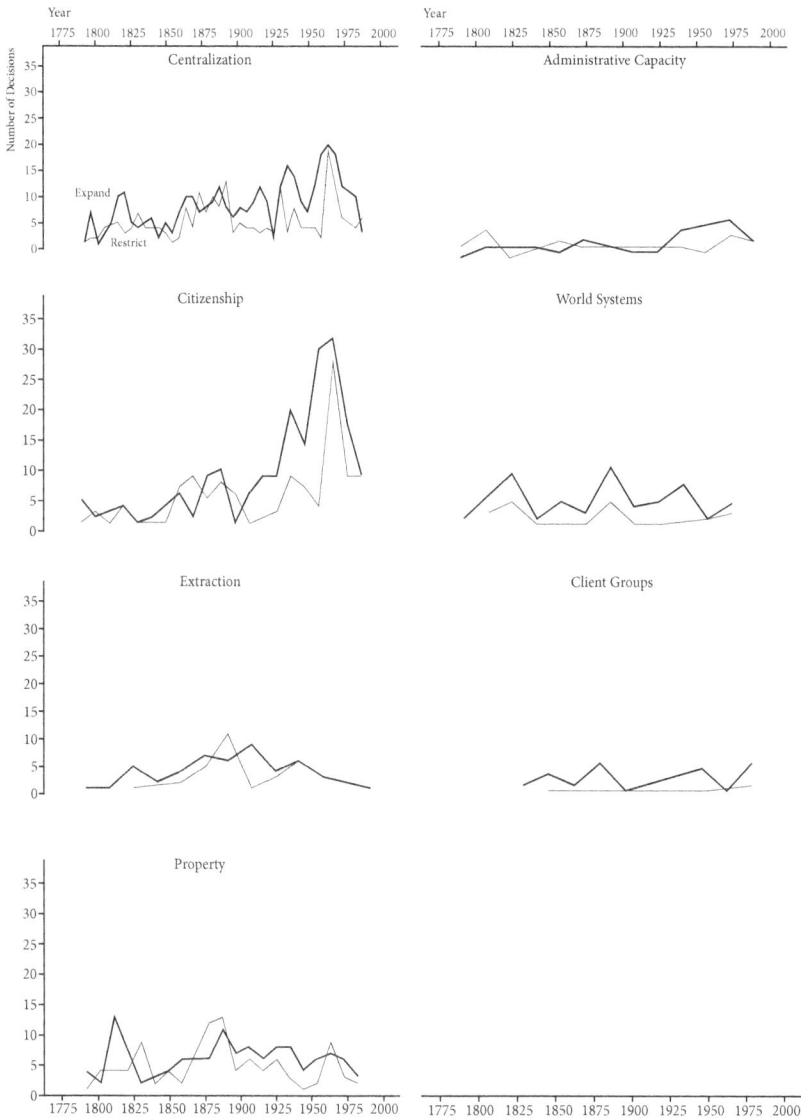

Figure 2.7. Central State Dimensions and Effect on Federal Authority across Time.

Note and Source: Compiled by author.

not comes as no surprise, but we do not yet know how this happens. Figure 2.9 seems to indicate that this expansion occurs largely through the channel of centralization, that is, through the transfer of decision-making authority from subordinate governments to the central government—a hallmark of

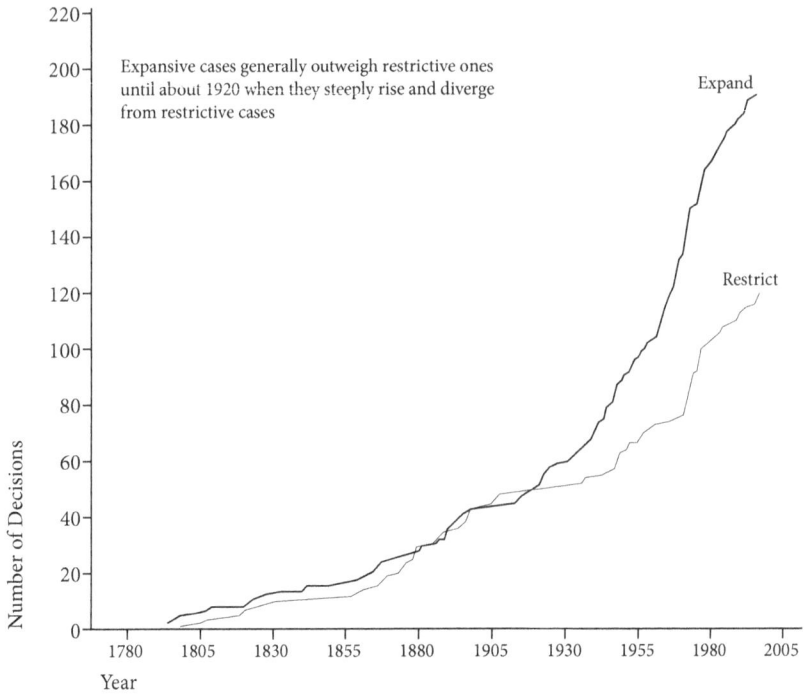

Figure 2.8. Cumulative Frequency of Citizenship Dimension, 1792–1997.

Notes and Source: Compiled by author. Expansive-restrictive decisions on citizenship grow at nearly the same rate until 1920, when these decisions diverge greatly. After 1920, decisions that expand the federal government's authority along the citizenship dimension grow sharply.

American constitutional development.[32] At bottom, constitutional development deals with who has the authority to decide,[33] and constitutional design enshrines this question.

Developments across Historical Periods

While the later chapters delve into further detail, below I present some key highlights and findings within each period of American political development, examining key constitutional issues and the effects on both judicial authority vis-à-vis effect on the states, and the effect on the coordinate branches. I elaborate on these short histories in chapters 3–5.

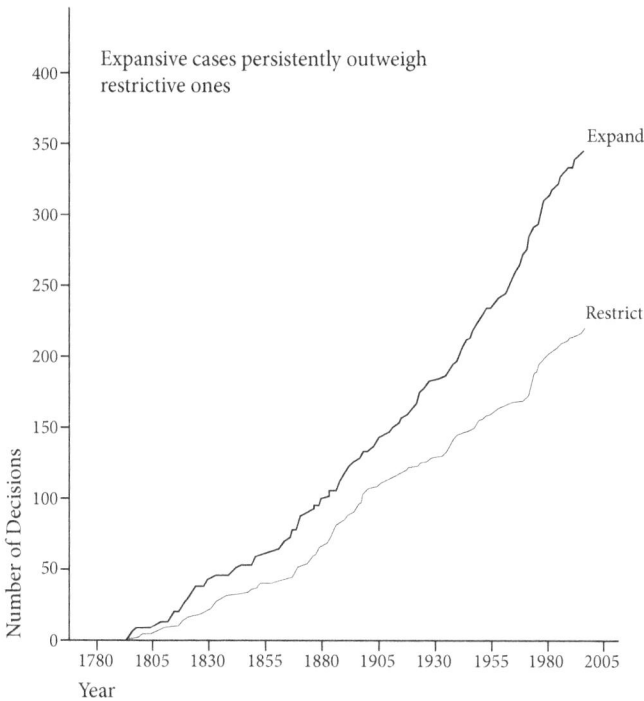

Figure 2.9. Cumulative Frequency of Centralization Dimensions 1792–1997.

Notes and Source: Compiled by author. Expansive decisions within centralization always outweigh restrictive decisions, which resembles the pattern of overall effect on state authority displayed above in Figure 2.4. N=565.

Early Republic (1789–1828)

Seventy-nine cases comprise this period, of which 48 (61%) expand central state authority. With 26 of 79 cases (33%), judicial power and jurisdiction issue represent a plurality. As expected for a fledgling republic, questions concerning its newly formed political institutions took center stage. In particular, the Supreme Court faced numerous questions that centered on the Court's own power: does the court have jurisdiction or the power to hear the case before it? Unlike in any subsequent period, the Court restricted central state authority more frequently vis-à-vis judicial power than it expanded federal authority, as seen in Figure 2.10 on page 48.

Number of Decisions

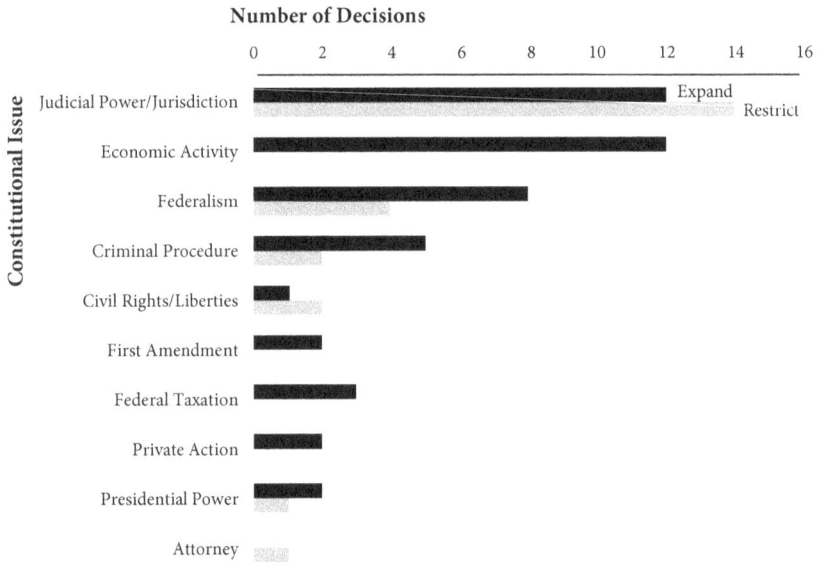

Figure 2.10. Constitutional Issues, Early Republic Era, 1789–1828.

Source: Compiled by author. N=79.

With respect to judicial power, the Court resisted early Congressional attempts to confer further federal judicial authority on the high court. In *Hayburn's Case* (1792) and *Marbury v. Madison* (1803), the Court rejected Congress's attempt to give it more authority. *Hayburn* concerned a 1792 Congressional Act that gave the US Circuit Courts the task of determining the pension claims of disabled war veterans.[34] William Hayburn went to the US Circuit Court for the District of Pennsylvania, but all those on the court held that the Congressional statute gave the courts nonjudicial powers and thus violated the Constitution and its separation of powers. Five of the then six Supreme Court justices also sat on Circuit Courts and penned opinions in the form of letters to President Washington, declining to serve as pension claim arbiters. Similarly, in *Marbury*, the Court rejected a Congressional statute, which conferred additional authority on the Court to hear particular types of cases. Most remembered for its first Supreme Court use of judicial review, *Marbury* invalidated Section 13 of the Judiciary Act of 1789,[35] a federal law that gave the Court original jurisdiction in writs of mandamus cases. Chief Justice Marshall declared that Congress did not have the authority to give the Supreme Court original jurisdiction in such cases, because the statute conflicted with Article III, Section 2, of the Constitution, which outlined the types of cases where the Court has original jurisdiction. By virtue of invalidating federal Congressional actions, these judicial-power cases restricted central state authority. However, when the Court's judicial authority juxtaposed state-level court jurisdiction, the Supreme Court often found for itself, as it did in *Martin v. Hunter's Lessee* (1816) and *Cohens v. Virginia* (1821).[36] I discuss these cases below in the "effects on states" section.

Effects on Federal Government

During this period, the Court did much to advance federal authority. It upheld federal laws or actions twenty-two times (or 28% of the decisions) while invalidating twelve federal laws or actions (15%) in this period (see Figure 2.11). Of these thirty-four decisions reviewing federal actions, fifteen pertained to the federal judiciary's own jurisdictional power, of which eight restricted the judiciary's federal authority. The remaining nineteen decisions examined coordinate branch powers, including *Hylton v. United States* (1796),[37] which upheld a Congressional tax on horse-drawn carriages. It also upheld the constitutionality of the Congressional passage of the Eleventh Amendment in *Hollingsworth v. Virginia* (1798),[38] despite the plaintiffs' claims that the Eleventh Amendment was invalid because the president had not approved it per the Presentment Clause in Article I, Section 7. The Court continued its affirmation and expansion of Congressional authority through the 1820s,

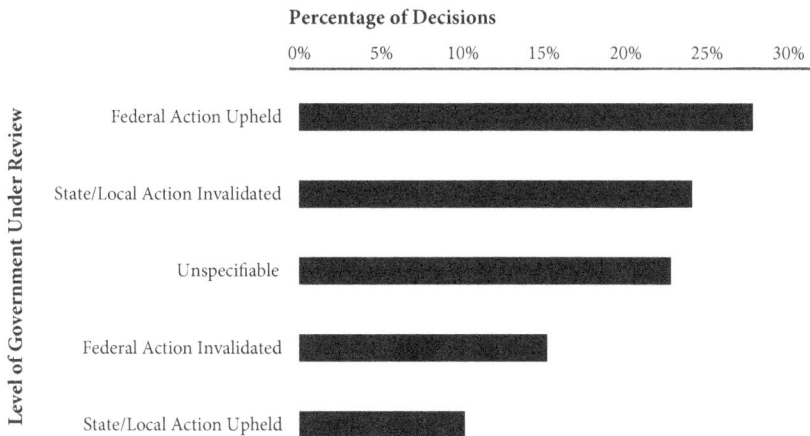

Figure 2.11. Level of Government Action under Review, Early Republic Era.

Source: Compiled by author.

as seen in *Anderson v. Dunn* (1821).[39] Here the Court upheld Congress's authority to punish nonmembers for contempt. *Anderson* dealt with a citizen (Anderson) who attempted to bribe a member of Congress, at which point the House's sergeant at arms (Dunn) arrested that person and brought him before the House to be reprimanded.

Effects on States

It also invalidated state or local laws in nineteen cases (24%) while only upholding eight (10%). In the realm of economic activity, the Marshall Court extended the Contracts Clause beyond private parties and toward the protection of the rights of corporations and the propertied class, as it did in *Fletcher v. Peck* (1810),[40] *New Jersey v. Wilson* (1812),[41] and *Dartmouth College v. Woodward* (1819).[42] These decisions represented central state expansion over the states through judicial review, extending the boundaries of the Contracts Clause.

Federalism was another chief constitutional issue that produced judicial invalidation and central state expansion. *Ware v. Hylton* (1796),[43] *McCulloch v. Maryland* (1819),[44] and *Osborn v. Bank of the United States* (1824),[45] for example, concerned federalism issues. In *Ware* the Court affirmed that the Treaty of Paris in 1783 overrode a Virginia law and that federal laws were supreme over state laws. *McCulloch* and *Osborn* also struck down state-level laws in Maryland and Ohio, respectively. Both cases struck down state-level taxes on branches of the United States Bank. The Court also remained vigilant in protecting its federal judicial power and jurisdiction against state-level courts. In *Martin v. Hunter's Lessee* (1816), for example, the Court declared—following the Jay Treaty—that Lord Fairfax was entitled to his property despite the Virginia legislature having voided the original land grant.[46] Nevertheless, the Virginia courts refused to follow the US Supreme Court's decision. Unanimously, the Court affirmed its ability to override state courts and establish a uniformity and supremacy in law.

Jacksonian Era (1829–1860)

By the mid-1820s, a new political party had emerged in the country, opposing concentrated wealth among the elites. Andrew Jackson and the new Democratic Party won the White House in 1828. Jackson and the Democratic Party championed democracy, extending the franchise to at least all adult white males, and despised privilege and wealth. The property-oriented and federal-supremacy tendency of the early-republic Marshall Court sat in stark contrast with the ethos of Jacksonian democracy's "unmistakable states' right aura" (S. Goldman 1991, 25). Yet even during the Jacksonian era twenty-six cases (54%) extended federal authority.

Economic activity was the only constitutional issue that restricted central state authority more often than expanded it—but just barely (eleven restricted while ten expanded, see Figure 2.12). The Taney Court gave states a great deal of autonomy in dealing with the Panic of 1837, a severe economic recession, partly because, without the Bank of the United States, the federal government had little ability to deal with national economic crises. Nearly 44% of all cases during this period dealt with economic activity. In 1837, for example, the Court restricted federal authority in a trilogy of decisions—*City of New York v. Miln*,[47] *Charles River Bridge v. Warren Bridge*,[48] and *Briscoe v. Bank of Kentucky*[49]—by leaving states the autonomy "to take appropriate actions they could on their citizens' behalf" to confront the economic crisis (S. Goldman 1991, 27). A number of federalism and economic activity cases later during this period expanded federal authority: *Bank of Augusta v. Earle* (1839),[50] *Bronson v. Kinzie* (1843),[51] and *Piqua Branch Bank v. Knoop* (1854) as detailed below.[52]

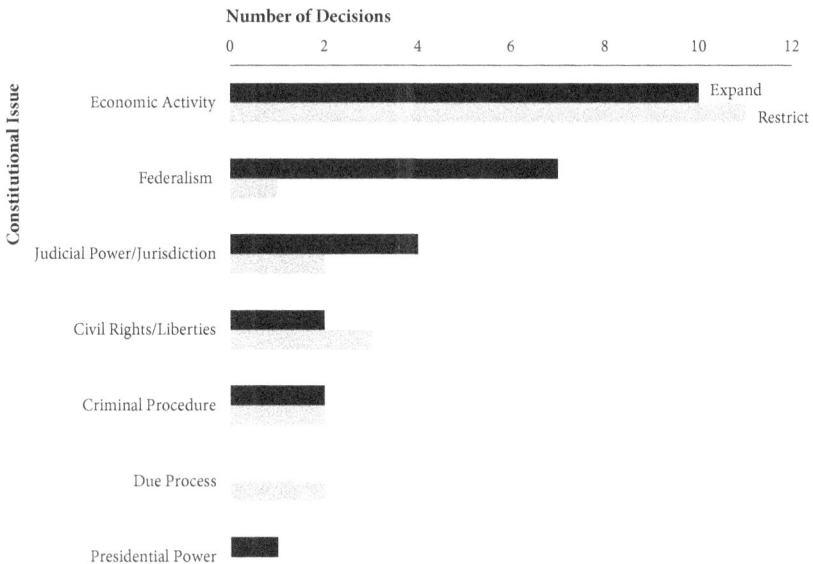

Figure 2.12. Constitutional Issues, Jacksonian Era, 1829–1860.

Source: Compiled by author. N=48.

Effects on Federal Government

During the Jacksonian era, the Supreme Court dealt with few cases that concerned federal action, but ten of these upheld federal action while only one invalidated federal action. Some key pieces of federal legislation on banking and internal improvements, all of which attempted to extend federal authority, were vetoed by Presidents Jacksons, Tyler, and Polk. Political commentators at the time, however, believed that had those presidents not vetoed those bills, the Taney Court would probably have declared that Congress did not have authority to incorporate a national bank or to legislate internal improvements related to rivers and harbors (Gillman, Graber, and Whittington 2017a, 185). With respect to slavery—the only rights issue that received substantial national judicial treatment during the Jacksonian era—the Taney Court expressed its proslavery, racist sentiments. In *Prigg v. Pennsylvania* (1842), the Court upheld the Fugitive Slave Clause of 1793.[53] However, in *Dred Scott v. Sandford* (1857),[54] the Court attempted to constrict federal authority by invaliding the Missouri Compromise, a federal law that prohibited slavery in the territories. For the most part, the Supreme Court reviewed few cases concerning federal action, and instead the vast majority of its focus concerned the states.

Effects on States

Thirty-four cases (71%) deal with state-level issues, outnumbering the eleven (23%) that concerned federal action. During this period, the Court was more likely to leave autonomy with the states, as was characteristic of Jacksonian era politics (nineteen cases upheld state action, while fifteen invalidated state laws). The Taney Court revealed its sympathy for states' rights in many of its economic-activity decisions. For example, in *Miln*, the Court dealt with a state law that required ships' masters, docking in New York City, to provide a passenger manifest and to post security for indigent passengers. Miln, the master of one these ships, refused to comply with the law. Rather than deal with the complicated issues of concurrent federal and state commerce, the Court suggested that Commerce Clause only deals with "goods" and not "persons," and thus the Court maintained the state police powers[55]—the first time the court invoked state police as a way to regulate a ship's contents traveling on interstate waterways (VanBurkleo 2005, 683). Similarly, *Charles River Bridge* upheld a Massachusetts law that rejected the exclusive bridge franchise in favor of market competition by allowing the Warren Bridge Company to build a bridge near the Charles River Bridge. In economic activity issues dealing with

Percentage of Decisions

| | 0% | 5% | 10% | 15% | 20% | 25% | 30% | 35% | 40% | 45% |

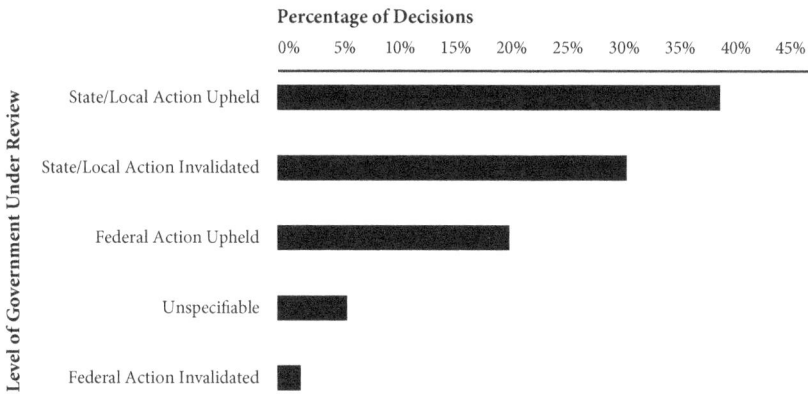

Figure 2.13. Level of Government Action under Review, Jacksonian Era
Source: Compiled by author.

banking, the Court—as it did in *Briscoe*—upheld the rise of "free banking" in the states: the Court essential gave states the ability to regulate their currency and banking as they saw fit, restricting national authority to control the money supply (M. Wilson 2008, 18).

Later decisions in the period expanded federal authority by upholding some of the Contracts Clause doctrines developed by the Marshall Court. For example, in *Bronson v. Kinzie* (1843) the Court protected private contracts against two Illinois statutes, which attempted to retroactively affect mortgages made before the acts were passed. Chief Justice Taney held that Illinois's attempt to change the terms of existing mortgages was unconstitutional because it violated the Contracts Clause. Likewise, in *Piqua Branch Bank* (1854), the Court confronted Ohio's attempt to change the terms of a corporate charter with a private bank; Ohio had passed a tax act that would increase the tax rate on banks in the state. The Taney Court invalidated the tax as an infringement of the Contracts Clause, upholding the Marshall Court's *New Jersey v. Wilson* (1812) decision.

Civil War and Reconstruction (1861–1876)

Fifty-three cases comprise this period, of which thirty (57%) expanded central state authority. With nineteen of fifty-three cases (36%), economic activity represented a plurality as it had during the Jacksonian era.

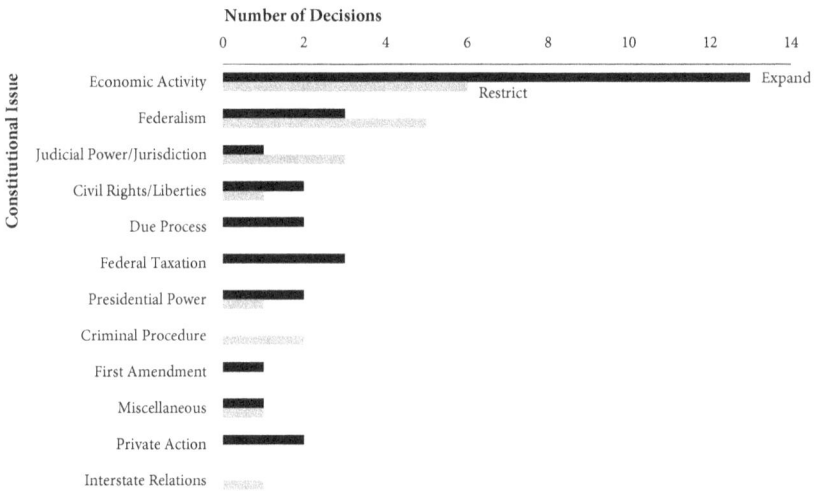

Figure 2.14. Constitutional Issues, Civil War and Reconstruction Eras, 1861–1876. *Source:* Compiled by author. N=53.

Effects on Federal Government

Of the nineteen cases dealing with federal action, ten upheld and expanded central state authority. The near fifty-fifty spilt among these nineteen cases suggests the difficult position the Court faced during and after the Civil War. During the war, President Lincoln took unprecedented action to suspend the writ of habeas corpus, detain citizens suspected of aiding the Confederate cause, and blockade southern ports. The Court affirmed Lincoln's blockade in the *Prize Cases* (1863),[56] but in other cases, such as *Ex parte Milligan* (1866), the Court struck down Lincoln's use of military commissions to try civilians suspected of supporting the Confederates.[57] Complicated questions of the Supreme Court's jurisdiction affected the boundaries of federal power, too. In *Ex parte Vallandigham* (1864),[58] the Court claimed that it had no jurisdiction over appeals made from military courts, thereby restricting its own power. But, in effect, the Court supported President Lincoln's use of military trials to try and convict Senator Clement Vallandigham for criticizing and urging resistance against Union military orders that prohibited expressing any support for the Confederacy. After conviction, President Lincoln banished Vallandigham beyond Confederate territory. The Court also affirmed Congress's withdrawal of the Court's jurisdiction in *Ex parte McCardle* (1869).[59] Federal authorities arrested McCardle for writing and publishing editorials criticizing

Reconstruction in a Mississippi newspaper. McCardle was convicted under the Reconstruction Act, which he claimed was unconstitutional and appealed to the Supreme Court. After the Court heard oral arguments, Congress stripped the Court of its jurisdiction to hear these types of habeas corpus cases, to which the Court acquiesced. The Court affirmed Congressional power in other ways as well. In the *Legal Tender Cases* (1871),[60] the Court broadly construed Article I, Section 8's Necessary and Proper Clause and affirmed the constitutionality of paper money.

Yet almost as often, the Court constricted federal authority by invalidating federal action. In *Collector v. Day* (1871),[61] the Court struck down a congressionally mandated tax on incomes over \$1,000. And, in *U.S. v. Cruikshank* (1875),[62] the Court greatly impeded Congress's ability to prosecute Ku Klux Klan vigilantes and other violent white supremacists, holding that the federal government could only prosecute these groups if the government could prove the white supremacists violated a specific federal right.

Effects on States

A greater number of cases dealt with state-level issues: thirty-two of fifty-three cases (60%). Many of these state issues dealt with economic activity. As with every period, the Court centralized power largely through reviewing and invalidating state-level laws. While the newly passed Thirteenth, Fourteenth, and Fifteenth Amendments gave the Court and the federal government greater power—on paper—to regulate state and local affairs than before the Civil War, the primary avenue for national state expansion remained questions of economic activity and commerce.

For example, decisions such as *Ward v. Maryland* (1871) and *Welton v. Missouri* (1876) struck down state statutes that required licenses for sellers of goods. In *Ward*, Maryland fined a New Jersey trader for selling goods in Baltimore without the license required by Maryland law.[63] The Court held that the Maryland law imposed a discriminating tax on nonresidents and thus it violated the privileges and immunities section of Article IV. According to Justice Clifford's majority opinion, the Maryland law "creates an unjust and onerous discrimination in favor of the citizens of the State enacting the statute" because it secures "to the citizens of that State, if not the exclusive control of the market, very important special privileges and immunities by exemption from burdensome requirements."[64] Likewise in *Welton*, the defendant salesman sold sewing machines in Missouri that were not manufactured in Missouri, without a license.[65] The Missouri law required a license whenever anyone (in state or out of state) sold goods that were not produced or manufactured in Missouri. The Court held that the Missouri statute ran afoul of the Commerce

Clause, and detailed the potential dangers of allowing "discriminating state legislation:" "The power of the state to exact a license tax of any amount being admitted, no authority would remain in the United States or in this Court to control its action, however unreasonable or oppressive."[66] From this the Court concluded, "all the evils of discriminating state legislation, favorable to the interests of one state and injurious to the interests of other states and countries, which existed previous to the adoption of the Constitution, might follow."[67] The Court used its economic activity decisions to bring uniformity across the states, but while much fewer in number, its federalism decisions (only eight total) restricted federal authority and left states with autonomy.

   Gilman v. Philadelphia restricted federal authority in that it left plenary power to the state in determining whether a bridge could be built on a Pennsylvania river.[68] The plaintiff in this case, a business owner in Philadelphia, sued the city of Philadelphia to prevent the building of a bridge that would make it impossible for some types of ships to load and unload at the business-owner's wharves. While the business owner claimed this bridge violated the interstate commerce clause of the Constitution, the Court, quoting from an earlier decision, held otherwise. Justice Swayne's majority opinion declared, "The right of eminent domain over the shores and the soil under the navigable waters *for all municipal purposes belongs exclusively to the states* within their respective territorial jurisdictions, and they and they only have the constitutional power to exercise it."[69] The Court, however, did leave room for national state expansion when it noted at the very end of the decision that

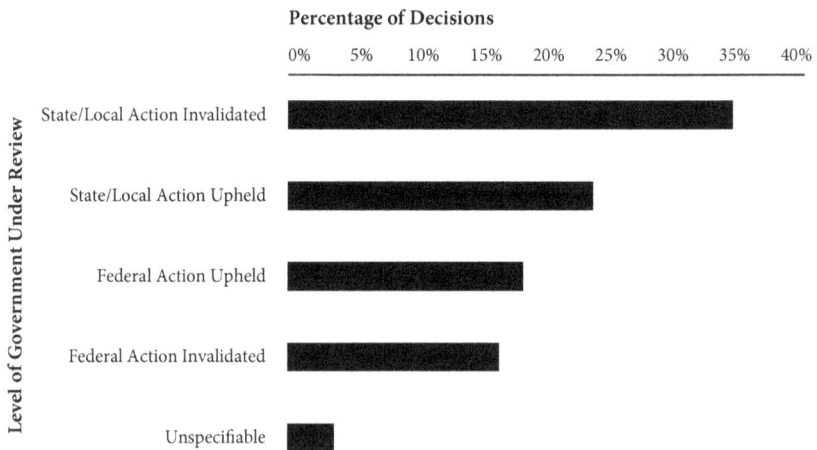

Percentage of Decisions

	0%	5%	10%	15%	20%	25%	30%	35%	40%

State/Local Action Invalidated

State/Local Action Upheld

Federal Action Upheld

Federal Action Invalidated

Unspecifiable

Level of Government Under Review

Figure 2.15. Level of Government Action under Review, Civil War and Reconstruction Eras.

Source: Compiled by author.

"until the dormant power of the Constitution is awakened and made effective by appropriate legislation, the reserved power of the states is plenary."[70]

Republican Era (1877–1932)

This period comprises 182 cases, of which 104 (57%) expand central state authority. The Republican era is often separated into two periods: the Gilded Age (up to the turn of the twentieth century), and the Progressive era (the early twentieth century). The Gilded Age, in particular, was a period of extraordinary economic expansion, with small businesses falling prey to monopoly capitalism. Indeed, 74 of those cases (41%) involved economic activity, which constitute a plurality of cases, as also in the previous two periods. Individual rights—primarily civil right/liberties and criminal procedure—also become more common on the Court's docket; both issue areas tended to expand central state authority. The primary way the Court expanded central state authority is through validating federal action, a phenomenon that only happened last in the Early Republic era; typically the Court expands central state authority through invalidating state-level laws.

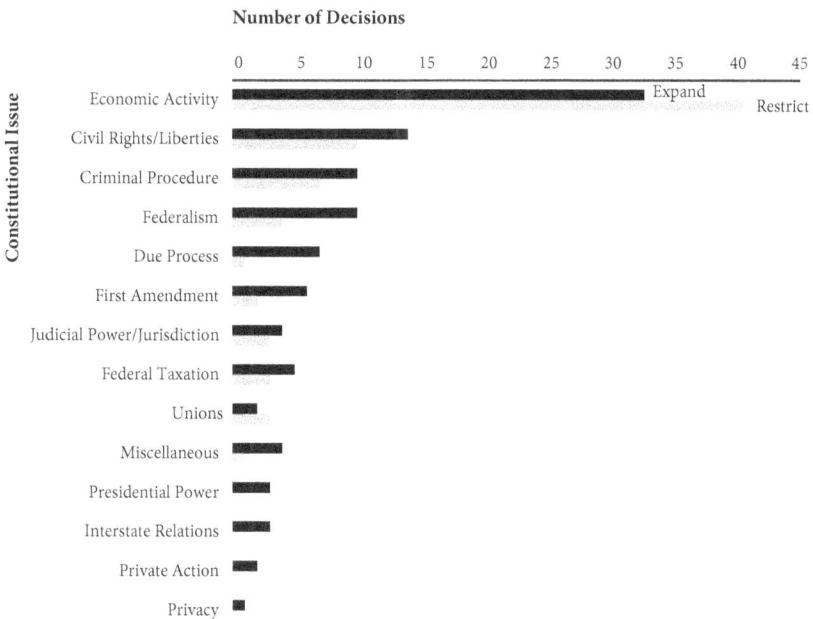

Figure 2.16. Constitutional Issues, Republican Era, 1877–1932.

Source: Compiled by author. N=182.

Effects on Federal Government

Of 182 cases, 73 (40%) reviewed some type of federal action. Fifty of those 73 decisions (68%) upheld some type of federal action; no single issue stands out as particularly prominent. Of these 73 cases, economic activity was the modal issue area (with fifteen cases). By the Progressive era, the Supreme Court began to support the federal government's antitrust efforts in decisions such as *McCray v. United States* (1904).[71] *McCray* upheld Congress's taxing power, which it used to regulate the production of oleomargarine. The Court also affirmed Congress's power to regulate the interstate sale of lottery tickets in *Champion v. Ames* (1903).[72] In addition to *Champion* and *McCray*, the Court upheld federal economic regulations in many other cases. It affirmed federal regulation of railroad rates that did not cross state borders,[73] the "White Slave Act" prohibiting interstate transport of women for prostitution or other "immoral purposes,"[74] the Pure Food and Drug Act of 1906,[75] and the Meat Inspection Acts of 1906 and 1907.[76]

In criminal procedure and civil rights cases, twenty of the seventy-three cases dealt with federal action. Here, too, as with economic activity, the Court was more likely to uphold federal action and centralize federal power. In *United States v. Ju Toy* (1905),[77] a case concerning criminal procedure and habeas corpus, the Supreme Court held that the secretary of commerce had the authority to make the final determination regarding a person of Chinese descent's readmission into the United States. Ju Toy's habeas corpus petition, the Court declared, should not be entertained unless he could demonstrate abuse of authority and a violation of due process, which the Court said he did not.

Another criminal procedure case, *United States v. Lanza* (1922),[78] also affirmed the federal government's authority over people and citizens. In this case, the two defendants were charged with five counts of alcohol possession and found guilty of violating both state and national laws concerning Prohibition. The defendants claimed that their two punishments for the same crime—one under the National Prohibition Act and the Eighteenth Amendment, and the other under a state law—amounted to double jeopardy, a violation of the Fifth Amendment. Chief Justice Taft held for the Court that both national and state governments may punish according to the laws of each government without violating the Fifth Amendment. He affirmed Congress's power to enforce the Eighteenth Amendment: "The first section of the amendment, the one embodying the prohibition, is operative throughout the entire territorial limits of the United States, [and] binds all legislative bodies, courts, public officers, and individuals within those limits"[79] (*Lanza*, 380).

A much smaller number of cases (twenty-three of seventy-three) restricted central state authority, but were nevertheless crucial, suggesting the Court's contradictory approach to rapid economic and industrial expansion.

For example, it narrowed the application of the Sherman Antitrust Act of 1890,[80] invalidated a federal law banning interstate transport of manufactured goods produced by children under sixteen,[81] invalidated the Civil Rights Act of 1875 banning racial discrimination by private businesses,[82] and limited Congress' power to impose income taxes.[83]

Effects on States

As with every period, the Court reviewed far more state than federal actions: 107 of 182 cases dealt with state issues. Here again, in every era except the Early Republic, economic activity is by far the most common issue reviewed: of the 59 state laws upheld, 38 of them were economic activity cases; and for the 48 state laws invalidated, 21 cases dealt with economic activity. The Court sometimes used the newly passed Fourteenth Amendment to strike down Progressive economic state regulations, centralizing federal authority in the judicial branch. For example, the Court in *Allgeyer v. Louisiana* (1897)[84] creatively used the "liberty of contract"—which emanated from the Fourteenth Amendment—to strike down a Louisiana law that prohibited out-of-state insurance corporations from doing business in the state without maintaining a place of business and an authorized agent in state. Almost twenty years later in *Coppage v. Kansas* (1915), the Court used the same doctrine to overturn a Kansas law that banned "yellow dog contracts"—employer agreements barring employees from joining labor unions.[85] But more often, the Court restricted federal authority by leaving state economic regulations standing, as in *Muller v. Oregon* (1908) and *Bunting v. Oregon* (1917).[86] Both of those decisions upheld Oregon's law prescribing a ten-hour workday.

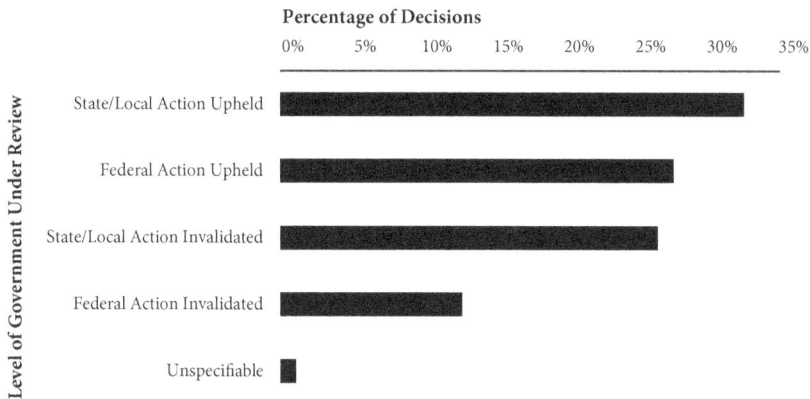

Figure 2.17. Level of Government Action under Review, Republican Era.
Source: Compiled by author.

New Deal and Great Society (1933–1968)

This period comprise 116 cases, of which 81 (70%) expand central state authority. Of those cases, 38 (33%) involve First Amendment rights, which represent a plurality of the cases in this period. Not too far behind were issues of civil rights and liberties, comprising 32 cases in this period. For the first time since the Early Republic, economic activity was not the primary constitutional issue. During the New Deal and Great Society eras, the Court expanded federal authority largely by invalidating state laws, centralizing authority in the judicial branch.

Effects on Federal Government

In this period 35 of 116 cases dealt with federal action, of which 26 affirmed national governing authority and the coordinate branches. The Court centralized federal authority and broadly interpreted the president's ability to conduct foreign affairs[87] and Congress's authority to regulate under the Commerce

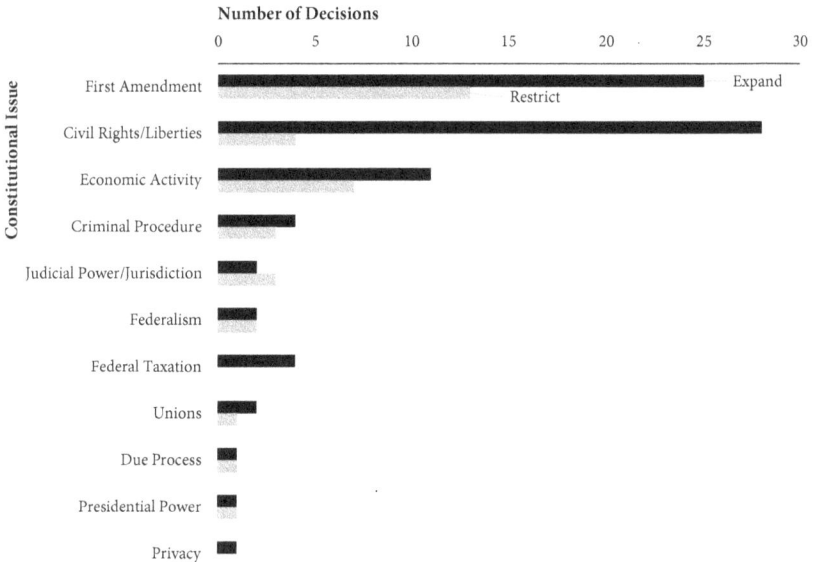

Figure 2.18. Constitutional Issues, New Deal and Great Society Eras, 1933–1968.
Source: Compiled by author. N=116.

Clause.[88] Indeed, between 1937 and 1995, the Supreme Court did not overturn any federal law as beyond Congress's Commerce Clause authority. The Court also supported the creation of the administrative state when it upheld the constitutionality of the Social Security Act in *Steward Machine Co. v. Davis* (1937) and *Helvering v. Davis* (1937).[89] It also affirmed Congress's growing involvement in civil rights issues, upholding Title II of the Civil Rights Act in *Katzenbach v. McClung* (1964) and *Heart of Atlanta Motel v. United States* (1964);[90] these decisions affirmed Congress's authority to ban racial discrimination in hotels and restaurants.

Effects on States

The Court reviewed state laws at a virtually unprecedented rate during this period: 77 of 116 cases (66%) reviewed state action, with 51 of those cases invalidating state laws. Thus this period marks a much more lopsided ratio of state actions upheld versus state action invalidated than the Republican era (where 59 cases upheld state laws and 48 invalidated laws). In the New Deal and Great Society eras, the Court centralized federal authority primarily by invalidating state laws pertaining to the First Amendment and civil rights (39 of 51 cases). This period marked the "rights revolution," as the Court now enforced a variety of noneconomic rights over the states.[91] Early in this period, the Court unanimously protected Jehovah's Witnesses who were arrested for violating a local Connecticut ordinance requiring a permit for solicitation. Writing for the Court, Justice Owen Roberts held that while regulation of solicitation was generally permissible, regulations based on religious speech were not.[92] The Court also overturned South Carolina's conviction of 187 African-American protesters who organized a march to the South Carolina State House grounds.[93] Justice Potter Stewart, writing for the Court, declared the arrests and convictions violated the defendants' freedom of speech and assembly.

The Court spoke equally forcefully with respect to civil rights issues, invalidating a variety of state action and laws that discriminated against African Americans. In *Shelley v. Kraemer* (1948),[94] for instance, the Court invalidated judicial enforcement of racial covenant laws—which prevented the sale of property to African Americans—for violating the Equal Protection Clause of the Fourteenth Amendment. Here, the Court centralized federal authority by preventing state courts from enforcing these restrictive covenants. By eliminating judicial enforcement of racial covenants, legal historian Francis Allen concluded, *Shelley* ended "one of the most devastating instrumentalities of racial segregation yet to emerge" (Allen 1989, 734). A decade later the Court,

Percentage of Decisions

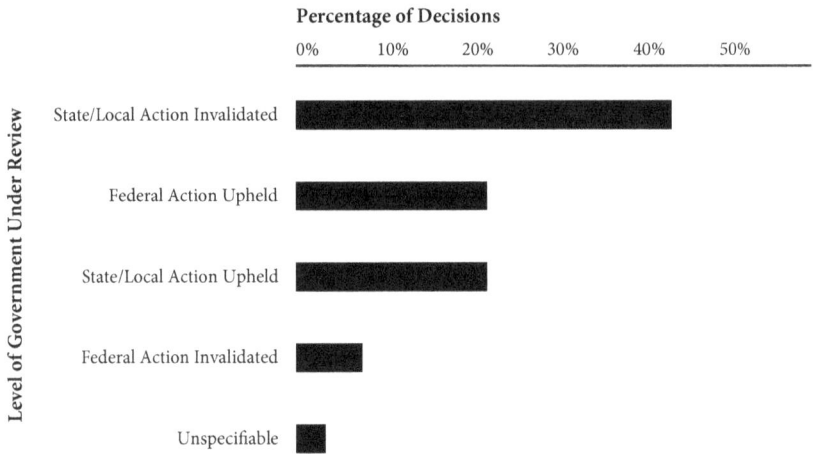

Figure 2.19. Level of Government Action under Review, New Deal and Great Society Eras.

Source: Compiled by author.

with ringing language in *Cooper v. Aaron* (1958),[95] asserted its authority over the states, citing Chief Justice John Marshall's opinion in *Marbury v. Madison* (1803): " 'It is emphatically the province and duty of the judicial department to say what the law is.' This decision [*Marbury*] declared the basic principle that the federal judiciary is supreme in the exposition of the law of the Constitution."[96] In *Cooper*, the Court emphasized its landmark desegregation decision, *Brown v. Board of Education* (1954), and declared that Arkansas school board officials were bound to obey federal court orders, which required schools to implement desegregation. The unanimous *per curiam* decision emphasized the power of the federal government, judiciary, and the Constitution over the states: "No state legislator or executive or judicial officer can war against the Constitution without violating his undertaking to support it."[97] The Court's centralization over noneconomic rights has continued into the contemporary era, and the effect of its decisions has limited the authority of state and local governments.

Contemporary Era (1969–1997)

This period comprises 146 cases, of which 84 (58%) expand central state authority. Of those cases, 47 (32%) deal with First Amendment rights, which represent a plurality of cases in this period. As in the previous period, civil

Number of Decisions

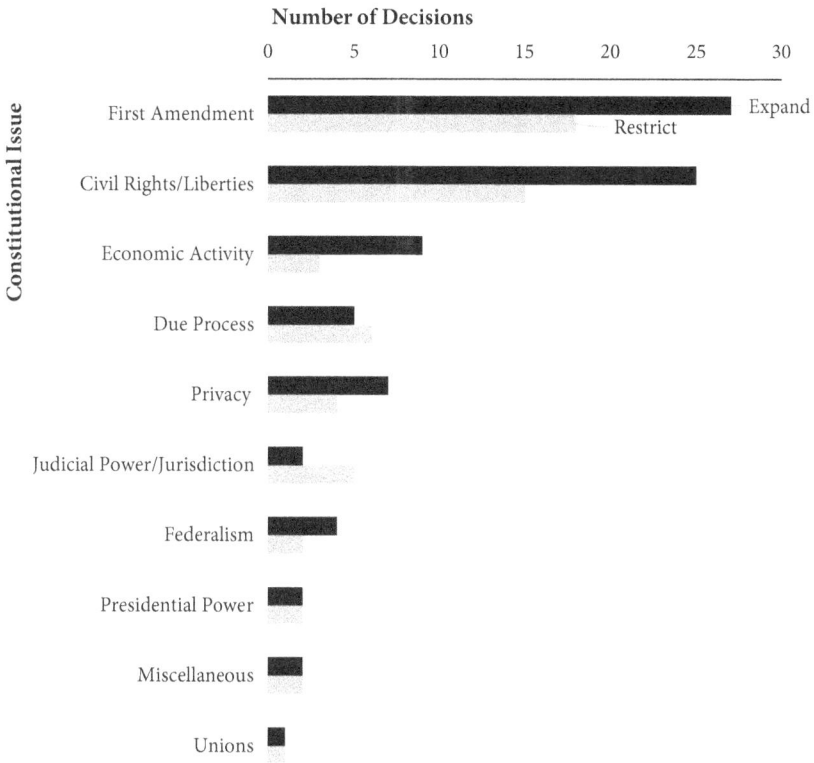

Figure 2.20. Constitutional Issues, Contemporary Era, 1969–1997.
Source: Compiled by author. N=146.

rights and liberties also mark a crucial issue area with 40 cases. Like the New Deal and Great Society eras, here, too, the Court expanded authority largely by invalidating state laws.

Effects on Federal Government

In this period 41 of 146 cases dealt with federal action, of which 23 affirmed national governing authority and the coordinate branches, which means the Court was almost just as likely to invalidate federal action (18 cases invalidated). *National League of Cities v. Usery* (1976) and *Garcia v. San Antonio Metropolitan Transit Authority* (1985) demonstrate the Court's back-and-forth nature on questions pertaining to national governing authority of the coordinate branches. *National League* declared Congress could not use the federal

Fair Labor Standards Act to regulate the labor market of state employees.[98] But nine years later in *Garcia*, the Court overruled *National League* and held that the Fair Labor Standards Act applied to the San Antonio Metropolitan Transit Authority.[99] It also limited the president's authority in *United States v. Nixon* (1974),[100] preventing President Nixon from invoking executive privilege as a reason not to obey a federal court subpoena. The Court also invalidated President Clinton's use of the line item veto in *Clinton v. City of New York* (1998).[101] Still other decisions empowered the coordinate branches, such as *South Dakota v. Dole* (1987),[102] which ordered the secretary of transportation to withhold 5% of federal highway funds from states that did not raise the drinking age to twenty-one. Just a year later, the Court affirmed Congress's authority yet again to empower parts of the executive branch. In *Morrison v. Olson* (1988),[103] a seven-to-one Court decision upheld Congress's authority to empower the attorney general to recommend an "independent counsel" to a special court created by the Ethics in Government Act of 1978.

Effects on States

The Court review of state laws greatly resembles that of the previous period: 94 of 146 cases (64%) reviewed state action with 58 of those cases invalidating state laws. The vast majority of its decisions concerning state action dealt with civil rights and First Amendment issues. It held that flag burning

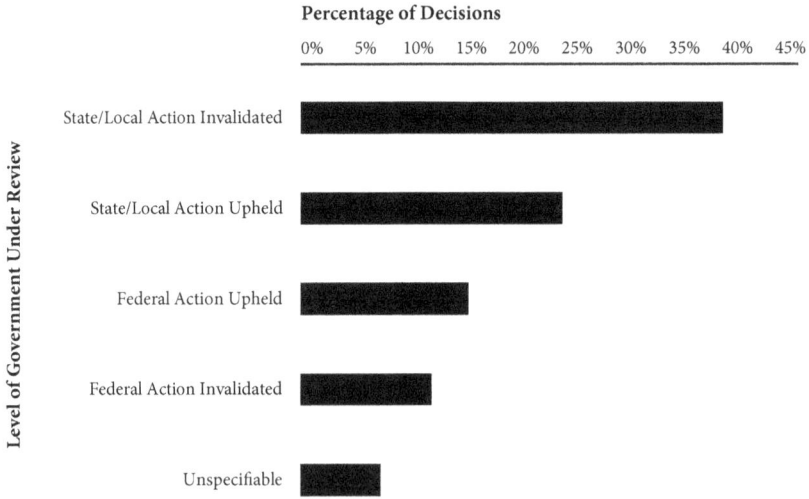

Figure 2.21. Level of Government Action under Review, Contemporary Era.
Source: Compiled by author.

was a form of protected expression under the First Amendment,[104] and that New Hampshire could not require citizens to display the state motto, "Live Free or Die," as it violated George Maynard's religious beliefs,[105] for example. In *Plyler v. Doe*, a civil rights case, the Court struck down a Texas law that allowed the state to withhold funds used to educate undocumented immigrants. In a close five-to-four decision, Justice William Brennan declared that the Fourteenth Amendment Equal Protection Clause provided protection against Texas state law, which disadvantaged children of undocumented immigrants. However, in some types of First Amendment cases, typically obscenity and child pornography cases, the Court upheld state-level speech restrictions, and thus constricted the reach and scope of federal authority.[106]

Conclusion

The data presented here reveal three characteristics of constitutional development: (1) there is persistent expansion of federal state authority; (2) it happens gradually and imperceptibly over time, often through the Court's use of its negative powers, invalidating lower-level state laws; and (3) it occurs through expanding federal authority to determine policy about citizens and people. Coding hundreds of decisions along seven dimensions of the federal government reveals when and where the federal government grew in authority. The persistent expansion of the "centralization" dimension begins to show us that the unsettled boundary between state and national authority was, and remains, an integral part of American constitutional development. Additionally, even decisions that were not overtly about centralization (such as the individual rights decisions) still had at their foundation questions about *who* (i.e., what level of government) had the authority to regulate individual rights. The data reveals similarities across periods of history and, as such, the benefit of considering the nature of the Constitution in structuring central state development and limiting constituent-state autonomy. The remaining substantive chapters examine how the Court has expanded federal authority from the founding until the end of the twentieth century.

Chapter 3

Strengths of the Early American State, 1789–1864

But where, say some, is the King of America? I'll tell you, friend, he reigns above, and doth not make havoc of mankind like the Royal Brute of Great Britain. Yet that we may not appear to be defective even in earthly honours, let a day be solemnly set apart for proclaiming the Charter; let it be brought forth placed on the Divine Law, the Word of God; let a crown be placed thereon, by which the world may know, that so far as we approve of monarchy, that in America the law is king.

—Thomas Paine, *Common Sense*, 1776[1]

Introduction

Scholars of the early American state characterize national authority in this period as extraordinarily decentralized and weak, or, at the least, unusual in comparison to European states.[2] This "exceptionalist" paradigm and the understanding that the early American state is distinctive remains, despite revisionist challenges.[3] The growth rate of the federal government belies the traditional scholarly interpretation that the United States lacked a central state that its European counterparts possessed.[4] And while individualistic and antistatist notions were (still) widely shared within American political culture,[5] the American federal government grew at a prodigious rate even in the pre–Civil War era, the time span examined in this chapter. As many scholars have noted, a powerful American state emerged before the Civil War,[6] and the Court's decisions helped extend national authority in the realms of economic activity, federalism, and control over territory and state membership, issues that concerned the world system, property, and extraction central state dimensions.

At the same time, other aspects of the federal state expanded, namely, the administrative capacity of the American state; communications, internal improvements, managing Indian affairs, and military authority were some areas of prodigious central state-building. With the Post Office Act of 1792, for example, the Congress established—for the next eight decades—an administrative institution "rivaled only by the military in its reach and cost" (M. Wilson 2008, 18). The 1792 Act also subsidized the circulation of newspapers and other sources of information on public life (John 1997, 372). Indeed, by the 1830s, because of postal subsides and low taxes on publishers, the United States had three times as many newspapers per capita as Britain (M. Wilson 2008, 18).

The strength and increasing independence of the Army Corps of Topographical Engineers—a division of the War Department—also revealed the strengths and expansion of the early American state. Especially in the nation's periphery—the West—the Corps of Topographical Engineers became "the most significant institutional actor with the greatest amount of power" (Adler 2012, 4). The Corps handled internal improvements, namely, the building of roads and canals. In the early republic, cabinet chiefs' desires to advance economic development, largely through railroad infrastructure, led secretaries of war to support the collaboration between the Corps and the private sector (Adler 2012, 8).[7]

Military authority over Indians revealed the federal state's strength both along administrative and world systems dimensions. The US military and the War Department also maintained direct oversight of all aspects of Indian affairs until the 1850s (M. Wilson 2008, 26). From 1796 to 1822, for example, Congress mandated that all Indian trade had to be conducted through official government "factories" or trading posts. Beyond routine administrative, the US military enforced Indian policy with pure physical coercion. The Indian Removal Act—signed into law by President Andrew Jackson on May 28, 1830—authorized the president to grant unsettled lands west of the Mississippi in exchange for Indian lands within existing state borders. Many tribes resisted the relocation policy, and during the fall and winter of 1838 and 1839, the Cherokees were forcibly moved west by the United States government, resulting in approximately 4,000 Cherokee deaths.[8] All told, the antebellum period saw increases in central state power in a number of policy areas, areas that pertained primarily to administrative bureaucratic capacities to control Indian affairs and build infrastructure.

As the central state expanded its territory, structure, and influence, it confronted constitutional issues regarding the boundaries of authority between state and national government, a byproduct of a constitution that enshrined a dual sovereign governing design. The ambiguity in the design of federalism left unanswered many questions of political authority that the Court would have to later address.[9] One place to examine these questions' effect on constitutional development is the Founding era and the Early Republic, when distributing powers between these two levels of governments was paramount. Despite the thorny debates set in motion because of this ambiguity, the Court regularly advanced federal authority. If the Court bowed to states' rights advocates, it typically did so by constricting its own authority to hear a case.

Some case examples will illuminate the Court's role in advancing federal authority. In 1769 the king of England granted a charter to Dartmouth College, located in what would become New Hampshire. The charter detailed the purposes of the college, outlined the governing structure, and gave it land. But, in 1816, the New Hampshire state legislature passed a law to change Dartmouth College from a private institution to a state university. This new law altered the school's corporate charter by giving the governor the power to appoint the college's trustees. The old trustees, however, filed suit, claiming that the New Hampshire laws violated Article 1, Section 10, of the Constitution, which prevented a state from "impairing" a contract. Thus, in *Dartmouth College v. Woodward* (1819),[10] the Court confronted the question, did New Hampshire unconstitutionally interfere with Dartmouth College's rights under the Contracts Clause of the Constitution? Marshall's Court answered affirmatively, in a five-to-one decision, striking down the New Hampshire statute and extending federal authority to protect business owners. If states could not pass laws to impair contracts and charters, then businesses would be more secure. By invalidating the state law, Marshall's Court helped lay the foundations for a strong national commercial union by encouraging "mobility, competition, and innovation" through its economic activity decisions (M. Wilson 2008, 16). Over the next half-century, the American economy would increase by a factor of eight, partly because of the Court's decisions.

This was not the only area where the Early Republic's federal authority expanded. Perhaps even more remarkably, the territory of the United States tripled from 864,000 square miles in 1800 to nearly 3 million square miles in 1850 (M. Wilson 2008, 3). The federal authority to govern these territories was a central question in many Court decisions. *American Insurance Company v. Canter* (1828) dealt with a ship carrying 584 bales of cotton from New Orleans to Havre de Grace, France, in 1825;[11] it was shipwrecked on the coast of what was then the US territory of Florida. The salvage company that saved the cargo later sold the cotton, but the insurers of the cargo brought a suit to recover a portion of it. After an unfavorable local territorial court ruling, the insurers appealed to the Supreme Court, maintaining that the territorial circuit court was neither legally organized nor of proper jurisdiction to adjudicate the case.

Beyond jurisdiction, *American Insurance Company* raised even larger questions about the power of Congress to acquire and control territories. In a unanimous ruling, Chief Justice Marshall affirmed Congressional action, holding that the Florida territorial courts were constitutional, contrasting these "legislative" courts (which Congress created through Articles I and IV) with the more typical "constitutional" courts (which Article III created). The Court found that the plenary congressional power over the territories (in Article IV) justified Congress' creation of non–Article III courts in the territories. In the territories, Marshall declared, "Congress exercises the combined powers of the general and of a state government," and so the jurisdiction of Article I courts in the territories "is not a part of that judicial power" that Article III constitutional courts like the Supreme Court define.[12] Thus, in *American Insurance*, the Marshall Court facilitated the growth of Article I "legislative" courts, which remained outside the reach of Article III constitutional courts' appellate review powers, yet simultaneously, it expanded the plenary powers of Congress to acquire and govern territory.

These questions of federalism and jurisdiction offered an important avenue for the extension of federal authority. They were not confined just to Marshall's Court; they played a key role during the Jacksonian era too. Chief Justice Roger Taney's Court confronted similar questions three decades later in *Ableman v. Booth* (1859),[13] a case concerning the relationship between federal and state governments. In this case, a federal marshal arrested an ardent abolitionist, Sherman Booth—an integral figure in the antislavery movement in Wisconsin—for violating the Fugitive Slave Act of 1850 when he aided an escaped slave, Joshua Glover. Despite being in federal custody, Booth successfully petitioned the Wisconsin State Supreme Court for his release through a writ of habeas corpus. He was later convicted in federal district court and detained again. But he successfully petitioned the Wisconsin Supreme Court for his release a second time, and the Wisconsin Supreme Court claimed that the Fugitive Slave Act was unconstitutional and that the federal district court lacked jurisdiction to try and detain Booth. The United States government appealed the Wisconsin Court's decision to the US Supreme Court under Chief Justice Taney, which faced the question, did the Supreme Court of Wisconsin have the authority to issue the writs of habeas corpus that released Booth?

Unanimously, the Court asserted the supremacy of federal courts on issues of federal laws. Invalidating the state-level action, Taney noted that the Constitution reads, "The laws of the United States . . . shall be the supreme law of the land, and the judges in every State shall be bound thereby."[14] He concluded, then, that "the supremacy thus conferred on this Government could not peacefully be maintained, unless it was clothed with judicial power, equally paramount in authority to carry it into execution; for if left to the courts of justice of the several states conflicting decisions would unavoidably take place, and the local tribunals could hardly be expected to be always free from the local influences of which we have spoken."[15] Through Taney's federalism decision, the Court asserted its power over state tribunals and thus extended federal authority to enforce the law.

State-Building during the Early Republic and Jacksonian Eras

From the founding until 1864 (Chief Justice Taney's final year in office), we see cumulative advancement of central state authority. Figure 3.1 demonstrates a persistent trend in expanding federal authority. The total number of decisions

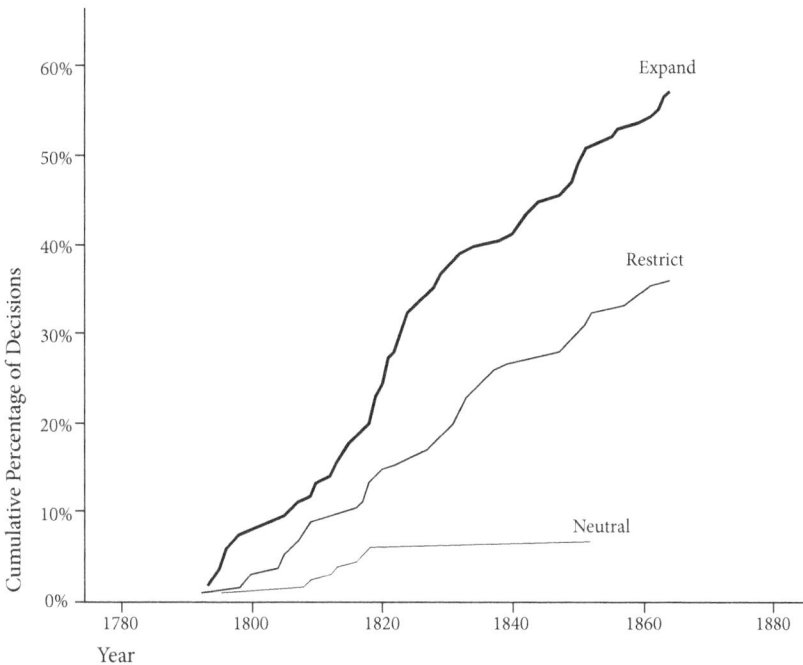

Figure 3.1. Cumulative Frequency of the Effect of Federal Authority, 1792–1864.
Source: Compiled by author. N=136.

expanding federal power rises at a much faster rate than those that restrict it. Breaking these data down into seven constitutional issue areas, economic activity and judicial power comprise 54% of decisions in this period; individual rights, surprisingly, make up 21% of the decisions the Court confronted through the end of the Civil War (see Table 3.1 below). Moreover, when examining the cases by chief justice tenures, we notice that under each chief justice, even under Chief Justice Roger Taney, decisions that expanded federal authority outweigh decisions constricting it (see Figure 3.2). All these graphics confirm patterns discussed in chapter 2: that the Supreme Court typically favored the growth of central state authority far more often than not. In fact, of the 136

Table 3.1. Constitutional Issue by Effect on Federal Authority, 1792–1864

| Constitutional Issue | | Effect on Federal Authority | | | |
		Restrict	Neutral	Expand	Total
Economic activity	Count	11	2	25	38
	% within row	32.4%	5.4%	62.2%	100.0%
Judicial power	Count	18	2	16	36
	%	47.2%	5.6%	47.2%	100.0%
Individual rights	Count	12	3	13	28
	%	42.9%	10.7%	46.4%	100.0%
Federalism	Count	5	1	15	21
	%	27.3%	4.5%	68.2%	100.0%
Taxation	Count	0	0	3	3
	%	0.0%	0.0%	100.0%	100.0%
Private action	Count	0	1	4	5
	%	0.0%	20.0%	80.0%	100.0%
Executive power	Count	2	0	3	5
	%	40.0%	0.0%	60.0%	100.0%
Total	Count	48	9	79	136
	%	36.0%	6.6%	57.4%	100.0%

Notes and Sources: Compiled by the author. Judicial power decisions constrict federal authority most frequently, with eighteen of forty-eight decisions, or 38% of the time. Conversely, economic activity expands federal authority most frequently, with twenty-five of seventy-nine decisions, or 32% of the time. There is no statistically significant relationship in this smaller subsample. The data as a whole reveal a significant relationship between constitutional issue and effect on authority (see Appendix 4, Figure A.3). I did not include here the one interstate relation decision in this period; it restricted federal authority. N=136.

Number of Decisions

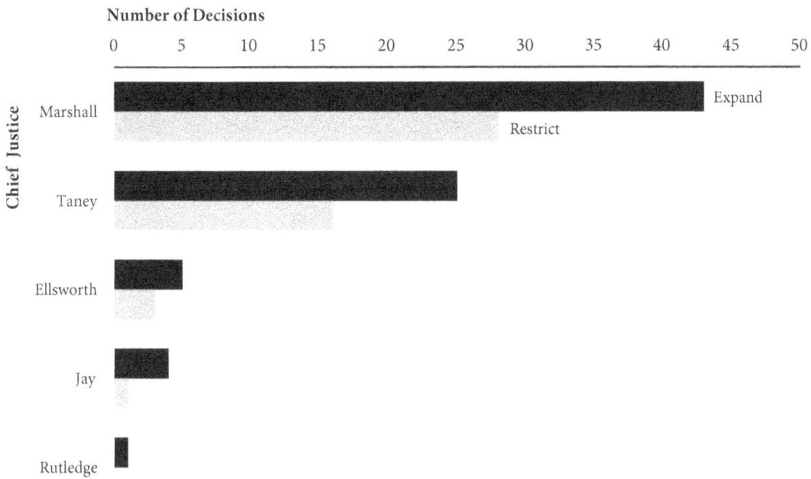

Figure 3.2. The Effect on Federal Authority across Chief Justice Tenures, 1792–1864.

Notes and Source: Compiled by author. I did not include neutral decisions, nine of which occurred in this period, six of them under Marshall's Court. Expansive decisions always outweigh restrictive ones. Of all the chief justices this graphic includes, Marshall sat the longest (thirty-five years); Taney sat for twenty-nine years. N=125.

total cases, 79 expand (57%) while 48 restrict (36%) federal authority during this almost eighty-year period. Thus, the Court's persistent expansion of federal authority is as old as the republic itself. Within the constitutional issues, economic activity and federalism issues most advanced federal authority (Table 3.1 on page 72 and Figure 3.3 on page 74), and world systems, extraction, and property were the central state dimensions that played the most important roles in building central state strength (Table 3.2 on page 74).

Having demonstrated that central state authority consistently grows, despite occasional examples of its restriction, the rest of this chapter details some of the legal doctrines and constitutional interpretations that facilitated this expansion. Ultimately, the empirical reality of the Court's constitutional decisions belies American skepticism of central state authority.

During this period, the Court expanded federal authority across all central state dimensions except for administrative capacity.[16] World systems, extraction, and property were vital to advancing early American state strength. Under the world system dimension, questions of territory, state membership, and control of ports and the high seas were prevalent, with 69% of the cases along this dimension expanding authority. Confronting issues of the control of ports, *The Passenger Cases* (1849) under the Taney Court, for

Economic activity is the
primary channel for
central state expansion.

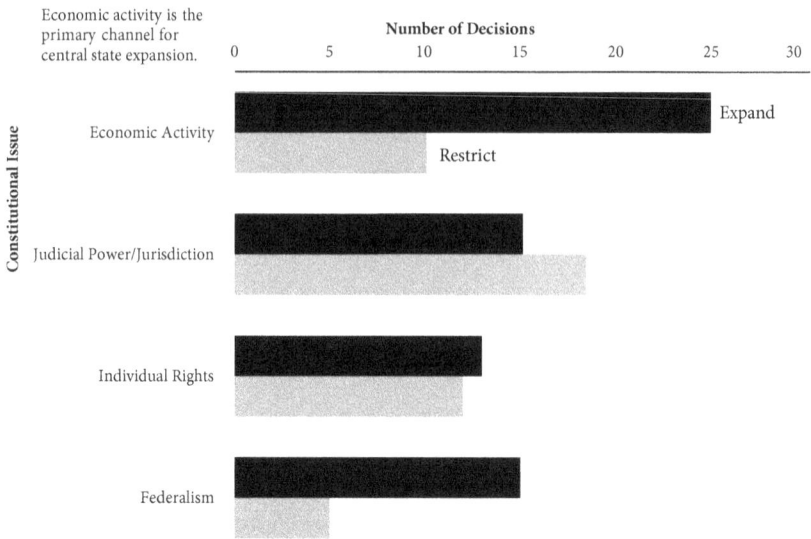

Figure 3.3. Constitutional Issue Areas and Effect on Federal Authority, 1792–1864.

Notes and Source: Compiled by the author. This graphic does not include neutral decisions. It contains the most abundant constitutional issues. "Individual rights" comprises civil rights, criminal procedure, due process, and First Amendment. Together, individual rights, economic activity, federalism, and judicial power comprise 84% of the issue areas. N=115.

example, invalidated state statutes that authorized the states to collect a tax on all passengers who arrived at a dock on a vessel arriving from a foreign port.[17] Here, the plaintiff passengers challenged the constitutionality of these state statutes, arguing that they violated the Commerce Clause. In a narrow five-four decision, the Taney Court expanded central state authority when it

Table 3.2. Frequency of Central State Dimensions, 1793–1864

Dimension	Expand	Restrict	Total	% Expanding
Client groups	8	1	9	88.89%
Extraction	11	3	14	78.57%
World systems	22	10	32	68.75%
Centralization	68	42	110	61.82%
Property	39	27	66	59.09%
Citizenship	19	16	35	54.29%
Admin. capacity	11	14	25	44.00%

Note and Source: Compiled by the author. Neutral decisions not included. N=125.

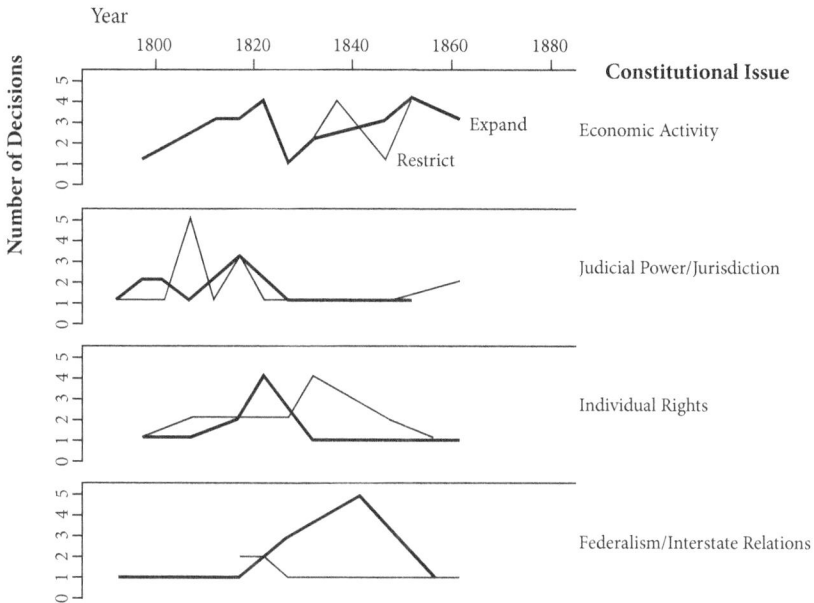

Figure 3.4. Most Abundant Constitutional Issues, 1792–1864.

Note and Source: Compiled by the author. Neutral decisions are not included. N=115.

held that collecting a tax on passengers from a foreign port amounted to a regulation on foreign commerce, which violated the Constitution.

While control of ports often dealt with economic issues, as in *The Passenger Cases*, the world system dimension also dealt with Congressional authority to regulate the high seas and individual rights. The Marshall Court, in *United States v. Smith* (1820),[18] upheld six to one an act of Congress that regulated piracy. In this case, Thomas Smith was part of a crew on the *Creollo*, a private armed ship commissioned by a Spanish colony at war with Spain. The *Creollo* then "seized by violence" another vessel, the *Irresistible*, and together they plundered and robbed a Spanish vessel in April 1819. Soon thereafter, the US Navy captured the crew members under a Congressional statute intended to "protect the commerce of the United States and punish the crime of piracy," which was punishable by death. The lower circuit court was divided on the question of whether these acts constituted "piracy" as the law of nations defined it, but Justice Story's majority opinion for the Supreme Court expanded central state authority by finding that Congress has broad latitude in defining piracy. He maintained that Congress should not be restricted "to a mere logical enumeration in detail of all the facts constituting the offence."[19] Story thus concluded and affirmed Congressional authority:

"The case is piracy, as defined by the law of nations, so as to be punishable under the act of Congress of the 3d of March, 1819."[20] The early republic Court—led by Marshall—did not merely define (as opposed to expand) central state authority. In fact, there was nothing neutral about early constitutional interpretation; defining the boundaries of federal power always resulted in either expanding or constricting federal state authority.

Another Marshall Court decision extending federal authority along the world system dimension was *Worcester v. Georgia* (1832),[21] a decision that deals with the individual rights of the criminally accused and territorial control. Here, a Congressional statute promoted the "civilization of Indian tribes," which allowed the president to appoint persons to "minister and educate Indians." However, a Georgia law prohibited white persons from living on Cherokee land without a license, while another Georgia law redrew the boundaries of Cherokee Nation. Thus, Samuel Worcester, who the president appointed, was convicted in Georgia court for living in the Cherokee Nation without a license and sentenced to "hard labour in the penitentiary for four years." Marshall's lengthy five-to-one decision expanded central state power when it struck down the Georgia laws because the "treaties and laws of the United States contemplate the Indian territory as completely separated from that of the states; and provide that all intercourse with them shall be carried on exclusively by the government of the union."[22] Chief Justice Marshall understood Indian tribes to be part of the world system dimension: "The Cherokee nation, then, is a distinct community occupying its own territory in which the laws of Georgia can have no force. The whole intercourse between the United States and this nation, is, by our constitution and laws, vested in the government of the United States."[23] While the world system dimension dealt with a variety of constitutional issues, including economic regulation, relations with Indian tribes, and the criminally accused, the majority of the decisions affirmed federal authority of Congress or invalidated state laws because they impinged on constitutional provisions.

Within the property and extraction dimensions, economic activity and federalism issues played a prominent role. For example, *Osborn v. Bank of United States* (1824) dealt with extraction and federalism.[24] At issue in *Osborn* was an Ohio state tax levied on the United States Bank. Ohio insisted on enforcing the tax, which defied a federal circuit court injunction. The circuit court then required the Ohio State Auditor, Ralph Osborn, to repay the amount seized, but he refused. On appeal, the Supreme Court expanded central state authority when it affirmed the lower federal court's decision and invalidated the Ohio law. First, Marshall held that because Congress can incorporate a national bank, federal courts had jurisdiction when suits were brought against the national bank. Second, and more substantively, Congress had the authority to create such a bank: "Why is it that Congress can incorporate or create a Bank? . . . It is an instrument which is 'necessary and proper' for carrying on the fiscal operations of government."[25]

Through economic activity cases, over two decades later, Chief Justice Taney's Court further extended federal authority in two cases dealing with the property dimension. In *Planters Bank v. Mississippi* (1848) and *Woodruff v. Trapnall* (1850),[26] the Taney Court held that the state statutes in both cases violated the Contracts Clause of the Constitution. At issue in these cases were state laws in Mississippi and in Arkansas that repealed previous laws that accepted promissory notes as repayment of debt. Justice Woodbury held for the Court in *Planters*, "The constitutional restrictions of the general government must control a statute of a state conflicting with them, and thus, for harmony and uniformity, make the former supreme, in compliance with the injunctions imposed by the people and the states themselves in the Constitution."[27] In effect, these economic decisions expanded federal authority by invalidating state laws that contravened the Constitution.

In contrast to the property, extraction, and world system dimensions, administrative capacity—since it concerns the structural design of the federal state—often dealt with the role of the judiciary among the national branches. The judiciary's reluctance to expand its own federal authority explains why administrative capacity is the only dimension of the seven that did not expand federal authority more often than not (nine of the thirteen administrative capacity decisions in Table 3.2 that constricted authority dealt with judicial power). It is these cases to which we now turn.

The Court's Placement in the Early American State

Before explaining the issues that helped expand federal authority, it is necessary to examine one area that neither drastically expanded nor constricted the central state: judicial power. Because 61% of judicial power decisions (thirty-six of fifty-nine decisions) happened between 1789 and 1864, they warrant further examination. Additionally, these cases demonstrate the unique institutional role of the Court within the broader federal government. The Court's cautious approach to judicial power cases is emblematic of the larger questions and hostilities the Court confronted during this period.

Take *Cohens v. Virginia* (1824), for example, which illuminates both Supreme Court cautiousness *and* an expansion of federal authority over state-level actions.[28] In *Cohens*, simply declaring that the Court would even hear the case ignited a "political firestorm" in Virginia, yet that was exactly what the Marshall Court did: it unanimously held that it had appellate jurisdiction over criminal proceedings.[29] In response, the Virginia legislature maintained that the Marshall Court had "no rightful authority under the Constitution to examine and correct the judgment for which the Commonwealth has been cited" (quoted in Graber 1995, 75). Nevertheless, despite Marshall's strategic politics and deference to the state of Virginia in the substance of his decision, the Court expanded central state authority by emphasizing federal judicial power: "The propriety of entrusting the construction of the Constitution, and laws made in pursuance thereof, to the judiciary of the Union has not, we believe, as yet, been drawn into question. It seems to be a corollary from this political axiom that the federal Courts should either possess exclusive jurisdiction in such cases, or a power to revise the judgment rendered in them, by the State tribunals."[30]

Brothers Philip and Mendes Cohen owned the Cohens Lottery and Exchange Offices of Baltimore, New York, Philadelphia, Charleston, and Norfolk. Approved by a Congressional act, the Cohen brothers began to sell lottery tickets within the District of Columbia, too. But on January 1, 1820, a Virginia state law took effect that prohibited the sale of lottery tickets. Shortly thereafter, the Cohen brothers were arrested at their Norfolk office and convicted of selling out these DC lottery tickets approved by federal law. Congress had delegated to the Corporation of Washington the power to hold lotteries, a common political practice in the late eighteenth and early nineteenth centuries. The Grand National Lottery was intended to generate funds to build a canal between Maryland and Washington. Marshall's assertion that the Grand National Lottery was local in scope—confined only to the District of Columbia—belied the common usage of lotteries; government officials often used proceeds from these lotteries to fund federal projects. More than that, anyone familiar with the nation's capital at this time knew Washington DC could not make good on the Grand National Lottery's $50,000 worth of prizes (Graber 1995, 73–81). Nevertheless, the justices adhered to a "highly implausible reading" of the congressional legislation that created the Grand National Lottery and concluded Congress did not intend to authorize the sale of tickets outside of DC (Graber 1995, 69).

At the same time, however, the Marshall Court affirmed central state authority (both of the Congress and the Court). More specifically, Marshall held that the Court had appellate jurisdiction to hear cases of individuals convicted of state crimes. He also ruled that the Supremacy Clause prevented states from impinging on Congress's authority to govern the nation's capital. Despite these affirmations of central state authority, the Court still held that the Grand National Lottery did not prevent Virginia's ban on out-of-state lottery sales and thus, after all that, Marshall upheld Virginia's conviction of the Cohen brothers. Still, and crucially, *Cohens* held that individuals convicted of state crimes had the right to appeal their judgments in federal courts.

The Court's implausible reading of the congressional and Virginia statutes resulted from its having no reason to believe that "Virginians would respect a decision in favor of the Cohen brothers" (Graber 1995, 86). One prominent Ohio attorney said at the time that ruling in favor of Virginia's law was an attempt to "allay the apprehensions" that the Court's assertion of jurisdictional authority would generate in Virginia (quoted in Graber 1995, 87). Fundamentally, the Marshall Court recognized its inability to declare laws—even state laws—unconstitutional if it lacked the support of the national political branches, as it did in *Cohens* because of Virginia's vigorous objections. Notwithstanding this inability, the Court still expounded on broad constitutional issues pertaining to supremacy and jurisdiction before it issued its much narrower edict on the constitutionality of Virginia's ban on lotteries. Ultimately, *Cohens* demonstrated how judicial power decisions involve much larger questions of federalism but also how the Court's cautious approach helped lay the foundation for expansion of national authority.[31]

The judiciary's position within the federal government is relatively precarious, and that was especially true during the pre–Civil War era. On the one hand, courts are supposed to be independent from the controversial politics of the day so their decisions will appear legitimate. In *Federalist* No. 78, Hamilton argued that the "complete independence of the courts of justice is peculiarly essential in a limited Constitution." Without independent courts, Hamilton contended, "all the reservations of particular rights or privileges would amount to nothing" (Kramnick 1987, 438). Yet, on the other hand, this independence leaves the judiciary highly susceptible to the criticism that it has pursued its own ideological interest under the guise of impartial adjudication. Thus, anti-Federalists objected to Hamilton's claims, fearing the power of an insulated judiciary; Brutus wrote, "There is no power above [judges] to controul any of their decisions. . . . In short, they are independent of the people, of the legislature, and of every power under heaven. Men placed in this situation will generally soon feel themselves independent of heaven itself" (Ball 2007, 525). This unique institutional placement has produced what some call the paradox of the "two faces of judicial power" (Bybee 2007, 1).

To protect itself from such criticism and to ensure its autonomy, the judiciary embraces legal reasoning and analysis, which is distinct from the decision-making processes of the legislative and executive branches. Thus a person is likely to reach different conclusions as a justice than he or she would as a legislator or executive.[32] Over time, the federal judiciary has imposed a set of doctrinal constraints that limit its judicial power and jurisdiction. In particular, the Court has implemented the principle of justiciability, according to which it can refuse to hear cases and with this refusal limit federal authority, grounding its federal jurisdiction in Article III of the Constitution with its language of "cases" and "controversies." This has led the Supreme Court to hold that federal courts may take jurisdiction only in "justiciable" disputes, that is, those "appropriate for judicial determination,"[33] thereby imposing limitations on jurisdictional authority.[34]

One such example occurred early in the country's history. In 1793, as the war between France and England grew more intense, President Washington's administration wondered what, if any, obligations it had to France under its treaty of alliance. Washington asked the Supreme Court for an advisory opinion on the French ambassador's outfitting of enthusiastic American volunteers as well as of French privateers in American ports. But in August 1793, in *Hayburn's Case*,[35] the Court unanimously refused Washington's request to issue an advisory opinion, referencing the separation of powers as well as the "strong arguments against the propriety of" answering questions extrajudicially (Holt 1998, 178–179).[36] The Court's refusal in this instance was odd given that the Court did not rule advisory opinions unconstitutional and that advisory opinions were common in the English tradition (Holt 1998, 179). It was this particular advisory opinion that the Court rejected, and for the calculated political reason that it would pull the Court into a hotly debated issue that pitted Washington's administration against itself, with Secretary of State Jefferson supporting the French and Secretary of Treasury Hamilton supporting the British (Holt 1998, 178). Thus, Washington's decision to remain neutral in the war "provoked the first open attacks on his previously untouchable character and judgment" (Ferejohn et al. 2006, 186). Determined early in the Court's history, the norm of refusing to issue advisory opinions provided an avenue for constitutional deference and thus maintained the Court's legitimacy and political capital, which in turn led it ultimately to restrict federal authority via the judiciary.

The political questions doctrine is another prominent way the Court can refuse power for itself and instead leave power with the political branches. This doctrine has emerged as a way for the Court to duck potential cases that might make them vulnerable. According to this doctrine, the Court removes from judicial consideration constitutional law questions that it deems beyond its constitutional authority to decide. The doctrine is as old as *Marbury v. Madison* (1803), on which Chief Justice Marshall said, "The province of the Court is solely to decide on the rights of individuals, not to inquire how the Executive or Executive officers perform duties in which they have a discretion. Questions, in their nature political or which are, by the Constitution and laws, submitted to the Executive, can never be made in this court."[37] Certainly, the Court applies this doctrine with little consistency (Pacelle 2002, 88), but the important point is that "political questions," and jurisdiction questions more broadly, result from the Court's unique institutional placement and produce a mechanism that constricts federal authority more often than any other constitutional issue.

The Court refined and advanced the political question doctrine under the Taney Court. For example, *Luther v. Borden* (1849) declared that the Court did not have the constitutional authority to determine which group—after a small civil war in Rhode Island—constituted the official government of that state.[38] The Court's invocation of the political question doctrine—or, really, any justiciable principle—is self-enforcing; it is the arbiter of its own rules and thus can ignore or invoke them (O'Brien 2003, 171). While the application of these jurisdictional principles—and other principles like diversity jurisdiction[39]—can be sporadic, the bottom line is that the Court relies on them when its legitimacy is at risk and when its decision would have little effect and, consequently, undermine its authority (Ferejohn and Kramer 2006, 193). These jurisdictional methods illuminate how the Court's judicial power cases affect federal authority.

Constitutional Design at the Founding: Federal versus State Sovereignty

All this expansion occurred in the context of a constitution designed by two main groups at the 1787 Constitutional Convention—broad nationalists and narrow nationalists. Broad nationalists such as James Madison of Virginia sought to build a very strong central government that had complete authority over taxes, commerce, and defense. These broad nationalists aimed to diminish state governments' powers and relegate states to a secondary role in American government. By contrast, narrow nationalists such as Roger Sherman of Connecticut supported only a few limited national powers.[40] Sherman and his supporters believed that states should remain the locus of power, governing most of American life, as the states did under the Articles of Confederation (Robertson 2012, 19).[41] The Convention, then, pivoted on negotiating between the preferences of broad and narrow nationalists, ensuring the Constitution would enshrine an amalgam of vague boundaries between state and national governing authority.

The compromise between these two groups produced what Madison called a "compound republic" that left the relationship between national and state authority imprecise (Robertson 2012, 34). This ambiguity—combined with the Tenth Amendment, which left the states with powers not specifically granted to Congress—made likely that clarifying the boundaries between state and national power would characterize constitutional development (Robertson 2012, 34).[42]

In other words, American constitutional design created an inherent tension[43] between the central and state-level governments, and the tension in those relationships created questions the Supreme Court—and other political institutions—would later have to address. Conflicts over the authority of subordinate governments and the national government became the sine qua non of constitutional development as well as the focus of the Constitutional Convention itself. William P. Murphy's (1968) extensive study of the making of the constitution finds, "The convention thus had before it a clear-cut choice between two systems . . . a national government of virtually unlimited powers, armed with complete and absolute supremacy over the states" and "a confederation in which the central authority had enforceable supremacy only in sharply limited areas, with the states retaining their sovereignty in all others" (Murphy 1968, 147). He concludes, "The convention rejected the continuation of a system based on state sovereignty and decided in favor of a system based on national supremacy. It was a decision which was never changed" (Murphy 1968, 148). Nevertheless, it was a decision that would be repeatedly challenged, at least until the Civil War, vis-à-vis economic questions largely pertaining to tax, property, and contracts issues that focused on the boundaries between state and federal sovereignty.

Both federalism and judicial power decisions—decisions that comprise over 40% of the Court's decisions in this period—had at their foundation unsettled questions about the boundaries between state and national government. The way the constitution designed sovereignty—and the way the Supreme Court interpreted the powers of each sovereign—facilitated the continued expansion of the American central state.[44] As the Court has adjusted its constitutional interpretation to modern conditions, this has created a bias toward central state expansion.[45] Indeed, the federal government has involved itself in a growing number of political issues, which in turn has made it necessary for the Court to review a growing corpus of legal questions.[46] To keep the coherence and legitimacy of the national regime intact, the Court has thus tended to support the aims of the political branches.

Yet as it attempts to define the boundaries between federal and state sovereignty, the Court's decisions fluctuate between expansion and restriction of federal authority. The Court faced the unenviable position of having to interpret the Constitution so as to grow federal power to meet new socials needs while simultaneously attempting to preserve the federalist design enshrined in the Constitution's language (Redish 1995, 61). Meeting new social needs has greatly contributed to the persistent central state expansion seen especially in the post–Civil War era, when the Supreme Court shifted from a prescriptive to prospective understanding of law.[47]

Beyond the overarching design of dual sovereignty, another design attribute helped create an ever-expanding federal state: the centrality of the national economy in the Constitution, which placed the federal state on an expansionary track especially within the realm of economics. Because the Constitutional Convention left the distribution of commercial authority deliberately unclear,[48] the Court could interpret the Commerce, Coinage, and Necessary and Proper[49] Clauses as vehicles for central state expansion, a fact revealed by the ubiquity of "economic activity" decisions in the data from chapter 2.[50] The economic goals of the Founders thus provided a foundation upon which the Court could affirm the expansion of congressional power via the Commerce Clause.

Economic Independence at the Founding

In drawing up the new Constitution, some of the founders sought to escape "their mercantile dependence" in a world of "predatory European states" (Rana 2010, 133). This helped make economic activity issues and the property dimension key drivers of central state expansion during this period. During the Convention, the desire for independence from Europe led the founders to create a federal system that could limit outside interference as well as insulate the central state from democratic pressure, a system that would enable strong national economic power.[51] Federalist constitutional architects like Alexander Hamilton and James Madison aimed to move away from a state-based idea of liberty and sovereignty (Rana 2010, 134). Many worried that if it did not become a strong union, America's fate would be the same as that of failed confederal republics in the past (Hendrickson 2003, 51). Delegates to the Constitutional Convention began to realize that ensuring independence from European states and securing American safety would require a federal government that was stronger and more centralized than in historical republics.[52]

A strong, centralized federal government could better assure America's safety and longevity in the international arena, Hamilton argued in *Federalist Papers* Nos. 6 and 7. Conversely, he maintained, a decentralized United States would produce competing European alliances among the separate colonies. In the *Federalist Papers*, Hamilton warned of this possibility: "America, if not connected at all, or only by the feeble tie of a simple league, offensive and defensive, would, by the operation of such jarring alliances, be gradually entangled in all the pernicious labyrinths of European politics and wars; and by the destructive contentions of the parts into which she was divided, would be likely to became a prey to artifices and machinations of powers equally the enemies of them all" (*Federalist* No. 7, 113). Creating a centralized federal government would help the United States defend against the "arms and arts of foreign nations" that would not be possible if America otherwise remained "in a state of disunion" (*Federalist* No. 6, 104).[53] A centralized government required a strong commercial union because commercial interests would create peace among the colonies, Hamilton believed. He wrote: "The genius of republics (say they) is pacific; the spirit of commerce has a tendency to soften the manners of men, and to extinguish those inflammable humors which have so often kindled into wars. Commercial republics, like ours, will never be disposed to waste themselves in ruinous contentions with each other. They will be governed by mutual interest, and will cultivate a spirit of mutual amity and concord" (*Federalist* No. 6, 106).

He went on to argue in *Federalist* No. 12 that "the prosperity of commerce is now perceived and acknowledged by all enlightened statesmen to be the most useful as well as the most productive source of national wealth, and has accordingly become a primary object of their political cares" (*Federalist* No. 12, 134). Accordingly he concluded, "one national government would be able, at much less expense, to extend the duties on imports, beyond comparison, further than would be practicable to the States separately, or to any partial confederacies" (*Federalist* No. 12, 137). To create a strong central state authority, the constitution would have to be designed to advance the property and commercial interests of speculators, merchants, and manufacturers. In the end, the federal state was designed in part to protect these financial interests, a fact that helps explain relatively persistent state expansion along economic issues.[54]

In *Federalist* No. 41, Madison reiterated Hamilton's argument that without a strong central state, the United States would be prey to powerful European states: "Should a war be the result of the precarious situation of European affairs, and all the unruly passions attending it be let loose on the ocean, our escape from insults and depredations, not only on that element, but every part of the other bordering on it, will be truly miraculous" (*Federalist* No. 41, 271). Because of this possibility, Madison argued for a vigorous union. In sum, as Rana points out, "In order to achieve not just juridical independence from foreign masters but substantive independence as well, the defenders of the new Constitution sought to develop a political system that was based on greater centralization and able to limit the internal and external challenges to freedom" (Rana 2010, 135).

Looking more closely at the Constitution's design reveals the areas that lent themselves to expansion, and it demonstrates how these calls for a mighty national economic power contributed to the debate over central state formation and expansion. Of course, disagreements over the vigor and energy of the central state were not confined to constitutional architects such as Hamilton and Madison. The Supreme Court, especially during the Marshall Court years, had the onerous task of determining the boundaries between the federal and state governments. Defining these powers mapped onto the debates over constitutional interpretation during the early republic and Jacksonian years, and it is these debates to which we now turn.

Constitutional Interpretation during the Early Republic

While these ideas made their way into the Constitution's text and design, the persistent state expansion seen in chapter 2 was far from guaranteed. The Constitution's text could have, depending on its interpretation, lent itself to an American state development story of persistent restriction rather than one of expansion. Indeed, the design of the Constitution facilitated economic centralization but did not make it certain and, thus, the Court's interpretation played a pivotal role in state development. Walter Licht put it this way: "Did the Constitution guarantee economic development? No. . . . What it did was *allow*. A political framework was laid down in the United States that placed no obstacles in the way of economic transformation and expansion" (Licht 1995, 93, emphasis original).[55] But how did the Court contribute to this economic development and, more broadly, to central state development?

The expansion and restriction of federal powers is due in part to the divide between those who view the Constitution as bestowing broad powers on the central state and those who interpret constitutional language more narrowly. In other words, the Federalists and the Republicans in the early republic debated whether there should be a strong central state or a weak central state. These interpretational philosophies did not necessarily deal with specific provisions, but imbued particular meaning to ambiguous constitutional clauses such as the Necessary and Proper and Commerce Clauses, as in *McCulloch v. Maryland* (1819) and *Gibbons v. Ogden* (1824), respectively.[56]

The Court expanded power, and did so exponentially, largely because the Marshall Court went to great lengths to employ broad interpretations of Congressional power. At issue in *Gibbons* was a New York state law that provided exclusive rights to operate steamboats on waters within its jurisdiction. But other states duplicated these kinds of laws and thus would require out-of-state boats to pay high fees for navigation privileges. Mr. Thomas Gibbons—a steamboat owner who conducted business between New York and New Jersey under a federal license—challenged the New York state law that granted Aaron Ogden a monopoly license. Marshall and the Court faced the question, did New York exercise authority in a realm reserved exclusively to Congress, the interstate commerce realm? Marshall answered in the affirmative and defended the Court's use of broad constitutional interpretation. When a lawyer urged the Court to use a narrow interpretation of Congress's commerce power, Chief Justice Marshall said that doing so would weaken the federal government.[57]

Gibbons structured Commerce Clause cases at least through the nineteenth century, which helps explain why the Court, via commerce and federalism decisions, persistently expanded central state authority across time.[58]

Defining the spheres of sovereignty (i.e., political authority) was also central to *McCulloch*. *McCulloch* concerned an 1818 Maryland state tax on the Second Bank of the United States. The cashier for the Baltimore branch of the Second Bank, James W. McCulloch, refused to pay the tax. In this case, the Court held that the sovereignty of the Union lies with the people of the United States, not with the individual states that comprise it. The United States is not a simple alliance of states, but rather is a "constitutional sovereign" with its authority resting exclusively with "the people" who created and are governed by the Constitution. To the Court, "the government of the Union is a government of the people; it emanates from them; its powers are granted by them; and are to be exercised directly on them, and for their benefit."[59] With this logic, Marshall's opinion struck down Maryland's tax on the bank as a violation of constitutional sovereignty because the tax acted against all the people in the United States and it was imposed by a state accountable only to some of the people. *McCulloch*—and cases like it[60] that determined the limits the Constitution placed on the sovereignty of states—primarily dealt with preserving the Union against powerful state sovereignty arguments that threatened its dissolution.[61] Marshall thus favored reading the Constitution as providing Congress wide discretion in determining the reach and scope of its expressed powers.[62]

Beyond its economic decisions, among them *Gibbons* and *McCulloch*, the Marshall Court also encouraged federal expansion in another area: territorial expansion. In particular, it decided each of a trilogy of Native American cases—*Johnson v. M'Intosh* (1823),[63] *Cherokee Nation v. Georgia* (1831),[64] and *Worcester v. Georgia* (1832)[65]—in favor of the federal power with respect to westward expansion. At issue in *Johnson* were competing claims on an 11,000-acre tract of land. In 1775, Thomas Johnson purchased the land from the Piankeshaw Indian tribe, a purchase arranged in a 1763 proclamation by the King of England. Then, in 1818, William M'Intosh purchased this same land from Congress. In *Johnson*, the Marshall Court held that the federal government had "sole right" to negotiation with native nations and that the Revolutionary War and the treaties that followed gave the United States the "exclusive right . . . to extinguish [the Indians'] title, and to grant the soil."[66]

Despite this unequivocal decision, it comes as no surprise that dual sovereignty proved a difficult concept to balance in practice. Looking more closely at the decisions of the Marshall Court, it becomes evident that drawing the boundaries between two sovereigns—defining federalism, essentially—occupied constitutional development; decisions from the data set reveal this fact.

Gibbons is known for expanding the central state's power to regulate commerce, but just five years later, in *Willson v. Blackbird Creek Marsh Company* (1829),[67] the Court's ruling left power with the states. A unanimous opinion in *Willson* allowed a Delaware state law regulating the navigation of Blackbird Creek to stand.[68] Other decisions during Marshall's tenure, such as *Providence Bank v. Billings* (1830),[69] also relegated power to the states, thus restricting central state authority and demonstrating that the Court both expanded and restricted federal power (Gunther 1969, 19–21).[70]

As Figure 2.5 shows, the rate of expansion was greatest from 1789 to 1824. *Gibbons* and *McCulloch* epitomize this general trend in which the Supreme Court affirmed its own review powers and secured the supremacy of the national government over the state governments. Yet restriction remained an important facet of constitutional development, and that restriction turned on the division of powers between state and national governments. Because the Court shifted its understanding of dual sovereignty during the final years of Marshall's tenure and the first years of Taney's, the era from 1824 to 1849 showed the slowest rate of state expansion in all of the data. This shift produced a growing number of restrictive cases that devolved power to state governments, but nevertheless—and contrary to how we typically remember it—Taney's Court still did more to expand than restrict central state power.[71]

The High Court during the Jacksonian Era

In 1831, two years into his presidency, Andrew Jackson appointed Roger Taney attorney general. Jackson needed Taney to help him dismantle the Second Bank of the United States, a controversial and difficult political task. Taney helped draft Jackson's statement vetoing the bank's renewal. In 1833, as Secretary of the Treasury, Taney withdraw all federal funds from the bank, something that two previous treasury secretaries had refused to do. His loyal service to Jackson's administration earned him the position of chief justice of the Supreme Court, which he assumed from 1836 until his death in 1864. The Senate refused to confirm Taney in 1835 because of his involvement in the national bank affair. It was not until a second nomination, after the Senate changed membership, that Taney became chief justice. Given Taney's historical reputation on issues of national power,[72] you might think that his Court would hand down more cases favoring states' rights and constrict federal power. Instead, following Marshall's judicial philosophy, Taney largely supported the primacy of federal power.

Still, even some of the Taney Court's decisions that sided with states' rights helped spur nation-building. For example, while in *Charles River Bridge v. Warren Bridge* (1837) the Court refused to extend the Constitution's Contracts Clause to protect the Charles River Bridge Company's monopoly over a toll bridge in Massachusetts, the decision's effect was to encourage states to charter new corporations that competed with older ones.[73] Thus, by supporting the Massachusetts law that created the new Warren Bridge Company (which built a free bridge), Taney's Court dealt a blow to old monopolies. By ruling against a steamboat monopoly that New York State chartered, Marshall's Court had done a similar thing in *Gibbons*.[74]

Since its very inception, the Court has reviewed state laws to determine if they impinged on federal interests. Taney's Court protected the federal government from the states by affirming national supremacy against nullification.[75] The Supreme Court did very little to restrict Congress's attempts to expand its power over the states until the turn of the twentieth century (Kramer 2000, 228). Take *Prigg v. Pennsylvania* (1842), for example.[76]

While Chief Justice Taney dissented in part in *Prigg*, the Court affirmed congressional power over the states, validating a federal statute that regulated fugitive slaves—even though the Constitution does not give Congress explicit authority to do so. Many northern states slowly outlawed slavery during the early decades of the nineteenth century. And some states—including Pennsylvania—enacted laws of gradual emancipation. Thus, southern slaves attempted to escape to freedom in the North. Congress's 1793 Fugitive Slave Law, however, gave slave owners the right to cross state lines to capture escaped slaves and force them back into slavery. The law trampled on the liberty of free African Americans in the North, whom slave catchers often seized. As a result, in 1826, Pennsylvania passed antikidnapping laws, stymieing slave-catchers trying to remove African Americans from the state.

A decade later, a slave-catcher named Edward Prigg entered Pennsylvania on behalf of Margaret Ashmore, a slave owner from Maryland. Prigg hunted for Ashmore's escaped slave, Margaret Morgan. Pennsylvania law required Prigg to acquire certain documents from local authorities to remove Morgan from Pennsylvania, but ultimately, Prigg did not furnish sufficient evidence of ownership to legally remove Morgan and her two children, according to state officials. On receiving this information, Prigg took matters into his own hands and kidnapped Morgan and her family without state permission. Pennsylvania then convicted Prigg under its antikidnapping statute. On appeal, Prigg argued that the law was unconstitutional as it violated both Article IV of the Constitution[77] and the federal Fugitive Slave Law of 1793.

At its core, *Prigg v. Pennsylvania* concerned not only individual rights but also sectional conflict, the instability of the antebellum Union, and the acrimony between the national government and the states. The case put in focus an important question: do states have the right to pass legislation concerning fugitive slaves or can only the federal government legislate this issue?

On appeal from the Pennsylvania Supreme Court, the US Supreme Court held that the Pennsylvania law contradicted both Article IV, Section 2, of the Constitution and the Fugitive Slave Law. Chief Justice Marshall's disciple Justice Joseph Story delivered the opinion of the Court, holding that the federal government had exclusive authority to regulate the capture and seizure of fugitive slaves:

> The right to seize and retake fugitive slaves, and the duty to deliver them up, in whatever state of the Union they may be found, and of course the corresponding power in Congress to use the appropriate means to enforce the right and duty, derive their whole validity and obligation exclusively from the Constitution of the United States . . . The natural inference deducible from this consideration certainly is, in the absence of any positive delegation of power to the state legislatures, that it belongs to the legislative department of the national government, to which it owes its origin and establishment.[78]

In cases like *Prigg* and many others that centered on contentious legal issues in which the Court could have "easily" decided the other way, Taney's Court affirmed congressional authority and left states to protect themselves.[79] *Prigg* expanded federal power and laid the groundwork for the Fugitive Slave Act of 1850, under the terms of which federal officials enforced the return of runaway slaves from non-slave-holding states.

While the Taney Court limited central power by leaving state laws to stand, as in *Charles River Bridge* (1837), in one case it directly limited congressional power to protect state sovereignty, in *Dred Scott v. Sandford* (1857).[80] *Dred Scott* held that Congress had no authority to naturalize slaves or regulate slavery in territories acquired after the adoption of the Constitution. Writing for the majority, Taney took the path of judicial supremacy, and the Court's decision has been reviled ever since. Many consider it to be among the worst, if not the worst, Supreme Court decision ever handed down (Whittington 2001, 366). The opinion deeply wounded the Court's legitimacy and authority for at least a generation.

Dred Scott was a slave in Missouri. From 1833 to 1843, he lived in the free state of Illinois and in an area of the Louisiana Territory that outlawed slavery per the Missouri Compromise of 1820. After returning to Missouri, Scott sued for his freedom unsuccessfully in that state's courts, claiming that living in free territory had made him a free man. Scott then brought a new suit in federal court. His master maintained that no African American or any descendant of slaves could be a citizen in the sense of Article III of the Constitution. Thus, the Court faced the question, was Dred Scott a free man or a slave?

Taney declared that Scott was a slave. Under Articles III and IV, he argued, no one but a citizen of the United States could be a citizen of a state. He reached the conclusion that no person descended from an American slave had ever been a citizen for Article III purposes. The Court ruled that because Scott was "a negro, whose ancestors were imported into this country, and sold as slaves," and thus "[not] a member of the political community formed and brought into existence by the Constitution," Scott was not a citizen and had no right to file a lawsuit in federal court.[81] Moreover, the Court argued that Scott was not free by virtue of his residency because Congress lacked the power to ban slavery in US territories, thus nullifying the Missouri Compromise. The Court viewed slaves as "property," and the Fifth Amendment forbids Congress from taking property away from individuals without just compensation.

The decision in *Dred Scott v. Sandford* exacerbated the growing tensions between the North and South. While the Missouri Compromise had already been repealed prior to the case, the decision validated the southern version of constricted national power and emboldened proslavery Southerners to expand slavery across the nation. The decision caused violence between slave owners and abolitionists on the frontier, and it strengthened the newly formed Republican Party.

After the Civil War, the Reconstruction Congress passed, and the states ratified, the Thirteenth, Fourteenth, and Fifteenth Amendments, all of which directly overturned *Dred Scott* and prodigiously expanded federal power over the states, a focus of chapter 4.

Conclusion

Both Marshall's and Taney's Courts represent the general historical trend that the judiciary more often than not extended federal authority and defended the national government from state laws. Constitutional development reflected the need to reconcile the tension between federal and state governments, which the Court did through its consistent support of the two political branches. If the Court had not resolved this tension in favor of the central state, then the unresolved issue would have constrained American political development and weakened the United States. The Court's decision may have been inevitable, as Shapiro suggested (1980, 361), but for the economy to modernize and grow commercially, it required a Court that would respond to the increasing economic pressures felt throughout the country. Thus the early republic witnessed rapid central state expansion because it comprised members sympathetic to creating a strong commercial republic. Yet the Court also sometimes restricted federal power, though it more often expanded it, because it took seriously the boundaries of the two sovereigns and because fitting constitutional doctrine to the ever-changing sociopolitical environment naturally produced these differing outcomes.[82]

Chapter 4

Building a Modern National Government, 1865–1932

> The great danger now will be that things will rush in the opposite direction, and the central authority, from being limited and straitened in all its powers and functions, and scarcely able to maintain a precarious existence, will be in danger of absorbing all the important functions of governmental administration.
>
> —Vermont State Supreme Court Judge Isaac F. Redfield, 1867[1]

Introduction

Scholars have often understood the period from 1865 to 1932 as the time when the modern American state formed, even though they tend to argue that during this period, the Court obstructed the emergence of this American state. In contrast, I have found that the Court's decisions helped consolidate the nation-state and reduced state autonomy as federal-state relations became ever more paramount in the wake of the Civil War. From around 1865 to 1932, the Court—because of its newly expanded jurisdictional powers and its interpretation of commerce—was not in fact a persistent inhibitor of state development.

Far from obstructing state-building, the Supreme Court provided much of the foundation on which subsequent political actors built the coercive apparatus of the federal government.[2] The Court is not outside of the central state[3] (and juxtaposed to this state); it is part and parcel of the central state. This understanding of state development shifts attention away from European-style welfare-state conceptions and toward a broader definition of development. Empirical analysis of a sample of 214 decisions during this period reveals that the Supreme Court as an institution had a complex relationship with federal authority, building it in the individual rights realm while neither greatly expanding nor constricting it within economic activity issues.

The founders cemented lexicon divisions between federal and state sovereignty and between narrow and broad constitutional interpretation within the constitutional lexicon, thus ensuring a persistent conflict between national and state power. While this conflict persists to the present day, its apotheosis was the Civil War. That war and the Reconstruction Amendments mark the most important constitutional change since the founding, and accordingly, the effects wrought by these changes warrant closer investigation. Significant legal changes along constitutional issue areas began at the end of the Civil War and the start of Chief Justice Salmon P. Chase's tenure. In this era, legal doctrine—porous and ever-changing—possessed more continuity across chief justice tenures more frequently than in the past.

Two examples exemplify the Court's role in economic activity cases during this period. In 1902, at the urging of dairy farmers, Congress passed an act imposing a tax of ten cents per pound on oleomargarine that was artificially colored yellow. Noncolored margarine was taxed only one-quarter of a cent per pound. McCray, a licensed dealer, did not pay the higher tax despite selling the yellow-colored form of margarine. After losing his case in lower courts, McCray appealed to the Supreme Court, arguing that the federal act exceeded Congress's taxing authority. In *McCray v. United States* (1904), the Court held in a six-to-three decision that "The right of Congress to tax within its delegated power being unrestrained," the federal statute was constitutional.[4] Thus, *McCray* positively expanded federal authority to regulate economic activity.

Contrast *McCray* with *Miller v. Schoene* (1928).[5] In the lush, green rolling hills of Virginia's Shenandoah Valley, Miller owned a property with a large stand of ornamental red cedar trees located near an apple orchard that he did not own. During the mid-1920s, a plant disease called cedar rust was spreading to apple orchards in the state, so the state legislature passed the Cedar Rust Act of Virginia (1924). Under the power of the law, the state entomologist, Schoene, asked Miller to cut down his red cedar trees because of their proximity to the apple orchard. Miller refused, claiming that the Virginia statute violated his Fourteenth Amendment due process rights. Unanimously, the Court disagreed with Miller, upholding the Virginia statute. The Court recognized Virginia's interest in preventing cedar rust from damaging apple orchards, since apple growing was a "principal agricultural pursuit" in Virginia[6] (*Miller*, 279). While the destruction of Miller's trees would be a taking of his property, Virginia "[did] not exceed its constitutional powers by deciding upon the destruction of one class of property in order to save another which, in the judgment of the legislature, is of greater value to the public."[7] Consequently, the Court constricted the application of the Fourteenth Amendment, thus limiting federal authority.

These two cases demonstrate an important trend during the Reconstruction and Republican eras that stretched from the Civil War to the Great Depression: with respect to economic activity, the Court expanded and constricted federal authority at an equal rate. In contrast, when it came to questions of individual rights, the Court greatly expanded federal authority. In 1873, for example, a West Virginia law declared that only whites may serve on juries. The Court held that this law violated the Equal Protection Clause of the Fourteenth Amendment because denying citizen participation based on race "is practically a brand upon them, affixed by the law, an assertion of their inferiority, and a stimulant to that race prejudice."[8] By invalidating this state statute in a seven-to-two decision, the Court advanced federal authority over civil rights.

In other cases, the expansion of federal authority actually limited individual rights. Almost forty years later, during World War I, Charles Schenck, as general secretary of the US Socialist Party, mailed circulars to military draftees, suggesting that capitalist greed motivated the draft. The circulars urged "Do not submit to intimidation," but advised only peaceful action such as petitioning to repeal the federal Conscription Act.[9] Because of these circulars, federal authorities charged Schenck with conspiracy to violate the Espionage Act. Unanimously, the Court held that the Free Speech Clause of the First Amendment did not protect Schenck. The Court maintained "the character of every act depends upon the circumstances in which it is done," and during wartime, Congress has the right to prevent some speech that might otherwise be permissible during peacetime.[10] Both *Strauder* and *Schenck* typify the expansion of federal authority concerning individual rights.

State-Building during the Reconstruction and Republican Eras

A few cases in particular evoke the commonly held view that the Court was primarily a restraint or check on central state-building. *E. C. Knight, In Re Debs*, and *Lochner v. New York*—dubbed the "unholy trinity of laissez-faire constitutional cases"—have assumed too much prominence in the constitutional canon (Novak 2002, 273). In these decisions, the Court sides with the sugar monopoly (*E. C. Knight*), stifles labor union strikes (*In Re Debs*), and invalidates New York's attempt to regulate maximum working hours for bakers (*Lochner v. New* York). Because *E. C. Knight* thwarted *federal* regulation over a sugar monopoly, this decision constricted central state authority. In contrast, *In re Debs* and *Lochner* represent expansions of central state authority of two different types.

In the first case, by supporting federal troops to quash a railroad strike, *Debs* expanded central state authority. *Debs* represents an expansion of central state authority through validating federal action. Justice David Brewer spoke for the Court, plainly asserting and advancing central state authority: "The strong arm of the national government may be put forth to brush away all obstructions to the freedom of interstate commerce or the transportation of the mails. If the emergency arises, the army of the Nation, and all its militia, are at the service of the Nation to compel obedience to its laws."[11] In the second case, *Lochner* struck down a state regulatory law as a violation of federally protected constitutional right. From the perspective of the national state, *Lochner* expands central state authority because it concentrates power in the federal judiciary and prevents state legislatures from creating laws that infringe on the "liberty of contract."

Perhaps we might think that the Court's most prominent decisions stymie expansion because they inhibited labor protections closely associated with European-style welfare states. Yet when we look at the totality of cases, we uncover a different story. When we shift our focus away from the creation of the administrative state and look more broadly at multiple dimensions of the federal state, we find that the Court and legal doctrine greatly advanced the power of the federal government, even in cases seen as hindering tradi- tional, Weberian state development.[12] Both *Debs* and *Lochner* fit this category.

Just as in the periods covered in the previous chapter, the Reconstruc- tion and Republican eras also experienced persistent advancement of central state authority. Figure 4.1 demonstrates this trend, revealing that expansive

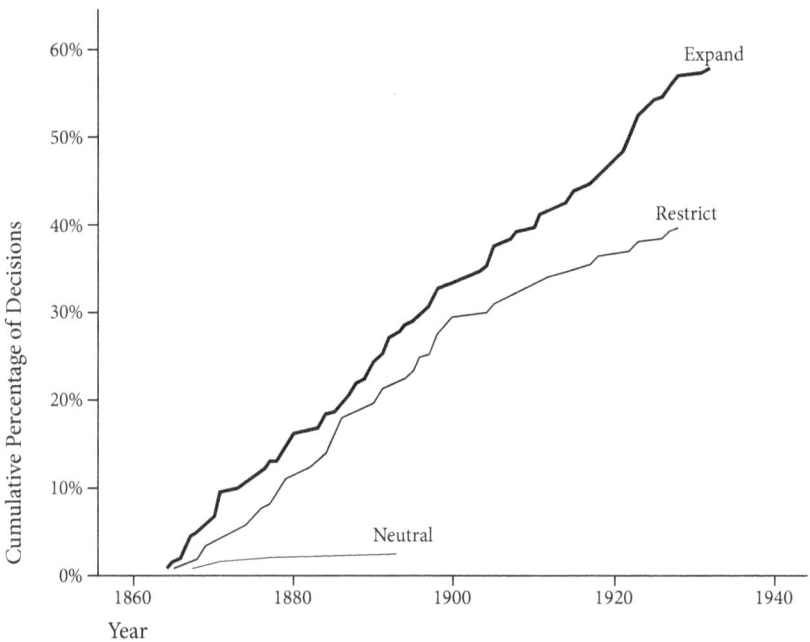

Figure 4.1. Cumulative Frequency of the Effect of Federal Authority, 1865–1932.
Source: Compiled by author. N=214.

and restrictive cases grew at a similar rate until about 1900, when expansive cases rose at a much steeper rate. Of the 214 decisions in the data between 1865 and 1932, 124 expanded (58%) and 85 restricted (40%) federal authority in this almost seventy-year period. Breaking these data down into seven constitutional issue areas, economic activity and individual rights comprise 73% of the decisions in this period (see Table 4.1 below). Within the constitutional issues, individual rights most advanced federal authority both in terms of raw count and as a proportion of all expansive case (44 of 124 cases). Moreover, when examining the cases by historical eras, we notice that under two of the three periods decisions that expanded federal authority outweigh

Table 4.1. Constitutional Issue by Effect on Federal Authority, 1865–1932

Constitutional Issue		Effect on Federal Authority			
		Restrict	Neutral	Expand	Total
Economic activity	Count	44	0	41	85
	% within row	51.8%	0.0%	48.2%	100.0%
Individual rights	Count	24	3	44	71
	%	33.8%	4.2%	62.0%	100.0%
Federalism/	Count	9	0	16	25
Interstate	%	36.0%	0.0%	64.0%	100.0%
Judicial power	Count	4	2	5	11
	%	36.4%	18.2%	45.5%	100.0%
Taxation	Count	2	0	7	9
	%	22.2%	0.0%	77.8%	100.0%
Private action	Count	2	0	7	9
	%	22.2%	0.0%	77.8%	100.0%
Executive power	Count	0	0	4	4
	%	0.0%	0.0%	100.0%	100.0%
Total	Count	85	5	124	214
	%	39.70%	2.30%	57.90%	100.00%

Notes and Source: Compiled by author. Individual rights generally expand while economic decisions generally constrict the federal government. This table collapses twelve issues areas into six. Most importantly, the "individual rights" issues comprise due process, criminal procedure, First Amendment, and civil rights/liberties issues. "Economic activity" and "federalism" largely deal with commerce and economic issues, but the conflict between state and federal spheres of power is central to the individual rights issue area, too. I observed a strong association between the constitutional issue area and the impact on federal power, $\chi^2(12) = 27.29$, $p = .007$. N=214.

Number of Decisions

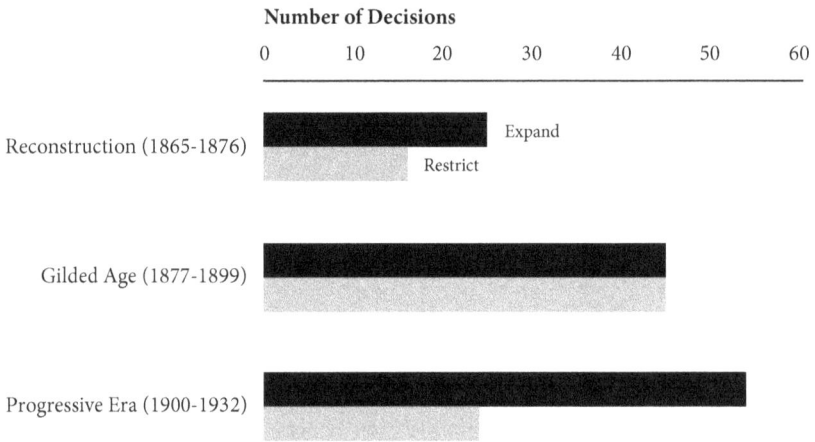

Figure 4.2. Effect on Federal Authority across Historical Eras, 1865–1932.
Source: Compiled by author. N=209.

decisions constricting it (see Figure 4.2 above). Of the central state dimensions, centralization, world systems, and extraction played important roles in building federal state authority (Table 4.2). These findings cast doubt on the story that the Court acted as a negative check on central state development, and instead, they suggest that the Court acted as more of an ally with other federal branches during the expansion of the new American state.

The Court's tendencies in the post-war era dealt primarily with economic activity and individual rights, issues that interacted with the centralization and citizenship dimensions. Decisions on these two constitutional issues often adjudicated among political institutions and decided which would decide

Table 4.2. Frequency of the Dimensions of the Central State, 1865–1932

Dimension	Expand	Restrict	Total	% Expanding
Centralization	118	84	202	58.42%
Property	49	48	97	50.52%
Citizenship	44	34	78	56.41%
Extraction	28	19	47	59.57%
World systems	26	8	34	76.47%
Admin. capacity	12	4	15	75.00%
Client groups	7	1	8	87.50%

Note and Source: Compiled by author. Neutral decisions not included. N=211.

the growing and complicated questions facing an industrializing republic. The postwar constitutional order had to reconcile the constitutional ideas of the previous state-centered agrarian society with a rapidly industrializing nation-state that was undergoing profound social and economic transformation.[13] Negotiating between these two constitutional orders required balancing federal versus state authority. The recurring question along these lines dealt with the centralization dimension: where does decision-making authority rest?

The citizenship dimension includes questions of individual rights. By relegating such rights to the federal government, the Court expanded central state authority over people. In this realm, the judiciary often advanced federal control of union strikers and draft protestors, for example. Notably, though, the Court constricted federal power over questions of enforcing Reconstruction Amendments in such decisions as *United States v. Cruikshank* (1876),[14] the *Civil Rights Cases* (1893),[15] and *Plessy v. Ferguson* (1896),[16] and it upheld state regulation of social behavior.[17]

Ultimately, the Court settled states' rights questions by constricting federal authority to enforce economic regulations, but it maintained relatively strong control over citizenship rights. In doing so, constitutional development moderated between those who sympathized with pre–Civil War models of federalism and those who believed the Civil War profoundly changed the conception of federalism and central state authority, advancing federal power over individual rights yet constricting it over economic rights.

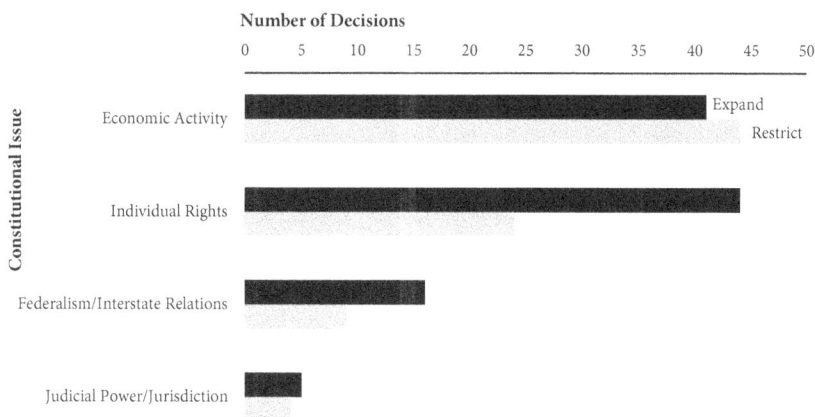

Figure 4.3. Constitutional Issue Areas and Effect on Federal Authority, 1865–1932.

Notes and Source: Compiled by author. This graphic does not include neutral decisions. It contains the most abundant constitutional issues. "Individual rights" comprises civil rights, criminal procedure, due process, and First Amendment. Together, individual rights, economic activity, federalism, and judicial power comprise 87% of the issue areas. N=187.

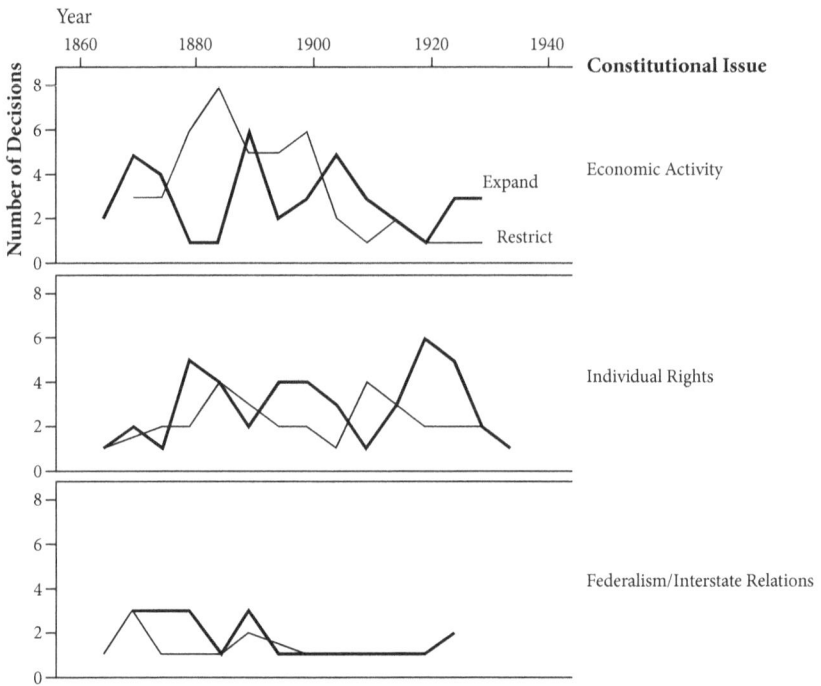

Figure 4.4. Most Abundant Constitutional Issues, 1865–1932.

Note and Source: Compiled by author. N=178.

As noted above, the expansion category embraces a broader under-standing of state-building, a form of state-building that not only lays the foundation for welfare-state arrangements but also advances myriad other structural and substantive apparatuses integral to a powerful central state. And this state-building took place primarily in the realm of individual rights and economic activity. With eighty-five decisions, "economic activity" is the issue that came before the Court most frequently, and after centralization, the property dimension appeared most frequently. Indeed, the majority of economic activity decisions fell within the property dimension.

Before 1900, the Court's economic activity decisions tend to constrict central state authority along the property dimension (thirty-six of sixty cases). Decisions such as *Powell v. Pennsylvania* (1888) exemplified the Court's inter-pretation, upholding a Pennsylvania regulation on the sale and manufacturing of oleomargarine.[18] The Court maintained that the federal government had no authority, via the Fourteenth Amendment, to invalidate these police power types of regulation: "it is the settled doctrine of this court that, as government is organized for the purpose, among others, of preserving the public health and the public morals, it cannot divest itself of the power to provide for those objects; and that the Fourteenth Amendment was not designed to interfere with the exercise of that power by the States."[19] Public sentiment at the time concurred with the Court's reasoning in these economic activity decisions. The *Washington Post* wrote, "It is the business of the State, and not of the United States, to determine what is good or bad for the people of a State. . . . Our Republican Supreme Court has become the fortress of State rights because it finds States rights in the Constitution. The process of centralization by interpretation of the fundamental law was, happily, checked in time to save the Government."[20]

After about 1900, the Court's economic activity decisions lent themselves to central state expansion, with seventeen of twenty-five advancing authority along the property dimension. In *Allgeyer v. Louisiana* (1897), for instance, the Court promulgated a decision that became key in establishing the idea of "liberty of contract."[21] In this case, a Louisiana statute regulated the insurance business. Louisiana required that out-of-state insurance corporations had to maintain at least one place of business and an authorized agent within the state. Justifying the statute as an exercise of its police powers, Louisiana sought to protect its citizens from deceitful insurance companies. Allgeyer and Company violated this statute by purchasing insurance from a firm based in New York, which did not meet the requirements of the Louisiana law. Thus the Court faced the question, did the Louisiana law violate the Fourteenth Amendment's Due Process Clause, which, according to Allgeyer and Company, protected its liberty to enter into contracts with businesses of its choice?

Unanimously, the Court found that the Louisiana statute deprived Allgeyer and Company of its liberty without due process of law: "To deprive the citizen of such a right as herein described without due process of law is illegal. Such a statute as this in question is not due process of law, because it prohibits an act which under the Federal Constitution the defendants had a right to perform."[22] The "liberty to contract" articulated in *Allgeyer*, as the Court noted, necessitated that the judiciary would have to determine "when and how far [state police] power may be legitimately exercised with regard to these subjects must be left for determination to each case as it arises."[23] Therefore, *Allgeyer* and the "liberty to contract" it promulgated advanced central state authority to determine questions pertaining to economic activity and the property dimension in the decades to come.

Individual rights issue areas—due process, civil rights/liberties, criminal procedure, and First Amendment—comprise another seventy-one decisions and mainly affect the citizenship dimension. Of these decisions, forty-four expanded the power of federal government, meaning that the Court either supported a Congressional statute or invalidated a state-level statute. The tally is more balanced with economic activity decisions: forty-four of eighty-five decisions constricted central authority. Such numbers indicate that the Court was preoccupied with navigating between economics and individual rights questions. Unlike with economic activity decisions, the Court steadily expanded central state authority over questions of individual rights from 1865 to 1932 for both liberal and conservative aims. With its decision on *In re Debs* (1898), for example, the Court extended federal authority by upholding a federal injunction, which prevented protestors from disrupting railroad operation during the Pullman strike. Detained labor-union officers sought a writ of habeas corpus from the Supreme Court. In a conservative decision, the Court denied the writ and held that Article 1, Section 8, gave the United States the power to regulate interstate commerce.

During this period, too, some liberal decisions also extended federal authority. For example, *Tumey v. Ohio* (1927) advanced federal power via the judiciary.[24] In this case, a unanimous Court overturned Tumey's conviction for violating the state's Prohibition Act. After police arrested Tumey, he was brought before Mayor Pugh, who convicted him. Tumey challenged his conviction under the Fourteenth Amendment, because Mayor Pugh had a direct economic interest in Tumey's conviction: the mayor could only be paid for his services as a judge if he convicted those who were brought before him.

In sum, the Court generally advanced state authority in the individual rights realm—whether to advance liberal or conservative aims—while taking a more balanced approach toward economic and commerce activity. Let us now take a closer look at the broader constitutional and political developments of the period.

Patterns of Central State Growth After the Civil War

The Civil War, however, definitively ended the idea that the United States was a confederate state, subject to the will of its individual states. Still, in the aftermath of the war, the country did not fully embrace the centralization implicit in a war based on union.[25] While there was no going back, the Civil War and Reconstruction were not enough to forge the modern American state. Instead, much of the building of the American state occurred as the Supreme Court balanced the new authority bestowed upon the federal government against the calls to return to a state-centered model of federalism.[26]

This fear of full centralization is aptly captured by Redfield's epigraph at the beginning of the chapter. The Civil War period had been a time of extraordinary growth in national power—a federal income tax, a new banking system, the beginning of national railroad control, and presidential suspensions of habeas corpus typified important growth in central state power. The central dilemma facing the Supreme Court as it confronted questions about the relationship between the states and the Union during the Reconstruction era was whether central authority would be limited as it had been before the Civil War, or whether the national government would continue to grow in power. During this time, therefore, America's federalist system came under close judicial scrutiny. Senator James Grimes[27] recognized that during the Civil War the Union drew to "the Federal Government authority which had been considered doubtful by all and denied by many of the statesmen of this country." But he was quick to urge his fellow senators "That time . . . has ceased and ought to cease. Let us go back to the original condition of things, and allow the States to take care of themselves."[28]

Beginning in 1865, the Supreme Court, through its decisions, navigated a balanced course of state development until 1900, when it began to expand federal authority more frequently. On the one side, the northern states wanted a unified national market (thus broad interpretation of the commerce clause) and little or no government regulation of private enterprise (thus narrow interpretation of the Due Process Clause). On the other side, the former Confederate states wanted local control of race relations and politics generally (thus, individual state control of citizenship/social policies). Still, looking at the period in total and across many issue areas, the Court's constitutional decision-making expanded federal power to control individual rights issues while slightly constricting its authority over economic matters. Intentionally or not, the Court ended up steering a moderate course between those who sought a return to a state-centered understanding of federalism and those who wanted to aggressively expand federal state power.

Two ideational and institutional changes greatly influenced the Court's complex relationship toward national state development. First, questions pertaining to federalism became ever more pressing and thus the dominant vehicle through which the Court expanded its own power as well as the powers of the other federal branches. The Court at this time, legal historian Stanley Kutler argues, should be remembered for its "remarkable tenacity and toughness," which enlarged its judicial power (Kutler 1968, vii). Second, the Court became the primary institution for resolving controversies over central state authority, whereas previously, other institutions had more influence in regulating the whole political system. These changes were important because they perhaps inadvertently created a Supreme Court strong enough to define federalist boundaries as the New Deal approached.

The mechanism through which the Court operated was both legal and institutional. In particular, the creation of the dormant Commerce Clause doctrine[29] enabled the Court to strike down state-level barriers to interstate commerce *even if* Congress had not passed a law governing the behavior a state law sought to regulate. The dormant Clause, in effect, allowed the Court to become a mouthpiece of the state, enhancing national authority in the name of economic expansion. Moreover, institutional developments enhanced the power of the Court itself, thereby enabling it to expand federal author-ity; during Reconstruction, the Court acquired "removal"[30] power, broader jurisdiction, and an extension of the federal courts' habeas corpus powers, to name a few examples.[31] Indeed, the congressional judicial reorganization bills of 1862, 1863, 1866, and 1869 were attempts to vest more power in the judiciary to help extend Republican Party power. Changes in federal court jurisdiction were not embarked upon because of antipathy to the institu-tion or to President Johnson, but instead because the Republican-controlled Congress sought to tailor the judiciary to satisfy the political objectives of the dominant regime (Kulter 1968, 62).[32] But before we discuss specific con-stitutional developments in this period, let us take a look at the broader state theories and changes in constitutional thought advanced in the last quarter of the nineteenth century, as these help explain the debates surrounding the advancement of central state authority.

In the late nineteenth century, changing constitutional and legal thought redefined the purposes of the central "state," and thus nationalized many legal questions that once remained under the purview of the individual states.[33] These changes gave the Court additional avenues and justifications for expanding central state authority, which the Court did not have during the pre–Civil War era. Questions concerning state police powers, for example, became thoroughly nationalized in the last quarter of the nineteenth century in decisions such as *Munn v. Illinois* (1877),[34] *Mugler v. Kansas* (1887),[35] and *Budd v. New York* (1892)[36] (Novak 2002, 268). All three cases examined the constitutionality of state laws under the Fourteenth Amendment, and, through striking these state laws down, the Court expanded central state authority. They represent how the Fourteenth Amendment created new avenues for court standing and thus enabled the federal judiciary to police state legislative bodies and its laws.[37] This nationalization, by its very nature, provided the foundation on which the Court's review power grew, which thus resulted in an expansion of the central state itself.[38] The growing number of legal issues coming before the Court resulted in the development of a federal police power, which was premised largely on issues of Commerce Clause and economic regulation. Indeed, then-retired Justice Charles Evans Hughes pointed out in a 1918 speech to the American Bar Foundation, "The extended application of the doctrine that federal rules governing interstate commerce may have the quality of police regulations" (Hughes quoted in Novak 2002, 270). Thus,

Hughes saw federal government expansion as a consequence of a modernizing industry and economy. The changes reflected in constitutional thought—with the justifications for a stronger federal government—also helped reconcile the debates over the Union witnessed in the aftermath of the Civil War.

Emerging Social Consensus: Fashioning Reconciliation

If ever the Court was faced with federal-state relationships as "a new question," as Woodrow Wilson phrased it, then the Civil War and Reconstruction years were such a time.[39] And on this altar of federalism the Court fashioned doctrine that helped fortify an emerging consensus in the country. As is true of any period, constitutional development during this period largely reflected the broader politics of the day. The commitment to a pre–Civil War understanding of federalism, with its emphasis on state rights, inhibited the radical Republican agenda from establishing full freedom and equality for newly freed African Americans (Les Benedict 1978, 47). For the rest of the nineteenth century, historians recognize, protection of citizenship rights (i.e., social control) remained the duty of the states and not the federal government.[40] Congressional debates indicate the centrality of federalism and states' rights in the construction of the Civil Rights Act of 1866. Republican Congressman John Bingham, for example, sought to strengthen Congressional power in the Civil Rights Act by allowing Congress power to impose criminal sanctions against state officers, but Democrats and moderate Republicans rebuffed him. They "opposed the transfer of sovereignty over civil rights to the federal government" (Belz 1976, 171). Essentially, in this period, neither radical Republicans nor Democrats steered Congressional policy; moderates did, which created a polity colored by the "interplay between the war-born ideals of strong central government and race-blind citizenship, and more traditional American beliefs in localism, limited government, and racial inequality" (Keller 1977, 37–38).

The Court reflected these trends of reconciliation and helped steer a moderate course of development. Chief Justice Salmon P. Chase (1864–1873), a Lincoln appointee, sought to bring about reconciliation. Chase was aware of the fragility of the Court and attempted to shift away from the Court's sullied image that Taney and *Dred Scott* produced (Chase 993, xvii). Indeed, the Court, because of the nature of law and precedent, confronts its historical and institutional memory far more often than any other political institution. Consequently, Chief Justice Chase expressed his support for an accommodating approach to former Confederates. Chase revealed this in a letter to George H. Hill, an Ohio legislative representative serving from 1870 to 1872: "I have always thought, too, that universal amnesty should be accorded, and the most liberal and generous policy should be adopted towards all who, having been enemies during the civil war, were willing to resume in good faith the relation of friends and fellow citizens when war was over. Hence, I very early adopted the motto, Universal Suffrage and Universal Amnesty. I felt sure that this policy would secure the peace of the whole country, and the highest prosperity of all the South."[41] Chase, in this same letter, recognized that universal suffrage via the Fifteenth Amendment would not expand central state authority, leaving it to state control. He argued that civil rights were to be a state-based project: "The Amendment gives no power to Congress to interfere with suffrage in any state unless it is denied or abridged by the state. . . . The full power of regulation, as it has existed heretofore will exist still in the states."[42] This remained the Supreme Court's interpretation long after Chase left the Court, and this sentiment assuaged the feelings of states' rights proponents who sought to keep in place the state-based, dual federalism understanding of the relationship between the national and state governments, as Chase's majority opinion in *Texas v. White* demonstrated.[43]

In *Texas v. White* (1869), Chase promulgated an idea about the nation that the Court perpetuated throughout the Reconstruction era. Chase held for the majority, "The Constitution in all its provisions looks to an indestructible Union composed of indestructible states."[44] Similarly, Justice Nelson held in *Collector v. Day* (1871) that the powers of states "remained unaltered and unimpaired" in most internal matters.[45] And again, in *Lane County v. Oregon* (1869) the Court advanced ideas concurrent with states' rights advocates: "in many of the articles of the Constitution, the necessary existence of the states, within their proper spheres, the independent authority of the states are distinctly recognized. To them nearly the whole charge of interior regulation is committed" (*Lane County*, 76).[46] These decisions recognized both the centralizing effect of Union victory and the need to recognize states' rights. Ultimately, Union victory relegated many questions upward to the Supreme Court. Consequently, building the modern American state became the particular province of the Court.[47]

At the same time, a rapid expansion of federal judicial power enabled the Court, on the one hand, to become an outlet for state expansion with respect to Commerce Clause and economic questions. The withdrawal of southern congressional delegations between 1861 and 1865 enabled Congress to make the judiciary the most Republican instrument of the federal government, protecting its favored constituencies, who called for the rapid expansion of central state power (Crowe 2012, 170).[48] On the other hand, the expansion of federal authority moved at a slower pace in the individual rights realm in the way Chase outlined.[49] Constitutional development, during this time, involved an ideological process that constructed a compromise between conceptions of federalism. This continued long after the Chase Court. Under Chief Justices Waite and Fuller (1874–1910), the Court aligned at least its civil rights decisions with a "state-centered federalism," but not the extreme Democratic version, as political scientist Pamela Brandwein emphasizes. Instead, the Court produced a more "moderate version" that allowed states to have local control over crime yet still gave Congress the power to punish alleged criminals if states "defaulted in their duty to redress wrongs against 'civil rights'"—a concept Brandwein calls "state neglect" (Brandwein 2006, 277; Brandwein 2011, 12).[50] Doing so helped create a climate of reconciliation between northern and southern interests and insured the Court's legitimacy in a tumultuous period in American state development (Brandwein 2007, 371).[51] Thus, the Court's doctrine produced an institution that expanded central state authority in some realms and constricted authority in others.[52]

The popular press lauded the Court's recognition of states' rights in economic cases, for instance its decision to uphold state liquor prohibition in *Mugler v. Kansas* (1877)[53] Citing *Mugler*, the *Washington Post*, in 1888, also celebrated an end to the "march of centralization" that took place in the twenty years immediately following the Civil War.[54] The late nineteenth century witnessed a number of additional articles praising Court decisions that left questions of social control to the states.[55] The steady calls to leave some policy areas—namely social policies—to the states, then, remained an important component in constitutional development during the emergence of the modern state. Indeed, the post–Civil War Court took care to establish "reasonably coherent" sets of categories to allocate regulatory authority between state and federal governments in order to preserve dual sovereignty (Compton 2014, 120).

The "genius" of Justice Harlan's opinion in *Mugler*, John Compton argues, was "that it defined the police power broadly enough to establish the constitutionality of liquor prohibition while at the same time leaving the door open to future constitutional challenges to industrial regulation" (Compton 2014, 115). In so doing, the Court created an avenue for the eventual national expansion of the police power seen later in the Progressive era, as the noted legal scholar Ernst Freund recognized. In his 1904 treatise, Freund helped shift the understanding of police power from its pre–Civil War, common-law definition to one centered on constitutional doctrine, "meaning the power of promoting the public welfare by restraining and regulating the use of liberty and property" (Freund 1904, iii).[56]

Let us now take a closer look at the Court's decisions at the turn of the twentieth century—and the legal issue areas of economics and individual rights—to see what the Court did in these realms.

Central State Expansion during the Gilded Age

Economic Activity and Moderate Central State Development

While the Court expanded central authority overall during this period, before 1900 it still embraced a more state-centered approach with respect to economic activity. Beginning with the *Slaughterhouse Cases* (1873),[57] the Court interpreted the new Fourteenth Amendment. Over a century's perspective makes it clear to us that these Reconstruction Amendments did, in fact, usher in a new constitutional order whereby the federal government protects the rights of individuals, but this new order was far from certain in 1873. *Slaughterhouse* narrowly interpreted citizenship and economic rights (especially the Privileges and Immunities Clause) of the Fourteenth Amendment, holding that a Louisiana law creating a monopoly over the slaughtering business was constitutional because of a state's police powers to protect health, safety, morals, and the general welfare.

Justice Miller upheld the validity of this monopoly on a state-centered understanding of federalism. He asked rhetorically, "Was it the purpose of the Fourteenth amendment, by the simple declaration that no State should make or enforce any law which shall abridge the privileges and immunities of citizens of the United States, to transfer the security and protection of all the civil rights which we have mentioned, from the States to the Federal government?"[58] Miller further questioned the issue of civil rights in relation to the Fourteenth Amendment: "And where it is declared that Congress shall have the power to enforce that article, was it intended to bring within the power of Congress the entire domain of civil rights heretofore belonging exclusively to the States?"[59] Miller's majority decision answered his own questions: if the Fourteenth Amendment did mean these things, then the Court would become "a perpetual censor upon all legislation of the States, on the civil rights of their own citizens, with authority to nullify such as it did not approve as consistent with those rights."[60] In making this argument, the Court created two separate spheres of citizenship: one state-based and one nation-based. Making such a distinction restricted the central state from enforcing subsequent civil rights legislation on state-level citizenship.

The Court's decision in *Slaughterhouse* clung to the state-centered model of federalism, thereby constricting central state authority. Miller rejected the possibility that the Reconstruction Amendments ushered in a new constitutional order: "[W]hen, as in the case before us, these consequences are so serious, so far-reaching and pervading, so great a departure from the structure and spirit of our institutions; when the effect is to fetter and degrade the State governments by subjecting them to the control of Congress, in the exercise of powers heretofore universally conceded to them of the most ordinary and fundamental character; when in fact it radically changes the whole theory of the relations of the State and Federal governments to each other."[61] Ultimately, this decision perpetuated a model of federalism that limited the ability of the central state to monitor state police power.

This pattern continued, too, in economic rights decisions. *Paul v. Virginia* (1869) and *Holden v. Hardy* (1898) typified the economic decisions whereby the Court allowed a state-level statute to stand.[62] Of the sixty economic decisions in this period, the Court upheld thirty-six of them (60%) while it only invalidated twenty-four (40%) state-level economic regulations. In *Paul v. Virginia* (1869), for example, Virginia convicted Samuel Paul—an insurance agent in New York—for issuing a fire insurance policy to a Virginia citizen when Paul had not obtained a license to do business in Virginia. The Court held that Virginia was within its rights to convict Paul; the law did not interfere with the Privileges and Immunities because corporations are not citizens within the understanding of this clause. The state law also did not violate the Commerce Clauses because issuance of an insurance policy was not commerce. The bottom line is that constitutional development in the economics realm often constricted central state authority by leaving state-level police power laws intact.[63]

Individual Rights and Expansive Central State Development

By contrast, before 1900, individual rights decisions expanded central state authority more frequently than economic activity decisions did. The federal government involved itself more frequently with individual rights than economic activity, and the Court has always been more likely to support coordinate branches of the central state. Within individual rights, thirty-four cases involved federal action (42%), while only fifteen economic activity cases involved federal action (19%). The Court largely supported the federal government's growing authority over individual rights, as seen in *Fong Yue Ting v. United States* (1893) and *Ex parte Virginia* (1880).[64] In *Ex parte Virginia*, the Court affirmed congressional authority under the citizenship dimension to enforce African Americans' rights to serve on juries in state courts. The case involved a Pittsylvania County, Virginia, judge, James D. Coles, who excluded black men from his juries, and as a result, Coles was indicted in a US district court for violating the federal Civil Rights Act of 1875. In *Fong Yue Ting*, the Court also affirmed congressional authority, but this time it dealt with using that authority within the world systems dimensions, too. The Court concluded that the right to expel noncitizens "rests upon the same grounds, and is as absolute and unqualified, as the right to prohibit and prevent their entrance into the country"[65] (*Fong Yue Ting*, 707).

Still, the Court often invalidated state-level laws that infringed on individual rights, as it did in *Strauder v. West Virginia* (1880), striking down a West Virginia law that allowed only whites to serve on juries.[66] A similar instance took place in *Yick Wo v. Hopkins* (1886), in which the Court overturned a San Francisco ordinance that, while neutral on its face, was administered in a prejudicial manner.[67] The law required all laundries in wooden buildings to hold a permit the city issued, but while workers of Chinese descent operated 89% of the city's laundry businesses, the city did not grant a single permit to a Chinese owner. Central state expansion took the form of limiting individual rights, as with *Fong Yue Ting*, just as often as it took the form of expanding citizenship rights, as in *Strauder*, but decisions like *Strauder* that aimed at protecting people of color against discrimination often had little positive effect.[68] In either ideological direction, however, the Court's decisions consolidated decision-making authority concerning questions around citizenship.

Central State Expansion from the Progressive Era to the New Deal

Economic Activity and Expansive Central State Development

While a majority of the Court's economic activity decisions before 1900 constricted federal authority, after that date, economic decisions expanded central state authority more frequently. The Court created the doctrinal foundation for this expansion, however, much earlier in the nineteenth century. Take the dormant Commerce Clause doctrine, for example. This doctrine enabled the Court to expand central authority, a doctrine refined in 1852 and solidified in 1886. By implication, the Commerce Clause prohibited states from passing legislation that discriminated against or excessively burdened interstate commerce even if Congress had not passed legislation explicitly prohibiting state action. An 1852 decision, *Cooley v. Board of Wardens*, laid the foundation for the dormant Commerce Clause when it recognized the constitutionality of a Philadelphia law requiring all ships entering or leaving the port of Philadelphia to hire a local pilot.[69] The Philadelphia law was permissible because, in 1789, Congress granted permission for states to govern pilotage laws: "The mere grant to Congress of the power to regulate commerce, did not deprive the States of power to regulate pilots. And that although Congress has legislated on this subject, its legislation manifests an intention, with a single exception, not to regulate this subject, but to leave its regulation to the several States."[70]

In other words, some subjects demanded a single uniform law for the whole nation, while others, like pilotage, demanded local laws that allowed for diverse local conditions. The power of Congress was therefore selectively exclusive.[71]

The dormant Commerce Clause, as a tool of central state expansion, took its most powerful form in an economic decision: *Wabash, St. Louis and Pacific Railway Company v. Illinois* (1886).[72] Penned by Justice Samuel Miller,[73] *Wabash* involved an Illinois state law that charged companies differing railroad rates depending on distance and cargo, which a railway company claimed was discriminatory. The Court concluded that this type of regulation, if established at all, had to be of general and national character; local regulations could not safely regulate it.[74] It declared that the Court could strike down state laws that interfered with the dormant (that is, yet-unexpressed) federal authority to regulate interstate trade.[75] The Court presumed that the United States would be an "internally free trade zone" (Gillman, Graber, and Whittington 2013, 390). It followed, then, that the states could not obstruct the free flow of goods without express permission from Congress (Gillman, Graber, and Whittington 2013, 390). The dormant Commerce Clause allowed the Court to be a mouthpiece for central state expansion within the economic and industrial realm, constructing the national marketplace by invalidating state regulations and, more importantly, denoting who held decision-making authority with respect to commerce. Writing in 1906, the *Wall Street Journal* said that, in the realm of commerce, state expansion was inevitable: "It has been inevitable that, with this mighty expansion in business operations and financial power, there should be a corresponding accumulation of political power. As our trade and commerce have outgrown state lines, so it has been inevitable that the political power of the country should have outgrown state lines and concentrated more and more in the national government."[76]

Other Commerce Clause cases, such as the *Shreveport Rate Case* (1914)[77] and the "stream of commerce" cases, extended federal authority over economic activity. In *Shreveport*, the Court upheld federal regulation of rates for rail transport between points within a state, reasoning that they bore a "close and substantial" relationship to interstate commerce. The Court similarly approved congressional supervision of "local" transactions in public stockyards because they were located in a "current" or "stream" of interstate commerce.[78]

Individual Rights and Expansive Central State Development

After 1900, the Court's pattern concerning individual rights looks similar to its pre-1900 decisions: expanded central state authority over citizens for both conservative and liberal aims. With America's involvement in World War

I, free-speech issues and the world systems dimension became ever more paramount, as seen in *Schenck v. U.S.* (1919) and *Abrams v. U.S.* (1919), and led to an expansion of central state authority that limited speech rights. In *Schenck*, the Court upheld Congress's Espionage Act, which enabled the federal government to suppress Schenck from circulating literature that criticized the military draft.[79] Similarly, in *Abrams*, the defendants were also convicted under the Espionage Act on the basis of two leaflets they printed and distributed that denounced sending American troops to Russia as well as the US war efforts to impede the Russian Revolution.[80] The Court upheld the Espionage Act and the defendants' twenty-year prison sentence.

Other free-speech issues also extend central state authority. *Gitlow v. New York* (1925) incorporated the Free Speech Clause of the First Amendment to the states.[81] Samuel Gitlow, a socialist, was arrested in New York for distributing copies of a "left-wing manifesto" that called for the establishment of socialism through strikes. New York convicted him under a state criminal anarchy law, which punished those who advocated the overthrow of the government by force. While the Court, on the merits in a seven-to-two decision, held that a state may forbid both speech and publication if they have a tendency to result in action dangerous to public security, thereby upholding the New York statute, the Court still extended central state authority by virtue of applying the First Amendment to the states via the Fourteenth Amendment Due Process Clause. In so doing, the Court extended its review authority over subsequent free speech cases.

In other cases, however, the Court used its power to expand central state authority to advance due process protections under the citizenship dimension. Decided during Chief Justice Taft's tenure, *Moore v. Dempsey* (1923), for example, represented a major legal victory for the NAACP in 1923.[82] Here, the Court expanded the power of federal district courts through the Due Process Clause of the Fourteenth Amendment. The Court held that the mob-dominated murder trial of a group of African American men—which led to death sentences for all twelve men—violated due process. The Taft Court, then, constructed extensive due process review powers that expanded federal court authority. Similar due process rights faced the Court under Chief Justice Hughes in 1932, in *Powell v. Alabama*.[83] Here, the Court held that the single-day trial and death sentence for nine black youths accused of raping two white women violated due process because the defendants' attorneys did not consult with their clients and had done little to actually defend them. In sum, the post-1900 period of individual rights cases consistently expanded federal authority, often resulting in constricted rights protection but nearly as often in advancing rights for citizens.

Conclusion

Across American history, the Court's most salient constitutional decisions have shaped the contours of the American central state. Through its constitutional decisions, the judiciary both expands and restricts this state, a pattern of development deeply rooted in the dual sovereign design of American federalism. In the aftermath of the Civil War, the Court's decisions helped chart a moderate course that pivoted on debates about varying conceptions of federalism, debates that reflect the Court's moderate record in enhancing national power, which prevailed more strongly in the individual rights realm than it did in questions over economic regulation. State-building in this era took a nonlinear path, generally expanding some policy areas while generally restricting others. The Court's role regarding state expansion rested largely within the structural dimension of central state authority, addressing, essentially, the question of who has the ultimate decision-making authority. Throughout this era, the Court's answer to this question was that it had the decision-making authority in individual rights cases, while in economic cases, states had that authority.

Still left to be explored is the Court's constitutional development in the remainder of the twentieth century. Chapter 5 explores the Court's role after this modern national government and its concomitant powers had been accepted.

Chapter 5

Legal Developments in the Modern American State, 1933–1997

The words of the Constitution . . . are so unrestricted by their intrinsic meaning or by their history or by tradition or by prior decisions that they leave the individual Justice free, if indeed they do not compel him, to gather meaning not from reading the Constitution but from reading life.

—Justice Felix Frankfurter, 1949[1]

Introduction

As the previous chapter detailed, the Court's constitutional output in the early twentieth century laid the foundations for and contributed to the rise of the modern regulatory state partly through judicial review and invalidation. I illustrate here the significant continuity in the advancement of the federal state before and after the New Deal, which turns out to be not as much of a "critical juncture" in the expansion of federal authority as is commonly believed. What changes from the 1930s onward is the ends the leaders of this more powerful state pursued. Indeed, before the New Deal, the Court's focus was not on erecting a national welfare state but on consolidating central state authority through expanding federal power at the expense of the individual states. The latter project can be considered a necessary (but largely unintended) precondition for the creation of the welfare state.

The constitutional patterns set in place during the New Deal era continued through the rest of the twentieth century. The Court's decisions largely expanded central state authority by asserting that the federal government would define the extent of individual rights and that states' rights over economic issues were limited. In *Helvering v. Davis* (1937), for example, the Court helped build the more typical, Weberian dimensions of the central state: its social welfare apparatuses. Writing for the Court, Justice Benjamin Cardozo affirmed Congress's Social Security Act and its authority to interpret the General Welfare Clause broadly.[2] Cardozo wrote, "Nor is the concept of the general welfare static. Needs that were narrow or parochial a century ago may be interwoven in our day with the well-being of the nation," and the Social Security Act represented just that: a federal response to a "nation-wide calamity."[3] Thus, Helvering entrenched the federal government's authority to protect its citizens from economic disaster.

At the same time, however, the Court's interpretation extended federal authority by asserting its authority over individual rights. Throughout the post–New Deal era, the Court persistently allowed the federal government to exercise power by constricting individual rights in the name of national security. For example, in one of the Court's most notorious decisions, *Korematsu v. U.S.* (1944),[4] Justice Hugo Black upheld Fred Korematsu's detention in an internment camp established by Presidential Executive Order 9066, an order that gave the military authority to exclude citizens of Japanese ancestry from areas deemed critical to national defense and potentially vulnerable to espionage. In the Court's 6-3 decision, Justice Black reasoned that wartime exigencies called for greater federal power. He argued that the need to protect against espionage outweighed Korematsu's rights and that compulsory exclusion, though constitutionally suspect, is justified during circumstances of "emergency and peril."[5] Korematsu clearly represented an important expansion of federal authority and illustrated the effects wartime has on this power. Due to the pressures of wartime, the Court largely deferred authority to the democratic branches, which extended federal authority to limit individual rights.[6]

The judiciary's decisions in federalism and economic activity cases provided another channel for central state growth. Take *Southern Pacific Co v. Arizona* (1945), for example.[7] Here, the Arizona Train Limit Law prevented any person or corporation from operating a railroad train of more than fourteen passenger cars or seventy freight cars long within the state. The Southern Pacific Company violated the Arizona law, and thus the state subjected the rail company to a monetary fine. Southern Pacific challenged the constitutionality of Arizona's law, claiming it violated the Constitution's Commerce Clause. The Court struck down Arizona's law, declaring, "[T]he Arizona Train Limit Law imposes a serious burden on the interstate commerce conducted by appellant [Southern Pacific Company]. It materially impedes the movement of appellant's interstate trains through that state and interposes a substantial obstruction to the national policy proclaimed by Congress, to promote adequate, economical and efficient railway transportation service."[8]

Chapter 5 reveals the Court's integral role, as seen previously, in expanding the powers of the federal government. But this role had less to do with any intent to develop an insulated bureaucracy and more to do with asserting and affirming central state authority to control citizens and states' rights. In the post–New Deal era, we see continuity across periods in the following general areas: affirming Congress's authority to curtail individual rights, invalidating state legislatures' infringement on individual rights, and invalidating state legislatures' economic regulations. By highlighting these patterns in development, chapter 5 moves beyond simply depicting the "modern state" as solely defined by its administrative and welfare capacity, and instead moves toward depictions of social and state control.

State-Building during the New Deal, Great Society, and Beyond

While 1933 to 1997[9] is a long period to summarize, it is worth noting the continuity and patterns of constitutional development seen in the post–New

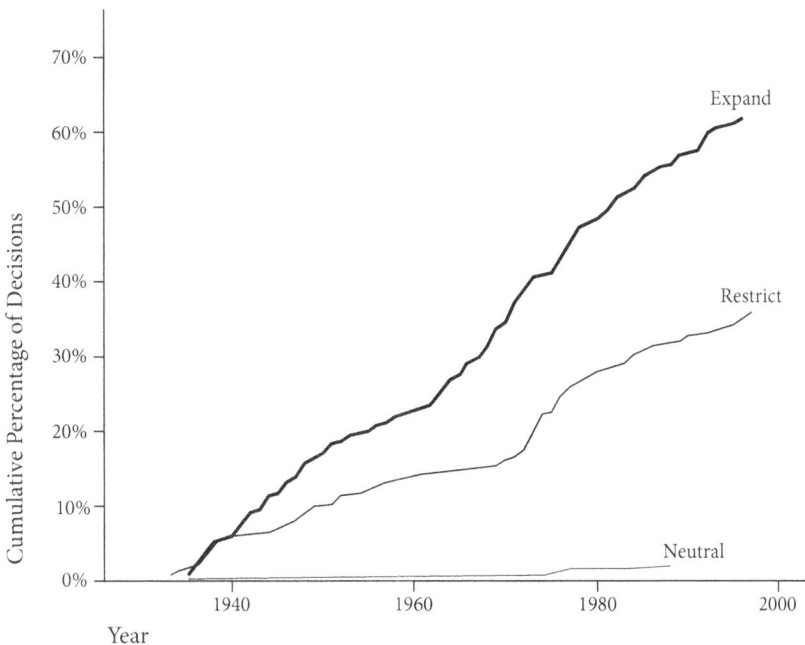

Figure 5.1. Cumulative Frequency of Effect on Federal Authority, 1933–1997.

Source: Compiled by author. N=274.

Deal Era. Still, I also separate out periods of development in Figure 5.2 below. During the post–New Deal period studied here, the Court's decisions drastically expanded the powers of the federal government, a quintessential feature of the modern state. Of 274 total cases, 170 (62%) advanced federal authority and 97 (35%) inhibited it. For a short period, until around 1940, the judiciary expanded and constricted federal authority at about the same rate. Restrictive cases also spiked briefly in the 1970s under Chief Justice Burger, with First Amendment restriction cases actually outweighing expansive ones for a brief period (see Figure 5.4 on page 120). Beginning in 1940, however, expansive decisions grow far more quickly than restrictive ones, as Figure 5.1 demonstrates. What propelled this steep rise? It has much to do with the fact that individual rights—civil rights, First Amendment issues—now comprised an extraordinary proportion of the Court's production; 158 of 274 cases (58%) dealt with these two issues areas. Of those, 105 extended federal authority over civil rights or First Amendment issues. This last period, from 1933 to 1997, is the only one in which the Court considered individual rights more frequently than economic activity. In fact, in the civil rights realm, expansive decisions dwarf restrictive ones; expansion decisions account for an astounding 73% of cases, the single greatest rate of expansion of any of the constitutional issues across history (see Figure 5.3 on page 120). Yet economic activity and due process and privacy have more moderate effects on federal authority, expanding and restricting at the same rate, as the line chart in Figure 5.4 reveals.

Within historical eras—four in total—during this period, expansive cases always outweigh restrictive ones. During the postwar and Great Society era (1945–1968), federal authority expanded more than it ever had in American history, just over 70% of the time (see Figure 5.2). These graphics

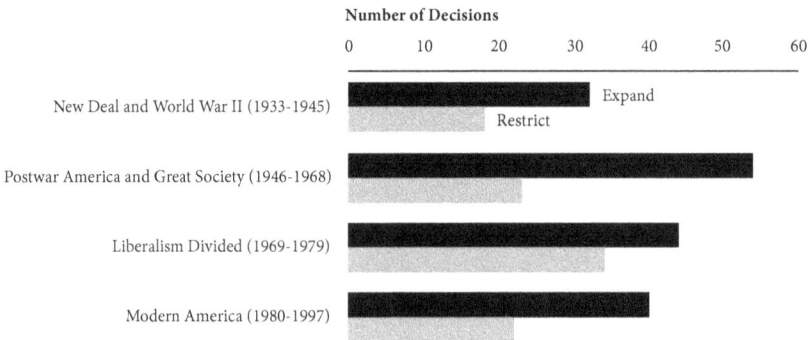

Figure 5.2. Effect on Federal Authority across Historical Eras, 1933–1997.

Note and Source: Compiled by author. The seven neutral decisions were not included. N=267.

confirm patterns we saw previously: the Supreme Court favored the growth of central state authority far more often than not, and from 1933 to 1997, it did do so with only slightly greater frequency than it had in earlier periods—62% expansion from 1933 to 1997, 58% from 1865 to 1932, and 57% from 1789 to 1864.

Table 5.1. Constitutional Issue by Effect on Federal Authority, 1933–1997

Constitutional Issue		Effect on Federal Authority			
		Restrict	Neutral	Expand	Total
First Amendment	Count	31	2	52	85
	% within row	36.5%	2.4%	61.2%	100.0%
Civil rights/liberties	Count	20	0	53	73
	%	27.4%	0.0%	72.6%	100.0%
Economic activity	Count	13	0	23	36
	%	36.1%	0.0%	63.9%	100.0%
Due process	Count	7	0	6	13
	%	53.8%	0.0%	46.2%	100.0%
Privacy	Count	4	0	8	12
	%	33.3%	0.0%	66.7%	100.0%
Judicial power	Count	8	0	4	12
	%	66.7%	0.0%	33.3%	100.0%
Federalism	Count	4	0	6	10
	%	40.0%	0.0%	60.0%	100.0%
Presidential power	Count	3	2	4	9
	%	33.3%	22.2%	44.4%	100.0%
Unions	Count	3	1	3	7
	%	42.9%	14.3%	42.9%	100.0%
Criminal procedure	Count	3	0	4	7
	%	42.9%	0.0%	57.1%	100.0%
Federal taxation	Count	1	0	5	6
	%	16.7%	0.0%	83.3%	100.0%
Miscellaneous	Count	0	2	2	4
	%	0.0%	50.0%	50.0%	100.0%
Total	Count	97	7	170	274
	%	35.4%	2.6%	62.0%	100.0%

Note and Source: Compiled by author. I observed a strong association between constitutional issue and effect on federal authority, $\chi^2(22) = 41.57$. $p = .007$. N=274.

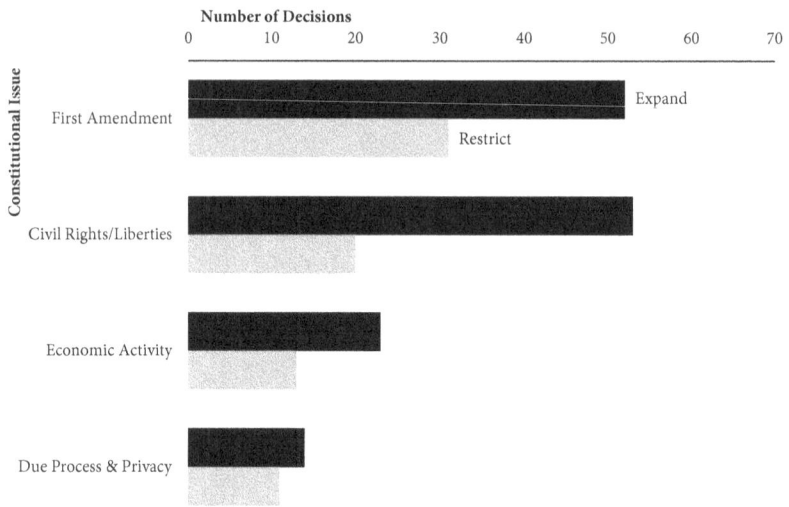

Figure 5.3. Constitutional Issue Areas and Effect on Federal Authority, 1933–1977.

Notes and Source: Compiled by author. This graphic does not include the two neutral decisions among these issue areas. It contains the most abundant constitutional issues. Together, the issues in this graphic comprise 79% of all the decisions in the period under study. N=217.

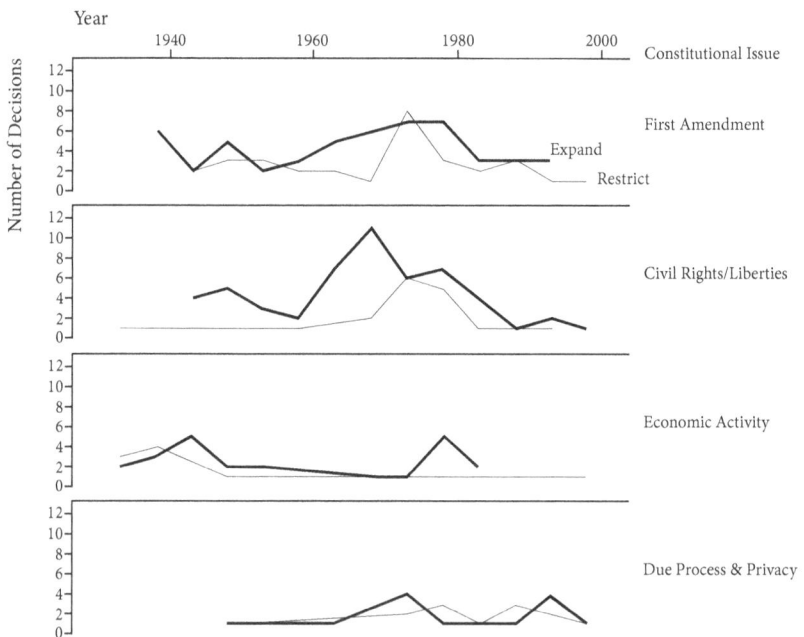

Figure 5.4. Most Abundant Constitutional Issues, 1933–1997

Note and Source: Compiled by author. Neutral decisions not included. N=217.

Table 5.2. Frequency of Dimensions of the Central State, 1933–1997

Dimension	Expand	Restrict	Total	% Expanding
Centralization	162	92	254	63.78%
Citizenship	131	68	199	65.83%
Property	42	26	68	61.76%
Admin. capacity	18	14	32	56.25%
World systems	15	5	20	75.00%
Extraction	10	7	17	58.82%
Client groups	12	3	15	80.00%

Note and Source: Compiled by author. N=274.

In this period, the judiciary advanced federal authority across all central state dimensions. Much of this advancement occurred through the citizenship dimension, given that the Court extended central state authority in 66% of its decisions in this area—up from 56% during the last period of study, 1865–1932. The property dimension saw the largest leap, expanding federal authority in 51% of cases from 1865 to 1932 but 62% from 1933 to 1997. And while world systems and client groups interact with only 20 and 15 decisions, respectively, they continued to lend themselves to the largest rate of central state expansion, at 75% and 80%.

Most of the citizenship dimension involved civil rights and First Amendment questions. Long before the civil rights revolution, the Court advanced federal authority over the interpretation of the First Amendment in several cases in the late 1930s and early 1940s. In *De Jonge v. Oregon* (1937), for example, a unanimous Court (eight to zero) invalidated Oregon's criminal syndicalism statute.[10] At a meeting held by the Communist Party, Dirk De Jonge was arrested during a police raid and charged with violating the statute, which defined criminal syndicalism as "the doctrine which advocates crime, physical violence, sabotage or any unlawful acts or methods as a means of accomplishing or effecting industrial or political change or revolution." Agreeing with De Jonge, Chief Justice Charles Evans Hughes held that "peaceable assembly for lawful discussion cannot be made a crime. The holding of meetings for peaceable political action cannot be proscribed. Those who assist in the conduct of such meetings cannot be branded as criminals on that score."[11] By holding that De Jonge's conviction violated the Due Process Clause of the Fourteenth Amendment, the Court extended federal authority over citizens.

Control over property also became a significant avenue for federal state expansion. During the New Deal, the Court upheld Congress's right to control property in economic activity cases such as *Ashwander v. TVA* (1936),[12] which affirmed Congress's authority to create the Tennessee Valley Authority

(TVA), a government corporation created as part of the New Deal to improve the economy. Among other things, the TVA helped improved navigation of Tennessee rivers, built flood control projects, and generated hydroelectric power. Decades later, the Court also advanced federal authority over economic issues and the property dimension to invalidate a North Carolina law that discriminated against out-of-state apple growers. In *Hunt v. Washington State Apple Advertising Commission* (1977),[13] the Court held unanimously that a North Carolina law that required all apples shipped into the state to display a USDA grade or nothing at all, violated the Commerce Clause because it discriminated against out-of-state growers but shielded local growers from the same burden. Using the dormant Commerce Clause, the Court held, "In the absence of conflicting legislation by Congress, there is a residuum of power in the state to make laws governing matters of local concern which nevertheless in some measure affect interstate commerce or even, to some extent, regulate it."[14] Thus, the Court effectively advanced federal authority through its negative powers, invalidating a state statute even though it did not contravene an existing Congressional statute.

Individual rights greatly preoccupied constitutional development during this period, and these issues followed a similar trend across each period of development. The remainder of this chapter looks more closely at subperiods during the era from 1933 to 1997.[15] These subperiods correspond to typical periods of American political development, and they roughly correspond to the tenures of certain chief justices. In each of these eras, the patterns of development look similar: the Court tended to affirm the federal government's right to control citizens in the name of national security or in the name of typical welfare state changes, to strike down state laws for nonsecurity violations of free speech and other individual rights, and to strike down state economic regulations.

New Deal Era and World War II

The Court in the 1930s and on the eve of World War II faced a litany of constitutional questions pertaining the Great Depression and civil liberties. President Franklin Roosevelt's ascension to office in 1932 ushered in a series of economic and administrative reforms, based on his campaign pledge of a "new deal," to remedy the severe economic crisis facing the country. The Court began reviewing many of these presidential actions and New Deal legislation; in the sixteen months following January 1935, the Court struck down eight of ten New Deal measures (S. Goldman 1991, 40). At the same time, the rise of Nazi Germany and World War II made questions of civil liberties a prominent concern under the leadership of Chief Justice Charles

Evans Hughes, whose tenure ended just months after the United States entered World War II.

Chief Justice Hughes possessed a penchant for administrative leadership and exercised it during the Court's most crucial days since Chief Justice Marshall.[16] When we consider the types of federal authority the Hughes Court advanced, we begin to see its role in the creation of the modern American state and its relationship to federal state powers. The Hughes Court did not simply acquiesce to the features of the modern American state with a "switch in time that saved nine," an about-face that some scholars claim occurred in *West Coast Hotel v. Parrish* (1937).[17] The data show that the Hughes Court both expanded and constricted federal authority. Before *West Coast*, seven decisions constricted while six decisions expanded the federal state, suggesting that the Hughes Court advanced some aspects of the federal government and not others.

In particular, the Court exerted great control over questions of individual rights. Starting in the 1930s, more and more such cases came before the Court, testing the reach of constitutional liberties. These cases sparked one of the major jurisprudential debates in constitutional history, a debate over incorporating the Bill of Rights so that they applied to the states. We see this debate plainly in *Palko v. Connecticut* (1937).[18] While *Palko* inhibited federal power by refusing to incorporate to the states the Fifth Amendment's protection against double jeopardy, it declared that the Court had the power to apply the Bill of Rights. Writing the majority opinion, Justice Cardozo put forward a theory of "selective incorporation" that held that the Court should only apply the Second through the Eighth Amendments if it determined they were "the very essence of a scheme of ordered liberty."[19] In contrast, he declared the First Amendment must be incorporated entirely because free expression is "the matrix, the indispensable condition" for nearly every other freedom.[20] Earlier, in 1931, the Hughes Court had incorporated one aspect of the First Amendment—the Free Press Clause—in *Near v. Minnesota*, a case that expanded the federal state along citizenship, as opposed to welfare state, dimensions.[21] *Near* demonstrated the protection that the First and Fourteenth Amendments provided against prior publication restraints and the extent to which Hughes would enforce these rights. The Court heard this case on appeal from a state court that had forbidden publication of *The Saturday Press*, which a Minnesota statute considered "largely devoted to malicious, scandalous and defamatory articles." *The Saturday Press* claimed Minneapolis officials were complicit in gambling, bootlegging, and racketeering, and many of the articles contained anti-Semitic rhetoric (Cox, in Levy and Karst 2000, 1,317). Nevertheless, in Chief Justice Hughes's majority opinion, he held that Minnesota's statute infringed upon the liberty of press that the First and Fourteenth Amendments guaranteed.

Similarly, in 1932, the Hughes Court protected individual due process rights by invalidating state action, as it had done in *Near*. As mentioned, *Powell* concerned Alabama's sentencing nine black teenage boys to death after a one-day trial. Justice Sutherland held, "The right of the accused, at least in a capital case, to have the aid of counsel for his defense, which includes the right to have sufficient time to advise with counsel and to prepare a defense, is one of the fundamental rights that the due process clause of the Fourteenth Amendment guarantees."[22] Archibald Cox concluded, "The Hughes Court infused the First Amendment with a new and broader vitality that still drives the expansion of the constitutional protection available to both individuals and speakers and institutional press" (Cox, in Levy and Karst 2000, 1,316). By doing so, the Hughes Court advanced the citizenship and individual rights dimensions of the federal state, but it also laid the groundwork to expand the Court's own judicial review power.

Even before this "switch," the Hughes Court also expanded some aspects of executive and legislative power, and it constricted similar power in other decisions. For example, *United States v. Curtiss-Wright* (1936) and *Ashwander v. Tennessee Valley Authority* (1936) enhanced the administrative capacity of the executive and Congress, respectively. *Curtiss-Wright* dealt with a joint resolution from Congress that authorized the president to ban the sales of arms to countries involved in the Chaco War between Bolivia and Paraguay.[23] The president immediately made an executive order banning such sales, and the defendant, Curtiss-Wright Corporation, a weapons manufacturer, was convicted of selling arms to warring nations in South America. The Court held that Congress could delegate great authority and discretion to the president in the conduct of foreign affairs: "[T]he President alone has the power to speak or listen as a representative of the nation. He makes treaties with the advice and consent of the Senate; but he alone negotiates. Into the field of negotiation the Senate cannot intrude, and Congress itself is powerless to invade it."[24]

Ashwander (1936) also expanded federal power by expanding the scope of administrative agencies.[25] In this case, the Court held that Congress had the power to establish the Tennessee Valley Authority. *Ashwander* concerned the creation of a federal agency, the TVA, to advance the long-term regional-planning capacity of the central state (administrative dimension), and it dealt with the TVA's acquisition of property and equipment from a private power company. The Court argued that the Wilson Dam, from which the TVA generated electricity, had been built originally for national defense—to produce materials involved in munitions manufacturing—and thus the federal government could assert its authority.

Yet another case, *United States v. Carolene Products Co* (1938), laid the foundation for the individual-rights revolution yet to come during the Warren

Court era.[26] In a seemingly unremarkable case concerning the shipment of "filled milk" (milk with skimmed milk and vegetable oil added), the Court upheld Congress's power, via the Commerce Clause, to regulate the shipment of this manufactured good and thus expanded central state authority.[27] While Footnote Four has turned out to be the most important facet of *Carolene Products*, and the note provides significant *potential* for central state expansion, Footnote Four is not the reason the decision extends federal authority. Instead, it does so because the Court affirmed Congress's commerce power and the federal law in question.

Ultimately, the leading decisions of the Hughes Court demonstrate how it advanced many aspects of the federal state, most significantly the citizenship dimension. But even through its most conservative years (before *West Coast*), it expanded federal power at almost the same rate as it constricted it. Overall, though, the Hughes Court favored expansion 54% of the time. These data show that the Court helped lay the foundations of the modern American state long before the New Deal. In its early years, the Court both expanded and restricted coercive statecraft and other forms of governance that have come to define the modern central state. The Court's complicated relationship with the state suggests we need a more nuanced depiction of the constitutional development of the federal state.

In the sweep of constitutional history, the Stone and Vinson Courts together marked an important transition period for the Court and federal power. From 1941 to 1953, Chief Justices Harlan Stone and Fred Vinson led the Court, Stone until 1946 and Vinson thereafter. In his history of the Supreme Court, Bernard Schwartz concluded, "In terms of their leadership abilities . . . Chief Justices Harlan F. Stone and Fred M. Vinson were the least effective Court heads during the present century" (Schwartz 1993, 246). While Stone, according to his biographer, "was not born to command equals" (Mason quoted in S. Goldman 1991, 115), he also had the misfortune of presiding over "one of the most cantankerous courts in the nation's history" (Urofsky 2005, 456). The Court divided into two intellectual factions: Justice Felix Frankfurter's advocated judicial restraint, and the faction that Justices Hugo Black and William Douglas led epitomized judicial activism and the expansion of individual rights. Indeed, Chief Justice Stone would come to characterize his colleagues as "a team of wild horses" (Cox, in Levy and Karst 2000, 2,548). Still, during wartime, Stone's Court extended federal authority to regulate the economy, but with respect to civil liberties, the Court began to use its authority to protect personal freedoms, especially regarding First Amendment issues; 77 percent (seventeen of twenty-two cases) expanded federal authority during Stone's tenure.

With respect to the Commerce Clause, the Stone Court supported Congressional authority to regulate local economic activities that only slightly, if at all, affected interstate commerce. Take *Wickard v. Filburn* (1941) for example.[28] Here, the Court upheld the constitutionality of a federal penalty on Roscoe Filburn, the owner of a small family farm. Filburn grew 11.9 acres of wheat in excess of the 11.1 acre federal allotment. In upholding Filburn's federal penalty, the Court reasoned that Congress could rationally conclude that small additions to the total wheat supply, even for home consumption as was the case with Mr. Filburn, could cumulatively affect the price of wheat in interstate markets. In another broad interpretation of the Commerce Clause, the Court invalidated in *Edwards v. California* (1941) a California law that prohibited knowingly bringing a nonresident "indigent person" into the state.[29] Writing for the Court, Justice James Byrnes declared the California law's "express purpose and inevitable effect is to prohibit the transportation of indigent persons across the California border. The burden upon interstate commerce is intended and immediate; it is the plain and sole function of the statute."[30] Commerce, as had been true at the turn of the twentieth century, proved to be an avenue through which federal power would expand.

Beyond the explicit authority of the federal branches, the Stone Court forayed deeply into the realm of individual rights. New constitutional issues that would contribute to the next major development in constitutional doctrine emerged during this time. The war against Nazi Germany brought to the fore questions about human dignity, equality, and democracy; the justices therefore began to reexamine their judicial deference to legislative statutes that threatened civil rights and liberties. Indeed, Chief Justice Stone himself began this reexamination when he penned Footnote Four in 1937, back when he was an associate justice. His footnote declared the Court would remain vigilant over legislative statutes prejudiced against "discrete and insular minorities." In *West Virginia State Board of Education v. Barnette* (1943),[31] for example, the Court struck down a state law that mandated a compulsory flag salute in all West Virginia public schools, and thus overturned a Supreme Court case of just three years earlier, *Minersville School District v. Gobitis* (1940).[32] While *Gobitis* upheld mandatory flag salute, the Court's opinion in *Barnette* held, "Compulsory unification of opinion," was doomed to failure and was antithetical to First Amendment values. Writing for the majority in a six-three decision, Justice Robert Jackson argued, "If there is any fixed star in our constitutional constellation, it is that no official, high or petty, can prescribe what shall be orthodox in politics, nationalism, religion, or other matters of opinion or force citizens to confess by word or act their faith therein."[33]

In addition to speech protection, the Stone Court also advanced federal power by curtailing states' ability to discriminate in the electoral process. In most of the states of the Old South, nomination as the candidate of the Democratic Party still assured election to office. Since a political party was regarded as a private organization, it was not subject to the Equal Protection Clause of the Fourteenth Amendment or to the Fifteenth Amendment's prohibition against denying voting rights by race. Thus, "white primaries" excluded African American voters from participating in elections (Cox, in Levy and Karst 2000, 2,550). In *Smith v. Allwright* (1944), the Stone Court undermined the use of "white primaries."[34] At issue in *Smith* was S. S. Allwright, a white election official, who denied Lonnie E. Smith, a black man, the right to vote in the 1940 Texas Democratic primary. The NAACP's Thurgood Marshall and William Hastie fought Smith's case all the way to the Supreme Court, which declared, "The right to vote in a primary for the nomination of candidates without discrimination by the State, like the right to vote in a general election, is a right secured by the Constitution."[35] *West Virginia v. Barnette* (1943) and *Smith v. Allwright* (1944) underscore that central state expansion can occur in either the protection or curtailment of individual rights. Both these free-speech issues advanced central state authority because, in *West Virginia v. Barnette*, the Court invalidated a lower-level state legislative body, and in *Smith v. Allwright*, the Court affirmed Congressional legislation. That the former expanded individual rights protection and the latter inhibited those protections matters not at all to the impact on central state authority.

Postwar America and the Great Society

Chief Justice Stone's tenure was brief, and after he died in April 1946, Fred Vinson took over as chief justice. Vinson presided over a trying era in constitutional development, dealing with serious and important issues regarding Cold War challenges to civil rights and liberties and to growing concerns about racial discrimination. When Chief Justice Earl Warren took over the Court in 1953, the Cold War, domestic subversives, and racial discrimination remained important policy and legal issues facing the Court and the country. Across the Vinson and Warren Court eras, federal power expanded enormously. Of the seventy-seven decisions in the data, 72% of the decisions under Vinson and Warren expanded federal power—a 9% increase from the previous two chief justices, Stone and Hughes.

At a time when Republicans accused President Truman's administration of sympathizing with and employing communists, the Vinson Court continued to extend federal power over citizens, but often in the name of stifling dissent. In *Dennis v. U.S.* (1951),[36] Chief Justice Vinson's majority opinion defended the constitutionality of Congress's Smith Act. In *Dennis*, leaders of the Communist Party of America were arrested and charged with violating provisions of the Smith Act. The Act made it unlawful to knowingly conspire to teach and advocate the overthrow or destruction of the United States government. In a six-two decision, the Court upheld the convictions of the Communist Party leaders and found that the Smith Act did not "inherently" violate the First Amendment. Similarly in *American Communications v. Douds* (1950),[37] the Vinson Court upheld the Taft-Hartley Act, which required labor union leaders to take anticommunist oaths. The Act stated that if labor union leaders did not file affidavits swearing they were not members of the Communist Party, then the protections and services afforded under the National Labor Relations Act did not apply to that union.

While the Cold War and anticommunism contributed to the expansion of federal powers to curtail civil rights under the Constitution, growing racial tension resulted in the protection of racial minorities. Both outcomes expanded federal power. In the realm of race discrimination, the Vinson Court built on the Stone Court's broad interpretation of the Commerce Clause and exercised judicial review through the Fourteenth Amendment. In *Morgan v. Virginia* (1946),[38] for example, the Vinson Court invalidated a state Jim Crow law that required racial segregation of passengers on public motor carriers, but the Constitutional ground, again, relied on interstate commerce rather than on equal protection. Then again, in *Shelley v. Kraemer* (1948), the Vinson Court declared that restrictive covenants—binding property owners not to sell to minorities—while within the legal rights of property owners, were unenforceable.[39] For a court to give effect to such a discriminatory contract, Vinson concluded, would amount to state action in violation of the Fourteenth Amendment. The Vinson Court also vigorously extended federal power, via judicial review, over segregation in higher education. For instance, the Court declared unconstitutional in *Sweatt v. Painter* (1950) the separate law school for blacks that Texas had established.[40]

In the end, as the United States emerged from World War II, it found itself both a consolidated administrative state and a crucial world power. This reality coupled with the growing racial tensions in the country thrust the Court into resolving novel constitutional issues, issues that produced an even more powerful federal state than previously seen. The individual rights issues decided during the Stone and Vinson years laid the foundation for the Warren Court's focus on race and equality. With Earl Warren as chief justice, the Court's focus now shifted from the economic issues witnessed during the Taft and Hughes Courts to equality. While in service of a different aim, the Court under Warren would continue to utilize its powers to expand federal power.

By Chief Justice Earl Warren's retirement in 1969, a Warren Court decision had had an impact on virtually everyone in the United States. The Warren Court's creative reinterpretation of law could only be matched by that of Marshall's Court over two centuries prior (Schwartz 1993, 263). As intimated in the previous section, civil rights now became the Court's chief focus. The Court, once focused on the "national-state relationship" and then, later, on the "business-government" relationship, now became increasingly "concerned with the relationship between the individual and government" (McCloskey 2005, 122). The Warren Court referred to fewer cases in its opinions; that is, it promulgated a larger number of cases without any citations than any Court in American history, a finding that demonstrates the well-documented activist nature of the Warren era (Fowler and Jeon 2008, 19).[41] Yet with regard to its impact on federal power, the Warren Court resembled the Stone and Vinson period. As in eras of Court history when either nation-state or business-government relations dominate, the Warren Court's solution to policy problems once again resulted in extending federal authority over both the lives of citizens and the workings of society.

Indeed, the Warren Court actively expanded federal power via individual rights. The Court enhanced federal power in nearly 80% of its decisions that I have included in this book. Examining these decisions along constitutional issue areas, we can see the Warren Court's focus on individual rights, primarily issues of civil rights and the First Amendment. Most remember the Warren Court for consolidating federal power over civil rights issues, as it did in *Brown v. Board of Education* (1954), in which it held segregation unconstitutional, and in *Loving v. Virginia* (1967), in which it invalidated a state prohibition on interracial marriage.[42] In the realm of criminal procedure, too, the Warren Court greatly expanded the application of the Bill of Rights. The key decisions, *Mapp v. Ohio* (1961) and *Gideon v. Wainwright* (1963),[43] spoke broadly about the need to incorporate the Bill of Rights to protect individuals—and thereby expand federal power via the judiciary. Thus, in the following decade, the Warren Court incorporated the rights against double jeopardy and self-incrimination, as well as the rights to jury trial in criminal cases, to a speedy trial, and to confrontation.[44] It comes as no surprise, then, that the vast majority of its decisions enhanced federal power.

The rate at which it expanded power does not differ much from the Stone and Vinson periods. Legal themes similar to those that expanded federal authority—egalitarianism, liberalism, and activism—motivated even the Warren Court decisions that constricted power (White, in Levy and Karst 2000, 2,853). For example, in *Powell v. McCormack* (1969), the Court constricted federal power by prohibiting the House of Representatives from excluding a duly elected member from office.[45] Adam Clayton Powell had a history of criticizing his House of Representatives colleagues, and when he did not heed civil proceedings against him in New York, a judge held him in criminal contempt. Nevertheless, he won reelection in 1966, but the House voted to exclude him. Chief Justice Warren concluded that Congress did not possess such authority because Powell's district lawfully elected him, and he met the constitutional requirements for membership in the House. Consequently, the legislature was powerless to exclude him, thus restricting federal power through egalitarian principles.

Similarly, in *Bolling v. Sharpe* (1954), the Court used egalitarian principles to constrict federal authority.[46] Here, the Court held that segregation in District of Columbia public schools (governed by federal law) deprived African Americans of their Fifth Amendment due process rights. Thus, the Court invalidated federal action, constricting power on the basis of egalitarianism. In the same vein, the Court extended individual rights through invalidating federal law in *Reid v. Covert* (1957).[47] In *Reid*, Clarice Cover had been convicted by a military tribunal of murdering her husband on an air base in England. An executive agreement between the United States and the United Kingdom allowed the US military courts to exercise exclusive jurisdiction over offenses committed in the UK by US servicemen and their dependents. Yet the Warren Court invalidated this federal agreement, holding that US citizen civilians, like Clarice Covert, have the right to Fifth and Sixth Amendment protections even while abroad, and their trials must be conducted in civilian, not military, courts. Ultimately, the Court's restrictive decisions embraced many of the principles that spurred on great constitutional expansion in its other criminal procedure, civil rights, and First Amendment decisions.

The constitutional development of the Warren Court took root long before Earl Warren ascended to the chief justiceship. As mentioned, Footnote Four in the *United States v. Carolene Products* (1938) decision provided the foundation on which the Warren Court would expand federal power in the name of the people. While activism—and expansion of federal power—are as old as the Court itself,[48] what differed during the Warren Court was whom expanded power served. No longer were entrenched elites the principle beneficiaries of enhanced federal power. With the Warren Court, federal power benefitted African Americans, atheists, criminals, pornographers, and the poor. As the Warren Court was put on a path toward greater federal expansion (and embraced it), so, too, the Burger Court would continue the tradition of federal expansion, though much to the chagrin of Chief Justice Burger. Still, the Burger Court, despite Burger's efforts, did not overturn any important Warren Court decisions, resulting in an ever-more-powerful federal state.

Liberalism Divided

The Warren Court's activism—especial its protection of the criminally accused—played an important role in the 1968 presidential campaign with the Republican Party candidate, Richard Nixon, vowing to bring "law and order" to the United States He criticized the Warren Court's jurisprudence, and sought to appoint "strict constructionists" to the bench, if elected. During this period, the Vietnam War raised important free speech issues as did the cultural-sexual revolution, which begin in the 1960s and continued in the 1970s, raising questions about obscenity and speech. The women's' rights movement also built on the cultural revolution at the time, which posed controversial questions for the Court concerning rights to sexual privacy.

Chief Justice Warren Burger's Court continued along the path of federal government expansion that we have seen previously. It extended federal power less often than the Warren Court, but the landmark decisions of the Warren Court remained virtually intact (Schwartz 1993, 314). While Burger and Rehnquist's conservative Courts expanded power at a slower rate than Warren's, they still expanded federal power more often than not—58% of the 138 landmark decisions evaluated advanced federal power. In this sense, the Burger and Rehnquist Courts returned us to the usual rate of federal expansion, and the Warren Court—by extending federal power in close to 80% of its most important decisions—represents an aberration in constitutional development.

The Burger and Rehnquist benches continued the Court's postwar focus on individual rights, a facet of rights consciousness. Rights consciousness represents a general awareness of individual rights that one can assert or claim against someone or something else, usually a government. The Burger and Rehnquist Courts followed the Warren Court's lead—58% of its cases deal with civil rights and liberties and the First Amendment (80 of 138 cases). In these realms of civil rights and First Amendment, the Court advanced federal power more often than it restricted power. While the Burger Court perpetuated the Warren Court's precedents, it also made important adjustments to Warren Court doctrine, thus producing a more even balance between advancement and restriction of federal power. We should expect such an outcome because the Warren Court's reimagining of public law could only last for so long; the Burger Court was destined to consolidate the legal changes created under Warren's leadership.

The Burger Court's First Amendment jurisprudence is a good example of this consolidation and balance. It extended the Warren Court's vigorous protection of speech to commercial forms. In *Buckley v. Valeo* (1976), for example, the Court restricted federal power in a seven-one decision.[49] It overturned part of the Federal Election Campaign Act of 1971 by holding that spending limits placed on individual electoral expenditures violated the First Amendment. Yet in *Cohen v. California* (1971), the Court wielded judicial review to extend federal power, a classic example of how rights claims became ever more frequent during the late twentieth century.[50] *Cohen* concerned a nineteen-year-old department store employee, Paul Cohen, who wore a jacket that protested the Vietnam War. His jacket read "FUCK THE DRAFT. STOP THE WAR." A California statute prohibited "maliciously and willfully disturb[ing] the peace and quiet of any neighborhood or person [by] offensive conduct."[51] In a narrow five-four decision, the Court overturned California's statute, holding that "one man's vulgarity is another's lyric. Indeed, we think it is largely because governmental officials cannot make principled distinctions in this area that the Constitution leaves matters of taste and style so largely to the individual."[52]

The Court extended federal protection not only to the dissenter but also to the journalist. In *Richmond Newspapers Inc. v. Virginia* (1980), Burger held, in a seven-to-one opinion, that the right to attend criminal trials was "implicit in the guarantees of the First Amendment."[53] Echoing Warren Court jurisprudence, Burger wrote, "Certain unarticulated rights are implicit in enumerated guarantees. For example, the rights of association and of privacy, the right to be presumed innocent . . . as well as the right to travel, appear nowhere in the Constitution or Bill of Rights. Yet these important but unarticulated rights have nonetheless been found to share constitutional protection in common with explicit guarantees."[54] In this way, the Burger Court largely continued in Warren's tradition, using the judiciary to extend federal power and protect individual rights.

In addition to speech protections, the Burger Court's ebb and flow between restriction and expansion is witnessed in its privacy and civil rights decisions. The Court built on *Griswold v. Connecticut*'s (1965) right to privacy in *Roe v. Wade* (1973) by invalidating Texas's restrictions on abortion access during the first trimester.[55] In so ruling, the Court continued its postwar tradition of enhancing federal power through the judicial branch. The Burger Court also advanced federal power in realms of civil rights where the Warren Court refused,[56] namely in sex discrimination cases. *Craig v. Boren* (1976), for instance, applied intermediate scrutiny to sex classifications for the first time.[57] In a seven-to-two opinion, the Court held that an Oklahoma statute that made gender classifications was unconstitutional. The statute prohibited the sale of "non-intoxicating" 3.2% beer to males under the age of twenty-one and to females under the age of eighteen. The plaintiffs, Curtis Craig, a male then between the ages of eighteen and twenty-one, and a female licensed beer vendor, challenged the law as discriminatory. The Burger Court also extended the protections of civil rights in *Goldberg v. Kelly* (1970).[58] *Goldberg* extended the social welfare state by advancing due process rights. The Court declared in *Goldberg* that a state needed to afford a public aid recipient an evidentiary hearing before deciding to discontinue that individual's social welfare aid.[59]

Still, nearly as frequently, the Burger Court restricted federal power via civil rights cases. In *San Antonio Independent School District v. Rodriguez* (1973), the Court declared that there was no fundamental right to education in the Constitution.[60] In addition to a statewide funding program, Texas public elementary and secondary schools relied on local property taxes for supplemental revenue. The San Antonio Independent School District, on behalf of students whose families resided in poorer districts, challenged Texas's funding scheme, arguing that the scheme underprivileged poorer students because their schools lacked the property tax revenue base that other, wealthier districts had. But the Court was not convinced, because Texas's system closely resembled those in other states. The Court also restricted federal power by invalidating Congressional laws concerning civil rights. *Frontiero v. Richardson* (1973), for example, concerned a federal statute that maintained "spouses of male members of the uniformed services are dependents" for purposes of receiving allowances and medical and dental benefits when the husband dies. But spouses of female military members "are not dependents unless they are in fact, dependent for over one-half of their support."[61] The Court recognized, "it can hardly be doubted that, in part because of the high visibility of the sex characteristic, women still face pervasive, although at times more subtle, discrimination in our educational institutions, in the job market and, perhaps most conspicuously, in the political arena." And so it concluded, "classifications based upon sex . . . are inherently suspect" and thus the federal statute differentiating between men and women was unconstitutional.[62] *San Antonio* and *Frontiero* reveal how the Court constricted federal power through both passive and active channels, that is, by on the one hand allowing a state law to stand and on the other invalidating a federal law.

All told, the Burger Court became "increasingly difficult" to distinguish from the Warren Court (Howard in Levy and Karst 2000, 272). The activism of the Warren Court continued—while the Warren Court invalidated 21 federal and 150 state statues, the Burger Court struck down·31 federal and 288 state laws (Schwartz 1993, 333). Still, a balance between expansion and restriction cases resumed during the Burger years. This suggests that we cannot model constitutional development through a series of constitutional moments or punctuated equilibria; the path-dependent nature of law requires that we recognize the more glacial and incremental habits of constitutional development.

Modern America

Following Burger's retirement in 1986, Chief Justice Rehnquist's Court continued to deal with many of the same issues: criminal procedures, affirmative action, and abortion. While neither the Burger nor Rehnquist Courts overruled some of liberal criminal procedures decisions like *Mapp v. Ohio* (1961)[63] and *Miranda v. Arizona* (1965),[64] they did institute many exceptions to these rulings. What did change, however, was that "constitutional debates would never again be contests between different liberals." Instead, from 1980 onward, "liberals and conservatives have debated on relatively equal terms the constitutional meaning of free speech, cruel and unusual punishment, and the due process clause" (Gillman, Graber, and Whittington 2017b, 576). In the 1980s and 1990s, the Republican Party sought to reign in growing federal power and give states greater autonomy. Presidents Reagan and George H. W. Bush appointed justices "committed to reinvigorating judicial enforcement of federalism" (Somin 2017, 458). Yet this enforcement represented what has not changed in the modern era: the Supreme Court's frequent and continued use of judicial activism. Thomas Keck has observed that justices appointed by Republican justices "exercise judicial review just as frequently" as their Democratic counterparts, and "they are no more reluctant to enter political thickets" (Keck 2004, 286).

Because of the case selection method employed, this book did not include all the Rehnquist Court decisions, but only those made through 1997[65]—eleven years into William Rehnquist's tenure as chief justice and eight years before he left office. Some have noted that "central to [Rehnquist's] agenda" was "curtailing federal power," but the data do not fully support this conclusion.[66] In the twenty-six decisions I evaluated, the Rehnquist Court continued the typical trend, expanding federal power in seventeen of these landmark decisions. When the Rehnquist Court did limit federal power, however, it did so forcefully.

Both *United States v. Lopez* (1995) and *City of Boerne v. Flores* (1997) are illuminating examples. In *Lopez*, for the first time since the 1937 constitutional crisis over New Deal legislation, the Court limited Congress's Commerce Clause power.[67] The federal statute in question—the Guns-Free School Zones Act of 1990—forbade "any individual knowingly to possess a firearm at a place that [he] knows . . . is a school zone."[68] Yet Alfonzo Lopez, a twelfth-grade high school student, brought a concealed weapon into his San Antonio, Texas, high school, and federal agents later charged him with violating the Guns-Free Act. Chief Justice Rehnquist's bare majority opinion did not mince words. Congress had justified its statute by claiming it regulated commercial or economic activity, and in his opening paragraph, Rehnquist declared, "The Act neither regulates a commercial activity nor contains a requirement that the possession be connected in any way to interstate commerce. We hold that the Act exceeds the authority of Congress" (*Lopez*, 551). Similarly, in *City of Boerne*, the Court rebuffed Congress, but this time in the realm of civil rights, invalidating Congress's Religious Freedom Restoration Act of 1993.[69]

Boerne involved the proposed expansion of a Catholic church in Boerne, Texas. The Catholic archbishop of San Antonio, Patrick Flores, applied for a permit to expand the church, but the City of Boerne denied it, maintaining that the church qualified as a historic structure under the city's historic preservation ordinances and that local zoning laws forbade the expansion. In response, the archbishop filed a lawsuit against the city in a local federal court. He claimed that the Religious Freedom Restoration Act (RFRA), which Congress passed in 1993, prohibited "governments" like the City of Boerne from "substantially burdening" a person's exercise of religion unless the government proves the burden "is in furtherance of a compelling governmental interest and is the least restrictive means of furthering that . . . interest."[70] Archbishop Flores's legal team argued that Congress had the power to pass the RFRA under Section 5 of the Constitution's Fourteenth Amendment, which allows Congress to enforce the First Amendment's provisions against the states. The Supreme Court disagreed and stressed that it alone defined the scope of constitutional rights: "The design of the [Fourteenth] Amendment and the text of Section 5 are inconsistent with the suggestion that Congress has the power to decree the substance of the Fourteenth Amendment's restrictions on the States. Legislation which alters the meaning of the Free Exercise Clause cannot be said to be enforcing the Clause. Congress does not enforce a constitutional right by changing what the right is. It has been given the power 'to enforce,' not the power to determine what constitutes a constitutional violation."[71]

Lopez and *Boerne* are thus striking examples of the Court's lack of deference to Congress, and they constrict federal power through bold judicial action. Rehnquist's Court continued this tradition in areas of presidential power, too, in *Clinton v. City of New York* (1998).[72] *Clinton* invalidated then–President Bill Clinton's use of Congress's Line Item Veto Act, which allowed the president to selectively cancel individual portions of a bill that came to him for signature. Legislation that passes both Houses of Congress, the Court held, must be entirely approved (signed) or rejected (vetoed) by the president.

All told, six Rehnquist Court cases in the data invalidated a Congressional statute. Yet the Court's bold judicial action contributed more heavily to expanded federal power than not,[73] but mainly vis-à-vis the judiciary, as its rulings invalidating state and local affirmative action programs demonstrate. For example, *Richmond v. Croson* (1989) struck down a City of Richmond law that required companies awarded city construction contracts to subcontract 30% of their business to minority-owned business enterprises.[74] In a six-three decision, the Court held that "generalized assertions" of past racial discrimination could not justify "rigid" racial quotas for the awarding of public contracts. Justice O'Connor's opinion noted that the 30% quota could not be tied to "any injury suffered by anyone"[75] (*Richmond*, 499). Thus, Richmond's law violated the Fourteenth Amendment's Equal Protection Clause. In *Shaw v. Reno* (1993),[76] the Court again exercised its own power to expand federal authority, holding that given an unusually shaped North Carolina electoral district, residents had raised a valid constitutional issue under the Equal Protection Clause of the Fourteenth Amendment and thus the Court had the power to hear the case. In the realm of Fifth Amendment property rights, too, the Rehnquist Court extended federal power by invalidating state laws. In *Lucas v. South Carolina Coastal Council* (1992) and *Nollan v. California Coastal Commission* (1987),[77] the Court reinvigorated the Fifth Amendment Takings Clause to protect the interests of property owners. Eleven of the twenty-six decisions I studied invalidated state or local laws. At bottom, by using its power of judicial review, the Court extended federal power to protect individual rights while it also, in new areas, limited congressional and presidential power.

Conclusion

Considering Court decisions in light of whether and how they expand governing authority adds to the portrayal of constitutional development that the punctuated equilibria model provides, which assumes transformative constitutional moments as well as collective action on the part of the electorate to effect constitutional change through informal, extraconstitutional means. While the theory is meant to explain the great paradigm shifts in constitutional interpretation that occurred at crucial points in our history, we rarely see bursts of either restriction or expansion, and we see periods of stasis even less often. The nature of constitutional development is one of steady incremental expansion of federal power.

While it is certainly true that a jurisprudential shift occured during the New Deal—as the Supreme Court broke with outmoded doctrines such as the liberty of contract—a constitutional moment theory does not tell us much beyond that. But what explains the Court's steady extension of federal authority across either side of these constitutional moments?

In the end, the punctuated equilibrium model of constitutional development involves a Whiggish historical bias, a bias that sees law developing along a linear track toward ever-expanding people's rights and sees the Court's function as simply to maintain these rights, as summarized by legal theorist Bruce Ackerman: "My second aim will be to convince lawyers and judges to adopt the regime perspective. . . . [The Court's] job is to preserve the higher law solutions reached by the People against their erosion during periods of normal politics" (Ackerman 1991, 60). Thus, this model portrays the Court's output, in each constitutional regime, as a rather simplistic affirmation of the prevailing time.

To better comprehend constitutional change, we must remain attuned to the constant expansion of federal authority. More than that, when we model constitutional change in relation to its effects on national authority and not just its effects on jurisprudential paradigm shifts, we can focus on the similarity across these constitutional moments rather than only on the differences.

Chapter 6

Comprehending Supreme Court Influence

The Framers of the Constitution built the United States on a foundation of limited government, and yet, as this book reveals, federal authority has expanded persistently throughout American history. The constitutional structure seems to have enabled, not limited, the authority of the federal government. Irrespective of ideology or era, the Supreme Court's rulings have steadily and persistently strengthened and consolidated the central state. The Court has expanded federal authority both by invalidating state-level regulations (such as abortion regulations) and by validating federal-level rules (such as the Affordable Care Act). Whether the problems facing the nation pertained to national-state relations issues over slavery, business-government relationships dealing with workplace and corporate regulation, or individual-government relations over issues of equality, the Court's—and the country's—answer has trended in one direction: toward more federal authority, more government. This is the unifying theme across every period of American constitutional development, both at critical junctures and during normal, noncritical periods. Indeed, in asking the questions that animate this book—how has the Court affected central state authority over time, and when and in what areas has the Court facilitated or restricted the federal government?—I deliberately avoided looking solely at critical junctures; instead, I systematically surveyed the entire arc of American constitutional development without imposing on it contemporary biases about which constitutional decisions are most worthy of study. By applying a common interpretive framework to the Court's decisions across time, I traced the Supreme Court's relationship to federal authority from the Founding to the modern day.

In this book, "development" describes the effect of constitutional decisions on federal authority, regardless of whether these decisions constrained or advanced a particular kind of state—the social-welfare or European-style central state.[1] This definition of state-building is based partially on the work of the anti-Federalist Brutus, who might have been the most prescient Founding-era statesman of all:[2] he wrote that the Supreme Court would "lean strongly in favour of the general government," and that it would interpret the Constitution so as to "favour an extension of its jurisdiction."[3] Brutus warned that because the Constitution contained "general and indefinite terms" and the high court is "authorized to explain the constitution," the Court would "extend the powers of the general government as much as possible."[4] Though it is not the traditional way to understand "state-building," seeing centralization of decision-making as a form of state development, as Brutus did, enables this book to trace the steady growth of federal authority as witnessed through Supreme Court decisions. This broad definition of state-building takes into account the fact that the American state is a legal entity. While not every aspect of state development has a significant legal component, much is lost when scholars view law and courts only as limiting and checking the broader political system. As this book shows, the legal branch actively contributes to the growth of the federal state.

This chapter summarizes the book's core findings, then discusses those findings' implications for constitutional development; finally, it explores some possible reasons for the persistence of central state expansion across American history.

Patterns of Development

In this book, I have coded hundreds of decisions according to three criteria: which of the seven dimensions of the central state they engage, which of fifteen constitutional issues they center on, and what effect each decision has on federal authority. By doing so, I have shown the persistent, expansive impact of the Court's decisions on the American state. My analyses of these decisions show that the Supreme Court, as a branch of the national government, has supported the development and expansion of national governmental power about twice as often as not; it has supported this expansion incrementally across periods and across almost every legal issue area and dimension of state authority.

Patterns in the data offer more information about the Supreme Court's role in expanding the central state.[5] The data indicate that while the Court's decisions tend to support national state expansion more often than they restrict federal government authority, the ratio between expansion and restriction of federal authority has remained relatively stable since around 1900; the Court's role in the story of American state development has been remarkably steady and consistent.

Based on the data, I reached four specific conclusions. (1) The Supreme Court, as an instrument of the national government, has been a powerful driver of the development of central state authority. (2) Consequently, the growth of central state authority has entrenched both liberal and conservative (in the American sense) uses of state power. (3) The growth of the central state has been gradual, expanding not at critical junctures but through accretion over time; it has also been uneven, expanding more in certain constitutional issue areas than in others. (4) Central state authority, at least where the Court's construction of it is concerned, began to grow in the United States long before the twentieth century. In sum, I find that, regardless of the historical era or the Court's ideology, it has persistently expanded federal authority across every constitutional issue area except judicial power.

Even early in its history, the American state gained strength through the Court's decisions. The constitutional design laid out by the Founders facilitated a judiciary that would largely support federal supremacy and thus tend toward national government expansion. In addition to this, two particular attributes of the Constitution—dual sovereignty and the Commerce Clause—created an inherent tension between the federal and state-level governments, and these tensions forced the Supreme Court to clarify the boundaries between federal and state power. The Constitution's design thus structured constitutional debates over central state power—debates that persisted during the emergence of the modern central state in the late nineteenth century and into the present day. The ambiguity inherent in the design of the federalist system—the lack of clear boundaries between the sets of powers allotted to the federal state and the constituent states—help to explain why the Court's constitutional development expanded federal state authority more often than it restricted that authority. For all their differences, both the Marshall and the Taney Courts attempted to reconcile the conflicts between federal and state governments while attending to the health of the nation; if the Court had not regularly resolved conflicts in favor of the federal government, the growth of the central state would have been constrained, weakening the United States as a nation. Although it would not reach its full strength until after the New Deal, the central state consistently grew in size and strength even before the Civil War: the Marshall Court laid the groundwork for continuing constitutional expansion.

The power the Court began to wield after the Civil War continued to lay the foundations of the modern state. From 1865 to 1932, the national state faced the recurring problem of how to reduce state autonomy, and conflicts over competing models of federalism were therefore paramount during this time; decisions on constitutional issues of individual rights and economic activity dominated the Court's business. In individual-rights cases, the Court's decisions advanced federal authority over civil rights and criminal procedure. In economic activity cases, the Court slightly restricted federal authority. However, the overall balance between expansion and restriction masks the striking disparity between these two issue areas, as the Court attempted to navigate new changes wrought by the Fourteenth Amendment and what it meant for supervising constituent states, citizenship rights, and corporate power. During this period, the Court expanded the power of the national government over the individual states; for example, the Court established in the *Lochner* decision that the federal government would supervise and scrutinize states' economic policies closely. While the Court's expansion of federal authority originally served to impede progressive, welfare-state causes, this centralized authority would eventually enable the prodigious expansion of the federal state for progressive aims; the Court's decisions were a necessary (but presumably unintended) precondition for the later development of the national welfare state.

The Court's constitutional output from 1933 to 1997, which laid the foundations for and contributed to the rise of the modern regulatory and administrative state, demonstrates how important it is to take seriously the work that the Supreme Court does in between critical junctures—the generally recognized watershed cases and moments of constitutional development. This book shows the continuity in the federal state's advancement both before and after the 1937 "switch in time"—a pattern that persists through post–New Deal era historical periods[6] and continues today. This book thus challenges the "constitutional moment" theory of change. During this entire 1933–1997 period, which saw the slow incorporation of the Bill of Rights, the Court used judicial review to greatly restrict constituent state autonomy and expand federal supervisory power. This expansion of the federal state's authority was continuous, even during eras known for the restriction of federal authority. Only the purpose to which the Court extended federal state power changed: the increased federal supervisory power has been used to advance both progressive and conservative causes. Examining the Court's decisions across the entirety of US constitutional development thus shows that from the beginning, as Brutus predicted, the Court has been a reliable and consistent collaborator in national state expansion.

Taken as a whole, this book reveals two important truths about how the Supreme Court influences American state development. First, the Court expanded the American state steadily, a finding that contrasts with the constitutional moment theory propounded by some in the American constitutional development school. For example, in Bruce Ackerman's (1991, 1998, 2014) three-volume *We the People*, "normal politics" are distinguished from "constitutional politics." Ackerman views "normal politics" as the day-to-day operations of the political system in which elected representatives make decisions for the People—a condition that political scientists might call equilibrium. Ackerman sees "constitutional politics" as occurring when the People become so engaged with political issues that they achieve a "constitutional moment."[7] Ackerman argues that only three of these "constitutional moments" have occurred, each during one of the three epochal "constitutional regimes" in US history: the Founding, the Civil War and Reconstruction, and the New Deal (1991, 59). During the long periods of normal politics, Ackerman sees the Court's role as "preservationist" (1991, 10). In views such as Ackerman's, during normal politics, the Court exerts a negative power on legal development; its primary duty is to protect the "hard-won principles" delineated by the People during a constitutional moment. However, I find no great differences among these three watershed moments of constitutional change and the periods of "normal politics" between them—at least in terms of the rate at which the central state grew in authority.[8] The Court's disposition toward federal state authority remained quite similar before, during, and after these constitutional moments, a finding that problematizes theories of constitutional change that rest on the notion of critical junctures.[9]

Second, this book found that the Court—through time and regardless of its ideological composition—has persistently acted as an important instrument of the broader central state, expanding federal authority over society. This finding supports the claim that judicial systems tend to expand national governing authority—a claim that begins with Brutus's suspicion that the federal judiciary would usurp state rights by continually expanding the powers of the national government, and that present-day scholarship continues to promulgate.[10] For example, comparative judicial scholars such as Martin Shapiro have detailed how judicial systems outside the US extended national state power to facilitate control of conquered territories (Shapiro 1981, 22–23), and historical institutionalists studying the United States have similarly found that federal courts enhance the power of the dominant regime (Gillman 2002; Whittington 2005). I buttress these literatures by showing the Court's tendency to expand central state power (its own power and the power of the coordinate branches) over that of state governments on economic and individual rights issues.

This book also revealed important patterns in when and in what areas the Court has facilitated American state expansion. To be precise, it did so most rapidly during the Early Republic, a finding that dovetails with historical accounts of the importance of the Marshall Court (Newmyer 1986; White 1988). Despite the common perception that the Court stymied central state authority most frequently during the *Lochner* era, it actually restricted federal authority most often between 1825 and 1849, a period that encompasses the end of Marshall's tenure and most of Chief Justice Taney's. Even during this most-restrictive period, however, the Court tended to expand national authority more often than it restricted it.

The Court most regularly interacts with the centralization dimension[11] of federal authority, removing authority from constituent states and lodging authority upward in the federal government. State-level laws are the ones most often before the Court, and the invalidation of state laws is the most frequent method by which the Court enhances federal state power; the judiciary is the national branch most often responsible for extending central state control into the periphery. Therefore, both the judiciary as an institution and judicial power should be treated as endogenous to models of central state development. This centralization tendency of the Court is in part a function of its institutional features, such as life tenure, which insulates it from popular control, and the norm of maintaining precedent. The Court's persistent expansion of the centralization dimension results from a federal constitutional design that makes political conflict between federal and constituent-states inevitable, conflicts that courts have to mediate (W. Wilson 1908, 173; Robertson 2012). However, I identified one important legal issue area in which the Court tends to inhibit central state expansion: questions of the Court's own jurisdiction. The Court was more likely to expand the central state when the case involved questions about the powers of the other two branches of government; it was less likely to expand the central state through jurisdictional questions that would increase its own power directly.

Redefining Federal–State Authority

At the foundation of this book's argument that the Court is an agent of central state development rests a conceptual intervention. Scholars working in the Hegelian and Weberian traditions have tended (at least tacitly) to assume that development means movement toward a European-style welfare state. This tendency has caused some to understand the courts as an obstacle to development, because it sometimes stymied Progressive era causes (Berk 1994; Hattam 1993; Orren 1991; Bensel 2000). This book argues that development means simply the expansion of federal authority irrespective of the goals of that authority, a definition that would reduce our tendency to measure development via European-welfare metrics and would therefore allow us to see the central role judicial power plays in the development of the American state.

Summarizing the prevailing perspective, Whittington notes that "The most notable feature of courts was their ability to obstruct. . . . Given a status quo ante of a limited state, judges operated to disempower state actors and preserve private interests" (Whittington 2016, 318). Recent scholarship along two separate lines of research has, however, challenged this traditional assumption, and this book bridges these two new schools of thought. First, "new state" scholars like Brian Balogh (2009), Max Edling (2003), and Mettler (2011) have found strength in "hidden" or "submerged" places in the American state. These scholars write against the idea that the United States lacks a strong central state; they say that the central state, which is perhaps less noticeable to the untrained eye, nevertheless thrives in the United States. Second, law and courts scholars have emphasized the positive capacity of courts—a position that underscores central state strength. Some law and courts scholars see the primary role of the Court as validating the actions of the dominant national political coalition (Dahl 1957; Shapiro 1964; Adamany 1980; Lasser 1985). Others have recognized that the courts' power of judicial review is desirable to elected officials, who can let the courts decide politically contentious questions by validating or invalidating laws rather than making potentially unpopular decisions themselves (Graber 1993; Whittington 2005, 2007). Political leaders may also find the courts useful in entrenching their ideas in legal doctrine (Pickerill and Clayton 2004; McMahon 2011; Gillman 2002). In these ways, then, law and courts scholars have recognized courts as an ally to other branches of government. However, law and courts scholars have not explicitly endorsed the "new state" scholars' contention that the American central state possesses considerable strength. This book, by showing persistent central state growth vis-à-vis the judiciary, merges these two literatures; it also casts new light on the court power literature, which argues that the courts "can almost never be effective producers of significant social reform" (Rosenberg 2008, 422).

Ultimately, this book revises our understanding of the American state and constitutional development in three ways. First, it shows that the pre–Civil War American central state was already growing in strength, gained through the Court's tendency to expand federal authority over states and over the citizenry.[12] Second, it shows that the Court did much to expand federal authority during the emergence of the modern state, during the period from 1865 to 1932. Third, it shows that the development of federal power is more continuous than constitutional moment theory allows.

The framework of central state authority described in this book changes how we define and conceptualize the central state and how we view the strength of the American state. Until now, scholars have defined state development in terms of the accretion of social welfare rights and the concomitant ability of the federal government to provide and protect these positive rights. Scholars have seen US citizens as deeply suspicious of government in comparison to

Western Europeans, and have categorized the United States as more devoted to protecting private property than to building a welfare state (Hartz 1955). Similarly, followers of the American Political Development (APD) movement partly inspired by the work of Hartz have tended to see the United States as comparatively weak and stateless. This claim pivots on the distinction between negative rights (things that the government cannot do) and positive rights (things that the government must do); most public officials see the American federal constitution as, in the words of Judge Richard Posner, "a charter of negative rather than positive liberties" (Posner, quoted in Zackin 2010, 15).[13] While this book offers no measure of the absolute strength or weakness of the central state, it has shown that the Court has consistently and steadily bolstered the federal government's authority. This fact encourages us to reconsider arguments about the weakness of the central state in the United States and to recognize the very real and consistent affirmation the federal government has received from the Supreme Court.

Revisionist scholars such as Balogh (2009) have also argued for the strength of the early American state. According to Balogh, the early American state provided social goods primarily through state and local intermediaries.[14] Balogh thus dispels a belief held by both progressives and conservatives: that "the national government only began to exercise significant influence over the lives of most Americans in the early twentieth century" (Balogh 2009, 8). But Balogh and other revisionist scholars (John 1997; Adler 2012; Novak 2002; Zackin 2010) still define state capacity using the same terms as the scholars whose accounts they oppose—the delivery of welfare state goods and positive rights through an autonomous bureaucracy. Not even these revisionist accounts deny that, on balance, "the Supreme Court has adopted an almost exclusively negative reading of the federal Constitution, consistently expressing the view that its purpose is to limit the government's scope and restrain its actions" (Zackin 2010, 34).

There is something unsatisfying about the way the current debate over "strong" and "weak" central states is framed. Just as older conceptions of the central state led scholars to look primarily at the development of individual rights rather than the development of central state powers, the current debate discourage scholars from studying the US central state before the Progressive era, because they define the central state in terms of its social-welfare provisions rather than in terms of pure aggrandizement of centralized authority.

Moreover, this book complicates these prevailing depictions of the Constitution and the state, conceptualizing the central state as an entity that has been in development since the Founding and thus moving us away from the negative-versus-positive rights distinction. In fact, in the terms of this book's argument, positive expansions of the federal government often do not include the federal government's capacity to provide, deliver, or guarantee social welfare goods. Instead, this book defines expansion of national government power far more broadly: any new power of the federal government that the Court has sustained represents an expansion of national government power. Whether the federal government uses this authority to deliver welfare state goods or some other form of governance is a question entirely separate from the development of state authority. This agnostic analysis, which is less concerned with identifying when, precisely, the modern state emerged and which rejects a welfare-centered understanding of the state, shows that the Court has, from the beginning, done much to develop the federal government.

This work also has important implications for understanding constitutional changes and evolution. As noted above, scholars of constitutional development usually explain state development by focusing on watershed moments of history. However, this book has shown that federal authority expands at roughly the same rate on either side of these watershed moments, underscoring the continuity in state development over time. The Court advanced federal authority 61% of the time, and it never strayed far from this average. Even during the slowest periods of state-building, the Court's decisions expanded governmental power more than half the time. Some periods of supposed restriction (e.g., the Republican Era, 1877–1932) were actually periods of significant expansions of state power; other periods known as periods of expansion, such as the New Deal Era (1933–1968), do not far exceed the mean rate of federal state expansion. The percentage of cases that this book has identified as expanding state authority also shows us that constitutional interpretation has not changed much over time; the interpretation of the federal government's specific powers has changed immensely, but the overall effect on the growth of the central state has not.

If the Court's constitutional interpretation has actually expanded national authority at a relatively stable rate, then why have studies of constitutional development focused on particular moments? Perhaps because these studies often center less on state power and more on constitutional law's effect on the rights afforded to citizens (Ackerman 1991, 1998; Zackin 2013; Brandwein 2011). So while political scientists have "brought the state back in" to studies of political institutions, they have not yet attended to how the Supreme Court shapes the state across the sweep of constitutional development.

Reasons for Central State Expansion

My purpose in demonstrating the Supreme Court's overwhelming tendency to expand the central state has been twofold: to reveal the empirical reality of this tendency and to examine its patterns. It remains to be seen, however, why this institutional tendency exists. While that question is beyond the scope and data of this book, I mention here some theoretical explanations from court and APD literature that dovetail with this book's findings. Future research should examine the causes of the Court's tendency to expand central state power.

The patterns this book presents could fit within current political science models of judicial decision-making, particularly the attitudinal model (Segal and Spaeth 1993) and the governing regime model (Dahl 1957; Whittington 2007). But neither of these models provides a fully satisfactory explanation for the Court's behavior. The attitudinal model explains judicial decisions based on a justice's ideological preferences, and ideology does not fully explain the patterns I have presented here; both liberal and conservative decisions expand central state authority, although conservative decisions do so at a slower rate.[15] At best, then, ideology can only partially explain these findings. Similarly, the regime model is only partially explanatory. This model, which posits that the national governing coalition dictates judicial outcomes, holds that the Court will behave in a particular way depending on who occupies the presidency (Whittington 2007). Within this model, the Court maintains the dominant governing coalition's agenda: the Court is expected to follow the preferences of a president affiliated with the dominant collation but to resist the preferences of a reconstructive or preemptive president, the kind that ushers in a new governing regime and era. If this theory were perfectly explanatory, we would expect the data to show Court resistance to federal state authority under reconstructive presidents such as Lincoln and Jackson, but this is not the case. The regime model works to explain highly visible decisions such as *Brown v. Board of Education* (1954) where the president has a known stance, but it does not explain more obscure jurisdiction cases in which the president does not have a position—cases that comprise a large proportion of the data. Although these cases are less well known,[16] these decisions have an important effect on central state authority. Neither regime nor ideology theory fully explain the constancy of expansion of central state power, suggesting that other forces are at work. What, then, might drive persistent central state expansion? According to the literature on the Supreme Court, two interrelated factors drive central state authority: constitutional/institutional design and law.

Institutional/Constitutional Design

This explanation argues that the Supreme Court (and the rest of the central state) grew in strength over time because of constitutional design. This argument was first made in the early republic, in the debate between Brutus and Hamilton; we also see it in the contemporary work of Martin Shapiro (1981) and in Max Edling's (2003) more recent scholarship on the Founding. Edling argues that the Constitution contained the basis for an expanded American state with powers similar to those of European states: the Framers were not trying to write a Constitution so that the central state would be weak.

While the traditional story of Madisonian federalism argues that the Constitution was designed to limit government and protect the rights and liberties of the American people, other Federalists, especially Hamilton, developed "a conceptual framework that made it possible to accommodate the creation of a powerful national government to the strong antistatist current in the American political tradition" (Edling 2003, 219). Essentially, the constitutional Framers laid the foundation for the institutional expansion of the federal branches. Among the Founders, Hamilton was the "premier state-builder in a generation of state-builders" (Kramnick 1987, 67), and his zeal for a strong central state was most clearly expressed in his writings on the American presidency, which, for Hamilton, was at the heart of the new American state (Kramnick 1987, 70). Hamilton's desire for an expansion of central state authority aimed at garnering for America the grandeur and the glory that history accords to empire. In *Federalist* 11, he discussed "what this country can become" and predicted glories for America of a "striking and animating kind." He wrote, "Under a vigorous national government, the natural strength and resources of the country, directed to a common interest, would baffle all the combinations of European jealousy to restrain our growth" (*Federalist* No. 11). Hamilton here expresses the fervor for a strong central government that he and many of his fellow Founders shared and built into the Constitution's design of the branches of government.

The Constitution itself reflects the divide between Madison and Hamilton's differing conceptions of central state power, leaving many ambiguities for the Court to resolve. In particular, the Founders' establishment of federal and state sovereigns left unanswered many questions of political authority that the Court had to later address.[17] But the fact that the Court needed to adjudicate these questions does not explain why it often decided in favor of the federal government when doing so.

Two institutional reasons may explain why the Court often sides with the federal branches, expanding central state authority. First, the design of the federal political system, typified by the interdependence among the branches, encourages expansion.[18] Indeed, the Court has never been "truly independent" of the other national branches of government (Pickerill 2011, 106); some have argued that judicial independence is impossible under any system of government (Peretti 1999, 103), and others have shown that politicians influence and manipulate the structure of the federal judiciary to entrench their policy and ideological preferences (Crowe 2007; Gillman 2002). This interdependence has been in existence since the Founding of the nation; the Constitutional

Convention of 1787 created a national government with interdependent, cooperating, comprising, and sometimes conflicting branches (Pickerill 2011, 109). Viewing the judiciary as an obstacle to state development misses the more intricate ways that the federal branches interact with each other.

Second, the Court may tend to confirm and centralize the power of the federal state because it fears reprisal from the other branches if its rulings deviate too far from Congress's or the president's preferences (Eskridge 1991; Harvey and Friedman 2006; Edwards 2006).[19] Aware of its relative fragility among the national branches, the Court behaves in ways that protect its authority, because it remains vulnerable to political retaliation, and it needs the federal branches to help enforce its decisions (Ferejohn 1999).[20] Public officials have often threatened to curb the Court's power by constitutional amendment, statute, impeachment, jurisdiction stripping, or the freezing of judicial salaries (Epstein and Knight 1998; Pickerill and Clayton 2004, 236; Clayton and Pickerill 2006, 1392; Rosen 2006, 7).[21] To be sure, Congress does not often deploy these methods, but the mere threat of them alters judicial behavior (Clark 2009; Ferejohn et al. 2006, 167).[22] This encourages the judiciary to side with the federal government and increases its tendency to expand federal authority.

Law

The second factor that drives constitutional development via the Court is the law:[23] simply put, the Court uses legal reasoning and logic to reach its decisions. Howard Gillman's (1993) *Constitution Besieged* demonstrates the importance of law and precedent to constitutional development. Gillman recognizes, as I do, that reading Supreme Court jurisprudence through a Weberian Progressive lens can impede a full understanding of constitutional development. He finds that the decisions of the *Lochner* era were not the product of "Neanderthal justices" advancing their preferences for laissez-faire constitutionalism but "a principled effort" to uphold a legal distinction that long predated the *Lochner* era. During this era, according to Gillman, substantive due process reflected "an overarching set of well-established legal doctrines and principles governing the legitimate exercise of police powers" that were established long before laissez-faire ideologies became dominant among America's legal and political elites (1993, 177).

Judicial opinions and the contestation over constitutional ideas are similarly placed as drivers of constitutional development in Tom Keck's (2004) study of the conservative justices from the 1970s to 1990s. Keck recognizes that the conservative justices of the Reagan era grounded their judicial behavior in legal practices inherited from the liberal Warren Court. Modern conservative justices practiced the same type of judicial activism that the Warren Court had embodied in the decades prior. In accordance with the findings in this book, Keck describes the Court's advancement of central state authority as acting in service of both progressive and conservative aims.

According to legal explanations, then, the Court limits or expands central state authority where Constitution and precedents dictate that it should, suggesting reasons for the patterns unearthed in this book. And as both legal historical and American political development scholarship have shown,[24] the Court's interpretation and precedent of constitutional clauses have enabled the expansion of some parts of the central state (e.g., the Commerce Clause) and have prohibited the expansion of other parts (e.g., judicial power). For example, as Paul Frymer (2008) has shown, the Court helped build and expand the state's authority in the realm of labor law: "Judges, lawyers, administrators, as well as the rules and procedures that define and influence their actions were absolutely vital to integrating labor unions during the latter stages of the twentieth century" (Frymer 2008, 75). And this book's findings similarly indicate that some areas of the law—particularly civil rights and the First Amendment—acted as a primary channel for central state expansion. Although the Founders built the American republic on limited government, and although the American people fear centralized government, this book has shown that the reality of constitutional development in the United States has always been the gradual accretion of central state authority.

Conclusion

Whatever the precise causes that drive central state expansion, the findings presented in this book suggest that the pattern of slow accretion of authority to the central federal state via Court decisions will continue. But what does this mean for American politics? Currently, a deep divide exists between those who want the Court to limit central state authority and those who want the Court to expand it. The vociferous disagreements over recent Court decisions exemplify this division: in 2012, for example, the court expanded central state authority in its decision in *National Federation of Independent Businesses v. Sebelius* (2012), which upheld the individual mandate provision of the Affordable Care Act[25] (Somin 2017, 480). In the same year, the court restricted central state authority in its decision in *Shelby County v. Holder* (2013), invalidating Section 4 of the Voting Rights Act, which had protected against racial dis-crimination in voting.[26] With these decisions (as with all of the decisions that preceded them since the Court's founding), the Court advanced progressive and conservative causes.

This divide also relates to issues in constitutional theory and interpretation (Somin 2017, 480-81). Typically, conservative jurists such as the late Justice Antonin Scalia and Justice Clarence Thomas subscribe to an "original meaning" constitutional philosophy, which they believe tends to limit federal power by enabling the Court to enforce limits on the central state—in this view, the purpose of the Supreme Court is as the Founders designed it. By contrast, liberal justices like Justice Stephen Breyer tend to support a "living Constitution" theory, which argues that the Constitution should be interpreted with contemporary needs and issues in mind—an interpretational philosophy that they believe often requires the Court to expand central state authority. Still, these differing interpretational philosophies do not always run along political party lines, because people generally do not object to the expansion of central state authority if it benefits them in a particular situation. For example, in recent decades, conservatives have advocated for the Court to overrule state-level laws that affect issues like property rights and the rights of gun owners—rulings that would, as this book has shown, expand the power of the central state (Somin 2017, 480–81). Both liberals and conservatives, regardless of their rhetoric, seek to advance their ideological agendas, and the Court is often an effective way for them to do so. In the last twenty-five years, while there has been a modest uptick in the Court's penchant to restrict federal power, the role the Court has played in constitutional development across the history of the United States suggests that this is a temporary blip, and that over time, the Supreme Court will continue to extend and consolidate the power of the federal state.

Appendix 1

Coding Decisions

Introduction

This appendix outlines the coding for the variables for each judicial decision. There are three key variables of interest for each judicial decision in this book:

1. "Effect on Central State Dimensions" with three outcomes: expand, restrict, or not affected

2. "Constitutional Issue Areas" with fifteen outcomes (outlined below)

3. "Effect on Federal Authority" with three outcomes: expand, restrict, or neutral

Seven variables comprise the seven dimensions of the central state ("central state" and "federal government" are interchangeable terms) that the Court might possibly expand or restrict in any judicial decision. These variables are outlined below. Additionally, below I provide four sample cases to illustrate how I interpreted each decision for its effect on federal authority—one expanded, two restricted, and one that did not alter central state authority.

General Coding Rules

The Court is tasked with reviewing laws by a legislative body. These laws typically come from the federal level or the state level. Different coding outcomes pertain to the level of legislature that created the law (see Figure A.1):

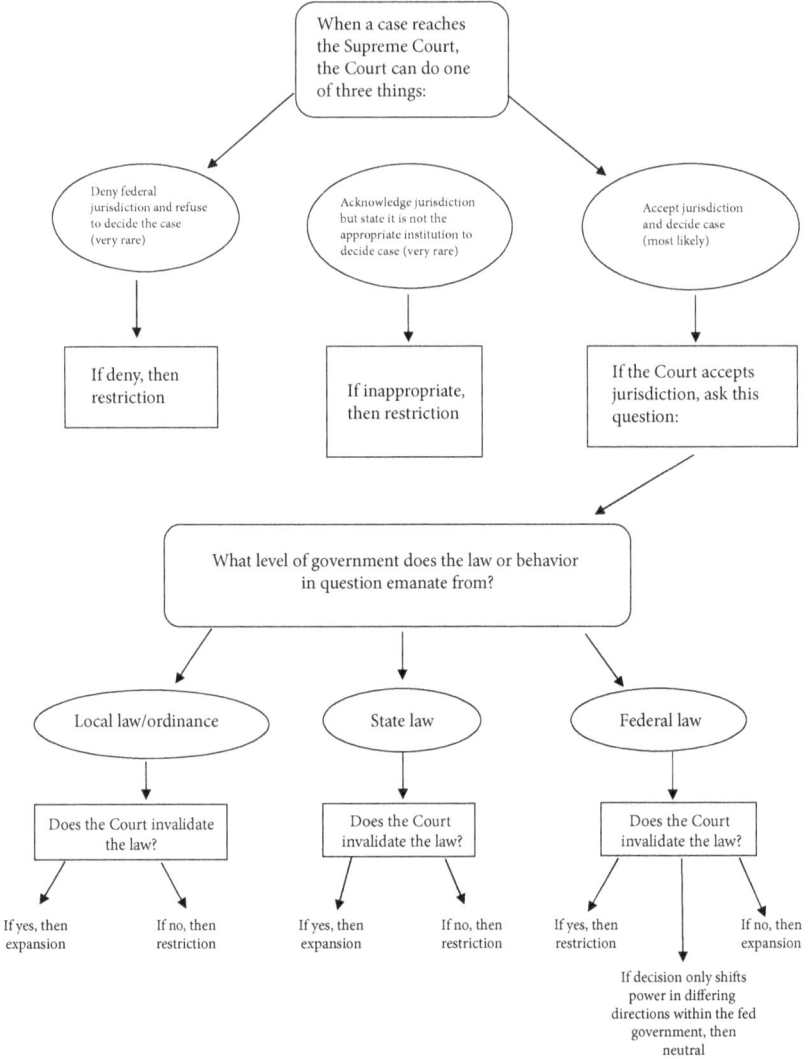

Figure A.1. Coding Process Flow Chart

When state and local-level laws/actions are reviewed by the Supreme Court:

1. If a Supreme Court decisions invalidates/overturns *any* law or action of a local *or* state-level government, then this is an expansion of federal authority.

2. If a Supreme Court decision upholds/sustains *any* law or action of local *or* state-level governments, then this is restriction of

federal authority (because the Court says a federal constitutional right does not apply to the state action).

When federal-level laws/actions are before the Supreme Court:

3. If the Supreme Court invalidates a federal law or action, then the decision restricts federal authority.

4. If the Supreme Court upholds/sustains a federal law or action, then this decision expands federal authority.

Coding for Effect on Seven Dimensions of Central State Authority

Seven dimensions comprise the entire federal government. A judicial decision could expand or restrict any one (or, theoretically, all) of these dimensions in a given case. These dimensions have the same outcome as the Effect on Federal Authority variable: expand/restrict/neutral. This variable is simply trying to uncover more information: which dimension does the Court typically expand/restrict over time?

1. Centralization of Authority. Measures involving the transfer of decision-making authority from subordinate governments and the citizenry to the central state; in the case of individual citizens, such measures do not involve a substantive expansion of central state activity, but only the allocation of influence and control over that activity. In the case of subordinate governments, such measures include the review of subordinate government decisions by central state institutions and the form of subordinate government participation in central state decision-making.

   • When decision-making power/authority is vested in the federal government and *not* in lower levels of government (states, municipalities—that is, "subordinate governments"), this is an expansion of central state authority = "1." Any decision that concentrates decision making in various branches of the federal government is an expansion of central state authority.

   Some of the following will signal that this dimension was considered by the Court:

   a. Discussion of an individual state law infringing on the power of Congress or infringing on a person.

b. Discussion of national unity, uniformity, paramount authority, or sustaining federal power—all of these are possible indications of an affirmation and expansion of central state authority.

c. Discussion of the "justiciability" or jurisdiction of a case—in other words, does the Supreme Court have the right to hear the case?

d. Any reference to "revising power," "review," or "violation of."

2. Administrative Capacity. Measures involving a broadening or narrowing of bureaucratic discretion and long-term planning capacity within the central state; these measures affect only institutions within the central state itself; in analyzing policy, reference is made to a hierarchy based on relative insulation from societal or outside political influence.

- This dimension is about locating decision-making authority among the national branches (and the bureaucracy). An expansion of central state authority occurs when a Court decision further insulates decision-making authority from societal influence. The federal branches, from least insulated to most insulated: Congress → President → Courts → Bureaucracy. Taking decision-making, for example, from Congress and giving it to the president is an expansion, while taking decision-making from bureaucracy and giving it to Congress is a restriction.

- When the Court sustains the federal administrative/bureaucratic authority (that is, the power to administer and execute procedure and rules), the decision expands central state authority = "1." A decision that affirms the creation of an agency or any other administrative structure design of the central state is an expansion of authority.

Indications that this dimension is implicated in a decision:

a. Discussion of commissions, agencies; validation of a federal commission's findings may indicate that administrative capacity is implicated.

b. Administrative procedure or procedural rules; any decision that pertains to allocating authority between *federal* branches of government and possibly insulating decisions from the more political branches of government (e.g., Congress).

   c. Discussion of the interior design of the state—who gets to make decisions over procedural questions.

3. Citizenship. Measures involving the religious practices, political beliefs, ethnic identity, and rights and duties of citizens in their relations with the state; this category excludes measures affecting property but includes all measures concerning the physical movement and labor of citizens (such as conscription).

- When the Court sustains the federal government's authority/power to control civil liberties or rights—either to curtail or provide further rights[1]—this decision expands central authority = "1."

- When the Court strikes the federal government's authority/power to control civil liberties or rights—either to curtail or provide further rights—this decision restricts central authority = "−1."

- When the Court strikes down state-level laws/power (often through the Fourteenth Amendment) that either curtail or provide further civil rights/liberties, this decision expands central authority = "1."

- When the Court sustains state-level laws/power (brought to the Court often via the Fourteenth Amendment), this decision is a restriction = "−1."

Indications that this dimension is implicated in a decision:

   a. Discussion of a person's individual rights with respect to federal and state government authority.

   b. Discussion of a person's right to "standing" to assert claims in a federal and state court.

4. Control of Property. Measures involving the control or use of property by individuals or institutions other than the central state itself, including expropriation, regulation of the marketplace, and labor contracts between private parties.

- When the Court upholds federal authority to use and own property, this is an expansion of the central state.

- When the Court upholds federal authority regulate private contracts involving property and the use of property (including, for example, environmental regulations).

  Indications that this dimension is implicated in a decision:

  a. Discussion of contracts, infrastructure, land use, property (even intangible property such as stocks and bonds), and so forth.

  b. Discussion of federal government regulation of private economic activity and marketplace relations.

5. Creation of Client Groups. Measures that increase the dependence of groups within society on the continued existence and viability of the central state; includes only measures that provide income or income substitutes to individuals (pensions, employment by central state institutions, welfare, and price-control programs for specific groups in society), that establish future-oriented obligations that depend on state viability (the issuance of long-term debt), and that control the value of the currency (the gold standard and redemption of paper money).

   - When the Court validates federal programs, statutes, and/or agencies that ensure the viability of the groups that depend on these parts of the federal government, this is an expansion of central state authority.

     Indications that this dimension is implicated in a decision:

   - Discussion of (1) pension and welfare systems, (2) salaries from government employment, (3) income substitutes (such as price controls on commodities sold to targeted groups), and (4) currency and federal debt.

6. Extraction. The coercive extraction of material resources from society into the central state apparatus; extraction measures skim wealth and resources from the flow of commerce and marketplace transaction without significantly redirecting or influence the volume of these transactions (unlike otherwise similar measures falling under the property, client-group, or world system dimensions); primarily forms of light taxation or manipulations of the financial system such as gradual inflation of the currency.

- When the Court enables the federal government to skim resources from citizens, businesses, and other aspects of society, this is an expansion of central state authority.

  Indications that this dimension is implicated in a decision:

  a. Discussion of any measures that support federal government operations within society.

  b. Discussion of taxation, duty, tonnage, fees, charges, and the like.

7. The Central State in the World System. Measures concerning the relationship of the central state and nation with other states and the world economy; these include access to foreign markets (licensing, import quotas, export subsidies, and tariffs), diplomatic relations (membership in international organizations, treaties, and military conflict), immigration restrictions, and broadly conceived polices of internal development (the construction of a railroad to the Pacific Ocean, the Homestead Act, and administration of territorial possessions).

   - When the Court enables the federal government to control its relations with other central states in the international arena, this decision expands central state authority.

     Indications that this dimension is implicated in a decision:

     a. Discussion of trade relations between national and world economics (tariffs, import quotas, export subsidies).

     b. Discussion of diplomatic relations with foreign nations (treaty negotiations, military conflicts, formal international alliances).

     c. Discussion of settlement/annexing of territory, territorial expansion, or the administration of territorial possessions.

     d. Discussion of the manipulation of immigration restriction and quotas.

Coding for Constitutional Issue Areas

This variable indicates the *central* constitutional issue/subject matter of the case at hand. It is a broad variable, and although multiple issues may exist in an individual case, I followed the coding outcomes provided in Harold

Spaeth's Supreme Court Legacy Database published July 12, 2016, for decisions between 1791 and 1945, and the Modern Supreme Court Database for decisions between 1946 and 2015, published July 12, 2016. The definitions for each issue come from Spaeth's variable 35, "Issue" in the Supreme Court Database Code Book, the version published on August 17, 2015.

1. Criminal procedure encompasses the rights of persons accused of crime, except for the due process rights of prisoners. This category includes such concerns as involuntary confession, habeas corpus, plea bargaining, search and seizure, self-incrimination, contempt of court, Miranda warnings, right to counsel, cruel and unusual punishment, double jeopardy, and retroactivity (of newly announced or newly enacted constitutional or statutory rights).

2. Civil rights/liberties includes non–First Amendment freedom and noncriminal cases that pertain to classifications based on race (including American Indians), age, indigency, voting, residency, military or handicapped status, gender, and alienage.

3. First Amendment encompasses the scope of this constitutional provision, including speech and religion:

   a. First Amendment: "Congress shall make no law respecting an establishment of religion, or prohibiting the free exercise thereof; or abridging the freedom of speech, or of the press; or the right of the people peaceably to assemble, and to petition the government for a redress of grievances."

4. Due process concerns civil and criminal due process. This deals with such concerns as prisoners' and defendants' rights, government taking of property for public use (Takings Clause), the requirement to have an impartial decision maker, and due process rights as written in the Fifth and/or Fourteenth Amendments.

5. Privacy deals with noncriminal privacy, abortion, use of contraceptives/birth control, the right to die, the Freedom of Information Act, and related federal or state statutes or regulations.

6. Attorneys' or governmental officials' fees includes compensation or licensees for attorneys or government officials.

7. Unions encompasses issues involving labor union activity.

8. Economic activity is largely commercial and business-related; it includes tort actions (suing business entities) and employee actions in relation to employers.

9. Judicial power and jurisdiction concerns the exercise of the judiciary's own power. To the extent that a number of these issues concern federal-state court relationships, I include them in the federalism category. This variable pertains to the reach and scope of the judiciary's power, namely, the extent of its jurisdiction and the justiciability of the case before them.

10. Federalism pertains to conflicts and other relationships between the federal government and the states, except for those between the federal and state courts.

11. Interstate relations does not relate to interstate commerce, but includes boundary disputes between states, miscellaneous interstate conflicts, and non–real property disputes (anything that is non–real property is personal property, and personal property is anything that isn't nailed down, dug into, or built onto the land. A house is real property, but a dining room set is not).

12. Federal taxation concerns the Internal Revenue Code and related statutes and the general extraction of material resources from citizens.

13. Miscellaneous contains cases that do not fit into any other category.

14. Private law relates to disputes between private persons involving real and personal property, contracts, evidence, civil procedure, torts, wills and trusts, and commercial transactions. Prior to the passage of the Judges' Bill of 1925 much—arguably most—of the Court's cases concerned such issues. The Judges' Bill gave the Court control of its docket, as a result of which such cases have disappeared from the Court's docket in preference to litigation of more general applicability.

15. Executive power pertains to the authority of the president to execute his/her office.

Coding for Effect on Federal Authority

Below, I demonstrate my coding scheme for the overall "effect on federal
authority" variable by applying it to four cases from the data set. Chronologi-
cally, the cases are as follows:

1. *Julliard v. Greenman* (1884) 110 U.S. 421

2. *Hurtado v. California* (1884) 110 U.S. 516

3. *Monongahela Navigation v. United States* (1893) 148 U.S. 312

4. *Coyle v. Smith* (1911) 221 U.S. 559

Case 1: Juilliard v. Greenman (1884)

Expansion by affirming federal statute

Step 1: Identify the background and context of case.

Juilliard made a contract with Greenman to sell 100 bales of cotton at a price
both parties agreed on: $5,122.90. Greenman, the defendant, agreed to pay
that sum on delivery of the cotton, at which time he paid Juilliard $22.90 in
gold and silver coins and the remaining $5,100 in US currency, one note of
$5,000 and one note of $100. Juilliard demanded the $5,100 be paid in coin,
too. Greenman refused. He claimed the US paper currency provided was as
good as coin, and the notes should be taken for their respective face values
for all debts, public and private.

Step 2: Identify the central legal claims.

Juilliard claimed Greenman's payment was a breach of their original contract
because the US notes were not equivalent to gold and silver coin.

Step 3: Identify the central legal question.

Are US treasury notes a tender of lawful money in payment of Greenman's debt?

Step 4: Identify the Supreme Court's outcome.

Yes. The Court held US treasury notes were a tender of lawful money in
payment of debt because the Congressional Act of May 31, 1878, under
which the Treasury issued the notes, was constitutional. The majority opinion
argued, "The constitutional authority of Congress to provide a currency for

the whole country is now firmly established" (445). And it went on to say, "The power of making the notes of the United States a legal tender in payment of private debts, being included in the power to borrow money and to provide a national currency, is not defeated or restricted by the fact that its exercise may affect the value of private contracts. If . . . a particular power or authority appears to be vested in Congress, it is no constitutional objection to its existence, or to its exercise, that the property or the contracts of individuals may be incidentally affected" (448).

Finally, the Court concluded that issuing treasury notes for payment of private debts is "conducive and plainly adapted to the execution of the undoubted powers of Congress" and within the meaning of the Necessary and Proper Clause (450).

Step 5: Code decision for impact on federal authority.

What, if anything, does this Court case say about the central government's authority? A federal statute allowed Greenman to repay his debt, lawfully, in cash. This congressional act, the Court maintained, fell within the scope of Congress's authority under the Constitution. In validating the act, the Supreme Court affirmed (or expanded) the purview of the central state's authority, the authority in this case being the ability to make treasury notes legal tender for debt repayment. **I coded the impact on central state authority "1," an expansion of state authority**, because the Court sustained a federal statute vis-à-vis both the property and the client group dimensions.

Case 2: Hurtado v. California (1884)

Restriction by allowing a state law to stand

Step 1: Identify the background and context of case.

The State of California accused Joseph Hurtado, the defendant, of murder in the first degree. The district attorney of Sacramento County, in particular, made and filed an information against Hurtado, charging him with the murder of Jose Antonio Stuardo. Accordingly, Hurtado was arraigned and tried. After the trial, the jury found Hurtado guilty of murder in the first degree. On conviction, the Supreme Court of California sentenced Hurtado to death. However, Hurtado appealed his conviction, claiming that it was unlawful to send him to trial based solely on the information the district attorney provided; Hurtado said he first needed to appear before a grand jury (twenty-three of his peers) before California could try him for murder. He appealed to the

US Supreme Court, claiming his death sentence was void because he was not indicted by a grand jury.

Step 2: Identify the central legal claims.

Joseph Hurtado claimed he did not receive his right of due process under the State of California Penal Code, which said "When a defendant has been examined and committed, as provided in section 872 of this Code, it shall be the duty of the district attorney, within thirty days thereafter, to file in the Superior Court of the county in which the offence is triable, an information charging the defendant with such offence. The information shall be in the name of the people of the State of California, and subscribed by the district attorney, and shall be in form like an indictment for the same offence."

This section of the penal code enabled the district attorney to avoid grand jury proceedings and to charge Hurtado based solely on information. On appeal, Hurtado argued that proceeding by information only in capital cases violated his Fourteenth Amendment right to due process, claiming that the due process clause of the Fourteenth incorporated his Fifth Amendment right to a grand jury indictment in federal capital cases.

Step 3: Identify the central legal question.

Does a state trial based on information from a district attorney rather than on a grand jury proceeding violate Hurtado's Fourteenth Amendment right of due process?

Step 4: Identify the Supreme Court's outcome.

No. The Court found that because Hurtado received both counsel and a fair trial by his peers, his due process rights were upheld.

Step 5: Code decision for impact on federal authority.

What, if anything, does this Supreme Court decision say about the limits of federal authority? What questions, if any, about the authority of the federal government did the Court decide? *Hurtado* prevented the Fourteenth Amendment from affecting a state-level law. Therefore, **I code a "−1" for this case**. The case is **a restriction on central state authority** because the Court allowed the State of California's interpretation to prevail, thereby leaving power in state government hands and preventing federal authority from altering California law.[2]

Case 3: Monongahela Navigation v. United States (1893)

Neutral

Step 1: Identify the background and context of case.

A federal statute passed on August 11, 1888, authorized the secretary of war to seize a dam in Pennsylvania at a cost of no more than $161,733.13:

> The Secretary of War be, and is hereby, authorized and directed to negotiate for and purchase, at a cost not to exceed one hundred and sixty-one thousand, seven hundred and thirty-three dollars, and thirteen cents, lock and dam number seven, otherwise known as "the Upper Lock and Dam," and its appurtenances, of the Monongahela Navigation Company, a corporation organized under the laws of Pennsylvania, which lock and dam number seven and its appurtenances constitute a part of the improvements in water communication in the Monongahela River, between Pittsburgh, in the State of Pennsylvania, and a point at or near Morgantown, in the State of West Virginia. And the sum of one hundred and sixty-one thousand, seven hundred and thirty-three dollars and thirteen cents, or so much thereof as may be necessary, is hereby appropriated, out of any moneys in the Treasury.

The Monongahela Navigation Company protested that the amount Congress offered was too small, claiming that the value of the lock and dam number seven was really $209,393.52. The lower amount in the statute, the Company claimed, did not did not take into consideration the right Pennsylvania granted the company to collect tolls.

Step 2: Identify the central legal claims.

The Monongahela Navigation Company asserted that the Fifth Amendment required the government to pay the entire value of the property taken from the company, including the value of the right to collect tolls.

Step 3: Identify the central legal question.

Does the Congressional Act of August 11, 1888, violate the Navigation Company's Fifth Amendment right to just compensation? Is the Navigation Company entitled to additional monies?

Step 4: Identify the Supreme Court's outcome.

Yes. The majority opinion declared that Congress does not have the authority to determine the amount of compensation:

> By this legislation, Congress seems to have assumed the right to determine what shall be the measure of compensation. But this is a *judicial* and not a legislative question. The legislature may determine what private property is needed for public purposes— that is a question of a political and legislative character; but when the taking has been ordered, then the question of compensation is judicial. (327, emphasis added)

The Court found the taking of the Navigation Company's property unconstitutional because the central state owed more money to the Navigation Company. The Court held:

> the right of the national government, under its grant of power to regulate commerce, to condemn and appropriate this lock and dam belonging to the navigation company, is subject to the limitations imposed by the Fifth Amendment that private property shall not be taken for public uses without just compensation, that just compensation requires payment for the franchise to take tolls, as well as for the value of the tangible property, and that the assertion by Congress of its purpose to take the property does not destroy the state franchise. (345)

Step 5: Code decision for impact on federal authority.

What, if anything, does this Court case say about the central government's authority? The Court's decision restricted the authority of the central state from acquiring lock and dam number seven under the existing congressional act. The Court's decision determined that Congress and the secretary of war did not offer just compensation to the Navigation Company. Moreover, Congress, the Court held, did not have the authority to determine the amount of compensation. As a result, the Court inhibited the Congress and the secretary of war from taking the property under the original congressional act. However, **I coded this "0" because** the decision merely said that the Courts (not Congress) have the authority to determine compensation, therefore **the overall central state (as a single entity) did not lose power.** For the same reason, the decision expanded the administrative capacity dimension because it left power with the more statist branch—the Court.

Case 4: Coyle v. Smith (1911)

Restriction by invalidating federal statute

Step 1: Identify the background and context of case.

In 1910, Oklahoma enacted a law (the Oklahoma Act) moving its state capital from Guthrie to Oklahoma City. In admitting Oklahoma to the Union, the Congressional statue (the Enabling Act of 1906) declared the temporary capital to be Briscoe and stated that a change to some other location would not occur until 1913. Citizens of Oklahoma attempted to prevent the enforcement of the act. The citizens seeking to prevent enforcement of the Oklahoma Act were owners of property interests in the former location of the state capital.

Step 2: Identify the central legal claims.

According to the petitioner citizens, the act, which provided for the immediate relocation of the state capital, violated a Congressional Act, the Enabling Act of Congress of June 16, 1906, 34 Stat. 267, ch. 3335, under which Oklahoma was admitted to the union.

Step 3: Identify the central legal question.

Does Oklahoma have the power to locate its seat of government when Congress has imposed conditions limiting that location?

Step 4: Identify the Supreme Court's outcome.

Yes. The Court decided this was congressional overreaching and that a state may determine its own location for the state-level seat of government. The constitutional duty of Congress to guarantee each state a republican form of government does not give Congress the authority to impose upon a new state, as a condition of its admission to the union, restrictions that render that state unequal to the other states, such as limitations on its power to locate or change its seat of government.

Step 5: Code decision for impact on federal authority.

What, if anything, does this Supreme Court decision say about the boundaries of federal authority? The Court's decision determined that Congress did not have the authority to mandate the location of a state's capital because this decision falls within the scope of the individual state's authority. Moreover, the Constitutional guaranty of a republican form of government does not necessitate that the central state determine lower states' capitals. Therefore, **I coded this case as a restriction, "−1," on central state authority** because the Court invalidated a Congressional statute.

Appendix 2

List of Cases in the Data

Case Name	Year	Effect on Federal Authority
Hayburn's Case	1792	Restrict
Chisholm v. Georgia	1793	Expand
Ravara, United States v.,	1793	Expand
Penhallow v. Doane's Administrators	1795	Expand
Van Horne's Lessee v. Dorrance	1795	Expand
Hamilton, United States v.,	1795	Expand
Talbot v. Jansen	1795	Neutral
Hylton v. United States	1796	Expand
Ware v. Hylton	1796	Expand
Wiscart v. Dauchy	1796	Expand
Hollingsworth v. Virginia	1798	Expand
Calder v. Bull	1798	Restrict
Worrall, United States v.,	1798	Expand
Fowler v. Lindsey	1799	Restrict
Cooper v. Telfair	1800	Restrict
Marbury v. Madison	1803	Restrict
Stuart v. Laird	1803	Expand
Little v. Barreme	1804	Restrict
Hepburn v. Ellzey	1805	Restrict
Moore, United States v.,	1805	Restrict
Fisher, United States v.,	1805	Expand
Bollman, Ex parte	1807	Expand
Burr, U.S. v.,	1807	Restrict

Case Name	Year	Effect on Federal Authority
Diggs v. Wolcott	1807	Restrict
Jennings v. Carson	1807	Expand
Chappedelaine v. Dechenaux	1808	Neutral
Bank of United States v. Deveaux	1809	Restrict
Owings v. Norwood	1809	Restrict
Peters, United States v.,	1809	Expand
Brent v. Chapman	1809	Neutral
Hope Insurance Company v. Boardman	1809	Restrict
Fletcher v. Peck	1810	Expand
Durousseau v. United States	1810	Expand
New Jersey v. Wilson	1812	Expand
Hudson, United States v.,	1812	Neutral
The Exchange v. M'Faddon	1812	Restrict
Brig Aurora, The	1813	Expand
Mills v. Duryea	1813	Expand
Jones, United States v.,	1813	Neutral
Terrett v. Taylor	1815	Expand
Pawlet v. Clark	1815	Expand
De Lovio v. Boit	1815	Expand
Martin v. Hunter's Lessee	1816	Expand
Coolidge, United States v.,	1816	Neutral
New Orleans v. Winter	1816	Restrict
Chirac v. Chirac	1817	Expand
Slocum v. Mayberry	1817	Restrict
Palmer, United States v.,	1818	Restrict
Bevans, United States v.,	1818	Restrict
Hampton v. McConnell	1818	Expand
Evans v. Eaton	1818	Neutral
Gelston v. Hoyt	1818	Restrict
Robinson v. Campbell	1818	Neutral
McCulloch v. Maryland	1819	Expand
Dartmouth College v. Woodward	1819	Expand
Sturges v. Crownshield	1819	Expand
McMillan v. McNiel	1819	Expand
Houston v. Moore	1820	Restrict
Loughborough v. Blake	1820	Expand
Smith, United States v.,	1820	Expand
Wiltberger, United States v.,	1820	Restrict

Case Name	Year	Effect on Federal Authority
Cohens v. Virginia	1821	Expand
Anderson v. Dunn	1821	Expand
McClung v. Silliman	1821	Expand
Farmers and Mechanics Bank v. Smith	1821	Expand
Kearney, Ex parte	1822	Expand
Corfield v. Coryell	1823	Restrict
Green v. Biddle	1823	Expand
Johnson v. McIntosh	1823	Expand
Society for Propagation of the Gospel. v. New Haven	1823	Expand
Gibbons v. Ogden	1824	Expand
Osborn v. Bank of the United States	1824	Expand
Perez, United States v.,	1824	Expand
Wayman v. Southard	1825	Expand
Brown v. Maryland	1827	Expand
Ogden v. Saunders	1827	Restrict
Martin v. Mott	1827	Expand
Mason v. Haile	1827	Restrict
American Insurance Co. v. Canter	1828	Expand
Willson v. Black Bird Creek Marsh Co.	1829	Restrict
Weston v. Charleston	1829	Expand
Foster v. Neilson	1829	Expand
Satterlee v. Mathewson	1829	Restrict
Craig v. Missouri	1830	Expand
Providence Bank v. Billings	1830	Restrict
Cherokee Nation v. State of Georgia	1831	Restrict
Worcester v. State of Georgia	1832	Expand
Green v. Neal's Lessee	1832	Restrict
Gassies v. Ballon	1832	Expand
Boyle v. Zacharie	1832	Restrict
Barron v. Baltimore	1833	Restrict
Turner v. Maryland	1833	Restrict
Watson v. Mercer	1834	Restrict
Wheaton v. Peters	1834	Expand
Charles River Bridge v. Warren Bridge	1837	Restrict
New York, City of v. Miln	1837	Restrict
Briscoe v. Bank, etc.	1837	Restrict
Kendall v. United States	1838	Expand
Bank of Augusta v. Earle	1839	Expand

Case Name	Year	Effect on Federal Authority
Holmes v. Jennison	1840	Expand
Dobbins v. Commissioner of Erie County	1842	Expand
Prigg v. Pennsylvania	1842	Expand
Swift v. Tyson	1842	Expand
Bronson v. Kinzie	1843	Expand
McCracken v. Hayward	1844	Expand
License Cases, The	1847	Restrict
Fox v. Ohio	1847	Restrict
Waring v. Clark	1847	Expand
West River Bridge Co. v. Dix	1848	Restrict
Planter's Bank v. Sharp	1848	Expand
Luther v. Borden	1849	Restrict
Passenger Cases, The	1849	Expand
PA v. Wheeling & Belmont Bridge Co.	1850	Expand
Woodruff v. Trapnall	1850	Expand
Marigold, United States v.,	1850	Expand
Butler v. Pennsylvania	1851	Restrict
Darrington v. Bank of Alabama	1851	Expand
East Hartford v. Hartford Bridge	1851	Restrict
Genesee Chief, The	1851	Expand
Cooley v. Board of Wardens	1852	Restrict
Ferreira, United States v.,	1852	Neutral
Veazie v. Moor	1852	Restrict
Piqua Branch Bank v. Knoop	1853	Expand
Wells, Ex parte	1855	Expand
Murray v. Hoboken Land & Improvement	1856	Expand
Dred Scott v. Sandford	1857	Restrict
Ableman v. Booth	1859	Expand
Kentucky v. Dennison	1861	Restrict
Almy v. California	1861	Expand
Merryman, Ex parte	1861	Restrict
Ohio R.R. Co. v. Wheeler	1861	Restrict
Conway v. Taylor's Lessee	1862	Expand
Prize Cases	1863	Expand
Baldwin v. Hale	1863	Expand
Gelpcke v. Dubuque	1864	Expand
Vallandigham, Ex parte	1864	Restrict
Bank Tax Cases	1864	Expand

Case Name	Year	Effect on Federal Authority
Binghamton Bridge Case	1865	Expand
Holliday, United States v.,	1865	Expand
Gilman v. Philadelphia	1865	Restrict
Milligan, Ex parte	1866	Restrict
Moses Taylor, The	1866	Expand
Crandall v. Nevada	1867	Expand
Mississippi v. Johnson	1867	Expand
Garland, Ex parte	1867	Neutral
Von Hoffman v. City of Quincy	1867	Expand
Cummings v. Missouri	1867	Expand
License Tax Cases	1867	Expand
Woodruff v. Parham	1868	Restrict
Georgia v. Stanton	1868	Restrict
Pacific Insurance Co. v. Soule	1868	Expand
McCardle, Ex parte	1869	Neutral
Paul v. Virginia	1869	Restrict
Veazie Bank v. Fenno	1869	Expand
Texas v. White	1869	Expand
Dewitt, United States v.,	1869	Restrict
Thomson v. Pacific Railroad	1869	Restrict
Hepburn v. Griswold	1870	Restrict
State Tonnage Tax Case	1870	Expand
Miller v. United States	1870	Expand
Van Allen v. Assessors	1870	Expand
Collector v. Day	1871	Restrict
Daniel Ball, The	1871	Expand
Legal Tender Cases	1871	Expand
Ward v. Maryland	1871	Expand
Tarble's Case	1871	Expand
Klein, United States v.,	1871	Expand
Pumpelly v. Green Bay Co.	1871	Neutral
Slaughterhouse Cases	1873	Restrict
State Freight Tax Case	1873	Expand
Railroad Co. v. Peniston	1873	Restrict
Loan Ass'n v. City of Topeka	1874	Expand
Bartemeyer v. Iowa	1874	Restrict
Minor v. Happersett	1875	Restrict
Walker v. Sauvinet	1875	Restrict

Case Name	Year	Effect on Federal Authority
Welton v. Missouri	1876	Expand
Inman Steamship Co. v. Tinker	1876	Expand
Kohl v. United States	1876	Expand
Cruikshank, United States v.,	1876	Restrict
Sherlock v. Alling	1876	Restrict
Munn v. Illinois	1877	Restrict
Pensacola Telegraph Co. v. Western Union Telegraph Co.	1877	Expand
Railroad Co. v. Husen	1877	Expand
Terry v. Anderson	1877	Neutral
Beer Co. v. Massachusetts	1878	Restrict
Davidson v. New Orleans	1878	Restrict
Hall v. De Cuir	1878	Expand
Fertilizing Co. v. Hyde Park	1878	Restrict
Reynolds v. United States	1879	Expand
Siebold, Ex parte	1879	Expand
Trade-Mark Cases	1879	Restrict
Tennessee v. Davis	1879	Expand
Kirtland v. Hotchkiss	1879	Restrict
Missouri v. Lewis	1879	Restrict
Strauder v. West Virginia	1880	Expand
Stone v. Mississippi	1880	Restrict
Virginia, Ex parte	1880	Expand
Hauenstein v. Lynham	1880	Expand
Kilbourn v. Thompson	1881	Restrict
Lee, United States v.,	1882	Expand
Greenwood v. Freight Co.	1882	Restrict
Civil Rights Cases	1883	Restrict
Escanaba Co. v. Chicago	1883	Restrict
New Hampshire v. Louisiana	1883	Expand
Hurtado v. California	1884	Restrict
Juilliard v. Greenman	1884	Expand
Head Money Cases	1884	Expand
Yarbrough, Ex parte	1884	Expand
Hagar v. Reclamation District	1884	Restrict
Brown v. United States	1885	Expand
Barbier v. Connolly	1885	Restrict
Brown v. Houston	1885	Restrict

Case Name	Year	Effect on Federal Authority
New Orleans Gas Light Co. v. Louisiana Light Co.	1885	Restrict
Fort Leavenworth R. Co. v. Lowe	1885	Restrict
Yick Wo v. Hopkins	1886	Expand
Wabash, St. Louis & Pacific Ry. Co. v. Illinois	1886	Expand
Coe v. Town of Errol	1886	Restrict
Boyd v. United States	1886	Restrict
Morgan's Steamship Co. v. Louisiana Board of Health	1886	Restrict
Presser v. Illinois	1886	Restrict
Mugler v. Kansas	1887	Restrict
Robbins v. Shelby County Taxing Dist	1887	Expand
Arjona, United States v.,	1887	Expand
Bowman v. Chicago & N. W. R. Co.	1888	Expand
Powell v. Pennsylvania	1888	Restrict
Leloup v. Mobile	1888	Expand
California v. Central Pac. R. Co.	1888	Expand
Chae Chan Ping v. United States	1889	Expand
Leisy v. Hardin	1890	Expand
Neagle, In re	1890	Expand
Minnesota v. Barber	1890	Expand
Hans v. State of Louisiana	1890	Restrict
Jones v. United States	1890	Expand
Home Ins. Co. v. New York	1890	Restrict
Rahrer, In re	1891	Restrict
Crutcher v. Kentucky	1891	Expand
Pullman Palace Car Co. v. Pennsylvania	1891	Restrict
Garnett, In re	1891	Expand
Maine v. Grand Trunk R. Co.	1891	Restrict
Field v. Clark	1892	Expand
Texas, United States v.,	1892	Expand
Chicago etc. R. Co. v. Wellman	1892	Restrict
Rapier, In re	1892	Expand
Logan v. United States	1892	Expand
Fong Yue Ting v. United States	1893	Expand
Monongahela Navigation Co. v. U.S.	1893	Neutral
Plumley v. Massachusetts	1894	Restrict
Lawton v. Steele	1894	Restrict
Luxton v. North River Bridge Co.	1894	Expand

Case Name	Year	Effect on Federal Authority
Reagan v. Farmers' Loan & Trust Co.	1894	Expand
Debs, In re	1895	Expand
Knight Co, E.C., United States v.,	1895	Restrict
Pollock v. Farmers' Loan & Trust Co.	1895	Restrict
Plessy v. Ferguson	1896	Restrict
Wong Wing v. United States	1896	Restrict
Geer v. Connecticut	1896	Restrict
Allgeyer v. Louisiana	1897	Expand
Chicago, Burlington & Q. R. Co. v., Chicago	1897	Expand
Robertson v. Baldwin	1897	Expand
Adams Exp. Co. v. Ohio State Auditor	1897	Restrict
Bauman v. Ross	1897	Expand
Holden v. Hardy	1898	Restrict
Wong Kim Ark, United States v.,	1898	Restrict
Thompson v. Utah	1898	Expand
Blake v. McClung	1898	Expand
Hawker v. New York	1898	Restrict
Thompson v. Missouri	1898	Restrict
Patapsco Guano Co. v. N.C. Board of Agriculture	1898	Restrict
Schollenberger v. Pennsylvania	1898	Expand
Smyth v. Ames	1898	Expand
Lake Shore etc. R. Co. v. Ohio	1899	Restrict
Addyston Pipe & Steel Co. v. United States	1899	Restrict
Knowlton v. Moore	1900	Expand
Austin v. Tennessee	1900	Restrict
Maxwell v. Dow	1900	Restrict
Downes v. Bidwell	1901	Expand
Connolly v. Union Sewer Pipe	1902	Expand
Champion v. Ames	1903	Expand
McCray v. United States	1904	Expand
Northern Securities Co. v. United States	1904	Expand
Missouri etc. R. Co. v. May	1904	Restrict
Lochner v. New York	1905	Expand
Jacobson v. Massachusetts	1905	Restrict
South Carolina v. United States	1905	Expand
Ju Toy, United States v.,	1905	Expand
Rassmussen v. United States	1905	Restrict
Union Refrigerator Transit Co. v. Kentucky	1905	Expand

Case Name	Year	Effect on Federal Authority
Hale v. Henkel	1906	Expand
Kansas v. Colorado	1907	Expand
Twining v. New Jersey	1908	Restrict
Muller v. Oregon	1908	Restrict
Young, Ex parte	1908	Expand
Adair v. United States	1908	Restrict
Galveston, H & S Ry. v. Texas	1908	Expand
International Textbook Co. v. Pigg	1910	Expand
Muskrat v. United States	1911	Restrict
Noble State Bank v. Haskell	1911	Restrict
Flint v. Stone Tracy Co.	1911	Expand
Coyle v. Smith	1911	Restrict
Bailey v. Alabama	1911	Expand
Southern R. Co. v. United States	1911	Expand
Pacific States Tel. & Tel. Co. v. Oregon	1912	Restrict
Second Employers' Liability Cases	1912	Expand
McDermott v. Wisconsin	1913	Expand
Shreveport Rate Cases	1914	Expand
German Alliance Insurance Co. v. Lewis	1914	Restrict
Coppage v. Kansas	1915	Expand
Truax v. Raich	1915	Expand
Guinn v. United States	1915	Expand
Sligh v. Kirkwood	1915	Restrict
Buchanan v. Warley	1917	Expand
Bunting v. Oregon	1917	Restrict
Clark Distilling Co. v. Western Maryland R.	1917	Expand
Hammer v. Dagenhart	1918	Restrict
United States Glue Co. v. Town of Oak Creek	1918	Restrict
Schenck v. United States	1919	Expand
Abrams v. United States	1919	Expand
Doremus, United States v.,	1919	Expand
Debs v. United States	1919	Expand
Missouri v. Holland	1920	Expand
Johnson v. Maryland	1920	Expand
Dillon v. Gloss	1921	Expand
Truax v. Corrigan	1921	Expand
Bailey v. Drexel Furniture Co.	1922	Restrict
Pennsylvania Coal Co. v. Mahon	1922	Expand

Case Name	Year	Effect on Federal Authority
Stafford v. Wallace	1922	Expand
Railroad Comm. Of Wisconsin v. Chicago, B. & Q. R. Co.	1922	Expand
Lanza, United States v.,	1922	Expand
Massachusetts v. Mellon	1923	Expand
Adkins v. Children's Hospital	1923	Restrict
Meyer v. Nebraska	1923	Expand
Pennsylvania v. West Virginia	1923	Expand
Moore v. Dempsey	1923	Expand
Terrace v. Thompson	1923	Restrict
Gitlow v. New York	1925	Expand
Pierce v. Society of Sisters	1925	Expand
Grossman, Ex parte	1925	Expand
Buck v. Kuykendall	1925	Expand
Euclid, Village of v. Ambler Realty Co.	1926	Restrict
Myers v. United States	1926	Expand
Whitney v. California	1927	Restrict
Buck v. Bell	1927	Restrict
McGrain v. Daugherty	1927	Expand
Tumey v. Ohio	1927	Expand
Di Santo v. Pennsylvania	1927	Expand
Miller v. Schoene	1928	Restrict
Foster-Fountain Packing Co. v. Haydel	1928	Expand
Ribnick v. McBride	1928	Expand
Near v. Minnesota	1931	Expand
Powell v. Alabama	1932	Expand
Nashville, C. & St. L. Ry. Co. v. Wallace	1933	Restrict
Nebbia v. New York	1934	Restrict
Home Building & Loan Association v. Blaisdell	1934	Restrict
A. L. A. Schechter Poultry Corp. v. United States	1935	Restrict
Baldwin v. G. A. F. Seelig Inc.	1935	Expand
Humphrey's Executor v. United States	1935	Neutral
Norman v. Baltimore & Ohio R. Co.	1935	Expand
Butler, United States v.,	1936	Restrict
California, United States v.,	1936	Expand
Curtiss-Wright Export Corp., United States v.,	1936	Expand
Carter v. Carter Coal Co.	1936	Restrict
Ashwander v. Tennessee Valley Authority	1936	Expand

Case Name	Year	Effect on Federal Authority
NLRB v. Jones & Laughlin Steel Corp	1937	Expand
West Coast Hotel v. Parrish	1937	Restrict
Steward Machine Co. v. Davis	1937	Expand
Palko v. Connecticut	1937	Restrict
DeJonge v. Oregon	1937	Expand
Helvering v. Davis	1937	Expand
Henneford v. Silas Mason Co.	1937	Restrict
Herndon v. Lowry	1937	Expand
James v. Dravo Contracting Co.	1937	Restrict
South Carolina State Highway Dept. v. Barnwell Brothers	1938	Restrict
Carolene Products Co., United States v.,	1938	Expand
Lovell v. City of Griffin	1938	Expand
Erie R. Co. v. Tompkins	1938	Restrict
Helvering v. Gearhardt	1938	Expand
Adams Mfg. Co., J. D. v. Storen	1938	Expand
Western Live Stock v. Bureau of Revenue	1938	Restrict
Hague v. Committee for Industrial Organization	1939	Expand
Coleman v. Miller	1939	Restrict
Graves v. New York ex rel. O'Keefe	1939	Restrict
Cantwell v. Connecticut	1940	Expand
Thornhill v. Alabama	1940	Expand
McGoldrick v. Berwind-White Coal Mining Co.	1940	Restrict
Darby, United States v.,	1941	Expand
Edwards v. California	1941	Expand
Bridges v. California	1941	Expand
Classic, U.S. v.,	1941	Expand
Wickard v. Filburn	1942	Expand
Skinner v. Oklahoma ex rel. Williamson	1942	Expand
Chaplinksy v. New Hampshire	1942	Restrict
Pink, United States v.	1942	Expand
Quirin, Ex parte	1942	Expand
West Virginia State Board of Ed v. Barnette	1943	Expand
Korematsu v. United States	1944	Expand
Smith v. Allwright	1944	Expand
McLeod v. JE Dilworth Co.	1944	Expand
South-Eastern Underwriters Assn, United States v.,	1944	Expand
Yakus v. United States	1944	Expand

Case Name	Year	Effect on Federal Authority
Ballard, United States v.,	1944	Restrict
Southern Pacific Co. v. Arizona	1945	Expand
Marsh v. Alabama	1946	Expand
Lovett, United States v.,	1946	Restrict
Causby, United States v.,	1946	Restrict
Prudential Life Ins. Co. v. Benjamin	1946	Expand
Morgan v. Virginia	1946	Expand
Colegrove v. Green	1946	Restrict
New York v. United States	1946	Expand
Everson v. Board of Ed of Ewing Township	1947	Expand
Adamson v. California	1947	Restrict
United Pub Workers of America v. Mitchell	1947	Expand
Shelley v. Kraemer	1948	Expand
McCollum v. Board of Education	1948	Expand
Toomer v. Witsell	1948	Expand
Takahashi v. Fish and Game Comm.	1948	Expand
Woods v. Miller Co.	1948	Expand
Railway Express Agency v. People of State of NY	1949	Restrict
Hood & Sons Inc. H.P. v. DuMond	1949	Expand
Terminiello v. Chicago	1949	Expand
Kovacs v. Cooper	1949	Restrict
California v. Zook	1949	Restrict
Lincoln Federal Labor Union v. Northwestern Iron & Metal Co.	1949	Restrict
Wolf v. Colorado	1949	Restrict
American Communications Association v. Douds	1950	Expand
Sweatt v. Painter	1950	Expand
Dean Milk Co. v. City of Madison	1951	Expand
Feiner v. New York	1951	Restrict
Dennis v. United States	1951	Expand
Spector Motor Service v. O'Connor	1951	Expand
Youngstown Sheet & Tube Co. v. Sawyer	1952	Restrict
Zorach v. Clauson	1952	Restrict
Beauharnais v. Illinois	1952	Restrict
Burstyn, Inc. v. Wilson	1952	Expand
Kahriger, United States v.,	1953	Expand
Terry v. Adams	1953	Expand
Brown v. Board of Education of Topeka	1954	Expand

Case Name	Year	Effect on Federal Authority
Bolling v. Sharpe	1954	Restrict
Williamson v. Lee Optical of Oklahoma	1955	Restrict
Brown v. Board of Education (II)	1955	Expand
Griffin v. Illinois	1956	Expand
Pennsylvania v. Nelson	1956	Expand
Roth v. United States	1957	Expand
Reid v. Covert	1957	Restrict
Yates v. United States	1957	Restrict
Watkins v. United States	1957	Restrict
Cooper v. Aaron	1958	Expand
NAACP v. Alabama ex rel. Patterson	1958	Expand
Bibb v. Navajo Freight Lines	1959	Expand
Burton v. Wilmington Parking Authority	1961	Expand
Poe v. Ullman	1961	Restrict
Braunfeld v. Brown	1961	Restrict
Mapp v. Ohio	1961	Expand
McGowan v. Maryland	1961	Restrict
Baker v. Carr	1962	Expand
Engel v. Vitale	1962	Expand
Sherbert v. Verner	1963	Expand
Douglas v. California	1963	Expand
Shuttlesworth v. City of Birmingham Ala.	1963	Expand
Edwards v. South Carolina	1963	Expand
Ferguson v. Skrupa	1963	Restrict
Heart of Atlanta Motel Inc. v. United States	1964	Expand
New York Times Co. v. Sullivan	1964	Expand
Reynolds v. Sims	1964	Expand
Katzenbach v. McClung	1964	Expand
Flast v. Cohen	1964	Expand
Griswold v. Connecticut	1965	Expand
Freedman v. Maryland	1965	Expand
Katzenbach v. Morgan	1966	Expand
Harper v. Viriginia Board of Elections	1966	Expand
Adderley v. Florida	1966	Restrict
Evans v. Newton	1966	Expand
South Carolina v. Katzenbach	1966	Expand
Loving v. Virginia	1967	Expand
Reitman v. Mulkey	1967	Expand

Case Name	Year	Effect on Federal Authority
O'Brien, United States v.,	1968	Expand
Jones v. Alfred H. Mayer Co.	1968	Expand
Duncan v. Louisana	1968	Expand
Amalgamated Food Employees Local v. Logan Valley Plaza	1968	Expand
Brandenburg v. Ohio	1969	Expand
Red Lion Broadcasting Co. v. FCC	1969	Expand
Powell v. McCormack	1969	Restrict
Shapiro v. Thompson	1969	Expand
Kramer v. Union Free School Dist. No. 15	1969	Expand
Stanley v. Georgia	1969	Expand
Tinker v. Des Moines Independent School Dist	1969	Expand
Dandrige v. Williams	1970	Restrict
Goldberg v. Kelly	1970	Expand
Oregon v. Mitchell	1970	Expand
Pike v. Bruce Church	1970	Expand
Evans v. Abney	1970	Restrict
Cohen v. California	1971	Expand
Swann v. Charlotte-Mecklenburg Bd. of Ed.	1971	Expand
Lemon v. Kurtzman	1971	Expand
Boddie v. Connecticut	1971	Expand
New York Times Co. v. United States	1971	Restrict
Perez v. United States	1971	Expand
Reed v. Reed	1971	Expand
Graham v. Richardson	1971	Expand
Moose Lodge No. 107 v. Irvis	1972	Restrict
Branzburg v. Hayes	1972	Expand
Eisenstadt v. Baird	1972	Expand
Wisconsin v. Yoder	1972	Expand
Board of Regents v. Roth	1972	Restrict
Gooding v. Wilson	1972	Expand
Lloyd Corp v. Tanner	1972	Restrict
Perry v. Sindermann	1972	Expand
Roe v. Wade	1973	Expand
Miller v. California	1973	Restrict
San Antonio Independent School Dist. v. Rodriguez	1973	Restrict
Frontiero v. Richardson	1973	Restrict
Paris Adult Theatre I v. Slaton	1973	Restrict

Case Name	Year	Effect on Federal Authority
Columbia Broadcasting System, Inc. v. Democratic Nat. Committee	1973	Restrict
Keyes v. School District No. 1	1973	Expand
U.S. Dept. of Agriculture v. Moreno	1973	Restrict
Broadrick v. Oklahoma	1973	Restrict
Doe v. Bolton	1973	Expand
Sugarman v. Dougall	1973	Expand
Nixon, United States v.,	1974	Neutral
Gertz v. Robert Welch Inc.	1974	Restrict
Miami Herald Pub Co. v. Tornillo	1974	Expand
DeFunis v. Odegaard	1974	Restrict
Jackson v. Metropolitan Edison Co	1974	Restrict
Milliken v. Bradley	1974	Restrict
Belle Terre v. Boraas	1974	Restrict
Lehman v. City of Shaker Heights	1974	Restrict
Warth v. Seldin	1975	Restrict
Cox Broadcasting Corp v. Cohn	1975	Expand
Buckley v. Valeo	1976	Restrict
Craig v. Boren	1976	Expand
Washington v. Davis	1976	Expand
Mathews v. Eldrige	1976	Expand
Virginia State Bd. Of Pharmacy v. Virginia Citizens Consumer Council Inc.	1976	Expand
National League of Cities v. Usery	1976	Restrict
Young v. American Mini Theatres Inc.	1976	Restrict
Bishop v. Wood	1976	Restrict
Hudgens v. NLRB	1976	Restrict
Nebraska Press Ass'n v. Stuart	1976	Expand
Paul v. Davis	1976	Restrict
Runyon v. McCrary	1976	Expand
Time Inc. v. Firestone	1976	Neutral
Moore v. City of East Cleveland	1977	Expand
Hunt v. Washington State Apple Advertising Com'n	1977	Expand
United States Trust Co. of New York v. New Jersey	1977	Expand
Wooley v. Maynard	1977	Expand
Arlington Heights v. Metropolitan Housing	1977	Restrict
Califano v. Webster	1977	Expand
Abood v. Detroit Board of Ed	1977	Neutral

Case Name	Year	Effect on Federal Authority
Linmark Associates Inc. v. Township of Willingboro	1977	Expand
Nixon v. Adminstrator of General Services	1977	Restrict
Whalen v. Roe	1977	Restrict
Philadelphia v. New Jersey	1978	Expand
Allied Structural Steel Co. v. Spannaus	1978	Expand
Regents of University of California v. Bakke	1978	Expand
Federal Communication Comm'n v. Pacifica Foundation	1978	Expand
Flagg Bros. Inc. v. Brooks	1978	Restrict
Penn Cent. Transp. Co. v. City of NY	1978	Restrict
Zablocki v. Redhail	1978	Expand
Personnel Admin of Mass v. Feeney	1979	Restrict
Goldwater v. Carter	1979	Restrict
Central Hudson Gas & Elec. Corp v. Public Serv. Comm'n	1980	Expand
Reeves Inc v. Stake	1980	Restrict
Richmond Newspapers Inc. v. Virginia	1980	Expand
Harris v. McRae	1980	Expand
Mobile, City of v. Bolden	1980	Restrict
Dames & Moore v. Regan	1981	Expand
Kassel v. Consolidated Freightways Corp of Delaware	1981	Expand
Michael M. v. Superior Court of Sonoma County	1981	Restrict
Rostker v. Goldberg	1981	Expand
Plyler v. Doe	1982	Expand
New York v. Ferber	1982	Restrict
Mississippi University for Women v. Hogan	1982	Expand
Nixon v. Fitzgerald	1982	Expand
Valley Forge Christian College v. Americans United for Separation of Church & State	1982	Expand
INS v. Chadha	1983	Neutral
Roberts v. United States Jaycees	1984	Expand
South Central Timber Development, Inc. v. Wunnicke	1984	Expand
Clark v. Community for Creative Nonviolence	1984	Expand
Hawaii Housing Authority v. Midkiff	1984	Restrict
Lynch v. Donnelly	1984	Restrict
United Bldg. and Const. Trades Council of Camden County and Vicinity v. Mayor and Council of City of Camden	1984	Expand
Allen v. Wright	1984	Restrict

Case Name	Year	Effect on Federal Authority
Cleburne, Tex., City of v. Cleburne Living Center Inc.	1985	Expand
Garcia v. San Antonio Metropolitan Transit	1985	Expand
American Booksellers Association Inc. v. Hudnut	1985	Expand
Cleveland Board of Ed. V. Loudermill	1985	Expand
Bowers v. Hardwick	1986	Restrict
Bowsher v. Synar	1986	Neutral
Renton, City of v. Playtime Theatre Inc.	1986	Restrict
South Dakota v. Dole	1987	Expand
Nollan v. California Coastal Commn.	1987	Expand
Board of Airport Com'rs of City of LA v. Jews for Jesus	1987	Expand
Edwards v. Aguillard	1987	Expand
Morrison v. Olson	1988	Expand
Hustler Magazine v. Falwell	1988	Neutral
Mistretta v. United States	1989	Expand
Texas v. Johnson	1989	Expand
Richmond, City of v. Croson Co.	1989	Expand
Michael H. v. Gerald D.	1989	Restrict
Ward v. Rock Against Racism	1989	Restrict
Employment Div. Dept of Human Resources Oregon v. Smith	1990	Restrict
Cruzan v. Director Missouri Dept of Health	1990	Restrict
Edmonson v. Leesville Concrete Co.	1991	Expand
Rust v. Sullivan	1991	Expand
Planned Parenthood v. Casey	1992	Expand
Lee v. Weisman	1992	Expand
Lujan v. Defenders of Wildlife	1992	Expand
New York v. United States	1992	Expand
RAV v. City of St. Paul Minn	1992	Expand
Lucas v. South Carolina Coastal Council	1992	Expand
International Soc. For Krishna Consciousness, Inc. v. Lee	1992	Restrict
Nixon v. United States	1993	Restrict
Church of the Lukumi Babalu Aye, Inc. v. City of Hialeah	1993	Expand
Shaw v. Reno	1993	Expand
Dolan v. City of Tigard	1994	Expand
Lopez, United States v.,	1995	Restrict
United States Term Limits, Inc. v. Thorton	1995	Expand

Case Name	Year	Effect on Federal Authority
Adarand Constructors, Inc. v. Pena	1995	Restrict
Romer v. Evans	1996	Expand
Virginia, United States v.,	1996	Expand
Boerne, City of v. Flores	1997	Restrict
Washington v. Glucksberg	1997	Restrict
Clinton v. City of New York	1998	Restrict
Printz v. United States	1997	Restrict
Clinton v. Jones	1997	Restrict

Appendix 3

List of Constitutional Casebooks
Used for Data Collection

1. Sergeant, Thomas. 1822. *Constitutional Law: Being a Collection of Points Arising upon the Constitution and Jurisprudence of the United States.* Philadelphia: A. Small.

2. DuPonceau, Stephen. 1824. *A Dissertation on the Nature and Extent of the Jurisdiction of the Courts of the United States.* Philadelphia: Abraham Small.

3. Rawle, William. 1825. *A View of the Constitution of the United States of America.* Philadelphia: H. C. Carey & I. Lea.

4. Kent, James. 1826. *Commentaries on American Law.* New York: O. Halstead.

5. Gordon, Thomas. 1827. *A Digest of the Laws of the United States: Including an Abstract of the Judicial Decisions Relating to the Constitutional and Statutory Law.* Philadelphia: Printed for the Author.

6. Story, Joseph. 1833. *Commentaries on the Constitution of the United States.* Boston: Hilliard, Gray and Company.

7. Baldwin, Henry. 1837. *A General View of the Origin and Nature of the Constitution and Government of the United States.* Philadelphia: J. C. Clark.

8. Curtis, George Ticknor. 1854. *Commentaries on the Jurisdiction, Practice, and Peculiar Jurisprudence of the Courts of the United States.* Philadelphia: T. & J. W. Johnson.

9. Pomeroy, John, and Edmund Bennett. 1868. *An Introduction to the Constitutional Law of the United States.* Cambridge, MA: Riverside Press.

10. Cooley, Thomas. 1868. *Treatise on Constitutional Limitations.* Boston: Little, Brown and Co.

11. Cooley, Thomas, and Andrew Cunningham McLaughlin. 1880. *General Principles of Constitutional Law in the United States of America.* Boston: Little, Brown and Co.

12. Lawson, John. 1882. *Leading Cases Simplified: A Collection of Leading Cases of the Common Law.* St. Louis: F. H. Thomas.

13. Thayer, James Bradley. 1895. *Cases on Constitutional Law.* Vols. 1–2. Cambridge, MA: Charles W. Sever.

14. Boyd, Carl Evans. 1898. *Cases on American Constitutional Law.* Chicago: Callaghan and Co.

15. Tucker, John Randolph. 1899. *The Constitution of the United States: A Critical Discussion of Its Genesis, Development, and Interpretation.* Vols. 1–2. Chicago: Callaghan and Co.

16. McClain, Emlin. 1900. *A Selection of Cases on Constitutional Law.* Boston: Little Brown.

17. Barnes, Edgar. 1910. *Selected Cases in Constitutional Law.* Philadelphia: Lyon & Amor.

18. Willoughby, Westel. 1912. *Principles of the Constitutional Law of the United States.* New York: Baker, Voorhis and Company.

19. Hall, James Parker. 1913. *Cases on Constitutional Law.* St Paul, MN: West.

20. Wambaugh, Eugene. 1914. *A Selection of Cases on Constitutional Law.* Cambridge, MA: Harvard University Press.

21. Evans, Lawrence. 1916. *Leading Cases on American Constitutional Law.* Chicago: Callaghan and Co.

22. Baker, Fred. 1916. *The Fundamental Law of American Constitutions.* Washington: J. Byrne.

23. Gerstenberg, Charles. 1926. *Constitutional Law: A Brief Text with Leading and Illustrative Cases.* New York: Prentice-Hall.

24. Long, Joseph. 1926. *Cases on Constitutional Law.* Rochester, NY: Lawyers Cooperative.

25. Field, Oliver Field. 1930. *A Selection of Cases and Authorities on Constitutional Law.* Chicago: Callaghan and Co.

26. McGovney, Dudley. 1930. *Cases on Constitutional Law*. Indianapolis: Bobbs-Merril.

27. Dodd, Walter. 1932. *Cases and Other Authorities on Constitutional Law: Selected from Decisions of State and Federal Courts*. St Paul, MN: West.

28. Dowling, Noel. 1937. *Cases on Constitutional Law*. Mineola, NY: Foundation Press.

29. Peirce, Joseph, and Harry Cook. 1938. *A Manual to the Constitution of the United States*. Charlottesville, VA: Michie.

30. Maurer, Robert Adam. 1941. *Cases on Constitutional Law*. Rochester, NY: Lawyers of Cooperative.

31. Strong, Frank R. 1950. *American Constitutional Law*. Buffalo, NY: Dennis and Co.

32. Frank, John P. 1950. *Cases and Materials on Constitutional Law*. Chicago: Callaghan and Co.

33. Sholley, John B. 1951. *Cases on Constitutional Law*. Indianapolis: Bobbs-Merrill.

34. Kauper, Paul. 1954. *Constitutional Law Cases and Materials*. New York: Prentice-Hall.

35. Freund, Paul. 1954. *Constitutional Law: Cases and Other Problems*. Boston: Little Brown.

36. Cushman, Robert. 1958. *Cases in Constitutional Law*. Englewood Cliffs, NJ: Prentice-Hall.

37. Forrester, Ray. 1959. *Constitutional Law Cases and Materials*. St. Paul, MN: West.

38. Lockhart, William, Yale Kamisar, and Jesse H. Choper. 1964. *The American Constitution: Cases and Materials*. St. Paul, MN: West.

39. Brest, Paul. 1975. *Processes of Constitutional Decision-making: Cases and Materials*. Boston: Little Brown.

40. Barron, Jerome, and Thomas Dienes. 1978. *Constitutional Law, Principles, and Policy: Cases and Materials*. Indianapolis: Bobbs-Merril.

41. Tribe, Laurence. 1978. *American Constitutional Law*. Mineola, NY: Foundation Press.

42. Nowak, John, Ronald Rotunda, and J. Nelson Young. 1978. *Handbook on Constitutional Law*. St Paul, MN: West.

43. Rotunda, Ronald. 1981. *Modern Constitutional Law*. St. Paul, MN: West.

44. Stone, Geoffrey R., Louis M. Seidman, Cass R. Sunstein, Mark V. Tushnet, and Pamela S. Karlan. 1986. *Constitutional Law*. Boston, MA: Little, Brown and Co.

45. Crump, David, Eugene Gressman, and Steven Reiss. 1989. *Cases and Materials on Constitutional Law*. New York: M. Bender.

46. Farber, Daniel A., William N. Eskridge, and Phillip P. Frickey. 1993. *Constitutional Law: Themes for the Constitution's Third Century*. St. Paul, MN: West.

47. Redlich, Norman, Bernard Schwartz, and John Attanasio. 1995. *Understanding Constitutional Law*. New York: M. Bender.

48. Araiza, William, Phoebe Haddon, and Dorothy Roberts. 1996. *Constitutional Law Cases, History, and Dialogues*. Newark, NJ: Lexis Nexis.

49. Chemerinsky, Erwin. 1997. *Constitutional Law Principles and Policies*. New York: Aspen.

50. Ides, Allan, and Christopher May. 1998. *Constitutional Law*. Vols. 1–2. New York: Aspen Law and Business.

51. Shanor, Charles. 2000. *American Constitutional Law: Structure and Reconstruction: Cases, Notes and Problems*. St. Paul, MN: West.

52. Massey, Calvin. 2001. *American Constitutional Law: Powers and Liberties*. New York: Aspen.

53. Parker, Wilson J., Douglas M. Davison, Paul Finkelman, and Michael Kent Curtis. 2003. *Constitutional Law in Context*. Durham, NC: Carolina Academic Press.

54. Choper, Jesse 2007. *Constitutional Law: Leading Cases*. St Paul, MN: Thomson West.

55. Barnett, Randy. 2008. *Constitutional Law: Cases in Context*. New York: Aspen.

56. Funk, William. 2008. *Introduction to American Constitutional Structure*. St. Paul, MN: West.

57. Odom, Thomas. 2009. *Cases and Materials on Federal Constitutional Law*. Vols. 1–3. Newark, NJ: LexisNexis.

58. Paulsen, Michael, Steven G. Calabresi, Michael W. McConnell, and Samuel L. Bray. 2010. *The Constitution of the United States: Text, Structure, History, and Precedent.* New York: Foundation Press.

Appendix 4

Characteristics of Constitutional Expansion

Figure A.2 presents the distributions of cases upon which this book's findings are based.

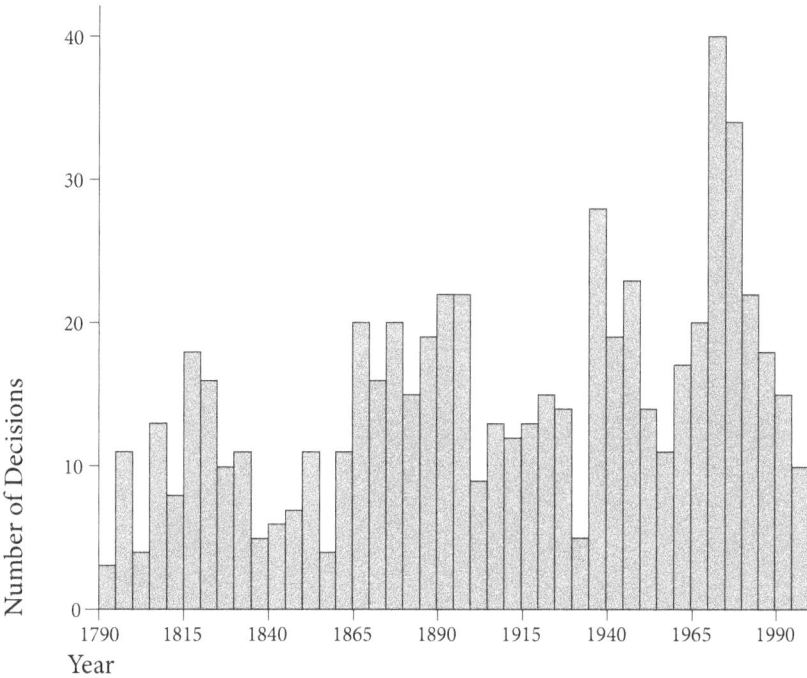

Figure A.2. Distribution of Landmark Decisions across Years, 1792–1997.

Source: Compiled by author. N=624.

Level of Government Action Under Review

To recall, generally speaking, when the Court's decision invalidates a state/ local action *or* upholds a federal action, the decision expands federal power. Conversely, if a Supreme Court decision upholds a state/local action, invalidates a federal action, *or* decides the judiciary lacked jurisdiction, then this decision restricts federal power. That is, the Court might expand federal power through its own institution by overturning state/local action, or it might expand national power by upholding the actions of coordinating branches. Indeed, the judiciary advanced federal power 56% of the time (in 210 of 372 decisions) by overturning state or local actions, declaring that the state or local action violated the federal Constitution. Still, at the same time, it constricted federal power 64% of the time (in 148 of 231 decisions) by allowing a state or local action to stand.

Table A.1 summarizes the mechanisms through which the Court's decisions affect national power. The judiciary expands federal power most frequently by invalidating a state/local action, while the Court constricts federal power most frequently by leaving a state/local law untouched. In other words, the Court most frequently extends federal authority through itself by invalidating state action and lodging decision-making authority with itself. Ultimately, the Court is a gradual state-builder with the unique ability to advance federal authority through its negative and positive uses of power.

Table A.1. Cross-Tabulation of Level of Government Action under Review by Effect on Federal Authority

Level of Government Action under Review		Effect on Federal Authority			
		Restrict	Neutral	Expand	Total
Federal action	Count	67	8	140	215
	% within row	31.2%	3.7%	65.1%	100.0%
State/local action	Count	147	3	219	369
	%	39.8%	.08%	59.3%	100.0%
Unspecifiable	Count	17	10	13	40
	%	42.5%	25.0%	32.5%	100.0%
Total	Count	231	21	372	624
	%	37.0%	3.4%	59.6%	100.0%

Source: Compiled by author. N=624.

Vote Outcomes

The Court extends federal authority with vigor and unanimity just as often as it expands authority more reluctantly with its split decisions. Its unanimous and split decisions are not any more likely to expand federal authority than the universe of cases. Of all the cases in the data (262 of 624), 42% were decided unanimously. The distribution of unanimous decisions mirrors, almost exactly, the distribution of all cases in the data: 58% expand (153 of 262), 37% constrict (98 of 262), and 4% (11 of 262) remain neutral to federal power. Conversely, in five-four decisions, the Court is more evenly split, but the sample size is small: 46% expand (11 of 24), and 54% constrict (13 of 24). When looking at the 211 decisions that are split seven-two or six-three, I notice trends very similar to those in the broader universe of cases (57% expand and 39% restrict power).

Ideology

Like constitutional issues, ideology influences judicial outcomes. As we might expect, liberal decisions are much more frequently associated with expanding federal power than conservative decisions. Yet conservative decisions still increase federal power in about half of cases (48%), while liberal decisions expand federal power 70% of the time. Thus, the Court advances federal state authority for both conservative and liberal ends, indicating the importance of evaluating federal state authority through a more agnostic lens (see Table A.2).

Table A.2. Cross-Tabulation of Ideology of Decision by Effect on Federal Authority

Ideology of Decision		Effect on Federal Authority			
		Restrict	Neutral	Expand	Total
Conservative	Count	127	11	126	264
	% within row	48.1%	4.2%	47.7%	100.0%
Liberal	Count	96	6	227	329
	%	29.2%	1.8%	69.0%	100.0%
Unspecifiable	Count	4	3	13	20
	%	20.0%	15.0%	65.0%	100.0%
Total	Count	227	20	366	613
	%	37.0%	3.3%	59.7%	100.0%

Notes and Sources: Compiled by author. The "decision direction" variable comes from the Spaeth US Supreme Court Database. I observed a strong association between ideology and effect on federal authority, $\chi^2(4) = 28.58$, $p = .000$. Eleven cases were missing from Spaeth's Database and thus not included in this table. N=613.

Across the fifteen constitutional issues there remains persistent expansion of federal authority, although there has been a greater rate of expansion in some areas of the Constitution than in others (see Figure A.3). Civil rights and liberties, the First Amendment, and federalism are three issues in which court decisions are twice as likely to expand federal authority as not. Economic activity has expanded power most frequently in terms of raw count, but it restricts federal authority at almost the same rate. Similarly, judicial power is the only constitutional issue that has seen more restriction of federal authority than expansion, though the balance is close to even.

Any central state dimension can theoretically involve any of the legal issue areas. The stacked bar chart (Figure A.4) shows the ubiquity of centralization across the constitutional issue areas. The bar chart represents the number of decisions (and their corresponding legal issue areas) that expand and constrict the centralization dimension; every legal issue area and nearly

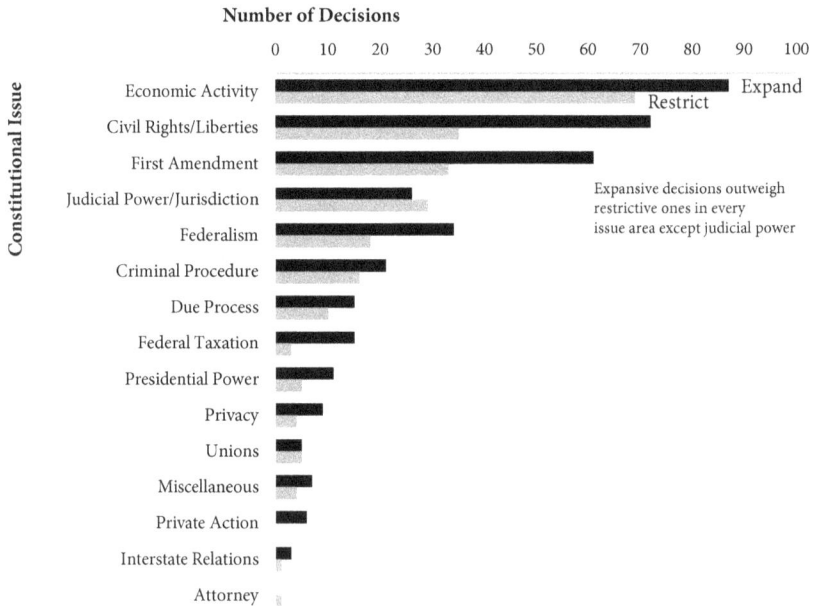

Figure A.3. Effect on Federal Authority by Constitutional Issue, 1792–1997.

Notes and Source: Compiled by author. This chart includes the fifteen constitutional issues utilized in Harold Spaeth's Supreme Court Database. Notably, in virtually every legal issue area, the Court expanded the powers of the national government. Neutral decisions are not included. I observed a strong association between the constitutional issue area and the effect on federal power, $\chi^2(12) = 23.20$, $p = .026$. N=603.

All 15 constitutional issues fall
under the centralization dimension.
Constitutional issues do not fall neatly
into the seven dimensions of the
federal state.

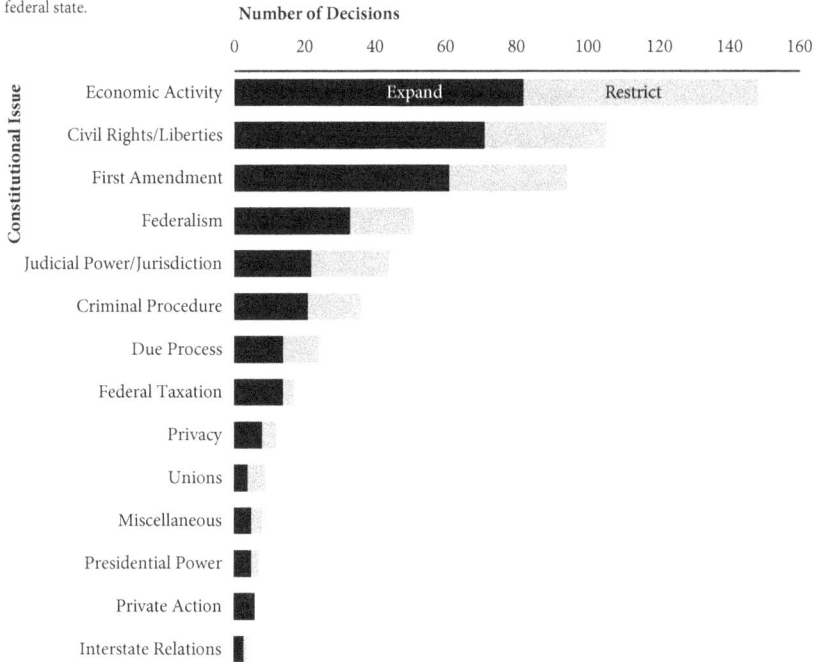

Figure A.4. Constitutional Issues as a Subset of Centralization.

Notes and Source: Compiled by author. Centralization is the primary mechanism through which a decision expanded or restricted central state authority. Of 624 decisions, 565 involved centralization, showing its prevalence in American constitutional development across a multitude of legal issues. N=565.

every judicial decision (565 of 624) interacts with centralization. Constitutional issues do not fall neatly into each of the seven policy dimensions of the state. For example, "federalism" does not fall *solely* under the centralization dimension, as one might think;[3] federalism is also seen as the primary legal issue in a small number of citizenship decisions (Figure A.5 on page 198). Similarly, individual rights decisions affect not only the citizenship dimension, as we might suspect, but also the centralization dimension. While centralization encompasses a broader set of constitutional issues, the citizenship dimension primarily comprises just two legal issue areas: civil rights/liberties and the First Amendment.

14 of 15 constitutional issues interact with
the citizenship dimension. Constitutional
issues do not fall neatly into the
seven dimensions of the federal state.

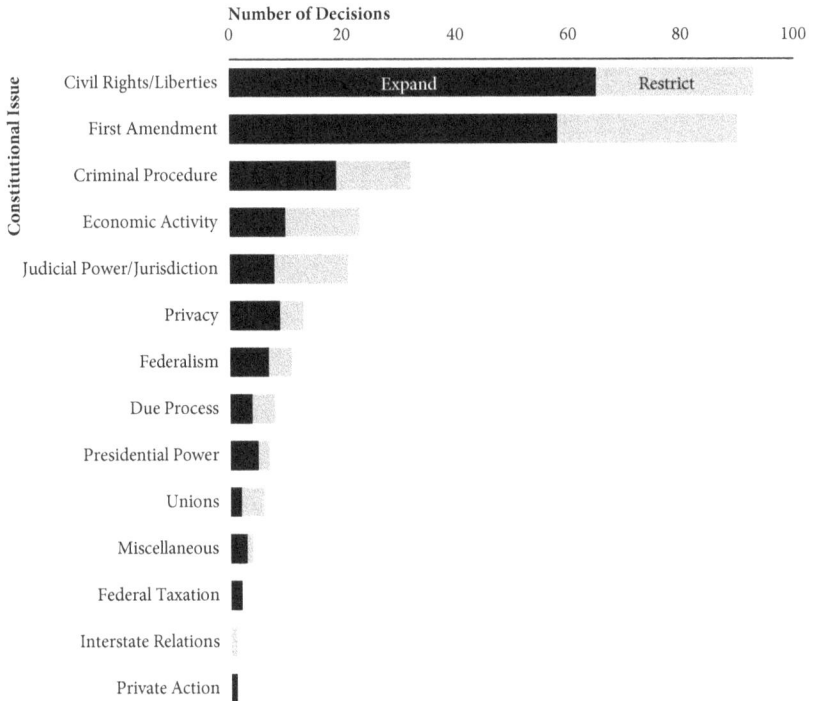

Figure A.5. Constitutional Issues as a Subset of Citizenship.

Notes and Source: Compiled by author. Because over 300 decisions did not implicate the citizenship dimension, I did not include them in the graphic. Much like centralization, citizenship does not solely subsume individual rights–related constitutional issue areas as we might expect. However, unlike in centralization, there is a far less even distribution of constitutional issues with the citizenship dimension; indeed, civil rights, the First Amendment, and criminal procedure comprise 69% of all the citizenship dimension decisions. Still, some noncitizenship issues, such as federalism and judicial power, for example, involve the citizenship dimension, albeit to a far lesser extent than the individual rights issue area. N=312.

Notes

Introduction

1. Obergefell v. Hodges, 576 U.S. _____ (2015) at 10 and 27 (slip opinion, Opinion of the Court. The official preliminary prints and finalized official bound volume have not yet been released by the Supreme Court Reporter's Office).

2. *Obergefell*, 576 U.S. at 2 and 3 (slip opinion, dissenting opinion).

3. *Obergefell*, 576 U.S. at 28.

4. When it comes to federal-state issues, the Court has often protected the federal government from the states by affirming national supremacy (Kramer 2000, 228). Of this depiction of the Court's role, Larry Kramer writes, "This claim may sound jarring to lawyers today, who have for decades been fed a story about the Supreme Court's uncompromising stand against federal growth until Justice Roberts spinelessly caved to pressure from the Roosevelt Administration. Yet [this] account is, in fact, the more accurate rendition of events" (Kramer 2000, 228).

5. "Kentucky Must Pay $224,000 After Dispute Over Same-Sex Marriage Licenses," *New York Times*, July 21, 2017. https://www.nytimes.com/2017/07/21/us/kentucky-taxpayers-gay-marriage.html.

6. "Roy Moore, Alabama Chief Justice, Suspended Over Gay Marriage Order," *New York Times*, September 30, 2016. https://www.nytimes.com/2016/10/01/us/roy-moore-alabama-chief-justice.html.

7. I understand "authority" in the way that Karen Orren and Stephen Skowronek detail. They define authority as first "something designated in advance"; second, as working "through institutions"; third as working "through mandates that are enforceable"; and last as working "through perceptions" of these institutions (2004, 125).

8. As Bensel (1990) also argues, Novak, too, sees centralization of authority as a crucial aspect of the "modern state." Novak's account challenges what he calls a "mythical American past"—one of a "golden age of liberalism, the nineteenth century Jeffersonian world of minimal government, low taxes, absolutely private property, individual rights, self interested entrepreneurship, and laissez-faire economics" (Novak 1996, ix). Contrary to prevailing thought, Novak argues, "The nineteenth century was not an era of laissez-faire or statelessness" (Novak 1996, 236). Instead, it "was home to

powerful traditions of governance, police, and regulation" (Novak 1996, ix). Relevant for this book is Novak's understanding that centralization indicated state-building toward the last quarter of the nineteenth century. For example, in looking at liquor prohibition, Novak concludes, "State prohibition involved a distinctively upward shift in the locus of public decision-making power." Once the province of local communities, state legislatures abolished local regulatory practices and created "a centralized, rule-based, and stream-lined enforcement apparatus" (Novak 1996, 188).

9. Nicholas Aroney and John Kincaid note, "By *national*, Madison meant 'unitary,' in the sense of a single location of sovereignty from which the constitution's authority is ultimately derived, in contrast to a 'federal' conception, in which the constitution is seen as an agreement between sovereign and independent states" (Aroney and Kincaid 2017, 16, emphasis in original).

10. For an analysis of the rise of rights argumentation in the US, see Keck (2004) and Teles (2008). Both scholars detail how conservatives either on the Court or through public interest law firms embraced rights-based judicial activism.

11. "Senate votes down Feinstein's assault weapons ban," *Los Angeles Times*, April 17, 2013. http://articles.latimes.com/2013/apr/17/news/la-pn-dianne-feinstein-assault-weapons-vote-20130417.

12. See Louis Michael Siedeman, "Let's Give Up on the Constitution," *New York Times*, December 30, 2012. http://www.nytimes.com/2012/12/31/opinion/lets-give-up-on-the-constitution.html?pagewanted=all&module=Search&mabReward=relbias%3Aw%2C%7B%222%22%3A%22RI%3A15%22%7D. Texas law professor Sanford Levinson makes a similar argument in "Our Imbecilic Constitution," *New York Times*, May 28, 2012. http://campaignstops.blogs.nytimes.com/2012/05/28/our-imbecilic-constitution/?module=Search&mabReward=relbias%3Aw%2C%7B%222%22%3A%22RI%3A15%22%7D.

13. I recognize that contemporary constitutional scholars have persuasively challenged Tocqueville's thesis that political questions often become legal ones. See Graber (2004). Nevertheless, many legal scholars have recognized the litigiousness that characterize American culture (Kagan 2001; Burke 2002).

14. See, for example, Michael Tanner, "Why the Size of Government Matters," *National Review*, March 20, 2013. http://www.nationalreview.com/articles/343419/why-size-government-matters-michael-tanner.

15. Scholars in American political development (APD)—a research community born in the 1980s—focus on the growth of the American state by examining changes in political institutions. APD has closely charted the growth of the presidency (Skowronek 1993) and the bureaucracy (Carpenter 2001; Skowronek 1982). Other studies have emphasized Congress as an important source of state development (Schickler 2001). Political party leadership, too, has been the focal point of studies of American state-building (Shefter 1994). Still others have focused on city or regional patterns as factors that contributed to state-building (Bridges 1997; Bensel 1990; Sanders 1999). But "a significant part of the field [has] pursued a delegalized study of the American state" (Skrentny 2006, 217). Skrentny argues, "The American exceptionalism question that dominated the field led to a focus on the lack of a national administrative welfare state structure and on the historical period—the Progressive era to the New

Deal—when Europe developed such state structures and the United States did not" (Skrentny 2006, 217). Consequently, law and courts played less of a role in studies of American state-building.

16. In his *Oxford Handbook on American Political Development* entry, Keith Whittington recognizes the typical depiction of the Court as an obstacle to state growth: "From the perspective of those who primarily study American political development, the courts have often appeared to be constraints on state-building" (Whittington 2016, 320). Paul Frymer (2008) argues that scholars have gone "too far in juxtaposing court power against other political institutions and . . . miss the important ways that courts contribute to the development of state power" (789). William Novak (2002) makes a similar argument. Looking at 1877 to 1937, he maintains that law and courts were not the "great bogeymen of liberal reform," persistently frustrating modern welfare-state building (251). Contrary to the progressive narrative, Novak contends that American public law was a "font of creative energy" at the state and local level, and therefore crucial to the development of the modern American state—a state comprised of a centralized, administrative, and regulatory government (260).

17. Segal and Spaeth (1993). This study is well known for putting forth the "attitudinal model," which sees justices as voting their ideological preferences when issuing Court rulings. For rational choice institutionalists, justices seek to maximize their preferences in a complex setting; justices must bargain, compromise, and consider institutional structures (rules/norms) both internal to the Court and external constraints when seeking to achieve their preferences (Epstein and Knight 1998; Murphy 1964). Rational choice scholars maintain that justices do not simply make decisions in a unidimensional context of ideological beliefs as behavioralists argue. Rational choice studies focus on the "collegial game" by modeling the strategic behavior of justices to create majority coalitions (Maltzman, Spriggs, and Wahlbeck 2001).

18. Howard Gillman and Cornell Clayton's (1999) edited volume *The Supreme Court in American Politics: New Institutionalist Interpretations* provides an excellent overview of the historical institutionalist research agenda. Looking more specifically at the Court and American political development, the contributors to Robert Kahn and Ken Kersch's (2006) edited volume also embrace an historical institutionalist approach to Supreme Court politics.

19. Paul Pierson recognizes the importance of studying politics as a long-term process. Pierson argues, "Contemporary social scientists are more likely to take a 'snapshot' view of political life" (Pierson 2005, 34). Too often, Pierson argues, social scientists focus on moments of specific policy enactments (or in this study's case, specific Court decisions), thereby blinding scholars to what happens before and after such decisions.

20. There are many courts and American political development scholars who have also emphasized development beyond critical moments, explaining these moments of watershed change not "through an analysis of the political conditions and allegiances of the time," but through examining "the developmental trajectories that led to the critical moment" (Novkov 2015, 820). See, for example, Mark Graber (2006a), who explains the landmark case of *Dred Scott* (1857) by detailing much earlier, nonjudicial developments such as the Northwest Land Ordinances and the land acquired

through the Mexican War. Similarly, Pamela Brandwein (2011) situates constitutional developments during the Reconstruction era as having roots in the earlier doctrinal framework of state neglect, which structured subsequent Congressional developments regarding civil rights.

Chapter 1

1. See also Heclo (1984, 30), who has described the American state as "an unmanaged affair," or Clemens (2006), who has described it as a "Rube Goldberg state."

2. On the tendency of the Supreme Court to promote unitarism over state autonomy, see Somin (2017), especially pages 477–80.

3. Because in my view development entails something other than the European-style welfare state and centralized Weberian structures, I do not use the progressive welfare-state dimension as the metric to assess the growth of the federal government. "Progressive" studies view the Court as an inhibitor of state development when the Court invalidates federal and state laws that attempted to create a stronger welfare state. Charles Beard's *Economic Interpretation of the Constitution* typifies this "Progressive" school of thought. Beard argued that the Constitution "was essentially an economic document based on the concept that the fundamental private rights of property are anterior to government and morally beyond the reach of popular majorities." Charles Beard, quoted in Wiecek (1998, 256).

4. There certainly have been contemporary and past scholars who push against this narrow conception of Court power, lending credence to taking a more dynamic view of constitutional development. In particular, Charles Warren (1922) defended the Court's decisions during the *Lochner* era, analyzing 790 state police power and tax decisions handed down between 1889 and 1918, and discovered that only 53 invalidated police-power regulations. Similarly, William Novak (2002) examined the period from 1877 to 1937 and concluded that law and courts were not the "great bogeymen of liberal reform," persistently frustrating modern welfare-state building (Novak 2002, 251). Novak contends that American public law, contrary to the progressive narrative, was a "font of creative energy" at the state and local level, and therefore crucial to the development of the modern American state—a state comprised of a centralized, administrative, and regulatory government (Novak 2002, 260).

5. Nevertheless, there exists a wealth of literature about how constitutional and other judicial decisions affect federal authority, but typically, this literature examines particular historical periods. To name just a few: see Brandwein (2011), which examines the Reconstruction period and the Court's state action doctrine that gave authority to the president and Congress to protect African-Americans' civil rights; Novkov (2001), who focuses on the *Lochner* era (1873 and 1937), which analyzes how gender shaped judicial outcomes and played into the balance between liberty and state authority to regulate; or Lovell (2003), who looks at early-twentieth-century labor law (1898–1935) and argues that scholars should recognize the symbiotic nature of federal authority: "electoral pressures on Congress lead legislators to empower judges" and thus "the

conventional divided between 'democratic' and 'counter-majoritarian' branches is too simplistic" (Lovell 2003, xix).

6. Briefly, here are the other dimensions of Bensel's taxonomy:

Administrative capacity: Measures involving a broadening or narrowing of bureaucratic discretion and long-term planning capacity within the central state.

Citizenship: Measures involving the religious practices, political beliefs, ethnic identity, and rights and duties of citizens in their relations with the state.

Control of property: Measures involving the control or use of property by individuals or institutions other than the central state itself.

Creation of client groups: Measures that increase the dependence of groups within society on the continued existence and viability of the central state.

Extraction: The coercive dimensions of material resources from society into the central state apparatus.

World system: Measures concerning the relationship of the central state and nation with other states and the world economy.

7. As an institution, however, the Court's own capacity—its ability to conduct its business effectively and efficiently—has grown over time; for a historical analysis of the Court's growing institutional capacity, see Crowe (2012).

8. For a critical examination of teleological or "Whiggish" interpretations of constitutional development, see Kersch (2004).

9. When the Court upholds a law and defers to other authorities, it sometimes does so because of its own fragility as an institution; the Court behaves in ways that protect its authority from political retaliation (Ferejohn 1999). The Court's institutional fragility probably contributes to why it often affirms federal law and thus persistently expands central state authority. Indeed, throughout American history, public officials have often threatened to curb the Court's power either by constitutional amendment, statute, impeachment, jurisdiction stripping, or holding judicial salaries constant, and these threats have frequently altered the Court's behavior (Epstein and Knight 1998; Pickerill and Clayton 2004, 236; Clayton and Pickerill 2006, 1392; Rosen 2006, 7). Robert Dahl's seminal article finds that the Court's "unique legitimacy attributed to its interpretations of the Constitution" is jeopardized if the Court "flagrantly opposes the major policies of the dominant alliance" (Dahl 1957, 293).

10. For example, the landmark voting rights case *Baker v. Carr*, 369 U.S. 186 (1962), centered on the Court's jurisdictional authority. In *Baker*, the question at

hand pertained to the Court's jurisdiction over state legislative apportionment issues. The Court answered in the affirmative, thus expanding the scope of the central state to supervise and effect state legislative apportionment throughout the United States, which opened up the floodgates for the Court to hear dozens of subsequent apportionment cases.

11. As Morgan (2016) notes, comparative studies follow this pattern, too. Comparative studies stemmed from scholarship examining Western European state-building, focusing on the role of war, economic development, and/or trade in producing the Weberian ideal–type of centralized authority and bureaucratic rationality (Morgan 2016, 175; see also Tily 1985).

12. See Vaubel's (2009, 205) literature review, citing Rydon (1993, 234f.) for Australia, Bednar, Eskridge, and Ferejohn (2001) for Canada, and McWhinney (1986, 176–83) for Canada and India.

13. Other studies, Vaubel (2009) notes, echo this finding. Chalmers and Haasbeek (2007, 63) write, "Central judicial institutions almost invariably have centralizing rather than particularistic tendencies." Similarly, Sweet (2004, 8) concludes, "Federal polities sustained through effective judicial review tend to evolve in ways that centralize power. The result hinges in part on the extent to which the court performs its assigned role."

14. Mettler and Valelly define the "state" as "a coherently (though not necessarily tightly) connected ensemble of legitimate, stable, and resilient (but also evolving) national and subnational institutions of representation and legislation, governance, and jurisprudence building" (Mettler and Valelly 2016, 7).

15. King and Lieberman assert that judicial review is "one of two main forms of constraint upon the American state," which they define as the "administrative structures created in the federal bureaucracy and executive branch" (King and Lieberman 2016, 239–40).

16. On these anti-Federalist fears regarding the Supreme Court and judicial review, see "Letters of Brutus" XI–XV (Ball 2007). See also "Centinel" XVI (http://teachingamericanhistory.org/library/document/centinel-xvi/). For a secondary source discussion of anti-Federalist views on the Constitution's design, see Herbert Storing (1981, 48–53).

17. "Letters of Brutus," Letter XI, 31 January 1788, in Ball (2007, 504).

18. Before the US Constitution was ratified, many US state constitutions recognized the importance of judiciary and judicial review. Massachusetts's Constitution of 1780, for example, guaranteed all citizens "an impartial interpretation of the laws . . . by judges as free, impartial, and intendent" (MA Constitution quoted in Aroney and Kincaid 2017, 7). Given the ubiquity of state-level judicial review, Alexander Hamilton presented a widely held view in *Federalist* 78 that "whenever a particular statute contravenes the constitution, it will be the duty of the judicial tribunals to adhere to the latter, and disregard the former" (Hamilton, quoted in Aroney and Kincaid 2017, 7).

19. On Madison's veto proposal and the subsequent Supremacy Clause, Charles Hobson argues, "Together, the supremacy clause, the judiciary article, and the restrictions on the states constituted the judicial substitute for the legislative negative on state laws" (Hobson 1979, 229).

20. Some scholars contest the idea of "judicial finality," arguing that constitutional decision-making "is decidedly polyarchic" (L. Fisher 2004, 153). Still, for much of American history, citizens, states, and national political authorities alike have looked on the Court as the branch that primarily interprets and evaluates the constitutionality of laws.

21. Thomas Jefferson, quoted in Balogh (2009, 251).

22. "Letters of Brutus," Letter XI, in Ball (2007, 504).

23. Gillman, Graber, and Whittington (2017b, 237). Some scholars argue that Reconstruction Republicans intended the Fourteenth to nationalize the Bill of Rights. See Curtis (1986) and Amar (1998). Earlier scholarship maintains just the opposite— that the Fourteenth Amendment never intended incorporation. See Fairman (1949).

24. In this quote, Richard Cortner refers to the Court's decisions—and the concomitant incorporation—that took place between 1925 and 1969.

25. See also McCurdy (1978), who also argues that Supreme Court helped build a unified national marketplace through its Commerce Clause decisions.

26. Santa Clara County v. Southern Pacific Railroad Co., 118 U.S. 394 (1886). For discussions of corporate personhood, see Friedman (2005, 455) and Bernard Schwartz (1993, 169–70).

27. In these quotes, William Wiecek refers specifically to the Court's ruling in Lochner v. New York (1905), and its subsequent effects.

28. Skowronek argues, "By the 1890s, the Supreme Court had articulated principles of nationalism, substantive due process, and constitutional laissez-faire that both extended and consolidated its traditional hold over governmental operations" (Skowronek 1982, 41). Thus, in a sense, the judiciary *was* the central state at least with respect to regulating the vast realm of industrialization.

29. Balogh notes, "Between 1875 and the 1890s, the Supreme Court walked a fine line between preserving government control over the structure of corporations chartered by the states and ensuring a national market" (Balogh 2009, 339).

30. Justice Samuel Blatchford's majority opinion is quoted in Bensel (2000, 334), from Chicago, Milwaukee and St. Paul Railway Company v. Minnesota, 134 U.S. 418 (1889). The other Supreme Court case referred to above is Minneapolis Eastern Railway Company v. Minnesota, 134 U.S. 467 (1889).

31. The "liberty of contract" doctrine first appeared in Allgeyer v. Louisiana, 165 U.S. 578 (1897), which struck down a state statute preventing out-of-state insurance companies from contracting with Louisiana citizens.

32. For an in-depth examination of railroad litigation between 1880s and 1910 that successfully helped create the substantive due process, see Cortner (1993, chs. 1–5). On the NAACP's public interest litigation that culminated in Brown v. Board of Education, 347 U.S., see Tushnet (1987).

33. Chapter 2—which summarizes the empirical findings of this book—demonstrates the Court's tendency toward unitarism. See Somin (2017), who makes a similar argument regarding the Court's tendency to promote centralization of federal power.

34. See note 6 above for a list of Bensel's dimensions.

35. Concerning judicial enforcement of limits on state power, Ilya Somin argues, "There has never been a prolonged period when the federal courts did *not*

use judicial review to impose substantial restrictions on state governments" (Somin 2017, 465, emphasis in original).

36. In his analysis of the Fourteenth Amendment and nationalization of the Bill of Rights, Richard Cortner recognizes that Lochner v. New York, 198 U.S. 45 (1905), and "liberty of contract" cases provided the foundation for the Court to incorporate other fundamental rights later in the twentieth century. Cortner notes that while the *Lochner* Court used the Due Process Clause of the Fourteenth Amendment to construct "substantive rights" related to property, these actions would "have a profound effect upon the nationalization of the Bill of Rights. For if the 'liberty' protected by the Due Process Clause embraced the right to be free to use one's faculties . . . such a broad right should also embrace the rights of free speech, freedom of the press, and freedom of religion, as well as other substantive liberties guaranteed in the Bill of Rights" (Cortner 1981, 23–24).

37. In Webber v. Virginia, 103 U.S. 344 (1880), for example, I. M Singer & Company successfully challenged a Virginia licensing tax. Using the dormant Commerce Clause, the Court reversed a conviction against I. M. Singer's out-of-state sales agent for selling goods without a license because "it was against legislation of this discriminating kind that the framers of the Constitution intended to guard when they vested in Congress the power to regulate commerce among the several states" (*Webber*, 103 U.S. at 350). The Court maintained that states may impose licensing taxes on sales agents, but states must impose the tax on *both* out-of-state and in-state sales agents—not on just out-of-state agents, as Virginia's law did.

38. Fletcher v. Peck, 10 U.S. 87 (1810).

39. Prigg v. Pennsylvania, 41 U.S. 539 (1842).

40. Ableman v. Booth, 62 U.S. 506 (1859).

41. See chapter 4 for further analysis of the dormant Commerce Clause.

42. For a more in-depth discussion of *Lochner* and its effects on central state authority, see the next section below.

43. Meyer v. Nebraska, 262 U.S. 390 (1923).

44. Pierce v. Society of Sisters, 268 U.S. 510 (1925).

45. Buchanan v. Warley, 245 U.S. 60 (1917).

46. Brown v. Board of Education of Topeka, Shawnee County, Kansas, 347 U.S. 483 (1954).

47. Some revisionist scholars also maintain that *Brown* and related cases represent "a modern version of the Court's old class legislation jurisprudence" of the *Lochner* era (Bernstein 2011, 111). For a discussion on the connections between *Lochner* and post–New Deal jurisprudence, see Bernstein (2011, ch. 7). The jurisprudential connection made between *Brown* and *Lochner* is not simply an invention of contemporary libertarian legal historians such as David Bernstein. As Bernstein notes even at the time of *Brown*, a 1952 memo written by a Supreme Court clerk who would later become Chief Justice William Rehnquist illuminates the connection. In the memo to Justice Robert Jackson, Rehnquist argued that the Court should rule against the pending segregation cases, otherwise it would write its own ideological views into law. Recalling the judicial activism of the *Lochner* era, Rehnquist wrote that the pre–New Deal Court, instead of heeding Justice Holmes's dissent "that the Fourteenth Amendment

did not enact Herbert Spence's [*sic*] Social Statics," it allowed "business interests" to "dominate the Court." If the Court overturned segregation laws, Rehnquist argued, "it differs from the McReynolds court only in the kinds of litigants it favors and the kinds of special claims it protects" (Rehnquist quoted in Bernstein 2011, 112–13).

48. Even if one wants to examine subsequent regulatory effects as a way to determine whether a decision expanded or constricted central state authority, then the historical record demonstrates that *Lochner* did not greatly inhibit bakeshop worker safety. *Lochner* had little effect on bakers' working hours, the aspect under review in the Court's decision. By 1909, four years after *Lochner*, fewer than 9% of bakers worked more than ten hours a day, and by 1919, only 3% worked more than ten hours. More specifically to New York's Bakeshop Act, *Lochner* left intact the act's sanitary provisions (Bernstein 2011, 37–38). Those who understand *Lochner* as restricting central state authority see the decision as preventing the Weberian state and its welfare components, but if we look at the ramifications of the decision, then *Lochner* might not even constitute a constriction on traditional, Weberian terms. Nevertheless, the coding schema in this book does not examine the ramifications of the judicial decision; it confines interpretation to the words promulgated by the Court in its majority decision.

49. Mapp v. Ohio, 367 U.S. 643 (1961) incorporated the "exclusionary rule" to the states, preventing states from using illegally obtained evidence at trial.

50. Miranda v. Arizona, 384 U.S. 436 (1966), while not included in the data, still has led to profound changes in state criminal procedures, requiring that police read defendants their "Miranda" rights before interrogating them in order to protect the accused's right against self-incrimination.

51. Gideon v. Wainwright, 372 U.S. 335 (1963), while not included in the data, established the right to counsel for indigent defendants.

52. On the Warren Court's influence on the criminal justice system, see Powe (2000, chs. 15–16). On the incorporation of the Bill of Rights, specifically, in the realm of criminal procedure, see Powe (2000, 412–20).

53. Brandenburg v. Ohio, 395 U.S. 444 (1969).

54. *Brandenburg*, 395 U.S. at 4445–46.

55. Allegheny County v. ACLU, 492 U.S. 573 (1989), while not included in the data, demonstrates the Court's reach into state and local matters through judicial review.

56. *Allegheny*, 492 U.S. at 598, 601. To be sure, in *Allegheny*, the Court upheld the display of a an eighteen-foot menorah because of its physical setting: placed outside the city courthouse building next to a forty-five-foot decorated Christmas tree (*Allegheny*, 492 U.S. at 575).

57. School District of Abington Township, Pennsylvania v. Schempp, 374 U.S. 203 (1963), while not included in the data, demonstrates how the Court's use of judicial review requires state and local governments to conform to national standards.

58. For a much lengthier discussion of how incorporation centralizes federal power, see Somin (2017, 473–77).

59. E. C. Knight Co v. United States, 156 U.S. 1 (1895), In Re Debs, 158 U.S. 564 (1895), and *Lochner*, 198 U.S. (1905) have been invoked as the "Holy Trinity of laissez-faire," decisions that advanced corporate interests over monopoly (*E. C. Knight*),

labor union strikes (*In Re Debs*), and workplace regulation (*Lochner*) (Novak 2002, 273). But central state development, properly understood, should not necessarily equate laissez-faire as an obstacle to state growth because two of these decisions (*Debs* and *Lochner*) significantly advanced some of the dimensions in the central state authority framework employed in this book (see chapter 2).

60. See chapter 2 for a discussion of the seven central state dimensions.

61. *Lochner*, 198 U.S. at 47.

62. *Lochner*, 198 U.S. at 53.

63. *Lochner*, 198 U.S. at 53, 58.

64. The typical treatment of *Lochner* represents scholars' "skepticism of courts," which has led us to go "too far in juxtaposing court power against other political institutions and . . . miss the important ways that courts contribute to the development of state power" (Frymer 2008, 789).

65. Legislation that singled out particular classes of people for state protection or regulation. For a critique of the class legislation explanation of *Lochner*, see Bernstein (2003, 13–31). Bernstein softens his critique of the class legislation explanation in his book, noting, "judicial hostility to class legislation likely played some role in liberty of contract cases after 1905" (Bernstein 2011, 16).

66. Juilliard v. Greenman, 110 U.S. 421 (1884).

67. *Juilliard*, 110 U.S. at 445.

68. *Juilliard*, 110 U.S. at 448.

69. *Juilliard*, 110 U.S. at 450.

70. See Appendix 1 for a detailed discussion of how I coded this case for "Effect on Federal Authority."

71. *Brown*, 347 U.S.

72. Plessy v. Ferguson, 163 U.S. 537 (1896).

73. *Brown*, 347 U.S. at 493.

74. *Brown*, 347 U.S. at 494.

75. The Court's judicial review in *Brown vs. Board of Education* provided a foundation for other federal actors—both the executive branch and Congress—to advance power over civil rights issues. Desegregation, and the Court's decision, took more than a decade to realize. Enforcement actions, such as President Dwight Eisenhower's use of the 101st Airborne to enforce desegregation in Little Rock, Arkansas, in 1957 and the Civil Rights Act of 1964, illustrate the Court's expansion of federal power, but these enforcement actions are simply a sign of the consolidation of federal power, not the power itself; the same expansion of federal authority would have occurred if state and local governments had simply complied with the Court's ruling in *Brown*, as they had in *Lochner*.

76. Coyle v. Smith, 221 U.S. 559 (1911).

77. See Appendix 1 for a detailed discussion of how I coded this case for "Effect on Federal Authority."

78. Barron v. Baltimore, 32 U.S. 243 (1833).

79. *Barron*, 32 U.S. at 247.

80. Of the Framers' intentions with respect the Bill of Rights, Marshall said:

[I]t is a part of the history of the day, that the great revolution which established the constitution of the United States, was not effected without immense opposition. Serious fears were extensively entertained that those powers which the patriot statesmen, who then watched over the interests of our country, deemed essential to union, and to the attainment of those invaluable objects for which union was sought, might be exercised in a manner dangerous to liberty. In almost every convention by which the constitution was adopted, amendments to guard against the abuse of power were recommended. These amendments demanded security against the apprehended encroachments of the general government—not against those of the local governments (1974, 250).

81. *Barron*, 32 U.S. at 247.

82. Howard Gillman, Mark Graber, and Keith Whittington assert, "The Fourteenth Amendment to the U.S. Constitution provided one important, but ill-defined, tool for lawyers to use to draw judges in political battles. This crucial Reconstruction amendment gave the federal courts a new basis on which to judge state actions, and over time it became one of the most litigated pieces of text in the U.S. Constitution" (Gillman, Graber, and Whittington 2013, 332).

83. 15 USCS § 41.

84. Humphrey's Executor v. United States, 295 U.S. 602 (1935).

85. *Humphrey*, 295 U.S. at 629. Writing for the opinion of the Court, Justice Sutherland dismissed the government's main line of defense in this case, which relied heavily on the Court's decision in Myers v. United States, 272 U.S. 52 (1926). In that case the Court upheld the president's right to remove officers who were "units in the executive department" (*Humphrey*, 295 U.S. at 627). Sutherland argued that the FTC was different because Congress created the agency to perform quasilegislative and judicial functions and hence it was not "subject to the exclusive and illimitable power of removal by the Chief Executive" (*Humphrey*, 295 U.S. at 627). The *Myers* precedent, therefore, did not apply in *Humphrey*.

86. Neutral outcomes, like *Humphrey*, make up 3% of the data: 21 of 624 decisions.

87. Since my book is concerned with how the Court allocated federal authority in over 600 cases, I do not examine the subsequent effects of each decision. Instead, its scope is to detail and outline the boundaries of authority promulgated by the judiciary. To understand which cases were self-executing and which required national political branch enforcement is ultimately a separate book project.

88. Brown v. Board of Education, 349 U.S. 294 (1955).

Chapter 2

1. Madison to Edmund Randolph, October 21, 1787, quoted in Ball (2007, 435).

2. For a discussion on the scholarship of Brutus's identity, see Ball (2003, 436).

3. Although the first reported US Supreme Court decision was in 1792, the first volume of the *US Supreme Court Reporter* contains decisions of the Supreme Court of Pennsylvania, which goes back to 1754 (Fowler and Jeon 2008, 17).

4. Indeed, the "canon," as Keith Whittington and Amanda Rinderle note, "is neither timeless nor natural" (Whittington and Rinderle 2012, 5).

5. The case date range differs from the casebook publication date range for methodological reasons detailed in this section.

6. This method is similar to how David Mayhew (2000) selected actions to study in *American Congress*. In his book, Mayhew sought to catalog Congressional members' "actions" in the "public sphere." To do so, Mayhew used thirty-eight secondary-source undergraduate history textbooks to identify 2,304 instances of members' actions in Congress. From this database, Mayhew offers insight on a variety of Congressional public actions, from the nature of congressional opposition to presidents and the surprising frequency of foreign policy actions to the timing of important activity within congressional careers (and the way that term limits might affect these behaviors).

7. Some critics might argue that by sampling landmark constitutional decisions, I potentially select on the dependent variable. Perhaps salient cases—those selected into leading casebooks—are more likely to contain cases that extend central state authority. Nevertheless, I do not see this as a serious research design problem because editors of these casebooks (lawyers) are far less concerned with central state power than political scientists, and thus they might not select cases primarily because of their effect on federal state authority. By contrast, lawyers (and their casebooks) select cases with an eye toward contemporary legal practice. Moreover, because of the Court's position in American politics as a final arbiter, it is highly probable that virtually all Supreme Court cases—salient or not—influence central state authority in some way. While other case selection methods such as random sampling would have generated a more representative list of the universe of Supreme Court cases, this book deliberately examines the Court's landmark constitutional cases for two reasons. First, these are the types of cases on which political scientists and historians have long focused. Second, since this book seeks to understand the Court's role in American state expansion, constitutional decisions are the appropriate starting point because they are the decisions that deal with the national state's relationship to its citizens and subnational governments. Thus, to satisfy the goal of sampling landmark constitutional decisions relatively free from contemporary bias, I used this casebook selection method. In further research, it will be interesting to see if the patterns found in this book hold constant for other fields of law and for less salient cases.

8. For most casebooks, except early in history, I specified Cornell Library holdings only. Cornell Library holds over eight million volumes and over a million e-books. https://www.library.cornell.edu/about/collections. Accessed 9 February 2016.

9. For details on this database, visit this site: http://gdc.gale.com/products/the-making-of-modern-law-legal-treatises-1800-1926/. This database is the world's most comprehensive full-text collection of Anglo-American legal treatises of the period 1800–1926.

10. The dean of Harvard Law School, Christopher Columbus Langdell, instituted the now-prototypical three-year casebook-method law school curriculum in 1876.

Langdell's casebooks were excerpts of actual cases arranged to illustrate the principles of law and how law developed. As a result, writes Lawrence Friedman in his seminal *A History of American Law*, "the classroom tone was profoundly altered" (Friedman 2005, 468). Before the rise of law schools, legal education took place through apprenticeships: "Most lawyers gained their pretensions by spending some time in training in the office of a member of the bar. . . . For a fee, the lawyer-to-be hung around an office, read Blackstone and Coke and miscellaneous other books, and copied legal documents" (Friedman 2005, 238). See Friedman, pp. 238–41, for an overview of legal education in America until the mid-nineteenth century. See LaPiana (1994) for a discussion of the sea changes in American legal education from its apprenticeship roots to the modern legal education system developed by Dean Langdell.

11. There is a well-documented history regarding the evolution of American legal education. For an extensive overview of this literature, see MacGill and Newmyer (2008). Of particular importance to American legal education, MacGill and Newmyer note that through the War of 1812 most of American law students educated themselves by reading primarily English treatises, especially Sir William Blackstone's (1764) four volume *Commentaries on the Laws of England*. They maintain that, up until the 1870s, Blackstone "did more to shape American legal education and thought than any other single work" (MacGill and Newmyer 2008, 40). Nevertheless, American treatises such as James Kent's (1826) *Commentaries on American Law* became progressively more widely used (MacGill and Newmyer 2008, 43). MacGill and Newmyer note that several developments—among them the steam press, cheap paper, and the establishment of subscription law libraries—enabled wide circulation long before the advent of law schools in the 1870s: "The treatise tradition, which did so much to shape law-office education, also greatly influenced the substance and methods of instruction in early law schools" (2008, 44).

12. In their analysis of Marbury v. Madison, 5 U.S. 137 (1803) and the constitutional canon, Whittington and Rinderle discuss key eighteenth-century constitutional treatises (2012, 848–49). Of the eleven treatises published between 1824 and 1868 that they discuss, I include the nine that had an index of cases.

13. See William Novak (2002) for a discussion of the importance of Thomas Cooley (1868), John Burgess (1890), and Westel Willoughby (1912) in the development of constitutional thought in the United States. Willoughby's and Cooley's work is included in my database.

14. Many casebooks in my database follow this pattern—William Lockhart et al.'s (1964) *The American Constitution* as well as Paul Brest et al.'s (1975) *Process of Constitutional Decision-Making*, to name a couple more examples. See Appendix 3, which lists all fifty-eight casebooks that comprise my database.

15. http://prawfsblawg.blogs.com/prawfsblawg/2007/05/choosing_a_case_1.html accessed 18 January 2016. I have included all the casebooks referenced in this blog entry.

16. http://prawfsblawg.blogs.com/prawfsblawg/2007/05/choosing_a_case_1.html

17. Casebook editors most frequently distinguish principal cases by italicizing the case name in the index. "Principal cases" are the Supreme Court decisions quoted and discussed at length in a casebook, whereas nonprincipal cases are merely cited in a footnote or parenthetically within the casebook. If a casebook distinguishes "principal" cases in its index, I listed only the "principal" cases in the spreadsheet.

18. This might indicate something about the canon—or lack thereof—of American constitutional law. For a discussion of the different kinds and objectives of constitutional canons, see Balkin and Levinson (1998).

19. *Brown*, 347 U.S.

20. See Rosenberg (2008, chs. 2–3).

21. In his study, Bensel (1990) compares Union- and Confederate-state strength along "seven dimensions of central state authority."

22. The table is taken directly from Bensel (1990, 114).

23. INS v. Chadha (1983) is a typical example of the small number of cases where the Court expands and contracts central state authority in the same decision, simply allocating power between branches of the national state. Here, the Court expanded the administrative capacity dimension and restricted the citizenship dimension. In INS v. Chadha, the Court declared that a one-House veto of the attorney general's decision regarding deportation, promulgated in the Immigration and Nationality Act, was unconstitutional because such a veto violated bicameralism. By ruling the one-House veto unconstitutional, the Court left decision-making authority power with the more statist branch, the executive, thus expanding the administrative capacity dimension. At the same time, this book's interpretation schema examines the actual law/action under judicial scrutiny: in this case, the Court reviewed a House of Representatives resolution that reversed the attorney general's decision to suspend Chadha's deportation. Since Congress had already delegated its authority over this issue to the executive branch, the Court held that the House's resolution was unconstitutional, thereby restricting the central state (i.e., Congress) along the citizenship dimension. Indeed, some cases expanded power for one branch of the national government while restricting for another (e.g., for example, a war power case giving power to the presidency instead of Congress). Such a case, like INS v. Chadha, would be denoted as having a neutral effect on the overall expansion of federal power, since the Court's decision just "allocate[s] authority between the various branches of the state itself," a defining feature of "administrative capacity" (Bensel 1990, 108). See Appendix 1 for a detailed description of a neutral case. See also Bensel (1990, 106–11) for a discussion of the "structural dimensions" of the central state, which includes centralization of authority and administrative capacity.

24. Landis and Koch (1977) suggest various effect sizes when interpreting the kappa statistic. If Kappa is greater than 0.60 and less than 0.80, they suggest this indicates "substantial agreement." More recently Elliot and Woodward (2016) echo Landis and Koch's (1977) interpretation of the kappa statistic.

25. Of 624 decisions in my database, 6 are lower federal court decisions and thus not included in the Spaeth Database. For these 6, I coded the issues following Spaeth's codebook. These issue areas, and their definitions, are derived from the "Issue Areas" variable of Harold Spaeth's Supreme Court Database. Accessed here: http://scdb.wustl.edu/documentation.php?var=issueArea.

26. On the issue variable, the Spaeth Codebook notes the problems and the accompanying solution for the presentist bias: "Because the database extends over four centuries of the Court's decisions during which time the Court's jurisdiction changed drastically, the description of many specific variables does not provide a good

fit. . . . We made a decision to retain the twentieth century listing and apply it as best we could to the eighteenth and nineteenth century decisions. We found it possible with the addition of only the seven common law decisions (variables 140010–140070), plus a couple of others." The 140010–140070 variables fall under the heading "private action"—see Table 2.2 for a fuller definition of private action.

27. Spaeth's Database does not include "executive power."

28. See Appendix 4 (figure A.2) for a distribution of cases in these data.

29. As discussed in detail above in the "Case Selection Method" section, the cases included for analysis, on the whole, are significant and authoritative in the sense that these cases are cited and used to guide lower-level courts at a higher rate than the average citation score for the universe of Supreme Court cases. While some landmark cases are not equally significant, this book does not parse out the precise significance for each and every case because its purpose is to understand constitutional development over a two-hundred-year span across several hundred constitutional decisions.

30. Cushman (1998) and White (2000) also push against the standard interpretation that the New Deal was an abrupt turning point in constitutional development.

31. Figure 2.4 graphs the overall impact on central state authority, that is, the change of any one of the seven central state dimensions. This overall impact is not separate from the seven central state dimensions. For example, if a decision restricted/expanded the centralization dimension, then that would also indicate a restriction/expansion of the overall impact on authority. However, simply because these two variables (central state dimensions and overall impact) are intimately linked does not explain why the centralization dimension—more than any other dimension—is the most abundant in these data.

32. Others have recognized that transferring governing authority typifies constitutional development, but that transference often centers of the emerging "modern state" of the New Deal era. For example, Keith Whittington argues that the "logic of the modern state" of the early twentieth century "favored centralization of political authority and influence" (Whittington 1997, 489). I agree with this interpretation, but I would also argue that the Court's interpretation of constitutional law began centralizing political authority long before the emergence of the "modern state."

33. This claim is supported by David Robertson's comprehensive study of American federalism, which argues that the Framers created "a double battleground." The first pertains to battles fought in every country, "whether the government should do something about health, welfare, the economy . . ." The second battleground touches on the question of who decides; Robertson says this battleground "turns on which level of government should have the power to choose whether to act" (Robertson 2012, 35).

34. Hayburn's Case, 2 U.S. 409 (1792).

35. *Marbury*, 5 U.S.

36. Martin v. Hunter's Lessee, 14 U.S. 304 (1816) and Cohens v. Virginia, 19 U.S. 264 (1821).

37. Hylton v. United States, 3 U.S. 171 (1796).

38. Hollingsworth v. Virginia, 3 U.S. 378 (1798).

39. Anderson v. Dunn, 19 U.S. 204 (1821).

40. *Fletcher*, 10 U.S.

41. New Jersey v. Wilson, 11 U.S. 164 (1812).

42. Dartmouth College v. Woodward, 17 U.S. 518 (1819).

43. Ware v. Hylton, 3 U.S. 199 (1796).

44. McCulloch v. Maryland, 17 U.S. 316 (1819).

45. Osborn v. Bank of the United States, 22 U.S. 738 (1824).

46. *Martin*, 14 U.S.

47. Mayor of the City of New York v. Miln, 36 U.S. 102 (1837).

48. Charles River Bridge v. Warren Bridge, 36 U.S. 420 (1837).

49. Briscoe v. Bank of Kentucky, 36 U.S. 257 (1837).

50. Bank of Augusta v. Earle, 38 U.S. 519 (1839).

51. Bronson v. Kinzie, 42 U.S. 311 (1843).

52. Piqua Branch Bank v. Knoop, 57 U.S. 369 (1853).

53. *Prigg*, 41 U.S.

54. Dred Scott v. Sandford, 60 U.S. 393 (1857).

55. State police powers are those that enable a sovereign entity to protect the health, safety, and welfare of its citizens.

56. Prize Cases, 67 U.S. 635 (1863).

57. Ex parte Milligan, 71 U.S. 2 (1866).

58. Ex parte Vallandigham, 68 U.S. 243 (1864).

59. Ex parte McCardle, 74 U.S. 506 (1869).

60. Legal Tender Cases, 79 U.S. 457 (1871).

61. Collector v. Day, 78 U.S. 113 (1871).

62. United States v. Cruikshank, 92 U.S. 542 (1876).

63. Ward v. Maryland 79 U.S. 418 (1871).

64. *Ward*, 79 U.S. at 425.

65. Welton v. Missouri, 91 U.S. 275 (1876).

66. *Welton*, 91 U.S. at 282.

67. *Welton*, 91 U.S. at 282.

68. Gilman v. Philadelphia, 70 U.S. 713 (1865).

69. *Gilman*, 70 U.S. at 726, emphasis original.

70. *Gilman*, 70 U.S. at 732.

71. McCray v. United States, 195 U.S. 27 (1904).

72. Champion v. Ames, 188 U.S. 321 (1903).

73. Shreveport Rate Case, 234 U.S. 342 (1914).

74. Hoke v. United States, 227 U.S. 308 (1913).

75. Hipolite Egg Co. v. United States, 220 U.S. 45 (1911).

76. Pittsburgh Melting Co. v. Totten, 248 U.S. 1 (1918).

77. United States v. Ju Toy, 198 U.S. 253 (1905).

78. United States v. Lanza, 260 U.S. 377 (1922).

79. *Lanza*, 260 U.S. at 380.

80. *E. C. Knight*, 156 U.S.

81. Hammer v. Dagenhart, 247 U.S. 251 (1918).

82. Civil Rights Cases, 109 U.S. 3 (1883).

83. Pollock v. Farmers' Loan and Trust Company, 157 U.S. 429 (1895).

84. *Allgeyer*, 165 U.S.

85. Coppage v. Kansas, 236 U.S. 1 (1915).

86. Muller v. Oregon, 208 U.S. 412 (1908) and Bunting v. Oregon, 243 U.S. 426 (1917).

87. United States v. Curtiss-Wright Export Corporation, 299 U.S. 304 (1936).

88. Wickard v. Filburn, 317 U.S. 111 (1941).

89. Steward Machine Co. v. Davis, 301 U.S. 548 (1937) and Helvering v. Davis, 301 U.S. 619 (1937).

90. Katzenbach v. McClung, 379 U.S. 294 (1964) and Heart of Atlanta Motel Inc. v. United States, 379 U.S. 241 (1964).

91. See Epp (1998).

92. Cantwell v. Connecticut, 310 U.S. 296 (1940).

93. Edwards v. South Carolina, 372 U.S. 229 (1963).

94. Shelley v. Kraemer, 334 U.S. 1 (1948).

95. Cooper v. Aaron, 358 U.S. 1 (1958).

96. *Cooper*, 358 U.S. at 18.

97. *Cooper*, 358 U.S. at 18.

98. National League of Cities v. Usery, 426 U.S. 833 (1976).

99. Garcia v. San Antonio Metropolitan Transit, 469 U.S. 528 (1985).

100. United States v. Nixon, 418 U.S. 683 (1974).

101. Clinton v. City of New York, 524 U.S. 417 (1998).

102. South Dakota v. Dole, 483 U.S. 203 (1987).

103. Morrison v. Olson, 487 U.S. 654 (1988).

104. Texas v. Johnson, 491 U.S. 397 (1989).

105. Wooley v. Maynard, 430 U.S. 705 (1977).

106. See for example Paris Adult Theatre I v. Slaton, 413 U.S. 49 (1973), Miller v. California, 413 U.S. 15 (1973), Young v. American Mini Theaters Inc., 427 U.S. 50 (1976), and New York v. Ferber, 458 U.S. 747 (1982).

Chapter 3

1. Thomas Paine, *The Writings of Thomas Paine*, Vol. 1 (1774–1779), p. 70. http://lf-oll.s3.amazonaws.com/titles/343/Paine_0548-01_EBk_v6.0.pdf (Conway 1894, 70).

2. Louis Hartz's (1955) *The Liberal Tradition* advanced this American exceptionalist paradigm. Soon after, in 1956, James Willard Hurst refined Hartz's argument. Like Hartz, and Tocqueville before him, Hurst suggested that the American state was unusual and distinctive, even if it was a state that sought to produce "the release of individual creative energy" that would expand state powers (Hurst 1956, 7). See Skowronek (1982) and Evans, Rueschemeyer, and Skocpol (1985) for examples of these comparative analyses of state strength. The American exceptionalism centered on the lack of a national administrative welfare state and thus on the historical period when the U.S. began to develop some semblance of a European welfare state: from around the Progressive era to the New Deal. The Court's constitutional evolution, however, challenges some of these narratives that focus more narrowly on the administrative welfare state.

Central state weakness and antistatism are not synonymous. Nevertheless, if the American state lacked strength, this was due in large part to the antistatist ideas that made their way into the design of the Constitution. As this chapter will discuss, the fear of a strong central state contributed greatly to America's federalist structure, a structure that created two sovereigns—the state governments and the federal government—whose boundaries of powers would be—and continue to be—determined largely by the Supreme Court.

3. See John (1997) and Katznelson (2003), for example. Also see footnote 6 below.

4. This sentiment is shared not just by APD scholars. German philosopher G. W. F. Hegel thought the United States had no state at all—without a bureaucracy, a national culture, or a monarch to represent the permanent interests of the national community (Hegel quoted in Skowronek 1982, 6–7). See also Hegel (1956, 84–87). Alexis de Tocqueville's *Democracy in America* commented on the relative statelessness in the United States. Of the "administration in New England," Tocqueville wrote, "Nothing is more striking to a European traveler in the United States than the absence of what we term the Government, or the Administration" (Tocqueville [1835] 2003, 51–52).

5. James Morone points out that both republican communitarian and liberal individualistic conceptions of democratic ideology share one thing: "each rests on a suspicion of government" (Morone 1998, 8). For a nice overview of the American "dread of government," see Morone (1998, 2–4). Like most studies within the APD tradition, Morone understands state-building as the creation of a centralized, bureaucratic administration. Moving beyond this conception, my book allows us to see where the tentacles of the central state expanded into other policy realms.

6. Revisionist studies of the American state have noted internal improvements (M. Wilson 2008), bureaucratic administrative authority to address Indians affairs (Rockwell 2010), and the Army Corps of Topographical Engineers as important sites of state-building and capacity in the early American state (Adler 2012).

7. Other scholars, such as John Larson (2001), have also detailed the extraordinary extent of internal improvements spearheaded by the national government, at least until Andrew Jackson assumed the presidency in 1828.

8. Library of Congress: https://www.loc.gov/rr/program/bib/ourdocs/Indian.html. For an overview of the relationship between the American state and Native Americans, see Prucha (1984). Stephen Rockwell (2010) has also argued that the early American state—through its bureaucratic administrative capacity—wielded considerable power over Native Americans. In particular, the Office of Indian Affairs possessed significant autonomy to enforce Indian policy in the antebellum period (Rockwell 2010, 31–34, 306–18).

9. David Robertson (2005b) recognizes this. For him, constitutional design acts as an independent variable, influencing the behavior of political actors by allocating authority and providing "legally defined constraints, opportunities, and incentives" (Simeon 2009, 242).

10. *Dartmouth College*, 17 U.S.

11. American Insurance Co. v. Canter, 26 U.S. 511 (1828).

12. *American Insurance*, 26 U.S. at 546.

13. *Ableman*, 62. U.S.

14. *Ableman*, 62. U.S. at 517.

15. *Ableman*, 62. U.S. at 518.

16. While some might say that, at least in the early republic, there might be a difference between expanding and defining central state authority, this book interprets expanding and defining as the same in the early republic. Judicial decisions that defined particular powers of the federal government invariably expanded the scope and reach of that government.

17. The Passenger Cases, 48 U.S. 283 (1849).

18. United States v. Smith, 18 U.S. 153 (1820).

19. U.S. v. Smith, 18 U.S. at 159.

20. U.S. v. Smith, 18 U.S. at 163.

21. Worcester v. State of Georgia, 31 U.S. 515 (1832).

22. *Worcester*, 31 U.S. at 557.

23. *Worcester*, 31 U.S. at 561.

24. *Osborn*, 22 U.S.

25. *Osborn*, 22 U.S. at 861.

26. Planter's Bank v. Sharp, 47 U.S. 301 (1848) and Woodruff v. Trapnall, 51 U.S. 190 (1850).

27. *Planter's*, 47 U.S. at 319.

28. *Cohens*, 19 U.S.

29. The Court held, "These States are constituent parts of the United States. They are members of one great empire—for some purposes sovereign, for some purposes subordinate." Thus, it was not "unreasonable" for the Supreme Court to "be empowered to decide on the judgment of a State tribunal enforcing such unconstitutional law," *Cohens*, 19 U.S. at 414.

30. *Cohens*, 19 U.S. at 415.

31. *Cohens* also demonstrated that the Court could not alone expand federal power; it often needs support from the political branches. There is a rich literature on the interdependence of America's national branches of government. This "governance as dialogue movement," as Mark Miller notes, rejects "the notion of either total legislative supremacy or total judicial supremacy in favor of a much more complicated and nuanced, continuous process of interaction among the institutions" (Miller 2009, 9). Despite the governance-as-dialogue school of thought, comparativist court scholars, examining thirteen federal or quasifederal countries, have found that the United States possesses "strong judicial review" in that a "court's declaration of unconstitutionality is final until the constitution is amended or the court overrules itself" (Aroney and Kincaid 2017, 9).

32. Graber (2006b) argues that "legal norms" explain Justice Miller's opinion in Roosevelt v. Meyer, 68 U.S. 512 (1863) and Chief Justice Chase's opinion in *Ex Parte McCardle*, 74 U.S., but "had Justice Miller or Chief Justice Chase been in the executive or legislative branches of the national government, they probably would have behaved differently" (Graber 2006b, 59).

33. Aetna Life Insurance Co. v. Haworth, 300 U.S. 227 (1937) at 240. Justiciability is a broad conceptual umbrella encompassing several interrelated doctrines, including standing, mootness, and ripeness. For the purposes of these data, all decisions dealing

with these doctrines were coded under the "jurisdiction/judicial power" legal issue area, and thus they are not discussed as separate doctrine below.

34. There is an important pragmatic side to jurisdictional denials, too. For much of the Court's history, the Court has advocated for reductions or stasis in federal rights because of their impact on federal court caseloads. Control over its own docket, and thus a reduction in caseload, was an impetus behind Chief Justice William Taft's efforts. See Crowe (2007).

35. *Hayburn's*, 2 U.S.

36. The quote is from a letter from Chief Justice John Jay to President Washington, August 8, 1793. Access here: http://press-pubs.uchicago.edu/founders/documents/a3_2_1s34.html.

37. *Marbury*, 5 U.S. at 170.

38. Luther v. Borden, 48 U.S. 1 (1849).

39. See also Strawbridge v. Curtiss, 7 U.S. 267 (1806)—another unanimous Marshall Court decision, which allowed the Court to duck certain cases through a jurisdictional rule known today as "complete diversity." In just a few sentences, Marshall held that, in lawsuits "where several parties represent several distinct interests," all parties of one side must be distinct and diverse from all parties on the other side of the suit. *Strawbridge*, 7 U.S. at 267.

40. Robertson (2012, ch. 2) carefully details the arguments for both the broad and narrow nationalists. For a detailed discussion of Roger Sherman's pivotal role at the Convention see Robertson's (2005b, 231–35).

41. Prominent anti-Federalist literature underscored the importance of states' rights. The anti-Federalist "John DeWitt" penned a number of articles circulated among his fellow Massachusetts citizens. He feared an enlarged central state, claiming the proposed Constitution asks the states and their citizens to "invest the new Congress with powers, which you have yet thought proper to withhold from your own present government" (John DeWitt, II, 27 October 1787), accessed 18 June 2016: http://www.constitution.org/afp/dewitt02.htm.

Other anti-Federalists agreed with DeWitt. After the Pennsylvania Convention ratified the new Constitution in December of 1787, a dissenting address appeared in the *Pennsylvania Packet and Daily Advertiser*, which was subsequently reprinted in many other states. Within his lengthy address, the probable author, Samuel Bryan, reiterated DeWitt's fear of a strong central state and the erosion of states' rights: "[T]he new government will not be a confederacy of states, as it ought, but one consolidated government, founded upon the destruction of the several governments of the states. . . . The powers of Congress under the new constitution, are complete and unlimited over the purse and the sword, and are perfectly independent of, and supreme over, the state governments" ("The Address and Reasons of Dissent of the Minority of the Convention of Pennsylvania to their Constituents," 12 December 1787, accessed 18 June 2016, http://www.constitution.org/afp/pennmi00.htm).

42. With respect to drawing the line between federal and state sovereignty, both the Marshall and Taney Courts had difficulty finding the precise boundaries of what Martin Shapiro called "the absurdity of two-sovereignty federalism" (Shapiro 1980, 360). This difficultly, I argue below, contributed to the Court restricting and

expanding central state authority at any given period in constitutional development. Constructing precise boundaries between these sovereigns is unrealistic and, more than that, such boundaries have never existed historically in America (Shapiro 1980, 367).

43. Scholars have noted that the Constitution creates conflicting governing prerogatives. Orren and Skowronek have recognized that "the Constitution stands midway between prescriptive and positive law and in that sense is a perfect example of multiple orders" (Orren and Skowronek 2004, 171). For Orren and Skowronek, the Constitution, in general, represents "intercurrence"—their idea that "the normal condition of the polity will be that of multiple, incongruous authorities operating simultaneously" (Orren and Skowronek 2004, 108). I embrace the general idea advanced by Orren and Skowronek that the Constitution creates conflicting spheres of governing authority.

44. The Early Republic (1789–1824) witnessed the greatest rate of state expansion whereby the Court attempted to ensure the national government's supremacy. Murphy maintains, "The Constitution was fatal to the sovereignty of the states . . . there was no misunderstanding as to the effect that the Constitution would have upon state sovereignty, for in the campaign for ratification one of the principal bases of opposition to the Constitution was that it would destroy the sovereignty of the states." Soon after ratification, however, people had "conveniently forgotten" that the Constitution destroyed state sovereignty, and from this grew doctrines of state interposition and nullification (Murphy 1968, 410–11).

45. On the ability of the federal courts to help the national political branches overcome thorny issues and thus expand federal power, see Whittington (2005).

46. The growth in law became particularly pronounced by the late nineteenth and early twentieth centuries. For example, the total amount of federal litigation in the United States rose from 47,553 cases in 1911 to 196,953 cases by 1930. Similarly, while the Supreme Court had only 253 cases pending before it in 1850, by 1890 the Court's docket swelled to 1,800 appellate cases. Moreover, the law profession grew, too: lawyers in the United States numbered around 39,000 in 1870 and 161,000 by 1930. Consequently, the number of law schools with a three-year program increased from 7 in 1890 to over 170 in 1931. All these numbers come from Novak (2002, 262–63).

47. Orren and Skowronek argue that the move from prescriptive to prospective law undergirds all of American political development (Orren and Skowronek 2004, 178–81). This sweeping theory has received scant attention in the literature, but with respect to the judiciary, it has long been held that the Civil War (and the subsequent passage of the Fourteenth Amendment) facilitated a move from prescriptive (based on common law precedent) to prospective (based on social circumstance) understandings of law. Yet even during the prescriptive era of American political development, the Court consistently expanded the powers of the federal government. The ways in which the Court expanded central state authority differed, however, during prescriptive versus prospective eras.

In the prescriptive era (before the Civil War), courts typically expanded central state authority vis-à-vis questions that had an established history within English common law, largely pertaining to property and contract rights and to taxing powers. *Dartmouth College* (1819) exemplified prescriptive lawmaking, invalidating a New

Hampshire state law that attempted to change Dartmouth College from a private institution to a state university. Marshall rooted his decision in a lengthy discussion of English common law concerning contracts (*Dartmouth College*, 17 U.S. at 707). Yet *Dartmouth College* still asserted judicial authority over the New Hampshire legislature and, in this sense, expanded federal power. Prescriptive-era decisions, while not based on broader questions of public welfare, nevertheless affirmed the enumerated powers of the federal government over state governments. For other prescriptive-era constitutional decisions that expanded central state authority, see *Ware*, 3 U.S., Terrett v. Taylor, 13 U.S. 43 (1815), and *Bronson*, 42 U.S.

But not until the twentieth century did the Court (and the other national political institutions) turn toward proscriptive lawmaking, an approach that accommodated a society looking more to the federal government for regulatory solutions than it had previously. Indeed, Brown v. Board of Education (1954) typified central state expansion through proscriptive lawmaking—a decision based less on precedent and more on the social and psychological consequences of racial segregation (Orren and Skowronek 2004, 179).

48. David Robertson finds, "The [constitutional] convention deliberately left the distribution of commercial authority ambiguous," which enabled the Court to interpret the Commerce Clause as a vehicle for state expansion (Robertson 2005a, 183).

49. For a history of the Necessary and Proper Clause and its effect on the development of federal power (especially with respect to the Bank of the United States), see Lawson, Miller, Natelson, and Seidman (2010, ch. 7).

50. Article I, Section 8: "To regulate commerce with foreign nations, and among the several states, and with the Indian tribes. . . . To coin money, regulate the value thereof, and of foreign coin, and fix the standard of weights and measures. . . . To make all laws which shall be necessary and proper for carrying into execution the foregoing powers, and all other powers vested by this Constitution in the government of the United States, or in any department or officer thereof."

51. According to Licht (1995), "The fortunes of the now former colonialist remained in the grips of the British commercial interests; the ups and downs of economic activity during and after the 1780s reflected the abilities of British merchants to flood the American market with goods or block American exports. . . . Hamilton and his allies sought to build a powerful nation through commerce" (Licht 1995, 18–19). Doing so helped produce a central state that would grow through constitutional issues of economic activity and through the property dimension.

52. *Federalist Papers* Nos. 18–20, penned by Madison, offer an account of the lessons gleaned from the history of previous republics. Madison's solution: "The general power whatever be its form if it preserves itself, must swallow up the State powers. Otherwise it will be swallowed up by them" (Farrand 1911, 287). David Hendrickson also details how the history of failed republics such as those of Italy, Greece, and Germany informed the preferences for a strong, centralized federal government among founders such as Madison and John Adams (Hendrickson 2003, 47–54).

53. Madison also echoed this sentiment during the federal convention. On 18 June 1787, in speaking to the committee of the whole house, Madison said, "Foreign

powers also will not be idle spectators. They will interpose, the confusion will increase, and a dissolution of the Union ensue" (*Records of Federal Convention*, 285).

54. For a discussion on how the founders sought to create an environment conducive to investment, see Holton (2007, 179–223).

55. Much like this chapter discusses below, Licht saw that the courts—not just the Supreme Court—as "occup[ying] a preeminent place in the nation's divided system of government" (Licht 1995, 93–95).

56. *McCullough*, 17 U.S., and Gibbons v. Ogden, 22 U.S. 1 (1824).

57. Marshall wrote that a "narrow construction" would "cripple the government, and render it unequal to the object, for which it is declared to be instituted." He thus concluded, "We cannot perceive the propriety of this strict construction, nor adopt it as the rule by which the constitution is to be expounded" (*Gibbons*, 22 U.S. at 187–88).

58. In their American legal history casebook, Kermit Hall, Paul Finkelman, and James Ely note, "*Gibbons* is the most important commerce clause case in Supreme Court history. All subsequent nineteenth-century commerce clause cases (and many twentieth-century ones) were, to a great extent, merely commentary on *Gibbons*" (2005, 155).

59. *McCullough*, 17 U.S. at 409.

60. These cases include *Gibbons* 22 U.S., Brown v. Maryland, 25 U.S. 419 (1827), Willson v. Blackbird Creek Marsh Co. 27 U.S. 245 (1829), Craig v. Missouri, 29 U.S. 410 (1830), and *Barron*, 32 U.S.

61. G. Edward White (1988) makes this argument. White argues that many of the Marshall Court's cases "did not so much promote federal sovereignty as restrict state sovereignty." The nationalism promulgated in Marshall's rulings "was not a nationalism in the modern sense of support for affirmative plenary federal regulatory power; the Court's posture can more accurately be described as a critique of reserved state sovereignty" (White et al. 1988, 486). Nonetheless, throughout Marshall's tenure, the Court was preoccupied with defining the boundaries between state and federal sovereignty, and the difficulty engendered by this duty produced decisions that restricted and expanded central state authority.

62. Charles F. Hobson, editor of *The Papers of John Marshall*, sees Marshall less as a proponent of broad constitutional interpretation and more as an opponent of the "restrictive construction" advocated by Maryland's counsel in *McCulloch*. Hobson notes that Marshall's primary concern with strict construction was that it "would inexorably transform the Union into a league of sovereign states—a belated triumph for Antifederalism" (Marshall et al. 1974, 258).

63. Johnson v. McIntosh, 21 U.S. 543 (1823).

64. Cherokee Nation v. State of Georgia, 30 U.S. 1 (1831).

65. *Worcester*, 31 U.S.

66. *Johnson*, 21 U.S. at 573–74.

67. In *Willson*, 27 U.S., Delaware authorized the Blackbird Creek Marsh Company to build a dam spanning the Blackbird Creek. This dam obstructed the creek and prevented a small sailing vessel, possessing a coastal license similar to the one held in *Gibbons*, from navigating the creek. During the course of his travel on the creek,

the licensed owner of the tiny sailing vessel broke part of the dam. Consequently, the Company successfully sued Willson for trespassing and obtained a Delaware court order requiring Willson to pay damages. Willson appealed to the Supreme Court, claiming that Delaware's law violated Congress's Commerce Clause. The Court disagreed, because Congress had taken no action with which the Delaware law could conflict: "We do not think that the Act . . . can . . . be considered as repugnant to the power to regulate commerce in its dormant state, or as being in conflict with any law passed on the subject" (*Willson*, 27 U.S. at 252). Thus, Marshall laid the ground for the "dormant" Commerce Clause, a constitutional interpretation of the Clause that allowed the Court to regulate commercial activity even when Congress had not promulgated a law intending to do so, which is discussed below.

68. The attorney for the sailor argued that the dam "unconstitutionally impeded" the boat "in use of her license." More than that, the Commerce Clause prevented Delaware from "closing a navigable river" (*Willson*, 27 U.S. at 248). In contrast, the attorney for the company argued that body of water being dammed was insignificant to water traffic: it was "one of those sluggish reptile streams, that do not run but creep, and which, wherever it possesses, spreads its venom, and destroys the health of all those who inhabit its marshes" (*Willson*, 27 U.S. at 249). Thus, the attorney for the company claimed that damming unhealthy waterways was a justifiable use of a state's police power to regulate healthy and safety of its citizens, especially since Congress had passed no legislation affecting the creek to which the Court agreed.

69. Providence Bank v. Billings, 29 U.S. 514 (1830). Influenced by the growing Jacksonian democracy sentiment, the Court limited the amount of protection afforded to corporate charters under the Contracts Clause (Hall, Finkelman, and Ely 2005, 801). Here Marshall rejected Providence Bank's argument that its charter exempted it from state taxation. Writing for the majority, Marshall held that the Constitution "was not intended to furnish the corrective for every abuse of power which may be committed by the state governments" (*Providence*, 29 U.S. at 563).

70. Gerald Gunther supports this claim. Gunther shows us that "The degree of centralization that has taken place since [Marshall's] time may well have come about in the face of Marshall's intent rather than in accord with his expectations. That centralization may be the inevitable consequence of economic and social changes. And this development may suggest the impossibility of articulating general constitutional standards capable of limiting those centralizing forces" (Gunther 1969, 20).

71. Michael Les Benedict notes that the "divergence between the Marshall and Taney Courts on matters of federalism has been exaggerated," and he emphasizes the Taney Court's "continued commitment to national supremacy" (Les Benedict 1978, 44), see also n. 13 on the same page.

72. See Crowe (2007, 120), referring to the Taney Court as "more likely [than the Marshall Court] to limit the sphere of central government authority."

73. *Charles River Bridge*, 36. US.

74. For a discussion of courts' role in expanding federal power through the economy, see M. Wilson (2008, 13–22).

75. Of this depiction of the Court's role, Larry Kramer writes, "This claim may sound jarring to lawyers today, who have for decades been fed a story about the

Supreme Court's uncompromising stand against federal growth until Justice Roberts spinelessly caved to pressure from the Roosevelt Administration. Yet [this] account is, in fact, the more accurate rendition of events" (Kramer 2000, 228).

76. *Prigg*, 41 U.S.

77. Article IV states, in part, "No Person held to Service or Labor in one State, under the Laws thereof, escaping into another, shall, in Consequence of any Law or Regulation therein, be discharged from such Service or Labor, but shall be delivered up on Claim of the Party to whom such Service or labor may be due."

78. *Prigg*, 41 U.S. at 622–23.

79. Kramer (2000, 229). See Kramer (2000) for a description of the Court's penchant for supporting federal power over states during the nineteenth century.

80. *Dred Scott*, 60 U.S.

81. *Dred Scott*, 60 U.S. at 403.

82. Loren Beth (1971) makes a similar argument of the interpretation of the Court during the Industrial Revolution. Beth writes: "It does not do, in this latter day, to take a simplistic view of the judges or the way the courts handled the resulting cases. . . . What emerges is what might be expected of a human institution: a fumbling and vacillating response which in the long run was astonishingly but accidentally successful in allowing both for *increasing* governmental regulation of the worst aspects of the Industrial Revolution and for the maintenance of the system (sometimes loosely called 'free enterprise') which was creating the revolution" (Beth 1971, 141).

Chapter 4

1. Redfield (1867).

2. In making this argument, I join APD scholars and legal historians who revise the obstructionist constitutional development narrative. For example, Paul Frymer (2008) argues that APD scholars' "skepticism of courts" leads these scholars to go "too far in juxtaposing court power against other political institutions and . . . miss the important ways that courts contribute to the development of state power" (Frymer 2008, 789). Similarly, sociologist John D. Skrentny also emphasizes the positive rather than obstructionist role courts play in the United States: "I argue here for increased attention to the positive role of law and courts in policymaking and statebuilding" (Skrentny 2006, 214).

Other APD scholars revise the obstructionist *Lochner* narrative. Howard Gillman (1993) argues that the *Lochner* era Court was not necessarily obstructionist. Instead, the Court invalidated state legislation not because of laissez-faire ideologies but because of state neutrality and aversions to class legislation, which had deep legal roots dating back to the nineteenth century. Legal historians such as Barry Cushman (1998) revise the obstructionist narrative by arguing against the "constitutional revolution of 1937"— the so-called switch in time that saved nine—marked by West Coast Hotel v. Parrish 300, U.S. 379 (1937). Finally, Julie Novkov (2001) adds further to these *Lochner* and New Deal revisionist interpretations; she emphasizes the continuity between *Lochner* and *West Coast Hotel*, noting the crucial role of gender and the social construction of gender at play in both cases.

3. It might be asked, who would place the Court outside of the central state? Narratives that view the Court as a persistent inhibitor, however, do just this—though not quite consciously. In viewing the Court as an obstacle during the *Lochner* era, for example, scholars have failed to recognize the very strength of the Court itself to rule over new questions and extend its reach into new areas of society. The increased power of the Court itself might also be an indication of greater judicial independence and insulation from other political institutions and society, indications of enhanced central state strength. Outside of the APD literature, judicial independence has also been recognized as a constitutional design principle that enhances economic growth; economic scholars have noted this causal connection (Feld and Voight 2006, 278).

4. *McCray*, 195 U.S. at 61.

5. Miller v. Schoene, 276 U.S. 272 (1928).

6. *Miller*, 276 U.S. at 279.

7. *Miller*, 276 U.S. at 279.

8. Strauder v. West Virginia, 100 U.S. 303 (1880) at 308.

9. Quote found at https://www.oyez.org/cases/1900-1940/249us47.

10. Schenck v. United States, 249 U.S. 47 (1919) at 52.

11. *In re Debs*, 158 U.S. at 582.

12. Decisions such as Lochner v. New York garner most of the scholarly attention, but the Court left much regulation intact in the states during this period. Two important law review articles penned by Charles Warren during the Progressive era, challenged the Progressive interpretation that the Court embodied a "judicial oligarchy." Warren argued, "The National Supreme Court, so far from being reactionary, has been steady and consistent in upholding all state legislation of a progressive type" (Warren 1913b, 295). He based this conclusion on looking at 560 decisions between 1887 and 1911 (inclusive), pertaining to the "Due Process" and "Equal Protection" Clauses of the Fourteenth Amendment. The Court invalidated only 3 state laws (including *Lochner*) relating to "social justice" questions of the Due Process Clause (Warren 1913b, 295). In another article from the same year, Warren found that of a total of 302 cases, only 36 state and local social and economic regulations were held unconstitutional in forty years. The vast majority of cases in Warren's study were upheld by the Court pertaining to a diverse set of issues: "anti-lottery laws; anti-trust and corporate monopoly laws; liquor laws; food, game, oleomargarine and other inspection laws; regulation of banks, telegraph and insurance companies; cattle, health, and quarantine laws; regulation of business and property of water, gas, electric light, railroad (other than interstate trains) and other public service corporations; regulation of rates of public service corporations, grain elevators; stockholders' liability laws; regulation of business of private corporations; negro-segregation laws; labor laws; laws as to navigation, marine lines, ferries, bridges, etc., pilots, harbors, and immigration" (Warren 1913a, 695). One thing Warren's study revealed was the explosion of law in the early twentieth century; the simple empirical reality was that there were more cases being adjudicated, falling under an ever-growing range of legal issues. This explosion led to an unprecedented expansion in the Court's review power, especially concerning federal police power (Novak 2002, 262).

13. For a list of the major impacts of this transformation, see William Wiecek (1998, 65–66).

14. *Cruikshank*, 92 U.S. *Cruikshank* constricted Congress's ability to prosecute individuals under the Enforcement Act of 1870. It also dealt with the incorporation of the Bill of Rights, holding that the First Amendment was not intended to limit the powers of state governments with respect to their own citizens as well as holding that the Second Amendment only restricts the national government not state governments.

15. *Civil Rights Cases*, 109 U.S. Here, the Court held that Congress had no authority under the Reconstruction Amendments to prohibit discrimination in privately owned public accommodations. More specifically, argued the Court, the Fourteenth Amendment restrained only state action. And the fifth section of the amendment empowered Congress only to enforce the prohibition on state action.

16. *Plessy*, 163 U.S. A Louisiana state law requiring separate railway cars for blacks and whites was constitutional. The majority, written by Justice Brown, declared "Laws permitting, and even requiring, their separation in places where they are liable to be brought into contact do not necessarily imply the inferiority of either race to the other, and have been generally, if not universally, recognized as within the competency of the state legislatures in the exercise of their police power" (*Plessy*, 163 U.S. at 544).

17. To be sure, as Brandwein (2011) details extensively, the Court's jurisprudence of "state neglect" let open the possibility for the federal government to expand its authority and protect African Americans during Reconstruction. However, simply because the Court endorsed the doctrine of state neglect—despite the fact that it allowed for the *possibility* of federal state expansion/intervention—does not translate to an expansion of central state authority in the way this book understands expansion. What matters for interpretation of these judicial decisions is what the Court says is permissible or impermissible in a *singular* case; not what *might be* possible given dicta from the justice(s) in their opinions.

18. Powell v. Pennsylvania, 127 U.S. 678 (1888).

19. *Powell*, 127 U.S. at 683.

20. "State Rights," *The Washington Post*, April 12, 1888, p. 4.

21. Earlier references to the "liberty of contract" can be found in Frisbie v. United States 157 U.S. 160 (1895). In *Frisbie*, Justice Brewer causally remarked "generally speaking, among the inalienable rights of the citizen is that of the liberty of contract" (*Frisbie*, 157 U.S. at 165). But *Allgeyer* 165 U.S. marked the first time the Court invalidated a state law as a violation of liberty of contract. See David E. Bernstein (2008), "Freedom of Contract," *George Mason University Law and Economics Research Paper Series* 08-51, accessed here: https://papers.ssrn.com/sol3/papers.cfm?abstract_id=1239749.

22. *Allgeyer* 165 U.S. at 591.

23. *Allgeyer* 165 U.S. at 590.

24. Tumey v. Ohio, 273 U.S. 510 (1927).

25. See, for example, "The State Rights Question," *The Boston Globe*, March 30 1876, p. 4, and "Nationality and the New South," *Chicago Daily Tribune*, January, 24 1909, p. G4. Both articles rejected persistent calls for a return to pre–Civil War understandings of federalism. Similarly, Johnson's (2007) work is built on the "curious puzzle" that the "crisis of the Civil War and Reconstruction was not enough to create

a centralized state, yet the key elements necessary for a modern state to form were already in place before the crisis of the Great Depression and the response of the New Deal" (Johnson 2007, 5). Johnson shows the ways in which Congress through "intergovernmental policies" helped foster the "development of interlocking bureaucracies at the national and state levels" during a period of "New Federalism," a period where the United States straddled a dual federalist system and a centralized modern state (Johnson 2007, 4, 6). While this book recognizes this puzzle, it disagrees with Johnson's view of the Court as a persistent inhibitor of state growth (Johnson 2007, 29–32) as well as with the conception that the pre-1877 era can be entirely dubbed as "dual federalist." Other scholars have objected to this dual federalism characterization, too. See Martin Redish (1995, 27–30). Redish finds little utility in the distinction between "dualist" and "cooperatist" federalism theories. Dualists see federalism where "each of the two sovereignties has its own exclusive area of authority and jurisdiction, with few powers held concurrently" (Elazar 1962, 22). Cooperatists, Edward Corwin notes in his seminal law review article, claim that "the National government and the States are mutually complementary parts of a single governmental mechanism" (Corwin 1950, 19).

26. Michigan Judge Thomas Cooley, arguably the most famous jurist and legal thinker of the post–Civil War decades, called for the return to the state-centered model of federalism: "The proper boundary between national and state powers was agreed upon after long discussion . . . and it has been found so satisfactory that we have willingly endured a most destructive war in its defence. The cost of that war has been expended in vain if at its conclusion we propose to treat that boundary as a shadowy line which none need regard. The only safety to our institutions consists in standing by their fundamental principles, of which the just division of local and general powers is, by the constitution, made first and most prominent" (Cooley 1875, 42).

27. A well-regarded Senate Republican from Iowa, Grimes served on the Joint Committee on Reconstruction, the committee that drafted the Fourteenth Amendment.

28. *Congressional Globe*, 39, 1, p. 2,446.

29. For an historical overview of the dormant Commerce Clause see Martin H. Redish and Shane V. Nugent (1987). The "dormant" Commerce Clause refers to the prohibition, *implied* in the Commerce Clause, against states passing legislation that discriminates against or excessively burdens interstate commerce. For a normative critique of the application of the dormant Commerce Clause over time, see Martin Redish (1995, ch. 3).

30. Congress permitted many cases that started in state courts to be removed into federal circuit courts. The courts used this new power, at first, to defend the rights of African Americans and federal officials in the South during the Reconstruction era, but this quickly changed. See William Wiecek (1969). For a list of the changes in Court powers see Wiecek (1969, 333).

31. Wiecek notes that these advancements "laid the groundwork" for subsequent judicial moments of state expansion of the late nineteenth and early twentieth centuries (Wiecek 1969, 334). For a close look at the Habeas Corpus Act's effect on Court power, see William Wiecek (1970). Wiecek highlights the new role the federal courts played in the post–Civil War era, a role that required building the central

state apparatuses: "[T]he expanded scope of federal activity during Reconstruction, together with the problems facing the freedmen, made it apparent that the objectives of the [Congressional-judicial] partnership would have to be expanded. By 1865 it had become obvious that the overriding result of the Civil War was the supremacy of the Union over the claims of state autonomy. Federal policy was to take precedence over state objectives in the event of a clash between the two, and the federal courts were to protect this precedence" (Wiecek 1970, 537).

32. For further discussion regarding the expansion of federal court jurisdiction, see Kutler (1968). Like Wiecek (1969), Kutler stresses the importance of congressional legislation that removed cases from state to federal courts (Kutler 1968, 143–44). More recently, and with a focus on judicial institutional development, Justin Crowe contends that congressional removal legislation "not only expanded the reach of judicial power but also unequivocally affirmed the federal judiciary as a crucial partner in the emerging economic regime" (Crowe 2012, 163).

33. For example, nationalistic treatises such as Orestes Brownson (1866) and John C. Hurd (1881) advanced vigorous arguments for a strong, centralized union. That is, the general trend of constitutional thought lent credence to the idea of an expanded, powerful central state. The treatises of Sidney Fisher (1862) and John Jameson (1867) also displayed a fundamental shift in the conceptualization of the American state. Together with Brownson and Hurd, these legal thinkers moved us away from a state-centered understanding of the American union and toward a more nationalistic, centralized conception, often criticizing the compact theory and state sovereignty arguments John C. Calhoun made in the mid-nineteenth century (Larsen 1959, 361).

34. Munn v. Illinois, 94 U.S. 113 (1877).

35. Mugler v. Kansas, 123 U.S. 623 (1887).

36. Budd v. New York, 143 U.S. 517 (1892).

37. Then-contemporary legal thinkers also observed these changes. For example, Ernst Freund—a Progressive-era law professor known for his treatises on police powers—noted the persistent expansion of central state power vis-à-vis law and the Court. Freund remarked, "The consolidation of our own nation has proved our allotment of federal powers to be increasingly inadequate; and had it not been aided by liberal judicial construction, our situation would be unbearable" (Freund quoted in Thompson 1923, 10).

38. For then-contemporary accounts of the centralization of federal judicial power and its effects on broader aspects of central state authority, see Powers (1890). Powers closely examines questions relating to commerce between the states and federal government and writes disapprovingly of the Court's jurisprudential changes (Powers 1890, 410). See also Pool (1902). The "strongest evidence" of the Court's expanding power, Pool claims, rests with the battle between the "common law of the United States" and the "preservation of the right of local self-government" (Pool 1902, 251). Navigating this battle became the Court's duty following the Civil War. In doing so, the Court expanded state authority along some realms (where it advanced US common law) and restricting it along others (where it preserved local self-rule).

39. W. Wilson (1908, 173).

40. Keller (1977, 31–81) and Herman Belz (1976, 113–37, 152–82.

41. Letter to George Hill, January 7, 1870, in the *Papers of Salmon P. Chase*, vol. V (Chase 1993, 323).

42. Letter to George Hill, January 7, 1870, in the *Papers of Salmon P. Chase*, vol. V (Chase 1993, 324). To be sure, Chase was an ardent proponent of suffrage for African Americans, but he failed to convince President Andrew Johnson or his fellow justices that the Thirteenth Amendment incorporated the Declaration of Independence or the Bill of Rights against national and state officials as well as private persons. In a letter to his son-in-law, William Sprague, Chase explained his "wide divergence" with President Johnson over African American rights, summarizing his views on these rights and his conversation with the president: "the blacks were citizens of the United States & of the States in which they live; that under an appeal from the President to the People to reorganize, the blacks as part of the people had a right their fair share of influence & control in the work of reorganization; that the People meant *all* People without respect to the color of the skin." Letter to William Sprague, September 6, 1865, *Papers of Salmon P. Chase*, vol. 5 (Chase 1993, 68, emphasis in original).

43. Texas v. White, 74 U.S. 700 (1869).

44. *Texas*, 74 U.S. at 725.

45. *Collector* 78 U.S. at 124. *Collector* represented a restriction of central state power, inhibiting Congress from imposing taxes on states and state officials because the states and national government were two separate entities, thus restricting central state authority along Bensel's extraction dimension.

46. Lane County, 74 U.S. 71 (1869) at 76. *Lane County* also pertained to issues of taxation. Lane County, Oregon, paid its county taxes to the state of Oregon in U.S. legal tender notes—not in gold and silver coin as stipulated by the Oregon legislature. Counsel for Lane County claimed that an 1862 Congressional statute authorizing US notes to be used as legal tender to pay debts enabled Lane County officials to pay taxes with such notes. The Court, however, disagreed, holding that the Congressional statute imposed no restriction on the requirements stipulated by the Oregon legislature on its counties.

47. Generally speaking, "the locus of constitutional power" shifted from the states to the federal government during this time. Beth (1971, 250).

48. In tracing the Court's institutional and administrative development, Crowe observes, "With the birth of central state authority came the rise of centralized *judicial* authority." Between 1870 and 1877, Congressional legislation greatly enhanced federal judicial power especially with the passage of the Jurisdiction and Removal Act of 1875. This Act granted the circuit courts both original and removal jurisdiction over the vast majority of cases arising under Constitutional and federal law (Crowe 2012, 161–62, emphasis in original). For a treatment of the important institutional developments that enhanced federal judicial power during this time, see Gillman (2002).

49. To be sure, the judiciary did not completely halt the expansion of congressional power in the civil rights realm, which is a large focus of Pamela Brandwein (2011). She stresses that Court decisions before and after the *Civil Rights Cases* held that Congress can reach private individuals, but only when what Brandwein terms "state neglect" is present—that is, if "State or local officers . . . refuse to extend to black citizens the protection to which they are entitled as citizens" (Brandwein 2011,

168). The Fifteenth Amendment, she argues, led to judicial decisions that "provided the federal government with broad possibilities for rights enforcement" in electoral rights decisions such as Ex Parte Siebold, 100 U.S. 371 (1880) and Ex Parte Yarbrough 110 U.S. 651 (1884) (Brandwein 2011, 12).

50. Brandwein (2006) revises the constitutional developmental narrative concerning the Court and civil rights, urging us not to view the Waite Court as "racial villains who lost interest in Reconstruction" (Brandwein 2006, 276). She offers a nuanced depiction of the Court as it navigated a moderate course in the broader political milieu, not fully abandoning blacks yet not fully embracing radical Republican agendas. Brandwein's (2011) concept of "state neglect" offered "protection against [private] race-based interference" and "provided the federal government with broad possibilities for rights enforcement" (Brandwein 2011, 12).

51. Brandwein (2007). Of the Court's decision in *Cruikshank*, 92 U.S., Brandwein speculates that the Court's "modulated expression" was a reflection of the Court's "sensitivity to the political context and a concern for its own institutional influence" (2007, 371).

52. This conception accords with Kersch's understanding of constitutional development. Writing against the fallacies of "Whig history," Kersch argues for a nonlinear understanding of constitutional development whereby development moved along two dimensions: institutional and ideological (Kersch 2004, 12).

53. *Mugler*, 123 U.S. *Mugler* concerned the prohibition of alcohol. Here the Court held that Kansas's prohibition of alcohol that led to the arrest of Mugler did not violate the Fourteenth Amendment.

54. "The Supreme Court," *The Washington Post*, March 25, 1888, p. 4.

55. "A Right Decision," *The Washington Post*, November 3, 1887, p. 2 (concerning criminal law); "An Important Result," *Washington Post*, December 12, 1887, p. 4 (concerning prohibition).

56. Ernst Freund helped usher in modern state development with his scholarship on legislative and police power. Areas of the law that were once left to the states and local governments—business, labor, and police powers—soon came under the purview of the national government. Freund recognized that the judiciary was crucial to this upward shift: "The consolidation of our nation has proved our allotment of federal powers to be increasingly inadequate; and had it not been aided by liberal judicial construction, our situation would be unbearable" (Freund 1920, 181).

57. Slaughterhouse Cases, 83 U.S. 36 (1873).

58. *Slaughterhouse*, 83 U.S. at 76.

59. *Slaughterhouse*, 83 U.S. at 77.

60. *Slaughterhouse*, 83 U.S. at 78.

61. *Slaughterhouse*, 83 U.S. at 78.

62. Paul v. Virginia, 75 U.S. 168 (1869) and Holden v. Hardy, 169 U.S. 366 (1898).

63. *Mugler*, 123 U.S.; *Muller*, 208 U.S.; *Holden*, 169 U.S.; Barbier v. Connolly, 113 U.S. 27 (1885); *Powell*, 127 U.S. (1888); Jacobson v. Massachusetts, 197 U.S. 11 (1905).

64. Fong Yue Ting v. United States, 149 U.S. 698 (1893) and Ex parte Virginia, 100 U.S. 339 (1880).

65. *Fong Yue Ting*, 149 U.S. at 707.

66. Strauder v. West Virginia, 100 U.S. 303 (1880).

67. Yick Wo v. Hopkins, 118 U.S. 356 (1886).

68. See Lucy E. Salyer (1995, chs. 2–4) for an account of the litigation Chinese immigrants and Chinese Americans brought against immigration exclusion acts. Despite some of these legal successes, the Bureau of Immigration "merged in 1924 virtually unscathed and fundamentally unchanged," able to resist the legal doctrines developed to help aliens and immigrants (Salyer 1995, 244). See also Mae M. Ngai (2004), who discusses the Supreme Court's rulings on Congress's "plenary power" over immigration, which facilitated exclusion laws that "declared Asians racially ineligible for naturalization" (2004, 18).

69. Cooley v. Board of Wardens, 53 U.S. 299 (1852).

70. *Cooley*, 53 U.S. at 320.

71. Justice Curtis, writing for the majority, held, "Now the power to regulate commerce, embraces a vast field, containing not only many, but exceedingly various subjects, quite unlike in their nature; some imperatively demanding a single uniform rule, operating equally on the commerce of the United States in every port; and some, like the subject now in question, as imperatively demanding that diversity, which alone can meet the local necessities of navigation." *Cooley* 53 U.S. at 319.

72. Wabash, St. Louis and Pacific Railway Company v. Illinois, 118 U.S. 557 (1886).

73. Justice Miller embodied the balance between differing understandings of federalism; he had possessed a strong commitment to the Union and used the Commerce Clause to achieve uniformity in federal regulation, yet he restricted the power of the central state in decisions such as *Slaughterhouse* 83 U.S., which limited the effectiveness of the Privileges and Immunities Clause to protect individual rights. In the 1870s and 1880s, then, it was Justice Miller whose voice pressed for federal government strength over Commerce Clause issues and a weakness in individual rights cases.

74. As a regulation of commerce, the Illinois law infringed on the central state's authority to decide rate regulation. *Wabash*, like much of the Commerce Clause jurisprudence, was fundamentally about who held decision-making authority. Justice Miller concluded for the majority: "And if it be a regulation of commerce, as we think we have demonstrated it is, and as the Illinois court concedes it to be, it must be of that national character, and the regulation can only appropriately exist by general rules and principles, which demand that it should be done by the Congress of the United States under the commerce clause of the Constitution" (*Wabash*, 118 U.S. at 577).

75. Writing for the majority, Justice Miller argued the importance of federal authority over state authority in establishing uniform laws: "It would be a very feeble and almost useless provision, but poorly adapted to secure the entire freedom of commerce among the States which was deemed essential to a more perfect union by the framers of the Constitution, if at every stage of the transportation of goods and chattels through the country, the State within whose limits a part of this transportation must be done could impose regulations concerning the price, compensation, or taxation, or any other restrictive regulation interfering with and seriously embarrassing this commerce" (*Wabash*, 118 U.S. at 573).

76. "The Growth of National Unity," *Wall Street Journal*, December 20, 1906, p. 1.

77. *Shreveport Rate Case*, 234 U.S.

78. See Tagg Brothers & Moorhead v. United States, 280 U.S. 420 (1930) at 436–37 (permitting regulation of livestock market agencies); Stafford v. Wallace, 258 U.S. 495 (1922) at 519 (permitting Congress to regulate transaction fees charged by intrastate packers and market agents); and Swift and Co v. United States, 196 U.S. 375 (1905) (approving the application of the Sherman Act to intrastate livestock traders).

79. Schenck v. United States, 249 U.S. 47 (1919).

80. Abrams v. United States, 250 U.S. 616 (1919).

81. Gitlow v. New York, 268 U.S. 652 (1925).

82. Moore v. Dempsey, 261 U.S. 86 (1923).

83. Powell v. Alabama, 287 U.S. 45 (1932).

Chapter 5

1. Frankfurter, quoted in Alpheus Thomas Mason (1979, 14).

2. *Helvering*, 301 U.S. at 6414.

3. *Helvering*, 301 U.S. at 641.

4. Korematsu v. United States, 323 U.S. 214 (1944).

5. *Korematsu*, 323 U.S. at 220. The Court was obviously deeply divided on the internment of Japanese Americans, because on the same day as *Korematsu*, the Court held in Ex Parte Endo, 323 U.S. 283 (1944), that once loyalty had been established, a person could no longer be kept at an internment camp.

6. On the Court's penchant to defer to the democratic branches during wartime and thus comprise civil rights and liberties, see Geoffrey Stone (2004).

7. Southern Pacific Co. v. Arizona, 325 U.S. 761 (1945).

8. *Southern Pacific*, 325 U.S. at 773.

9. This book did not include cases after 1997 because of the inductive case selection method used. Because this book, in part, measures salience of cases in terms of their frequency of citation in constitutional casebooks, more recent, twenty-first-century cases would not have the opportunity to appear in casebooks. See chapter 2 for a discussion of why 1997 is the end date.

10. DeJonge v. Oregon, 299 U.S. 353 (1937).

11. *DeJonge*, 299 U.S. at 365.

12. Ashwander v. Tennessee Valley Authority, 297 U.S. 288 (1936).

13. Hunt v. Washington State Apple Advertising Commission, 432 U.S. 333 (1977).

14. *Hunt*, 432 U.S. at 350.

15. See note 9 above.

16. For a discussion of Hughes's effective leadership, see Schwartz (1993, 227) and S. Goldman (1991, 104).

17. *West Coast Hotel*, 300 U.S. *West Coast* sustained minimum wage laws for women in Washington state and abolished the *Lochner*-era "liberty of contract" doctrine used to strike down economic-based legislation.

18. Palko v. Connecticut, 302 U.S. 319 (1937).

19. *Palko*, 302 U.S. at 325.

20. *Palko*, 302 U.S. at 327.

21. Near v. Minnesota, 283 U.S. 697 (1931).

22. *Powell*, 287 U.S. at 71.

23. *Curtiss-Wright*, 299 U.S.

24. *Curtiss-Wright*, 299 U.S. at 319.

25. *Ashwander*, 297, U.S.

26. United States v. Carolene Products Co., 304 U.S. 144 (1938).

27. The most remembered and influential aspect of *Carolene Products* is Justice Harlan Stone's famous "footnote four." Here, the Court declared it would not inhibit economic policies as it once had in the decades preceding, but Stone asserted that certain types of legislation might not merit such deference. Thus, he noted in Footnote Four that prejudice against "discrete and insular minorities," for example, may call for a "more searching judicial inquiry," thereby continuing to advance the judiciary's review power (*Carolene Products*, 304 U.S. at 155).

28. *Wickard*, 317 U.S.

29. Edwards v. California, 314 U.S. 160 (1941).

30. *Edwards*, 314 U.S. at 174.

31. West Virginia State Board of Education v. Barnette, 319 U.S. 624 (1943).

32. Minersville School District v. Gobitis, 310 U.S. 586 (1940).

33. *West Virginia*, 319 U.S. at 641–42.

34. Smith v. Allwright, 321 U.S. 649 (1944).

35. *Smith*, 321 U.S. at 662.

36. Dennis v. United States, 341 U.S. 494 (1951).

37. American Communications Association v. Douds, 339 U.S. 382 (1950).

38. Morgan v. Virginia, 328 U.S. 373 (1946).

39. *Shelley*, 334 U.S.

40. Sweatt v. Painter, 339 U.S. 629 (1950).

41. Fowler and Jeon (2008) dub this a lack of "outward citations" (2008, 18). Their "network of citations"—measured from 30,288 majority opinions contained in the US Reports from 1754 to 2002—concludes that the Warren Court demonstrated a "significant deviation from the norm of *stare decisis*," a conclusion that dovetails with qualitative historical accounts of the Court (Sangick and Jeon 2008, 17; Schwartz 1993; Powe 2000).

42. *Brown*, 347 U.S. and Loving v. Virginia, 388 U.S. 1 (1967).

43. *Mapp*, 367 U.S. and Gideon v. Wainwright, 372 U.S. 335 (1963).

44. Benton v. Maryland, 395 U.S. 784 (1969); Malloy v. Hogan, 378 U.S. 1 (1964); Duncan v. Louisiana, 391 U.S. 145 (1968); Klopfer v. North Carolina, 386 U.S. 213 (1967); and Pointer v. Texas, 380 U.S. 400 (1965), respectively.

45. Powell v. McCormack, 395 U.S. 486 (1969).

46. Bolling v. Sharpe, 347 U.S. 497 (1954).

47. Reid v. Covert, 354 U.S. 1 (1957).

48. Take Marbury v. Madison (1803), McCulloch v. Maryland (1819), Dred Scott v. Sandford (1857), Legal Tender Cases (1871), Pollock v. Farmers Loan and

Trust (1895), and Lochner v. New York (1905), for example. All these cases can be considered "activist," but who these cases benefitted—entrepreneurs, businesses that sought avoid government regulation, slave owners, and so forth—differed from the beneficiaries of activism during the Warren era (White, in Levy and Karst 2000, 2,858).

49. Buckley v. Valeo, 424 U.S. 1 (1976).

50. Cohen v. California, 403 U.S. 15 (1971).

51. Statute quoted from https://www.oyez.org/cases/1970/299.

52. *Cohen*, 403 U.S. at 25.

53. Richmond Newspapers Inc. v. Virginia, 448 U.S. 555 (1980) at 556.

54. *Richmond Newspapers*, 448 U.S. at 579–80.

55. Griswold v. Connecticut, 381 U.S. 479 (1965) and Roe v. Wade, 410 U.S. 113 (1973).

56. Hoyt v. Florida, 368 U.S. 57 (1961) represents the Warren Court's overall position on sex discrimination. *Hoyt* dealt with a Florida law that made jury service for women, but not for men, completely voluntary. If a woman wanted to participate in a jury, she had to volunteer and register for jury duty. The Warren Court held, unanimously, that this Florida law was constitutional.

57. Craig v. Boren, 429 U.S. 190 (1976).

58. Goldberg v. Kelly, 397 U.S. 254 (1970).

59. Because *Goldberg* invalidated a state law, it expanded central state authority. Contrast Powell v. McCormack, 395 U.S. 486 (1969). There, the Court prohibited the House—a coordinate branch of government—from excluding a duly elected legislative member. Since *Powell* inhibited a federal action, it constricted central state authority.

60. San Antonio Independent School District. v. Rodriguez, 411 U.S. 1 (1973).

61. Frontiero v. Richardson, 411 U.S. 677 (1973). Frontiero, 411 U.S. at 677.

62. Frontiero, 411 U.S. at 686 and 688.

63. Mapp v. Ohio, 367 U.S.

64. Miranda v. Arizona, 384 U.S.

65. The selection criteria intentionally ended the case sample date at 2000 because the last casebook used to select judicial decisions was published in 2010. Since this book selected cases based on their appearances in six or more constitutional casebooks, 2000 was set as the last possible year for data-set inclusion because only eight books appeared after 2000. A 1999 decision, for example, would have to appear in six of the eight twenty-first-century casebooks to appear in the data set. Thus, 1997 ended up being the latest case in these data because of this inductive case-selection method

66. Sue Davis's "William Rehnquist" entry in Hall, Ely, and Grossman (2005, 835). See also Sue Davis, "The Chief Justice and Judicial Decision-Making: The Institutional Basis for Leadership on the Supreme Court," in *Supreme Court Decision-Making: New Institutionalist Approaches*, edited by Cornell W. Clayton and Howard Gillman (1999).

67. United States v. Lopez, 514 U.S. 549 (1995).

68. *Lopez*, 514 U.S. at 549.

69. City of Boerne v. Flores, 521 U.S. 507 (1997).

70. *Boerne*, 521 U.S. at 507.

71. *Boerne*, 521 U.S. at 519.

72. *Clinton*, 524 U.S.

73. Thomas Keck (2004) makes this same argument throughout his book. He argues that as the Warren Court's "rights-based constitutional became entrenched in the American polity, it would prove increasingly difficult to dislodge" (Keck 2004, 65). Thus, he concludes, "When constitutional conservatives have sought to build upon, rather than disavow, the rights-protecting function of modern constitutionalism, they have been much more successful" (Keck 2004, 230).

74. City of Richmond v. Croson Co., 488 U.S. 469 (1989).

75. *Richmond*, 488 U.S. at 499.

76. Shaw v. Reno, 509 U.S. 630 (1993).

77. Lucas v. South Carolina Coastal Council, 505 U.S. 1003 (1992) and Nollan v. California Coastal Commission, 483 U.S. 825 (1987).

Chapter 6

1. Some scholars might define "development" in terms of its ideological valence, advancing particular ideological commitments. See Kahn (2006), "Social Constructions, Supreme Court Reversals, and American Political Development: *Lochner*, *Plessy*, *Bowers*, but not *Roe*."

2. While this pattern Brutus prophesized holds strongly in the US case, it is also seen in federal nation-states around the world. See the volume edited by Aroney and Kincaid (2017) comparing federal courts across the world, *Courts in Federal Countries: Federalist or Unitarists?* Looking at multiple nation-states, they conclude the evidence regarding Brutus's prediction "is mixed, though leaning in Brutus's direction" (Aroney and Kincaid 2017, 483).

3. "Brutus Letter XI" (31 January 1788), in Ball (2007, 504).

4. "Brutus Letter XI" (31 January 1788), in Ball (2007, 504) and "Brutus Letter XII" (7 February 1788), in Ball (2007, 506–7).

5. Certainly, there are myriad ways to understand American constitutional development and change. This project has taken a top-down perspective, but political scientists such as Emily Zackin (2013) have offered a more bottom-up perspective on changes in constitutional rights and the concomitant effects on state development. She examines how social movements and interest groups at the state level, with their focus on positivist rights, helped build a more activist, welfare state.

6. Banks and Blakeman (2012) also recognizes that the Rehnquist Court did not diminish central state authority as much as we think, despite some high-profile federalism cases. In particular, see chapter 5 on federalism and foreign affairs.

7. Constitutional moments constitute higher lawmaking because the People engage in an extended and better-informed process of coming to a new political consensus.

8. Work in political development has questioned the periodization employed by Ackerman. A number of authors argue that the standard periodization overemphasizes temporal discontinuities and overlooks continuities (Kersh 2005; Orren and Skowronek 2004; Thelen 2003).

9. Other scholars have also stressed how the growth of judicial power—and its growing caseload—creates issues for understanding constitutional development as resting on a theory of constitutional moments. Legal historian David Strauss underscores the empirical reality of the growth of constitutional law. Consider, as Strauss says, "expansive federal power; expansive presidential power, particularly in foreign affairs; the current contours of freedom of expression; the federalization of criminal procedure; a conception of racial equality that disapproves de jure distinctions and intentional discrimination; the rule of one person, one vote; a (somewhat formal) principle of gender equality; and reproductive freedom protected against criminalization" (Strauss 1996, 929). None of these changes map onto an obvious " 'moment' at which a strong popular consensus crystallized behind them" (Strauss, 1996, 929).

10. Brutus detailed his opposition to the federal judiciary in Letters XI–XV. See *The Federalist with Letters of "Brutus,"* Terence Ball, ed. (2007): New York: Cambridge University Press. For contemporary scholarship, see Nicholas Aroney and John Kincaid (2017).

11. For a discussion of the seven dimensions of central state authority, see chapter 2.

12. In this way, my book joins a growing literature that reveals the American central state's strength and power. See Balogh (2009) and Adler (2012), for example.

13. Zackin provides an excellent overview of the legal and APD literature concerning the negative rights tradition in the United States (Zackin 2010, 23–36). Her work uncovers the positive rights tradition in American constitutional development, but she admits that at the federal level a negative rights tradition prevails (Zackin 2010, 36).

14. For an examination of how national and state governments worked together to expand the modern state, see Johnson (2007), in particular her concept of "intergovernmental policy" (4–6).

15. See Appendix 4 for a presentation of the Court's ideology and its effect on central state authority.

16. While many cases in this book are less salient than cases such as *Brown*, all the decisions included in this book are considered landmark and salient in the sense that they have a much greater than average influence on lower-court opinions. The cases in this book are cited by lower courts (federal and state alike) at much higher frequency than the average US Supreme Court decision. See chapter 2 for a detailed discussion of case selection.

17. Robertson (2005b) recognizes this. See chapter 3 of this book for further discussion.

18. The contributions to Bruce Peabody's edited volume *The Politics of Judicial Independence* all espouse this interdependent characterization, seeing judicial "independence" as essentially a shibboleth. Peabody's volume seeks to understand judicial independence in the wake of growing Court criticisms occurring over the last fifty years: "how does the current era of court criticism help us to understand the circumstances under which judicial independence can be compromised by 'improper' political influences?" (Peabody 2011, 17). See also L. Fisher (1988). For Fisher, constitutional meaning is the product of ongoing discursive negotiations among the three national branches.

19. Court reprisal can happen through various mechanisms available to the executive and the Congress. One mechanism in particular looms largest among judges: the political branches could simply ignore Court mandates. Former chief judge for the District of Columbia Circuit Harry T. Edwards finds this mechanism the most effective in encouraging the judiciary to exercise restraint and affirm the coordinate branches (Edwards 2006, 231).

20. Indeed, Dahl's influential article concludes that, "By itself, the Court is almost powerless to affect the course of national policy," but the Court maintains public support by "confer[ring] legitimacy on the fundamental policies" of the dominant political alliance (Dahl 1957, 293–94). This kind of institutional behavior explains why the Court often sides with the federal branches, thus increasing the Court's tendency to expand federal authority.

21. Data on court-curbing legislation indicate the rise in attacks on the judiciary (Clark 2009). The legislative proposals comprising Clark's data represent an "institutional assault on the Court rather than a case-specific effort to reverse a Court decision" (Clark 2009, 979). From 1946 to 1966 he finds that Congress averaged just under five court-curbing proposals a year, but from 1967 to 1983, this average jumped to about nineteen proposals a year, and in the twenty-first century from 2003 to 2008, Congress has averaged thirteen proposals a year (Clark, cited in Peabody 2011, 7).

22. Some political scientists, however, see the Court as less concerned about the behaviors of other institutional actors. The paradigmatic example is Segal and Spaeth (1993). They primarily understand judicial outcomes as the product of a justice's ideology.

23. The "legal explanation" has its foundations in a theoretical approach to the study of law and courts rather than in specific scholars. In fact, the "legal" approach encompasses much of what Shapiro's body of scholarship sought to debunk: assuming that the legal features of courts distinguished them from conventional political institutions. In contrast to the legal approach, Shapiro's work, broadly speaking, viewed American politics as made up of many centers of decision-making and asked how courts fit into these decision-making centers (Gillman 2004, 364–65). See Gillman's 2004 *Annual Review* article on Shapiro for a longer discussion.

24. Similarly, Gillman (1997) shows how changes in constitutional interpretation helped advance the modern American state. He argues that the Court largely abandoned its doctrine of originalism during the New Deal era to "cope with the innovative challenges of managing a national industrial economy" (Gillman 1997, 192–93).

25. National Federation of Independent Business v. Sebelius, 567 U.S. 519 (2012).

26. Shelby County v. Holder, 570 U.S. 2 (2013).

Appendix

1. The coding application does not distinguish the *purpose* of a federal statute—whether it expands or restricts the rights of citizens. The coding application *only* concerns whether the central state has control over citizens—whether the central state uses that control to give more civil rights or to take civil rights away does not affect the coding outcome.

2. In Fourteenth Amendment (or any amendment) cases, where the Court strikes down one or more *state-level* laws this constitutes *an expansion* of central state authority because the Court has asserted national authority to declare that its interpretation overrules lower-level authority. Conversely, when the Court upholds a state or local-level law the decision restricts national authority because the Court has declared that a *federal* constitutional right does not apply to the subordinate government's authority in question.

3. Since federalism is a question about national versus state governing authority, one might logically assume that it would fall entirely within the centralization dimension. While federalism nearly always pertains to centralization, there are a couple decisions where it involves a dimension other than centralization.

For example, Ashwander v. Tennessee Valley Authority 297 U.S. 288 (1936) involved not the centralization but the administrative, property, and world system dimensions. In this case, the Court held that Congress did not exceed its power by creating the Tennessee Valley Authority (TVA), a government corporation created as part of the New Deal to improve the economy. *Ashwander* concerned the creation of a federal agency, the TVA, to advance the long-term regional planning capacity of the central state (administrative dimension), and it dealt with the TVA's acquisition of property and equipment from a private power company (property dimension). Last, the Court argued that the Wilson Dam—from which the TVA generated electricity—had been built originally for national defense, to produce materials involved in munitions manufacturing, and thus the federal government could assert authority (world system dimension).

Nevertheless, eighty-three of eighty-five federalism decisions implicated the centralization dimension. However, the vast majority touched on more than simply centralization: forty-nine decisions affected two central state dimensions, and nineteen dimensions concerned three central state dimensions.

References

Ackerman, Bruce. 1991. *We the People: Foundations*. Vol. 1. Cambridge, MA: Belknap Press of Harvard University.

———. 1998. *We the People: Transformations*. Vol. 2. Cambridge, MA: Belknap Press of Harvard University.

———. 2014. *We the People: The Civil Rights Revolution*. Vol. 3. Cambridge, MA: Belknap Press of Harvard University.

Adamany, David. 1980. "The Supreme Court's Role in Critical Elections." In *Realignment in American Politics: Toward a Theory*, edited by Bruce A. Campbell and Richard J. Trilling, 229–59. Austin, TX: University of Texas Press.

Adler, William. 2012. "State Capacity and Bureaucratic Autonomy in the Early United States: The Case of the Army Corps of Topographical Engineers." *Studies in American Political Development* 26 (2): 107–24.

Allen, Francis A. 1989. "Remembering *Shelley v. Kraemer*: Of Public and Private Worlds." *Washington University of Law Quarterly* 67: 709–35.

Amar, Akil Reed. 1998. *The Bill of Rights: Creation and Reconstruction*. New Haven, CT: Yale University Press.

Aroney, Nicholas, and John Kincaid, eds. 2017. *Courts in Federal Countries: Federalist or Unitarists?* Toronto, ON: University of Toronto Press.

Baldwin, Peter. 2005. "Beyond Weak and Strong: Rethinking the State in Comparative Policy History." *Journal of Policy History* 17 (1): 12–33.

Balkin, Jack and Sanford Levinson. 1998. "The Canons of Constitutional Law." *Harvard Law Review* 111: 963–1024.

Ball, Terrence, ed. 2007. *Hamilton, Madison, and Jay: The Federalist with Letters of "Brutus."* New York: Cambridge University Press.

Balogh, Brian. 2009. *A Government Out of Sight: The Mystery of National Authority in Nineteenth-Century America*. New York: Cambridge University Press.

Banks, Christopher, and John Blakeman. 2012. *The U.S. Supreme Court and New Federalism*. Lanham, MD: Rowman & Littlefield.

Bednar, Jenna, William Eskridge, and John Ferejohn 2001. "A Political Theory of Federalism." In *Constitutional Culture and Democratic Rule*, edited by John Ferejohn, Jack Rackove, and Jonathan Riley, 223–70. Cambridge, UK: Cambridge University Press.

Belz, Herman. 1976. *A New Birth of Freedom: The Republican Party and Freedmen's Rights, 1861 to 1866.* Westport, CT: Greenwood Press.

Benedict, Michael Les. 1978. "Preserving Federalism: Reconstruction and the Waite Court." *The Supreme Court Review* 1978: 39–79.

Bensel, Richard. 1990. *Yankee Leviathan: The Origins of Central State Authority, 1859–1877.* New York: Cambridge University Press.

———. 2000. *The Political Economy of American Industrialization, 1877–1900.* New York: Cambridge University Press.

Berk, Gerald. 1994. *Alternative Tracks: The Constitution of American Industrial Order, 1865–1917.* Baltimore, MD: Johns Hopkins University Press.

Bernstein, David E. 2003. "*Lochner* Era Revisionism, Revised: *Lochner* and the Origins of Fundamental Rights Constitutionalism." *Georgetown Law Review* 92 (1): 1–60.

———. 2008. "Freedom of Contract." George Mason Law & Economics Research Paper No. 08–51: 1–10.

———. 2011. *Rehabilitating* Lochner: *Defending Individual Rights against Progressive Reform.* Chicago: University of Chicago Press.

Beth, Loren P. 1971.*The Development of the American Constitution, 1877–1917.* New York: Harper & Row.

Brandwein, Pamela. 2006. "The *Civil Rights Cases* and the Lost Language of State Neglect." In *The Supreme Court and American Political Development*, edited by Ronald Kahn and Ken Kersch, 275–329. Lawrence: University Press of Kansas.

———. 2007. "A Judicial Abandonment of Blacks? Rethinking the 'State Action' Cases of the Waite Court." *Law & Society Review* 41(2): 343–86.

———. 2011. *Rethinking the Judicial Settlement of Reconstruction.* New York: Cambridge University Press.

Bridges, Amy. 1997. *Morning Glories: Municipal Reform in the Southwest.* Princeton, NJ: Princeton University Press.

Brownson, Orestes A. 1866. *The American Republic: Its Constitution, Tendencies, and Destiny.* New York: P. O. Shae.

Burgess, John W. 1890. *Political Science and Comparative Constitutional Law.* 2 vols. Boston: Ginn & Company.

Burke, Thomas. 2002. *Lawyers, Lawsuits and Legal Rights: The Struggle Over Litigation in American Society.* Berkeley: University of California Press.

Bybee, Keith, ed. 2007. *Bench Press: The Collision of Courts, Politics, and the Media.* Stanford, CA: Stanford University Press.

Carpenter, Daniel. 2001. *The Forging of Bureaucratic Autonomy: Reputations, Networks, and Policy Innovation in Executive Agencies, 1862–1928.* Princeton, NJ: Princeton University Press.

Chalmers, Damian, and Luke Haasbeek. 2007. "The Legal Dimension in European Integration." In *The European Union: Economics and Policies*, edited by Ali El-Agraa, 62–83. Cambridge, UK: Cambridge University Press.

Chase, Salmon. 1993. *Papers of Salmon P. Chase.* Vol. 5, *Correspondence: 1865–1873*, edited by John Niven. Kent. OH: Kent State University Press.

Clark, Thomas. 2009. "The Separation of Powers, Court Curbing, and Judicial Legitimacy." *American Journal of Political Science* 53 (4): 971–89.

Clayton, Cornell, and Howard Gillman, eds. 1999. *Supreme Court Decision-Making: New Institutionalist Approaches.* Chicago: University of Chicago Press.

Clayton, Cornell, and J. Mitchell Pickerill. 2006. "The Political Determinants of the Supreme Court's Criminal Justice Jurisprudence: How the New Right Regime Has Shaped the Rehnquist Court." *Georgetown Law Journal* 94 (5): 1,385–425.

Clemens, Elisabeth. 2006. "Lineages of the Rube Goldberg State: Building and Blurring Public Programs, 1900–1940." In *The Art of the State: Rethinking Political Institutions,* edited by Ian Shapiro, Stephen Skowronek, and Daniel Galvin, 187–216. New York: New York University Press.

Compton, John W. 2014. *The Evangelical Origins of the Living Constitution.* Cambridge, MA: Harvard University Press.

Conway, Moncure Daniel, editor. 1894. *The Writings of Thomas Paine.* Vol. I. New York: G. P. Putnam's Sons.

Cooley, Thomas M. 1875. "The Legal Aspects of the Louisiana Case." *Southern Law Review* 1: 18–44.

Cortner, Richard. 1993. *The Iron Horse and the Constitution: The Railroads and the Transformation of the Fourteenth Amendment.* Westport, CT: Greenwood Press.

———. 1981. *The Supreme Court and the Second Bill of Rights: The Fourteenth Amendment and the Nationalization of Civil Liberties.* Madison: University of Wisconsin Press.

Corwin, Edward S. 1950. "The Passing of Dual Federalism." *Virginia Law Review* 36 (1): 1–24.

Crowe, Justin. 2007. "The Forging of Judicial Autonomy: Political Entrepreneurship and the Reforms of William Howard Taft." *The Journal of Politics* 69 (1): 73–87.

———. 2012. *Building the Judiciary: Law, Courts, and the Politics of Institutional Development.* Princeton, NJ: Princeton University Press.

Curtis, Michael Kent. 1986. *No State Shall Abridge: The Fourteenth Amendment and the Bill of Rights.* Durham, NC: Duke University Press.

Cushman, Barry. 1998. *Rethinking the New Deal: The Structure of a Constitutional Revolution.* New York: Oxford University Press.

Dahl, Robert A. 1957. "Decision-Making in a Democracy: The Supreme Court as a National Policy-Maker." *Journal of Public Law* 6: 279–95.

Davis, Sue. 2005. "William Rehnquist." In *The Oxford Companion to the Supreme Court of the United States,* edited by Kermit L. Hall, James W. Ely, Jr., and Joel B. Grossman, 832–35. New York: Oxford University Press.

Edling, Max. 2003. *A Revolution in Favor of Government: Origins of the U.S. Constitution and the Making of the American State.* New York: Oxford University Press.

Edwards, Harry T. 2006. "Judicial Norms: A Judge's Perspective." In *Norms and the Law,* edited by John N. Drobak, 230–47. New York: Cambridge University Press.

Elazar, Daniel Judah. 1962. *The American Partnership: Intergovernmental Co-Operation in the Nineteenth-Century United States.* Chicago: University of Chicago Press.

Elliot, Alan C., and Wayne A. Woodward. 2016. *IBM SPSS by Example: A Practical Guide to Statistical Data Analysis.* 2nd ed. Los Angeles: Sage Press.

Ellis, Richard E. 2007. *Aggressive Nationalism: McCulloch v. Maryland and the Foundation of Federal Authority in the Young Republic.* New York: Oxford University Press.

Epp, Charles. 1998. *The Rights Revolution*. Chicago: University of Chicago Press.

Epstein, Lee, and Jack Knight. 1998. The Choices Justices Make. Washington: CQ Press.

Eskridge, William N. 1991. "Overriding Supreme Court Statutory Interpretation Decisions." *Yale Law Journal* 101: 331–455.

Evans, Peter, Dietrich Rueschemeyer, and Theda Skocpol, eds. 1985. *Bringing the State Back In*. New York: Cambridge University Press.

Farhang, Sean. 2010. *The Litigation State*. Princeton, NJ: Princeton University Press.

Fairman, Charles. 1949. "Does the Fourteenth Amendment Incorporate the Bill of Rights? The Original Understanding." *Stanford Law Review* 2 (1): 5–139.

Farrand, Max, ed. 1911. *The Records of the Federal Convention of 1787*. New Haven, CT: Yale University Press.

Feld, Lars P., and Stefan Voight. 2006. "Judicial Independence and Economic Development." In *Democratic Constitutional Design and Public Policy*, edited by Roger D. Congleton and Birgitta Swedenborg, 251–89. Cambridge, MA: MIT Press.

Ferejohn, John. 1999. "Independent Judges, Dependent Judiciary: Explaining Judicial Independence." *Southern California Law Review* 72 (2/3): 353–84.

Ferejohn, John, Carolyn Mungro, Larry Kramer, and Richard Lang. 2006. "Judicial Independence in a Democracy: Institutionalizing Judicial Restraint." In *Norms and the Law*, edited by John N. Drobak, 161–207. New York: Cambridge University Press.

Fisher, Louis. 1988. *Constitutional Dialogues: Interpretation as Political Process*. Princeton, NJ: Princeton University Press.

———. 2004. "Judicial Finality or an Ongoing Colloquy." In *Making Policy, Making Law: An Interbranch Perspective*, edited by Mark C. Miller and Jeb Barnes, 153–70. Washington: Georgetown University Press.

Fisher, Sidney George. 1862. *The Trial of the Constitution*. Philadelphia: J. B. Lippincott.

Forbath, William. 2008. "Politics, State-Building, and the Courts, 1870–1920." In *The Cambridge History of Law in America*. Vol. II, edited by Michael Grossberg and Christopher Tomlins, 643–97. New York: Cambridge University Press.

Fowler, James, and Sangick Jeon. 2008. "The Authority of Supreme Court Precedent." *Social Networks* 30: 16–30.

Freund, Ernst, 1904. *The Police Power: Public Policy and Constitutional Rights*. Chicago: Callaghan & Company.

———. 1920. "The New German Constitution." *Political Science Quarterly* 35: 177–203.

Friedman, Lawrence. 2005. *A History of American Law*. 3rd ed. New York: Simon & Schuster.

Frymer, Paul. 2003. "Acting When Elected Officials Won't: Federal Courts and Civil Rights Enforcement in U.S. Labor Unions, 1935–1985." *American Political Science Review* 97: 483–99.

———. 2008. "Law and American Political Development." *Law and Social Inquiry* 33: 779–803.

Gillman, Howard. 1993. *The Constitution Besieged: The Rise and Demise of Lochner Era Police Powers Jurisprudence*. Durham, NC: Duke University Press.

———. 1997. "The Collapse of Constitutional Originalism and the Rise of the Notion of the 'Living Constitution' in the Course of American State-Building." *Studies in American Political Development* 11: 191–247.

———. 2002. "How Political Parties Can Use the Courts to Advance Their Agenda: Federal Courts in the United States, 1875–1891." *American Political Science Review* 96 (3): 511–24.

———. 2004. "Martin Shapiro and the Movement from 'Old' to 'New' Institutionalist Studies in Public Law Scholarship." *Annual Review of Political Science* 7: 363–82.

Gillman, Howard, and Cornell Clayton, eds. 1999. *The Supreme Court in American Politics: New Institutionalist Interpretations.* Lawrence, KS: University Press of Kansas.

Gillman, Howard, Mark A. Graber, and Keith E. Whittington. 2013. *American Constitutionalism.* Vol. I: *Structures of Government.* 1st ed. New York: Oxford University Press.

———. 2017a. *American Constitutionalism.* Vol. I: *Structures of Government*, 2nd ed. New York: Oxford University Press.

———. 2017b. *American Constitutionalism.* Vol. II: *Rights and Liberties*, 2nd ed. New York: Oxford University Press.

Goldman, Jerry. 1992. "Is There a Canon of Constitutional Law?" *Law and Politics Book Review* 2 (10): 134–37.

———. 2005. "The Constitutional Law Canon Revisited." *Law and Politics Book Review* 15 (8): 648–56.

Goldman, Sheldon. 1991. *Constitutional Law: Cases and Essays.* 2nd ed. New Yorker: Harper Collins Publishers.

Graber, Mark. 1993. "The Nonmajoritarian Difficulty: Legislative Deference to the Judiciary." *Studies in American Political Development* 7 (Spring): 35–73.

———. 1995. "The Passive-Aggressive Virtues: *Cohen v. Virginia* and the Problematic Establishment of Judicial Power." *Constitutional Commentary* 12: 67–92.

———. 2004. "Resolving Political Questions into Judicial Questions: Tocqueville's Thesis Revisited." *Constitutional Commentary* 21: 485–545.

———. 2006a. *Dred Scott and the Problem of Constitutional Evil.* New York: Cambridge University Press.

———. 2006b. "Legal, Strategic or Legal Strategy: Deciding to Decide during the Civil War and Reconstruction." *The Supreme Court and American Political Development*, edited by Ronald Kahn and Ken Kersch, 33–67. Lawrence, KS: University Press of Kansas.

Greve, Michael. 2012. *The Upside-Down Constitution.* Cambridge, MA: Harvard University Press.

Gunther, Gerald. 1969. *John Marshall's Defense of McCulloch v. Maryland.* Palo Alto: Stanford University Press.

Hall, Kermit L., James W. Ely, Jr., and Joel B. Grossman, eds. 2005. *The Oxford Companion to the Supreme Court of the United States.* New York: Oxford University Press.

Hall, Kermit L., Paul Finkelman, and James W Ely, Jr., eds. 2005. *American Legal History: Cases and Materials.* New York: Oxford University Press.

Hartz, Louis. 1955. *The Liberal Tradition in America: An Interpretation of American Political Thought Since the Revolution.* New York: Harcourt, Brace & World.

Harvey, Anna, and Barry Friedman. 2006. "Pulling Punches: Congressional Constraints on the Supreme Court's Constitutional Rulings, 1987–2000." *Legislative Studies Quarterly* 31 (4): 533–62.

Hattam, Victoria. 1993. *Labor Visions and State Power: The Origins of Business Union-ism in the United States*. Princeton, NJ: Princeton University Press.

Heclo, Hugh. 1984. "In Search of a Role: America's High Civil Service." In *Bureaucrats and Policy Making: A Comparative Overview*, edited by Ezra N. Suleiman, 8–35. New York: Holmes and Meier.

Hegel, Georg Wilhelm Friedrich. 1956. *The Philosophy of History*. New York: Dover Publications.

Hendrickson, David C. 2003. *Peace Pact: The Lost World of the American Founding*. Lawrence: University Press of Kansas.

Hobson, Charles. 1979. "The Negative on State Laws: James Madison, the Constitution, and the Crisis of Republican Government." *The William and Mary Quarterly* 36 (2): 215–35.

Holt, Wythe. 1998. "John Blair, 'A Safe and Conscientious Judge.'" In *Seriatim: The Supreme Court before John Marshall*, edited by Scott Douglas Gerber, 155–97. New York: New York University Press.

Holton, Woody. 2007. *Unruly Americans and the Origins of the Constitution*. New York: Hill and Wang.

Howard, Christopher. 2007. *The Welfare State Nobody Knows: Debunking Myths About U.S. Social Policy*. Princeton, NJ: Princeton University Press.

Hurd, John C. 1881. *The Theory of Our National Existence, as Shown by the Action of the Government of the United States Since 1861*. Boston: Little Brown.

Hurst, John. 1956. *Law and the Conditions of Freedom*. Madison: University of Wisconsin Press.

Jameson, John Alexander. 1867. *The Constitutional Convention*. New York: C. Scribner & Company.

John, Richard S. 1997. "Governmental Institutions as Agents of Change: Rethinking American Political Development in the Early Republic, 1787–1835." *Studies in American Political Development* 11: 347–80.

Johnson, Kimberly. 2007. *Governing the American State: Congress and the New Federalism, 1877–1929*. Princeton, NJ: Princeton University Press.

Kagan, Robert. 2001. *Adversarial Legalism: The American Way of Law*. Cambridge, MA: Harvard University Press.

Kahn, Ronald. 2006. "Social Constructions, Supreme Court Reversals, and American Political Development: *Lochner, Plessy, Bowers,* but not *Roe.*" In *The Supreme Court and American Political Development*, edited by Ronald Kahn and Ken Kersch, 67–117. Lawrence, KS: University Press of Kansas.

Kahn, Ronald, and Ken I. Kersch, eds. 2006. *The Supreme Court and American Political Development*. Lawrence, KS: University Press of Kansas.

Katznelson, Ira. 2003. "On Rewriting the Epic of America," In *Shaped by War and Trade: International Influences on American Political Development*, edited by Ira Katznelson and Martin Shefter, 3–23. Princeton, NJ: Princeton University Press.

Keck, Thomas. 2004. *The Most Activist Supreme Court in History: The Road to Modern Judicial Conservatism*. Chicago: University of Chicago Press.

———. 2007. "Party, Policy, or Duty: Why Does the Supreme Court Invalidate Federal Statutes?" *American Political Science Review* 101 (2): 321–38.

Keller, Morton. 1977. *Affairs of the State: Public Life in Late Nineteenth Century America.* Cambridge, MA: Belknap Press of Harvard University Press.

Kersch, Ken. 2004. *Constructing Civil Liberties: Discontinuities in the Development of American Constitutional Law.* New York: Cambridge University Press.

Kersh, Rogan. 2005. "Rethinking Periodization? APD and the Macro-History of the United States." *Polity* 37 (4): 513–24.

King, Desmond, and Robert Lieberman. 2008. "Finding the American State: Transcending the 'Statelessness' Account." *Polity* 40 (3): 368–78.

———. 2009. "Ironies of State Building: A Comparative Perspective on the American State." *World Politics* 61: 547–88.

———. 2016. "The American State." In *The Oxford Handbook of American Political Development*, edited by Richard M. Valelly, Suzanne Mettler, and Robert C. Lieberman, 231–59. New York: Oxford University Press.

King, Desmond, and Marc Stears. 2011. "How the U.S. State Works: A Theory of Standardization." *Perspective on Politics* 9 (3): 505–18.

Kramer, Larry. 2000. "Putting the Politics Back into the Political Safeguards of Federalism." *Columbia Law Review* 100: 215–93.

Kramnick, Isaac, ed. 1987. *The Federalist Papers.* London:: Penguin Books Limited.

Kutler, Stanley I. 1968. *Judicial Power and Reconstruction Politics.* Chicago: University of Chicago Press.

Landis, Richard J., and Gary. G. Koch. 1977. "The Measurement of Observer Agreement for Categorical Data." *Biometrics* 33 (1): 159–74.

LaPiana, William. 1994. *Logic and Experience: The Origin of Modern American Legal Education.* New York: Oxford University Press.

Larsen, Charles E. 1959. "Nationalism and States' Rights in Commentaries on the Constitution after the Civil War." *The American Journal of Legal History* 3 (4): 360–69.

Larson, John. 2001. *Internal Improvement: National Public Works and the Promise of Popular Government in the Early United States.* Chapel Hill: University of North Carolina Press.

Lasser, William. 1985. "The Supreme Court in Periods of Critical Realignment." *Journal of Politics* 47: 1174–87.

Lawson, Gary, Geoffrey Miler, Robert Natelson, and Guy Seidman. 2010. *The Origins of the Necessary and Proper Clause.* New York: Cambridge University Press.

Les Benedict, Michael. 1978. "Preserving Federalism: Reconstruction and the Waite Court." *The Supreme Court Review* (1978): 39–79.

Levy, Leonard, and Kenneth Karst. 2000. *Encyclopedia of the American Constitution.* 6 vols. New York: Macmillan Reference.

Licht, Walter. 1995. *Industrializing America: The Nineteenth Century.* Baltimore: Johns Hopkins University Press.

Lovell, George I. 2003. *Legislative Deferrals: Statutory Ambiguity, Judicial Power, and American Democracy.* Cambridge, UK: Cambridge University Press.

MacGill, Hugh C., and R. Kenty Newmyer. 2008. "Legal Education and Legal Thought." In *The Cambridge History of Law in America.* Vol. II, edited by Michael Grossberg and Christopher Tomlins, 36–68. New York: Cambridge University Press.

Maltzman, Forrest, James Springs II, and Paul Wahlbeck. 2001. *Crafting Law on the Supreme Court: The Collegial Game.* New York: Cambridge University Press.

Marshall, John, et al. 1974. *The Papers of John Marshall.* Chapel Hill: University of North Carolina Press.

Mason, Alpheus. 1979. *The Supreme Court from Taft to Burger.* 3rd ed. Baton Rouge: Louisiana State University Press.

Mayhew, David. 2000. *America's Congress: Actions in the Public Sphere, James Madison through Newt Gingrich.* New Haven, CT: Yale University Press.

McCloskey, Robert. 2005. *The American Supreme Court.* 4th ed. Chicago: University of Chicago Press.

McCurdy, Charles. 1978. "American Law and the Marketing Structures of the Large Corporation, 1875–1890." *Journal of Economic History* 38 (3): 631–49.

McMahon, Kevin J. 2011. *Nixon's Court: His Challenge to Judicial Liberalism and Its Political Consequences.* Chicago: University of Chicago Press.

McWhinney, Edward. 1986. *Supreme Courts and Judicial Law-Making: Constitutional Tribunals and Constitutional Review.* Dordrecht, Netherlands: Springer Netherlands.

Mettler, Suzanne. 2011. *The Submerged State: How Invisible Government Polices Undermine American Democracy.* Chicago: University of Chicago Press.

Mettler, Suzanne, and Richard Valelly. 2016. "Introduction: The Distinctiveness and Necessity of American Political Development." In *The Oxford Handbook of American Political Development*, edited by Richard Valelly, Suzanne Mettler, and Robert Lieberman, 1–27. New York: Oxford University Press.

Miller, Mark C. 2009. *The View of the Courts from the Hill: Interactions between Congress and the Federal Judiciary.* Charlottesville: University of Virginia Press.

Morgan, Kimberly J. 2016. "Comparative Politics and American Political Development." In *The Oxford Handbook of American Political Development*, edited by Richard Valelly, Suzanne Mettler, and Robert Lieberman, 166–85. New York: Oxford University Press.

Morone, James A. 1998. *The Democratic Wish: Popular Participation and the Limits of American Government.* New Haven, CT: Yale University Press.

Murakawa, Naomi. 2014. *The First Civil Right: How Liberals Built Prison America.* New York: Oxford University Press.

Murphy, William P. 1964. *Elements of Judicial Strategy.* Chicago: University of Chicago Press.

———. 1968. *The Triumph of Nationalism: State Sovereignty, the Founding Fathers, and the Making of the Constitution.* Chicago: Quadrangle Books.

Nettl, J. P. 1968. "The State as Conceptual Variable." *World Politics* 20 (4): 559–92.

Ngai, Mae M. 2004. *Impossible Subjects: Illegal Aliens and the Making of Modern America.* Princeton, NJ: Princeton University Press.

Novak, William. 1996. *The People's Welfare: Law and Regulation in Nineteenth-Century America.* Chapel Hill: University of North Carolina Press.

———. 2002. "Legal Origins of Modern American State." In *Looking Back on Law's Century*, edited by Austin Sarat, Bryant Garth, and Robert Kagan, 249–87. Ithaca, NY: Cornell University Press.

———. 2008. "The Myth of the Weak American State." *American Historical Review* 113: 752–72.

———. 2015. "The Concept of the State in American History." In *Boundaries of the State U.S. History*, edited by James T. Sparrow, William J. Novak, and Stephen W. Sawyer, 325–49. Chicago: University of Chicago Press.

Novkov, Julie. 2001. *Constituting Workers, Protecting Women: Gender, Law, and Labor in the Progressive Era and New Deal Years.* Ann Arbor, MI: University of Michigan Press.

———. 2015. "Understanding Law as a Democratic Institution through U.S. Constitutional Development." *Law & Social Inquiry* 40 (3): 811–32.

O'Brien, David. 2003. *Storm Center: The Supreme Court in American Politics.* New York: W. W. Norton & Company.

Orren, Karen. 1991. *Belated Feudalism: Labor, the Law, and Liberal Development in the United States.* New York: Cambridge University Press.

Orren, Karen, and Stephen Skowronek. 2004. *The Search for American Political Development.* New York: Cambridge University Press.

Pacelle, Richard L. 2002. *The Role of the Supreme Court in American Politics: The Least Dangerous Branch?* Cambridge, MA: Westview Press.

Peabody, Bruce. 2011. "Introduction." In *The Politics of Judicial Independence: Courts, Politics, and the Public*, edited by Bruce Peabody, 1–19. Baltimore: Johns Hopkins University Press.

Peretti, Terri. 1999. *In Defense of a Political Court.* Princeton, NJ: Princeton University Press.

Pickerill, J. Mitchell, and Cornell W. Clayton. 2004. "The Rehnquist Court and the Political Dynamics of Federalism." *Perspectives on Politics* 2 (2): 233–48.

———. 2011. "Institutional Interdependence and the Separation of Powers." In *The Politics of Judicial Independence: Courts, Politics, and the Public*, edited by Bruce Peabody, 100–23. Baltimore: Johns Hopkins University Press.

Pierson, Paul. 2005. "The Study of Policy Development." *Journal of Policy History* 17: 34–51.

Pool, L. H. 1902. "Judicial Centralization." *Yale Law Journal* 11 (5): 246–55.

Powe, Lucas, Jr. 2000. *The Warren Court and American Politics.* Cambridge, MA: Harvard University Press.

Powers, Fred Perry. 1890. "Recent Centralizing Tendencies in the Supreme Court." *Political Science Quarterly* 5 (3): 389–410.

Prucha, Francis Paul. 1984. *The Great Father: The United States Government and the American Indians.* Lincoln: University of Nebraska Press.

Rana, Aziz. 2010. *The Two Faces of American Freedom.* Cambridge, MA: Harvard University Press.

Redfield, Isaac. 1867. "The Proper Limits between State and National Legislation and Jurisdiction. Speculations and Monopolies in the Staples of Subsistence. Railways a Matter of National Interest." *The American Law Register* 15 (4), New Series Vol. 6: 193–202.

Redish, Martin H. 1995. *The Constitution as Political Structure.* New York: Oxford University Press.

Redish, Martin H, and Shane V. Nugent. 1987. "The Dormant Commerce Clause and the Constitutional Balance of Federalism." *Duke Law Journal* 4: 569–617.

Robertson, David Brian Robertson. 2005a. *The Constitution and America's Destiny.* New York: Cambridge University Press.

———. 2005b. "Madison's Opponents and Constitutional Design." *American Political Science Review* 99 (2): 225–43.

———. 2012. *Federalism and the Making of America.* New York: Routledge.

Rockwell, Stephen J. 2010. *Indian Affairs and the Administrative State in the Nineteenth Century.* New York: Cambridge University Press.

Rosen, Jeffrey. 2006. *The Most Democratic Branch: How the Courts Serve America.* Oxford, UK: Oxford University Press.

Rosenberg, Gerald N. 2008. *The Hollow Hope: Can Courts Bring about Social Change?* 2nd ed. Chicago: University of Chicago Press.

Rydon, J. 1993. "The Australian Tradition of Federalism and Federation." In *Comparative Federalism and Federation*, edited by Michael Burgess and Alain Gagnon, 227–43. New York: Harvester Wheatsheaf.

Salyer, Lucy E. 1995. *Laws Harsh as Tigers: Chinese Immigrants and the Shaping of Modern Immigration Law.* Chapel Hill, NC: University of North Carolina Press.

Sanders, Elizabeth. 1999. *Roots of Reform: Farmers, Workers, and the American State, 1877–1917.* Chicago: University of Chicago Press.

Schickler, Eric. 2001. *Disjointed Pluralism: Institutional Innovation and the Development of the U.S. Congress.* Princeton, NJ: Princeton University Press.

Schwartz, Bernard. 1993. *A History of the Supreme Court.* New York: Oxford University Press.

Segal, Jeffrey, and Harold Spaeth. 1993. *The Supreme Court and the Attitudinal Model.* New York: Cambridge University Press.

Shapiro, Martin. 1980. "American Federalism." In *Constitutional Government in America: Essays and Proceedings from Southwestern University Law Review's First West Coast Conference on Constitutional Law*, edited by Ronald K. Collins, 359–73. Durham: Carolina Academic Press.

———. 1981. *Courts: A Comparative and Political Analysis.* Chicago: University of Chicago Press.

———. 1964. *Law and Politics in the Supreme Court.* New York: Free Press.

Shefter, Martin. 1994. *Political Parties and the State: The American Historical Experience.* Princeton, NJ: Princeton University Press.

Shklar, Judith N. 1998. "Positive Liberty, Negative Liberty in the United States." In *Redeeming American Political Thought*, edited by Stanley Hoffmann and Dennis F. Thompson, 111–27. Chicago: University of Chicago Press.

Simeon, Richard. 2009. "Constitutional Design and Change in Federal Systems: Issues and Questions." *Publius* 39 (2): 241–61.

Skowronek, Stephen. 1982. *Building a New American State: The Expansion of National Administrative Capacities, 1877–1920.* New York: Cambridge University Press.

———. 1993. *The Politics Presidents Make: Leadership from John Adams to George Bush.* Cambridge, MA: Belknap Press of Harvard University Press.

Skrentny, John David. 2006. "Law and the American State." *Annual Review of Sociology* 32: 213–44.

Somin, Ilya. 2017. "The Supreme Court of the United States: Promoting Centralization More than State Autonomy." In *Courts in Federal Countries: Federalist or Unitarists?* edited by Nicholas Aroney and John Kincaid, 440–82. Toronto, ON: University of Toronto Press.

Sparrow, James T. 2011. *Warfare State: World War II Americans and the Age of Big Government.* New York: Oxford University Press.

Stone, Geoffrey R. 2004. *Perilous Times: Free Speech in Wartime from the Sedition Act of 1798 to the War on Terrorism.* New York: W. W. Norton Company

Storing, Herbert J. 1981. *What the Anti-Federalists Were For: The Political Thought of the Opponents of the Constitution.* Chicago: University of Chicago Press.

Strauss, David A. 1996. "Common Law Constitutional Interpretation." *University of Chicago Law Review* 63 (3): 877–935.

Sweet, Alec Stone. 2004. *The Judicial Construction of Europe.* Oxford, UK: Oxford University Press.

Teles, Steven. 2008. *Rise of the Conservative Legal Movement: The Battle for Control of the Law.* Princeton, NJ: Princeton University Press.

Thelen, Kathleen. 2003. "How Institutions Evolve: Insights from Comparative Historical Analysis." In *Comparative Historical Analysis in the Social Sciences,* edited by James Mahoney and Dietrich Rueschemeyer, 208–41. Cambridge, UK: Cambridge University Press.

Thompson, Walter. 1923. *Federal Centralization: A Study and Criticism of the Expanding Scope of Congressional Legislation.* New York: Harcourt, Brace and Company.

Tily, Charles. 1985. "War Making and State Making as Organized Crime." In *Bringing the State Back In,* edited by Peter Evans, Dietrich Rueschemeyer, and Theda Skocpol, 169–92. New York: Cambridge University Press.

Tocqueville, Alexis de. (1835) 2003. *Democracy in America.* New York: Penguin Books.

Tushnet, Mark V. 1987. *The NAACP's Legal Strategy against Segregated Education, 1925–1950.* Chapel Hill: University of North Carolina Press.

Urofsky, Melvin I. 2005. "History of the Court: Depression and the Rise of Legal Liberalism." In *The Oxford Companion to the Supreme Court of the United States,* edited by Kermit L. Hall, James W. Ely, Jr., and Joel B. Grossman, 450–58. New York: Oxford University Press.

VanBurkleo, Susan. 2005. "*Fletcher v. Peck.*" In *The Oxford Companion to the Supreme Court of the United States,* edited by Kermit L. Hall, James W. Ely, Jr., and Joel B. Grossman, 352. New York: Oxford University Press.

———. 2005. "*New York v. Miln.*" In *The Oxford Companion to the Supreme Court of the United States,* edited by Kermit L. Hall, James W. Ely, Jr., and Joel B. Grossman, 683. New York: Oxford University Press.

Vaubel, Roland. 2009. "Constitutional Courts as Promoters of Political Centralization: Lessons for the European Court of Justice." *European Journal of Law and Economics* 28: 203–22.

Warren, Charles. 1913a. "A Bulwark to the State Police Power—The United States Supreme Court." *Columbia Law Review* 13: 667–95.

———. 1913b. "The Progressiveness of the United States Supreme Court." *Columbia Law Review* 13: 294–313.

———. 1922. *The Supreme Court in United States History, 1836–1918.* Boston: Little, Brown, and Company.

White, G. Edward. 1988. *The Marshall Court and Cultural Change, 1815–35.* Vols. III–IV. New York: Macmillan.

———. 2000. *The Constitution and the New Deal.* Cambridge, MA: Harvard University Press.

Whittington. Keith. 1997. "Dismantling the Modern State? The Changing Structural Foundations of Federalism." *Hastings Constitutional Law Quarterly* 483 (1997): 483–528.

———. 2001. "The Road Not Taken: Dred Scott, Judicial Authority, and Political Questions." *Journal of Politics* 63 (2): 365–91.

———. 2005. " 'Interpose Your Friendly Hand': Political Supports for the Exercise of Judicial Review by the United States Supreme Court." *American Political Science Review* 99: 584–96.

———. 2007. *Political Foundations of Judicial Supremacy: The Presidency, the Supreme Court, and Constitutional Leadership in U.S. History.* Princeton, NJ: Princeton University Press.

———. 2016. "Law and the Courts." In *The Oxford Handbook of American Political Development,* edited by Richard Valelly, Suzanne Mettler, and Robert Lieberman, 309–27. New York: Oxford University Press.

Whittington, Keith, and Amanda Rinderle. 2012. "Making a Mountain Out of a Molehill? *Marbury* and the Construction of the Constitutional Canon." *Hastings Constitutional Law Quarterly* 39 (4): 823–60.

Wiecek, William M. 1970. "The Great Writ and Reconstruction: The Habeas Corpus Act of 1867." *The Journal of Southern History* 36 (4): 530–48.

———. 1998. *The Lost World of Classical Legal Thought: Law and Ideology in America, 1886–1937.* New York: Oxford University Press.

———. 1969. "The Reconstruction of Federal Judicial Power, 1863–1875." *The American Journal of Legal History* 13 (4): 333–59.

Wilson, Mark R. 2008. "Law and the American, from the Revolution to the Civil War: Institutional Growth and Structural Change." In *The Cambridge History of Law in America.* Vol. II, edited by Michael Grossberg and Christopher Tomlins, 1–36. New York: Cambridge University Press.

Wilson, Woodrow. 1908. *The Constitutional Government in the United States.* New York: Columbia University Press.

Zackin, Emily. 2010. *Positive Constitutional Rights in the United States.* PhD diss., Princeton University. ProQuest.

———. 2013. *Looking for Rights in All the Wrong Places: Why State Constitutions Contain America's Positive Rights.* Princeton, NJ: Princeton University Press.

Index

Page numbers in *italics* refer to figures; page numbers in **bold** refer to tables.

Ableman v. Booth (1859), 11, 70–71
abortion, 132, 133–34
Abrams v. U.S. (1919), 111–12
Ackerman, Bruce, 136–37, 143
Adler, William, 68
administrative capacity
  during Early Republic (1789–1828), 73, **74**, 77
  during Jacksonian Era (1829–1860), 73, **74**, 77
  during Republican Era (1877–1932), 23, **98**
  during New Deal and Great Society (1933–1968), **98**, **121**
  during Contemporary Era (1969–1997), **121**
  coding rules for, 156–57
  definition of, 35–36, **35**, 203n6, 212n23
  overview of overall findings on, *43*, **44**, *45*
  scholarship on, 5–6
Affordable Care Act, 151
Allegheny County v. ACLU (1989), 14
Allen, Francis, 61–62
Allgeyer v. Louisiana (1897), 59, 101, 205n31
Allwright, S. S., 127
American Bar Association, 29

American Communications v. Douds (1950), 128
American exceptionalism, 67
American Insurance Company v. Canter (1828), 69–70
American Political Development (APD) movement, 25, 146, 147–48, 200–201n15, 216n5, 223–24n2
Anderson v. Dunn (1821), 49–50
Anti-Federalists, 7, 27–28, 79. *See also* Brutus
Arizona Train Limit Law, 116
Army Corps of Topographical Engineers, 68
Aroney, Nicholas, 200n9, 234n2
Articles of Confederation, 81–82
Ashmore, Margaret, 88
Ashwander v. Tennessee Valley Authority (1936), 124, 237n3
Ashwander v. TVA (1936), 121–22
Association of American Law Schools, 29
attitudinal model, 148
attorneys' and governmental officials' fees, **38**, *48*, 160
authority scores, 33

Baker v. Carr (1962), 203–204n10
Ball, Terrence, 27–28

Balogh, Brian, 7, 145, 146, 205n29
Bank of Augusta v. Earle (1839), 51
Bank of the United States, 51
Banks, Christopher, 234n6
Barron v. Baltimore (1833), *15*, 21–22
Beard, Charles, 202n3
Belz, Herman, 105
Bensel, Richard, 199n8, 212n23. *See also* dimensions of central state authority (Bensel)
Bernstein, David, 206–207n47, 208n65
Beth, Loren, 223n82
Bill of Rights, 8–10, 13–14, 22, 123. *See also specific Amendments*
Bingham, John, 105
Black, Hugo, 116, 125
Blackstone, William, 211n11
Blakeman, John, 234n6
Blatchford, Samuel, 205n30
Bolling v. Sharpe (1954), 130
Booth, Sherman, 70–71
Boston Globe (newspaper), 225n25
Brandenburg v. Ohio (1969), 14
Brandwein, Pamela, 107, 202–203n5, 202n20, 225n17, 228–29nn49–51
Brennan, William, 65
Brest, Paul, 211n14
Brewer, David Josiah, 95–96, 225n21
Breyer, Stephen, 152
Briscoe v. Bank of Kentucky (1837), 51, 52–53
broad nationalists, 81–82
Bronson v. Kinzie (1843), 51, 53
Brown, Henry Billings, 225n16
Brown v. Board of Education of Topeka (1954)
    citizenship and, 19–20
    Cooper v. Aaron and, 62
    effect on federal authority and, 34
    enforcement interventions and, 24–25
    Fourteenth Amendment and, 19–20
    judicial review and, 13
    significance of, 129, 148, 220n47
    typology of judicial decisions and, *15*

Brown v. Board of Education of Topeka II (1955), 24–25
Brownson, Orestes, 211n13, 227n33
Brutus (Anti-Federalist), 7–8, 27–28, 44, 79, 140, 148
Brutus, Marcus Junius, 27
Bryan, Samuel, 218n41
Buchanan v. Warley (1917), 13
Buckley v. Valeo (1976), 131
Budd v. New York (1892), 104
Bunting v. Oregon (1917), 59
Burger, Warren, 131, 132
Burger Court (1969–1986), 118, 130–33
Burgess, John, 211n13
Bush, George H. W., 134
Byrnes, James, 126

Calhoun, John C., 227n33
Cardozo, Benjamin, 116
Cedar Rust Act of Virginia (1924), 94
central state development, 1–2, 25
centralization of authority
    during Early Republic (1789–1828), **74**, 78–79
    during Jacksonian Era (1829–1860), **74**
    during Civil War and Reconstruction (1861–1876), 98–99
    during Republican Era (1877–1932), 16–18, 21, 98–99, **98**
    during New Deal and Great Society (1933–1968), 21–22, **98**, **121**
    during Contemporary Era (1969–1997), **121**
    coding rules for, 155–56
    definition of, 3–4, **35**
    Novak on, 199–200n8
    overview of overall findings on, 43–46, *43*, **44**, *45*, *47*, 144
Champion v. Ames (1903), 58
Charles River Bridge v. Warren Bridge (1837), 51, 52, 87–88, 89
Chase, Salmon P., 94, 105–107
Cherokee Nation, 68, 76, 86

Cherokee Nation v. Georgia (1831), 86

Chicago Daily Tribune (newspaper), 225n25

citizenship
during Early Republic (1789–1828), **74**
during Jacksonian Era (1829–1860), 19–20, **74**
during Civil War and Reconstruction (1861–1876), 98–99
during Republican Era (1877–1932), 98–99, **98**
during New Deal and Great Society (1933–1968), **98**, 121, **121**
during Contemporary Era (1969–1997), 121, **121**
coding rules for, 157
definition of, **35**, 203n6
ideology and, 197
overview of overall findings on, 43–46, *43*, **44**, *45–46*

City of Boerne v. Flores (1997), 134–35

Civil Rights Act (1866), 105

Civil Rights Act (1875), 59, 109

Civil Rights Act (1964), 61, 208n75

civil rights and liberties
during Early Republic (1789–1828), *48*, 76
during Jacksonian Era (1829–1860), *51*, 76
during Civil War and Reconstruction (1861–1876), *54*, 97, **97**
during Republican Era (1877–1932), 57, *57*, 58, 97, **97**
during New Deal and Great Society (1933–1968), 60, *60*, 101–102, **119**, *120*, 121, 122–36
during Contemporary Era (1969–1997), 62–63, **119**, *120*, 121
coding rules for, 160
definition of, **37**
Due Process Clause and, 13
ideology and, 196, 197
See also *Brown v. Board of Education of Topeka* (1954)

Civil Rights Cases (1893), 99

Civil War and Reconstruction (1861–1876)
centralization of authority in, 98–99
citizenship in, 98–99
civil rights and liberties in, *54*, 97, **97**
criminal procedure in, *54*
due process in, *54*
economic activity in, 53, *54*, 55–56, 94–95, 97–100, **97**
effect on federal authority in, *96*, *98*
executive power in, **97**
extraction in, 98
federal taxation in, *54*, **97**
federalism in, *54*, **97**, 102–108
First Amendment in, *54*
individual rights in, 95, 97–100
interstate relations in, *54*, **97**, 102–103
judicial power and jurisdiction in, *54*, **97**
level of government action under review in, *56*
miscellaneous in, *54*
overview of state-building in, 53–57, *54*, *56*, 93–102, 113, 141–42
presidential power in, *54*
private action in, *54*, **97**
world system in, 98

Clark, Thomas, 236n21

class legislation, 17

Clayton, Cornell, 201n18

Clemens, Elisabeth, 202n1

Clifford, Nathan, 55

Clinton, Bill, 135

Clinton v. City of New York (1998), 64, 135

Cohen, Paul, 132

Cohen, Philip and Mendes, 78–79

Cohen v. California (1971), 131–32

Cohens v. Virginia (1821), 49

Cohens v. Virginia (1824), 77–79

Coinage Clause, 83

Coles, James D., 109

Collector v. Day (1871), 55, 106

Commerce Clause
  dormant Commerce Clause doctrine
    and, 12, 103–105, 106–107, 110–11,
    122, 206n37
  Edwards v. California and, 126
  Gibbons v. Ogden and, 85–86
  Hunt v. Washington State Apple
    Advertising Commission and, 122
  Lochner v. New York and, 206n37
  Miln and, 52
  Morgan v. Virginia and, 128
  Passenger Cases and, 73–75
  role of, 10–11, 60–61, 83, 141
  Shelley v. Kraemer and, 128
  Southern Pacific Co. v. Arizona and,
    116
  Sweatt v. Painter and, 128
  United States v. Carolene Products Co
    and, 125
  United States v. Lopez and, 134
  Welton v. Missouri and, 55–56
  Wickard v. Filburn and, 125–26
  Willson v. Blackbird Creek Marsh
    Company and, 221–22nn67–68
Compton, John, 107
Conscription Act, 95
Constitution Besieged (Gillman), 150
Constitutional Convention (1787),
  81–85, 149–50
constitutional issue areas
  coding rules for, 159–61
  overview of, 33, 37, **37–38**
  See also specific issue areas
constitutional law casebooks and legal
  treatises, 28–33, *31*, 187–91,
  227n33
constitutional politics, 143
Contemporary Era (1969–1997)
  administrative capacity in, **121**
  centralization of authority in, **121**
  citizenship in, 121, **121**
  civil rights and liberties in, 62–63,
    119, *120*, 121
  control of property in, 121–22, **121**
  creation of client groups in, 121, **121**

criminal procedure in, **119**
due process in, **119**, *120*
economic activity in, **119**, *120*
effect on federal authority in, *117–18*,
  120
extraction in, **121**
federal taxation in, **119**
federalism in, **119**
First Amendment in, 62, 64–65, 118,
  119, *120*, 121
individual rights in, 122
judicial power and jurisdiction in,
  119
level of government action under
  review in, *64*
miscellaneous in, **119**
overview of state-building in, 62–65,
  63, 115–22, *117–18*, 136–37, 142
presidential power in, **119**
privacy in, **119**, *120*
property in, **121**
unions in, **119**
world system in, 121, **121**
Contracts Clause
  Bronson v. Kinzie and, 53
  Charles River Bridge v. Warren Bridge
    and, 87–88
  Fletcher v. Peck and, 11
  Piqua Branch Bank v. Knoop and, 53
  Planters Bank v. Mississippi and, 77
  Providence Bank v. Billings and,
    222n69
  Woodruff v. Trapnall and, 77
control of property
  during Early Republic (1789–1828),
    73, **74**, 76–77
  during Jacksonian Era (1829–1860),
    73, **74**, 76–77
  during Republican Era (1877–1932),
    16–18, **98**, 100–101
  during New Deal and Great Society
    (1933–1968), 21–22, **98**, 100–101,
    121–22, **121**
  during Contemporary Era (1969–
    1997), 121–22, **121**

coding rules for, 157–58
constitutional design and, 83–85
definition of, **35**, 203n6
overview of overall findings on, *43*,
    44, **44**, *45*
Cooley, Thomas, 29–30, 226n26
Cooley v. Board of Wardens (1852),
    110–11
Cooper v. Aaron (1958), 61–62
Coppage v. Kansas (1915), 59
Cortner, Richard, 8, 206n36
Corwin, Edward, 226n25
Cover, Clarice, 130
Cox, Archibald, 124
Coyle v. Smith (1911), *15*, 20–21,
    167–68
Craig, Curtis, 132
Craig v. Boren (1976), 132
creation of client groups
    during Early Republic (1789–1828), **74**
    during Jacksonian Era (1829–1860),
        19, **74**
    during Republican Era (1877–1932),
        98
    during New Deal and Great Society
        (1933–1968), **98**, 121, **121**
    during Contemporary Era (1969–
        1997), 121, **121**
    coding rules for, 158
    definition of, **35**, 203n6
    overview of overall findings on, *43*,
        44, **44**, *45*
criminal procedure
    during Early Republic (1789–1828),
        48, 76
    during Jacksonian Era (1829–1860),
        51, 76
    during Civil War and Reconstruction
        (1861–1876), *54*
    during Republican Era (1877–1932),
        57, *57*, 58
    during New Deal and Great Society
        (1933–1968), *60*, 101–102, **119**
    during Contemporary Era (1969–
        1997), **119**

coding rules for, 160
definition of, **37**
Crowe, Justin, 222n72, 228n48
Cruikshank, United States v., (1876), 55,
    99, 225n14, 229n51
Curtis, Benjamin Robbins, 230n69
Curtiss-Wright Corporation, 124
Cushman, Barry, 213n30, 223n2

Dahl, Robert A., 203n9, 236n20
Dartmouth College, 69
Dartmouth College v. Woodward (1819),
    50, 69, 219–20n47
De Jonge, Dirk, 121
De Jonge v. Oregon (1937), 121
Debs, In re (1895), 95–96, 102,
    207–208n59
Delaware, 87
Democracy in America (Tocqueville),
    216n4
Democratic Party, 50
Dennis v. U.S. (1951), 127–28
desegregation. See *Brown v. Board of
    Education of Topeka* (1954)
DeWitt, John (Anti-Federalist), 218n41
dimensions of central state authority
    (Bensel)
    coding rules for, 154–59
    overview of, 33, 34–36, **35**–**36**
    overview of overall findings on,
        43–46, *43*, **44**, *45–47*
    See also specific dimensions
Douglas, William, 125
Dowling, Noel, 30
Dred Scott v. Sandford (1857), 52,
    89–90, 105–106, 201–202n20
dual sovereignty, 69, 82, 86–87, 107,
    113, 141
due process
    during Jacksonian Era (1829–1860),
        51
    during Civil War and Reconstruction
        (1861–1876), *54*
    during Republican Era (1877–1932),
        57

due process *(continued)*
  during New Deal and Great Society
    (1933–1968), *60*, 101–102, **119**, *120*
  during Contemporary Era (1969–
    1997), **119**, *120*
  coding rules for, 160
  definition of, **37**
Due Process Clause
  Allgeyer v. Louisiana and, 101
  De Jonge v. Oregon and, 121
  Gitlow v. New York and, 112
  Lochner and, 17, 206n36
  Miller v. Schoene and, 94
  Moore v. Dempsey and, 112
  role of, 9, 13
  C. Warren on, 224n12

Early Republic (1789–1828)
  administrative capacity in, 73, **74**, 77
  centralization of authority in, **74**,
    78–79
  citizenship in, **74**
  civil rights and liberties in, *48*, 76
  control of property in, 73, **74**, 76–77
  creation of client groups in, **74**
  criminal procedure in, *48*, 76
  economic activity in, *48*, 50–51, 69,
    72, **72**, 73, *74–75*, 76–77, 82–83,
    85–87
  effect on federal authority in, 71–72,
    71, **72**, *73–74*
  executive power in, 72, **72**
  extraction in, 73, **74**, 76–77
  federal taxation in, *48*, **72**
  federalism in, *48*, 69–70, **72**, 73,
    74–75, 76, 82–83, 85–87
  First Amendment in, *48*
  individual rights in, 72, **72**, *74–75*
  judicial power and jurisdiction in,
    47–48, *48*, **72**, *74–75*, 77–81, 82–83
  level of government action under
    review in, 49–50, *49*
  overview of state-building in, 47–50,
    48–49, 67–70, 71–77, *71*, **72**,
    73–75, **74**, 141, 143–44, 217n44

presidential power in, *48*
private action in, *48*, **72**
world system in, 73–76, **74**
See also Marshall Court (1801–1835);
  specific cases
economic activity
  during Early Republic (1789–1828),
    48, 50–51, 69, 72, **72**, 73, *74–75*,
    76–77, 82–83, 85–87
  during Jacksonian Era (1829–1860),
    51, *51*, 52–53, 72, **72**, 73, *74–75*,
    76–77
  during Civil War and Reconstruction
    (1861–1876), 53, *54*, 55–56, 94–95,
    97–100, *97*
  during Republican Era (1877–1932),
    57–59, *57*, 94–95, 97–100, *97*,
    99–100, 108–109, 110–11
  during New Deal and Great Society
    (1933–1968), 60, *60*, 99–100,
    99–100, 101, 102, **119**, *120*
  during Contemporary Era (1969–
    1997), **119**, *120*
  coding rules for, 161
  constitutional design and, 83–85
  definition of, **38**
  ideology and, 196
Edling, Max, 145, 148–49
Edwards, Harry T., 236n19
Edwards v. California (1941), 126
effect on federal authority
  during Early Republic (1789–1828),
    71–72, *71*, **72**, *73–74*
  during Jacksonian Era (1829–1860),
    71–72, *71*, **72**, *73–74*
  during Civil War and Reconstruction
    (1861–1876), *96*, *98*
  during Republican Era (1877–1932),
    96, *98*
  during New Deal and Great Society
    (1933–1968), *117–18*, *120*
  during Contemporary Era (1969–
    1997), *117–18*, *120*
  coding rules for, 162–68
  definition of, 33, 34

overview of overall findings on, 38–42, *39–42*

See also constitutional issue areas (variable)

Eighteenth Amendment, 58

Eisenhower, Dwight, 208n75

Eleventh Amendment, 49

Elliot, Alan C., 212n24

Ellis, Richard E., 7

Ely, James, 221n58

Enabling Act (1906), 20–21, 167

Enforcement Act (1870), 225n14

Equal Protection Clause
  Miller v. Schoene and, 95
  Plyler v. Doe and, 65
  Richmond v. Croson and, 135–36
  Shelley v. Kraemer and, 61–62
  Stone Court and, 126–27
  C. Warren on, 224n12

Espionage Act, 95, 112

Establishment Clause, 14

Ethics in Government Act (1978), 64

executive power
  during Early Republic (1789–1828), 72, **72**
  during Jacksonian Era (1829–1860), 72, **72**
  during Civil War and Reconstruction (1861–1876), **97**
  during Republican Era (1877–1932), **97**
  coding rules for, 161
  definition of, **38**

extraction
  during Early Republic (1789–1828), 73, **74**, 76–77
  during Jacksonian Era (1829–1860), 73, **74**, 76–77
  during Civil War and Reconstruction (1861–1876), 98
  during Republican Era (1877–1932), 98, **98**
  during New Deal and Great Society (1933–1968), **98**, **121**
  during Contemporary Era (1969–1997), **121**

coding rules for, 158–59

definition of, **35**, 203n6

overview of overall findings on, *43*, **44**, *45*

Fair Labor Standards Act (1938), 64

Federal Election Campaign Act (1971), 131

federal taxation
  during Early Republic (1789–1828), *48*, **72**
  during Jacksonian Era (1829–1860), **72**
  during Civil War and Reconstruction (1861–1876), *54*, **97**
  during Republican Era (1877–1932), *57*, **97**
  during New Deal and Great Society (1933–1968), *60*, **119**
  during Contemporary Era (1969–1997), **119**
  coding rules for, 161
  definition of, **38**

Federal Trade Commission Act (1914), 23

federalism
  during Early Republic (1789–1828), *48*, 69–70, **72**, 73, *74–75*, 76, 82–83, 85–87
  during Jacksonian Era (1829–1860), *51*, 70–71, **72**, 73, *74–75*, 76, 86–90
  during Civil War and Reconstruction (1861–1876), *54*, **97**, 102–108
  during Republican Era (1877–1932), *57*, **97**, *99–100*, 103–108
  during New Deal and Great Society (1933–1968), *60*, *99–100*, **119**
  during Contemporary Era (1969–1997), **119**
  coding rules for, 161
  definition of, **38**
  ideology and, 196, 197
  typology of judicial decisions and, 15–16

The Federalist Papers, 79, 83–85, 149, 220n52

Feldman, Noah, 30
Fifteenth Amendment, 90, 126–27
Fifth Amendment
  Barron v. Baltimore and, 21–22
  Bolling v. Sharpe and, 130
  incorporation and, 13–14
  Lanza, United States v. and, 58
  Palko v. Connecticut and, 123
  Takings Clause of, 136
Filburn, Roscoe, 126
Finkelman, Paul, 221n58
First Amendment
  Cohen v. California and, 131–32
  Cruikshank and, 225n14
  De Jonge v. Oregon and, 121
  Dennis v. U.S. and, 127–28
  Establishment Clause of, 14
  Free Exercise Clause of, 14
  Free Press Clause of, 123
  Free Speech Clause of, 14, 95, 112
  Loving v. Virginia and, 129
  Near v. Minnesota and, 123
  Palko v. Connecticut and, 123
  Powell v. Alabama and, 124
  Richmond Newspapers Inc. v. Virginia
    and, 132
  *West Virginia State Board of
    Education v. Barnette* and, 126
First Amendment (as variable)
  during Early Republic (1789–1828), *48*
  during Civil War and Reconstruction
    (1861–1876), *54*
  during Republican Era (1877–1932),
    57
  during New Deal and Great Society
    (1933–1968), 60, *60*, 61, 101–102,
    118, **119**, *120*, 121
  during Contemporary Era (1969–
    1997), 62, 64–65, 118, **119**, *120*,
    121
  Brown v. Board of Education and, 129
  Buckley v. Valeo and, 131
  coding rules for, 160
  definition of, **37**
  ideology and, 196, 197

Fisher, Louis, 205n20, 235n18
Fisher, Sidney, 227n33
Fletcher v. Peck (1810), 11, 50
Flores, Patrick, 135
Fong Yue Ting v. United States (1893),
  109, 110
Forbath, William, 12
Fourteenth Amendment (1868)
  Brown v. Board of Education and,
    19–20
  Budd v. New York and, 104
  Dred Scott v. Sandford and, 90
  Due Process Clause in, 206n36
  Equal Protection Clause of, 61–62,
    65, 95, 126–27
  "liberty of contract" interpretation
    and, 9–11, 12–13, 59, 101
  Lochner and, 17
  Morgan v. Virginia and, 128
  Mugler v. Kansas and, 104
  Munn v. Illinois and, 104
  Near v. Minnesota and, 123
  Powell v. Alabama and, 124
  Powell v. Pennsylvania and, 100–101
  Privileges and Immunities Clause of,
    108–109
  role of, 4, 8–10, 142, 237n2
  Shelley v. Kraemer and, 128
  Slaughterhouse Cases and, 108–109
  substantive interpretation of rulings
    and, 5
  Sweatt v. Painter and, 128
  See also Due Process Clause
Fourth Amendment, 14
Fowler, James, 33, 232n41
Frankfurter, Felix, 125
Free Exercise Clause, 14
Free Press Clause, 123
Free Speech Clause, 14, 95, 112
Freund, Ernst, 107, 227n37, 229n56
Friedman, Lawrence, 210–11n10
Frisbie v. United States (1895), 225n21
Frontiero v. Richardson (1973), 133
Frymer, Paul, 151, 201n16, 208n64,
  223n2

Fugitive Slave Act (1850), 70–71, 89
Fugitive Slave Clause (1793), 52
Fugitive Slave Law (1793), 88–89
fugitive slaves, 11, 52, 70–71, 88–90,
    105–106
Fuller Court (1888–1910), 107

*Garcia v. San Antonio Metropolitan
    Transit* (1985), 63–64
General Welfare Clause, 116
Gibbons, Thomas, 85–86
Gibbons v. Ogden (1824), 85–86, 87, 88
Gideon v. Wainwright (1963), 129,
    207n51
Gilded Age (1877–1899), 57, *98*, 108–10
Gillman, Howard, 134, 150, 201n18,
    209n82, 223n2, 236n24
Gilman v. Philadelphia (1865), 56
Gitlow, Samuel, 112
Gitlow v. New York (1925), 112
Glover, Joshua, 70–71
Goldberg v. Kelly (1970), 132
Goldman, Jerry, 32, 50–51
governing regime model, 148
Graber, Mark, 201–202n20, 209n82,
    217n32
Grand National Lottery, 78–79
Great Society. *See* New Deal and Great
    Society (1933–1968)
Greve, Michael, 12
Grimes, James, 103
Griswold v. Connecticut (1964), 132
Guns-Free School Zones Act (1990), 134
Gunther, Gerald, 222n70

Habeas Corpus Act, 226n31
Hall, Kermit, 221n58
Hamilton, Alexander, 79, 80, 83–85,
    148, 149, 204n18
Harlan, John Marshall, 107
Hartz, Louis, 146, 215n2
Hastie, William, 127
Hayburn's Case (1792), 48, 80
*Heart of Atlanta Motel Inc. v. United
    States* (1964), 61

Heclo, Hugh, 202n1
Hegel, G. W. F., 216n4
Helvering v. Davis (1937), 61, 116
Hill, George H., 105–106
Hobson, Charles F., 204n19, 221n62
Holden v. Hardy (1898), 109
Hollingsworth v. Virginia (1798), 49
Holmes, Oliver Wendell, Jr., 206–207n47
Holton, Woody, 7
Hoover, Herbert, 23
Hoyt v. Florida (1961), 233n56
Hughes, Charles Evans, 104–105, 121,
    122–23
Hughes Court (1930–1941), 112,
    122–25, 127
Humphrey's Executor v. United States
    (1935), 23
*Hunt v. Washington State Apple
    Advertising Commission* (1977), 122
Hurd, John C., 227n33
Hurst, James Willard, 215n2
Hurtado, Joseph, 163–64
Hurtado v. California (1884), 163–64
Hylton v. United States (1796), 49

I. M. Singer & Company, 10–11
Immigration and Nationality Act
    (1952), 212n23
incorporation, 8–10, 13–14, 22, 123
Indian Removal Act (1830), 68
individual rights
    during Early Republic (1789–1828),
        72, *72*, *74–75*
    during Jacksonian Era (1829–1860),
        72, *72*, *74–75*, 88–89
    during Civil War and Reconstruction
        (1861–1876), 95, 97–100
    during Republican Era (1877–1932),
        57, 95, 97–100, *99–100*, 109–10,
        111–12
    during New Deal and Great Society
        (1933–1968), 99–100, *99–100*,
        101–102, 122–36
    during Contemporary Era (1969–
        1997), 122

individual rights *(continued)*
  typology of judicial decisions and,
    15–16
  See also civil rights and liberties;
    economic activity
INS v. Chadha (1983), 212n23
interracial marriage, 129
interstate relations
  during Civil War and Reconstruction
    (1861–1876), *54*, **97**, 102–103
  during Republican Era (1877–1932),
    57, **97**, *99–100*
  during New Deal and Great Society
    (1933–1968), *99–100*
  coding rules for, 161
  definition of, **38**

Jackson, Andrew, 50, 68, 87
Jackson, Robert, 126
Jacksonian Era (1829–1860)
  administrative capacity in, 73, **74**, 77
  centralization of authority in, **74**
  citizenship in, 19–20, **74**
  civil rights and liberties in, *51*, 76
  control of property in, 73, **74**, 76–77
  creation of client groups in, 19, **74**
  criminal procedure in, *51*, 76
  due process in, *51*
  economic activity in, 51, *51*, 52–53,
    72, **72**, 73, *74–75*, 76–77
  effect on federal authority in, 71–72,
    71, **72**, *73–74*
  executive power in, 72, **72**
  extraction in, 73, **74**, 76–77
  federal taxation in, **72**
  federalism in, *51*, 70–71, **72**, 73,
    74–75, 76, 86–90
  individual rights in, 72, **72**, *74–75*,
    88–89
  judicial power and jurisdiction in, *51*,
    72, *74–75*, 81
  level of government action under
    review in, *53*
  overview of state-building in, 50–53,
    51, *53*, 71–77, *71*, **72**, *73–75*, **74**, 141
  presidential power in, *51*
  private action in, **72**
  world system in, 73–76, **74**
  See also Marshall Court (1801–1835);
    Taney Court (1836–1864)
Jameson, John, 227n33
Jefferson, Thomas, 7, 80
Jehovah's Witnesses, 61
Jeon, Sangick, 33, 232n41
Johnson, Andrew, 228n42
Johnson, Kimberly, 225–26n25
Johnson, Thomas, 86
Johnson v. M'Intosh (1823), 86
Ju Toy, United States v., (1905), 58
judicial decisions
  examples of, *15*, 16–22, 23
  list of, 169–85
  neutral cases and, 22–23, 165–66
  potential objections to typology of,
    24–25
  typology of, 15–16, *15*
judicial finality, 7–8
judicial power and jurisdiction
  during Early Republic (1789–1828),
    47–48, *48*, **72**, *74–75*, 77–81,
    82–83
  during Jacksonian Era (1829–1860),
    51, **72**, *74–75*, 81
  during Civil War and Reconstruction
    (1861–1876), *54*, **97**
  during Republican Era (1877–1932),
    57, **97**, *99*
  during New Deal and Great Society
    (1933–1968), *60*, *99*, **119**
  during Contemporary Era (1969–1997),
    119
  coding rules for, 161
  definition of, **38**
  ideology and, 196
judicial review, 10–15, 22
Judiciary Act (1789), 48–49
Juilliard v. Greenman (1884), *15*, 18–19,
    162–63
Jurisdiction and Removal Act (1875),
    228n48

justiciability, 79–80. *See also* judicial power and jurisdiction

Kahn, Robert, 201n18
Karst, Kenneth, 125
Katzenbach v. McClung (1964), 61
Keck, Thomas, 134, 150–51, 234n73
Kent, James, 29, 211n11
Kersch, Ken, 201n18, 229n52
Kincaid, John, 200n9, 234n2
King, Desmond
    on citizenship rights, 19
    on Dahlian procedural conception of democracy, 2
    on judicial review, 204n15
    on Weberian model, 1, 5, 6, 26
Knight Co, E.C., United States v., (1895), 95–96, 207–208n59
Koch, Gary. G., 212n24
Korematsu, Fred, 116
Korematsu v. U.S. (1944), 116
Kramer, Larry, 199n4, 222–23n75
Kramnick, Isaac, 149
Ku Klux Klan, 14, 55
Kutler, Stanley I., 103, 227n32

Landis, Richard J., 212n24
Lane County v. Oregon (1869), 106
Langdell, Christopher Columbus, 210–11n10
Lanza, United States v., (1922), 58
Larson, John, 216n7
legal education, 28–29. *See also* constitutional law casebooks and legal treatises
legal reasoning and logic, 150
Legal Tender Acts (1862), 18
Legal Tender Cases (1871), 55
legal treatises. *See* constitutional law casebooks and legal treatises
Les Benedict, Michael, 222n71
level of government action under review
    during Early Republic (1789–1828), 49–50, *49*
    during Jacksonian Era (1829–1860), *53*

    during Civil War and Reconstruction (1861–1876), 56
    during New Deal and Great Society (1933–1968), *62*
    during Contemporary Era (1969–1997), *64*
    definition of, 33, 36–37
Levy, Leonard, 125
The Liberal Tradition (Hartz), 215n2
"liberty of contract" interpretation, 9–11, 12–13, 59, 101
Licht, Walter, 85, 220n51, 221n55
Lieberman, Robert
    on citizenship rights, 19
    on Dahlian procedural conception of democracy, 2
    on judicial review, 204n15
    on Weberian model, 1, 5, 6, 26
Lincoln, Abraham, 54
Line Item Veto Act (1996), 135
"living Constitution" theory, 152
Lochner v. New York (1905)
    APD scholars on, 25–26, 223–24n2
    centralization of authority and, 16–18, 95–96, 142
    check, 206n36
    control of property and, 16–18
    "liberty of contract" interpretation and, 10–11, 12–13
    typology of judicial decisions and, *15*
Lockhart, William, 211n14
Lopez, Alfonzo, 134
Lovell, George I., 202–203n5
Loving v. Virginia (1967), 129
Lucas v. South Carolina Coastal Council (1992), 136
Luther v. Borden (1849), 81

MacGill, Hugh C., 29, 211n11
Madison, James, 7, 27, 81–85, 149, 220–21nn52–53
Making of Modern Law (database), 29
Mapp v. Ohio (1961), 129, 134, 207n49
Marbury v. Madison (1803), 48–49, 61–62, 80–81, 211n12

Marshall, John, 61–62, 89. *See also*
    Marshall Court (1801–1835)
Marshall, Thurgood, 127
Marshall Court (1801–1835)
    centralization of authority and,
        21–22, 78–79
    Contracts Clause and, 11, 53
    control of property and, 21–22
    Dartmouth College v. Woodward and,
        219–20n47
    economic activity and, 50–51, 69,
        85–87
    extraction and, 76–77
    federalism and, 69–70, 76–77, 85–87,
        88
    judicial power and jurisdiction and,
        48–49, 77–81
    McCulloch v. Maryland and, 86
    overview of state-building in, 143–44
    racial segregation and, 61–62
    state expansion and, 90–91, 141
    Supremacy Clause and, 7, 78–79
    world system and, 75–76
    See also Early Republic (1789–1828)
Martin v. Hunter's Lessee (1816), 49, 50
Mason, Alpheus, 125
Mayhew, David, 28, 210n6
Maynard, George, 65
McCardle, Ex parte (1869), 54–55
McCray v. United States (1904), 58,
    94–95
McCulloch, James W., 86
McCulloch v. Maryland (1819), 50, 85,
    86, 87
McCurdy, Charles, 10–11, 205n25
Meat Inspection Acts (1906 and 1907),
    58
Mettler, Suzanne, 3, 145, 204n14
Miller, Mark, 217n31
Miller, Samuel, 108, 111
Miller v. Schoene (1928), 94–95
Milligan, Ex parte (1866), 54
Minersville School District v. Gobitis
    (1940), 126

M'Intosh, William, 86
Miranda v. Arizona (1966), 134, 207n50
miscellaneous
    during Civil War and Reconstruction
        (1861–1876), *54*
    during Republican Era (1877–1932),
        57
    during New Deal and Great Society
        (1933–1968), **119**
    during Contemporary Era (1969–
        1997), **119**
    coding rules for, 161
    definition of, **38**
Missouri Compromise (1820), 89–90
Modern Supreme Court Database,
    159–60
Monongahela Navigation v. United States
    (1893), 165–66
Moore v. Dempsey (1923), 112
Morgan, Kimberly J., 5, 204n11
Morgan, Margaret, 88
Morgan v. Virginia (1946), 128
Morone, James, 216n5
Morrison v. Olson (1988), 64
Mugler v. Kansas (1887), 104, 107
Muller v. Oregon (1908), 59
Munn v. Illinois (1877), 104
Murphy, William P., 82, 219n44
Myers v. United States (1926), 209n85

NAACP Legal Defense Fund, 9–10
narrow nationalists, 81–82
*National Federation of Independent
    Businesses v. Sebelius* (2012), 151
National Labor Relations Act, 128
National League of Cities v. Usery
    (1976), 63–64
National Prohibition Act, 58
Native Americans, 68, 76, 86, 214n8
Near v. Minnesota (1931), 123, 124
Necessary and Proper Clause, 18, 55,
    83, 85, 163
negative rights, 146
Nelson, Samuel, 106

New Deal and Great Society (1933–1968)
  administrative capacity in, **98**, **121**
  centralization of authority in, 21–22,
    98, **121**
  citizenship in, **98**, 121, **121**
  civil rights and liberties in, 60, *60*,
    101–102, **119**, *120*, 121, 122–36
  control of property in, 21–22, **98**,
    100–101, 121–22, **121**
  creation of client groups in, **98**, 121,
    121
  criminal procedure in, *60*, 101–102,
    119
  due process in, *60*, 101–102, **119**, *120*
  economic activity in, 60, *60*, 99–100,
    99–100, 101, 102, **119**, *120*
  effect on federal authority in, *117–18*,
    120
  extraction in, **98**, **121**
  federal taxation in, *60*, **119**
  federalism in, *60*, *99–100*, **119**
  First Amendment in, 60, *60*, 61,
    101–102, 118, **119**, *120*, 121
  individual rights in, 99–100, *99–100*,
    101–102, 122–36
  interstate relations in, *99–100*
  judicial power and jurisdiction in, *60*,
    99, **119**
  level of government action under
    review in, *62*
  miscellaneous in, **119**
  overview of state-building in, 60–62,
    60, *62*, 115–22, *117–18*, 136–37,
    142
  presidential power in, *60*, **119**
  privacy in, *60*, **119**, *120*
  property in, **121**
  redefinition of federal-state authority
    in, 147
  unions in, 59, *60*, **119**
  world system in, **98**, 121, **121**
New Jersey v. Wilson (1812), 50, 53
New York, City of v. Miln (1837), 51, 52
New York Court of Appeals, 17

New York Journal (newspaper), 27
Newmyer, R. Kenty, 29, 211n11
Nixon, Richard, 130–31
Nixon v. United States (1993), 64
Nollan v. California Coastal Commission
  (1987), 136
normal politics, 143
Novak, William, 199–200n8, 201n16,
  202n4
Novkov, Julie, 201n20, 202–203n5,
  223–24n2
nullification, 88–90

O'Connor, Sandra Day, 135–36
Office of Indian Affairs, 216n8
Ogden, Aaron, 85–86
Ohio Criminal Syndicalism, 14
Oklahoma Act (1910), 167
Oklahoma Enabling Act (1906), 20–21,
  167
Orren, Karen, 3, 5, 34, 199n7, 219n43,
  219n47
Osborn, Ralph, 76–77
Osborn v. Bank of the United States
  (1824), 50, 76–77

Palko v. Connecticut (1937), 123
Panic of 1837, 51
Passenger Cases, The (1849), 73–75
Paul, Samuel, 109
Paul v. Virginia (1869), 109
Peabody, Bruce, 235n18
Peckham, Rufus Wheeler, 17
*Pennsylvania Packet and Daily
  Advertiser* (newspaper), 218n41
Pennsylvania Supreme Court, 89
Philadelphia Constitutional Convention
  (1787), 27
Piankeshaw Indians, 86
Pierson, Paul, 201n19
Piqua Branch Bank v. Knoop (1853),
  51, 53
piracy, 75–76
Planters Bank v. Mississippi (1848), 77

Plessy v. Ferguson (1896), 19, 99
Plyler v. Doe (1982), 65
political development, 3, 34
The Politics of Judicial Independence
(Peabody), 235n18
Pool, L. H., 227n38
positive rights, 146
Posner, Richard, 146
Post Office Act (1792), 68
Powe, Lucas, Jr., 14
Powell, Adam Clayton, 129–30
Powell v. Alabama (1932), 112, 124
Powell v. McCormack (1969), 129–30,
233n59
Powell v. Pennsylvania (1888), 100–101
Powers, Fred Perry, 227n38
Presentment Clause, 49
Presidential Executive Order 9066
(1942), 116
presidential power
during Early Republic (1789–1828),
48
during Jacksonian Era (1829–1860),
51
during Civil War and Reconstruction
(1861–1876), *54*
during Republican Era (1877–1932),
57
during New Deal and Great Society
(1933–1968), *60*, **119**
during Contemporary Era (1969–
1997), **119**
Prigg, Edward, 88
Prigg v. Pennsylvania (1842), 11, 52,
88–89
privacy
during Republican Era (1877–1932),
57
during New Deal and Great Society
(1933–1968), *60*, **119**, *120*
during Contemporary Era (1969–
1997), **119**, *120*
coding rules for, 160
definition of, **37**

private action
during Early Republic (1789–1828),
48, **72**
during Jacksonian Era (1829–1860),
72
during Civil War and Reconstruction
(1861–1876), *54*, **97**
during Republican Era (1877–1932),
57, **97**
coding rules for, 161
definition of, **38**
Privileges and Immunities Clause, 108–109
Prize Cases (1863), 54
Progressive Era (1900–1932), 57, *98*,
110–12
Prohibition Act (1918), 102
Providence Bank v. Billings (1830), 87
Pullman Strike (1894), 102. See also
Debs, In re (1895)
Pure Food and Drug Act (1906), 58

racial covenant laws, 61–62
racial discrimination, 59, 151
racial segregation, 13, 61–62, 128, 129,
130. See also *Brown v. Board of
Education of Topeka* (1954); *Plessy
v. Ferguson* (1896)
Railroad and Warehouse Commission
(Minnesota), 9
Rana, Aziz, 83
Reagan, Ronald, 134
Reconstruction. *See* Civil War and
Reconstruction (1861–1876)
Reconstruction Act (1867), 55
Reconstruction Amendments, 94, 108–
109. *See also specific amendments*
Redfield, Isaac F., 93
Redish, Martin, 226n25
Rehnquist, William, 134, 206–207n47
Rehnquist Court (1986–2005), 14, 131,
133–36
Reid v. Covert (1957), 130
Religious Freedom Restoration Act
(1993), 134–35

Republican Era (1877–1932)
  administrative capacity in, 23, **98**
  centralization of authority in, 16–18,
    21, 98–99, **98**
  citizenship in, 98–99, **98**
  civil rights and liberties in, 57, *57*, 58,
    97, **97**
  control of property in, 16–18, **98**,
    100–101
  creation of client groups in, **98**
  criminal procedure in, 57, *57*, 58
  due process in, *57*
  economic activity and, 94–95
  economic activity in, 57–59, *57*,
    94–95, 97–100, **97**, *99–100*,
    108–109, 110–11
  effect on federal authority in, *96*, **98**
  executive power in, **97**
  extraction in, 98, **98**
  federal taxation in, *57*, **97**
  federalism in, *57*, **97**, *99–100*,
    103–108
  First Amendment in, *57*
  individual rights in, 57, 95, 97–100,
    99–100, 109–10, 111–12
  interstate relations in, *57*, **97**, *99–100*
  judicial power and jurisdiction in, *57*,
    97, *99*
  miscellaneous in, *57*
  overview of state-building in, 57–59,
    57, *59*, 93–102, 113
  presidential power in, *57*
  privacy in, *57*
  private action in, *57*, **97**
  redefinition of federal-state authority
    in, 147
  unions in, *57*
  world system in, 98, **98**
  See also Gilded Age (1877–1899);
    Progressive Era (1900–1932)
Richmond Newspapers Inc. v. Virginia
  (1980), 132
Richmond v. Croson (1989), 135–36
"rights revolution," 61–62

Rinderle, Amanda, 210n4, 211n12
Roberts, Owen, 61
Robertson, David Brian, 213n33, 216n9,
    218n40, 220n48
Rockwell, Stephen, 216n8
Roe v. Wade (1973), 132
Roosevelt, Franklin, 23, 122–23

Salyer, Lucy E., 230n68
*San Antonio Independent School District
    v. Rodriguez* (1973), 133
The Saturday Press (newspaper), 123
Scalia, Antonin, 152
Schenck, Charles, 95
Schenck v. United States (1919), 95,
    111–12
*School District of Abington Township,
    Pennsylvania v. Schempp* (1963),
    207n57
Schwartz, Bernard, 125
Scott, Dred, 89–90
Second Bank of the United States, 86,
    87
Segal, Jeffrey, 201n17
Seventh Amendment, 13–14
sex discrimination, 233n56
Shapiro, Martin, 90–91, 143, 148,
    218–19n42
Shaw v. Reno (1993), 136
Shelby County v. Holder (2013), 151
Shelley v. Kraemer (1948), 61–62, 128
Sherman, Roger, 81–82
Sherman Antitrust Act (1890), 59
Shreveport Rate Case (1914), 111
Singer & Company, 10–11
Sixth Amendment, 14, 130
Skowronek, Stephen
  on authority, 199n7
  on Constitution, 219n43
  on political development, 3, 34,
    219n47
  on role of Supreme Court, 5, 10,
    205n28
  on state actors, 6

Skrentny, John David, 200–201n15, 223n2

Slaughterhouse Cases (1873), 108

slavery, 11, 52, 88–90

Smith, Lonnie E., 127

Smith, Thomas, 75–76

Smith Act, 127–28

Smith v. Allwright (1944), 127

Social Security Act, 61, 116

Somin, Ilya, 13–14, 134, 205–206n35, 205n33

South Dakota v. Dole (1987), 64

Southern Pacific Co. v. Arizona (1945), 116

Spaeth, Harold, 37, 201n17

Sprague, William, 228n42

state capacity, 3, 4

state development, 3

state-building
  concept of, 1–2, 25, 139–40
  See also Supreme Court and state-building; *specific periods*

Steward Machine Co. v. Davis (1937), 61

Stewart, Potter, 61

Stone, Harlan F., 125, 126

Stone Court (1941–1946), 125–27, 128, 129

Storing, Herbert J., 7

Story, Joseph, 29, 89

Strauder v. West Virginia (1880), 95, 110

Strauss, David, 235n9

Strawbridge v. Curtiss (1806), 218n39

Sullivan, Kathleen, 30

Supremacy Clause, 7, 78–79

Supreme Court and state-building
  case selection method, 28–33, *31*, 187–91
  characteristics of constitutional expansion and, 65, 193–98, *193*, **194–95**, *196–98*
  coding rules for, 153–61, *154*
  ideology and, 195–96, **195**
  key variables studied, 33–37, **35–36**, **37–38**

overview of, 1–4, 26, 139–40, 151–52

patterns of development in, 140–44

reasons for central state expansion and, 4–15, 147–51

redefinition of federal-state authority and, 144–47

vote outcomes and, 195

See also constitutional issue areas; dimensions of central state authority (Bensel); effect on federal authority; level of government action under review

Supreme Court Database, 37

Supreme Court Legacy Database, 159–60

Sutherland, George, 124, 209n85

Swayne, Noah Haynes, 56

Sweatt v. Painter (1950), 128

Taft, William Howard, 58, 218n34

Taft Court (1921–1930), 58, 112

Taft-Hartley Act, 128

Taney, Roger, 70–71, 87, 89

Taney Court (1836–1864)
  Contracts Clause and, 52–53
  economic activity and, 51, 52–53, 77
  federalism and, 70–71, 87–90
  fugitive slaves and, 11, 52, 70–71, 88–90, 105–106
  judicial power and jurisdiction and, 81
  state-building and, 72–75, *73*, 90–91, 141, 144
  world system and, 73–75

Tennessee Valley Authority (TVA), 121–22, 237n3

Tenth Amendment, 81–82

territorial expansion, 86

Texas v. White (1869), 106

Thayer, James Bradley, 29–30

Third Amendment, 13–14

Thirteenth Amendment, 90

Thomas, Clarence, 152

Tocqueville, Alexis de, 200n13, 215n2, 216n4

Treaty of Paris (1783), 50
Truman administration, 127
Tumey v. Ohio (1927), 102

unions
    during Republican Era (1877–1932),
        57
    during New Deal and Great Society
        (1933–1968), 59, *60*, **119**
    during Contemporary Era (1969–
        1997), **119**
    coding rules for, 161
    definition of, **38**
unitarism, 1, 10
United States Bank, 50, 76–77
United States v. Carolene Products Co
    (1938), 124–25, 130
United States v. Curtiss-Wright (1936),
    124
United States v. Lopez (1995), 134, 135
United States v. Smith (1820), 75–76
Urofsky, Melvin I., 125
U.S. Circuit Courts, 48

Valelly, Richard, 3, 204n14
Vallandigham, Clement, 54
Vallandigham, Ex parte (1864), 54
Vaubel, Roland, 6, 204n13
Vietnam War, 131–32
Vinson, Fred M., 125, 127–28
Vinson Court (1946–1953), 125,
    127–28, 129
Virginia, 77–79, 94, 109
Virginia, Ex parte (1880), 109
Voting Rights Act, 151

*Wabash, St. Louis and Pacific Railway
    Company v. Illinois* (1886), 111
Waite Court (1874–1888), 107
Wall Street Journal (newspaper), 111
War Department, 68
Ward v. Maryland (1871), 55
Ware v. Hylton (1796), 50
Warren, Charles, 202n4, 224n12

Warren, Justice Earl, 127, 128–30
Warren Bridge Company, 88
Warren Court (1953–1969)
    Burger Court and, 132, 133
    civil rights and liberties and, 124–25,
        127, 128–31
    incorporation and, 14
    Keck on, 150–51
Washington, George, 80
Washington Post (newspaper), 101,
    107
We the People (Ackerman), 143
Webber v. Virginia (1880), 206n37
welfare state, 145–47
Welton v. Missouri (1876), 55–56
West Coast Hotel v. Parrish (1937), 123,
    125, 223–24n2
*West Virginia State Board of Education
    v. Barnette* (1943), 126, 127
White, G. Edward, 213n30, 221n61
Whittington, Keith, 145, 201n16,
    209n82, 210n4, 211n12, 213n32
Wickard v. Filburn (1941), 125–26
Wiecek, William M., 8, 226–27nn31–32
Willoughby, Westel, 29–30, 211n13
*Willson v. Blackbird Creek Marsh
    Company* (1829), 87
Wilson, Mark R., 68
Wilson, Woodrow, 105
Wisconsin State Supreme Court, 11,
    70–71
women's' rights movement, 131
Woodbury, Levi, 77
Woodruff v. Trapnall (1850), 77
Woodward, Wayne A., 212n24
Worcester, Samuel, 76
Worcester v. Georgia (1832), 76, 86
world system
    during Early Republic (1789–1828),
        73–76, **74**
    during Jacksonian Era (1829–1860),
        73–76, **74**
    during Civil War and Reconstruction
        (1861–1876), 98

world system *(continued)*
  during Republican Era (1877–1932),
    98, **98**
  during New Deal and Great Society
    (1933–1968), **98**, 121, **121**
  during Contemporary Era (1969–
    1997), 121, **121**
  coding rules for, 159
  definition of, **36**, 203n6

World War I, 111–12
World War II, 122–23, 126

Yates, Robert, 27. *See also* Brutus
  (Anti-Federalist)
yellow dog contracts, 59
Yick Wo v. Hopkins (1886), 110

Zackin, Emily, 146, 234n5, 235n13

www.ingramcontent.com/pod-product-compliance
Lightning Source LLC
Chambersburg PA
CBHW020339270326
41926CB00007B/243